FROM DESPAIR
TO HOPE

Harvey Reynolds (left) and Michael Reynolds sit in the window of their ninth-floor Cabrini-Green apartment in 1992. They were best friends of Dantrell Davis, a 7-year-old boy killed by a sniper as he walked to school.

Photo by John H. White, as published in *The Chicago Sun-Times*. Reprinted with permission.

To the generations of Americans whom the public housing system failed, left to struggle against despair and to sustain courageously the hope for a better future that everyone deserves.

FROM DESPAIR TO HOPE

HOPE VI and the New Promise of Public Housing in America's Cities

Henry G. Cisneros
Lora Engdahl, editors

BROOKINGS INSTITUTION PRESS
Washington, D.C.

Library of Congress Cataloging-in-Publication Data

From despair to hope : HOPE VI and the new promise of public housing in America's cities / Henry G. Cisneros and Lora Engdahl, editors.
    p.   cm.
  Includes bibliographical references and index.
  Summary: "Documents the evolution of HOPE VI, exploring what it accomplished replacing severely distressed public housing with mixed-income communities and where it fell short. Reveals how a program conceived to address a specific problem triggered a revolution in public housing and solidified principles that still guide urban policy today"— Provided by publisher.
  ISBN 978-0-8157-1425-5 (pbk. : alk. paper)
  1. Public housing—United States—Finance. 2. Housing policy—United States. 3. Housing rehabilitation—United States. 4. Urban renewal—United States. I. Cisneros, Henry. II. Engdahl, Lora.

  HD7288.76.U5F76 2009
  363.5'850973   2009000779

9 8 7 6 5 4 3 2 1
Printed on acid-free paper

Typeset in FontFont Scala
Font designed by Martin Majoor

Design and composition by Nancy Bratton Design
Washington, DC

Printed by Taylor Specialty Books
Dallas, Texas

CONTENTS

PART 3. BROADER IMPACTS OF THE MODEL

PART 4. LEARNING FROM CRITIQUES AND PLANNING FOR THE FUTURE

FOREWORD

Providing decent and affordable housing to low-income people has been a challenge to officials at all levels of government for decades. During my twelve-year tenure as mayor of Baltimore, I worked with the housing secretaries of three U.S. presidents on this challenge, particularly as it relates to those living in public housing. It was under President Bill Clinton's housing secretary, Henry Cisneros, that creative policy development and wise decisionmaking converged to produce an innovative approach that helped to improve the quality of life for many of the country's poorest citizens. That innovative approach came to be known as HOPE VI.

In Baltimore, as in many cities, much of the public housing was built shortly after World War II, designed to be transitional housing for the large number of military veterans and their families. In Baltimore, these new high-rise buildings replaced aging housing with poor sanitation and other unsafe living conditions. Unfortunately, over time those once welcoming structures became warehouses of poverty. Rather than being places for families to get a fresh start, the public housing high-rises were transformed into poverty traps characterized by high crime rates, significant unemployment, and deteriorating physical plants.

For far too long, the government's response to the condition of public housing was predictable and uncreative. Money was given to local housing authorities to maintain the buildings at the lowest possible level of habitability. For the most part, public housing became second-class housing and the people living there felt that the government treated them as second-class citizens. They had no incentive to treat the facilities with care. An attitude of indifference and sometimes outright hostility emerged from a significant number of residents of public housing.

However, under HOPE VI, things began to change. The program reflected a new view—that cities were centers of opportunity and not just massive shelters for the poor. Cisneros walked through public housing projects, joined by government officials and residents who reported that they liked the neighborhoods in which they lived but despised the housing. Residents had asked government officials for help in the past without expecting—or receiving—much, but this time, the response was both surprising and inspiring. They were offered a new type of partnership through a vehicle called HOPE VI.

Although created at the federal government level, HOPE VI had at its heart the belief that the solution to public housing problems was not to be found in the nation's capital but in the communities where public housing was located. Those who designed HOPE VI believed that local residents and government officials, in partnership, could transform public housing projects into attractive, livable communities. Residents were encouraged to dream their fondest dreams for themselves, their families, and their neighbors. They then were asked to work with housing experts and government leaders to envision a plan for a new community. With skepticism at first and then with enthusiasm, Baltimore's public housing residents embraced the opportunities offered by HOPE VI.

Lafayette Courts, a housing project less than a mile from Baltimore's central business district, was the first of the city's public housing communities to be transformed. Under a plan developed in partnership with the residents, the old high-rises were imploded and a new neighborhood was born, complete with rental apartments, for-sale town houses, a senior citizen apartment complex, a youth recreation center, and a community center that included headquarters for a police unit dedicated to patrolling only that neighborhood. At a community association meeting after the new buildings were completed, a woman was heard to say that with the new buildings, the residents now had such a pleasant view of downtown. Her observation led the residents to vote to change the name of Lafayette Courts to Pleasant View Gardens.

The second of the city's public housing redevelopments transformed the Lexington Terrace high-rises on the western edge of downtown, whose residents were among the first in the nation to share their concerns with Cisneros when he visited there early in his term. Thanks to HOPE VI, the site is now a welcoming mixed-income community of traditional Baltimore row houses, new retail and office space, and apartments for the elderly.

With the redevelopment of Lafayette Courts, Lexington Terrace, and four subsequent communities under HOPE VI, the program brought hope to thousands of Baltimore's low-income residents. Of course, the program was not a cure-all for all people and for all housing challenges. Because the plans for Baltimore's public housing facilities called for a reduction in population density, some families could not return to the redeveloped sites. Those families received vouchers to relocate to other neighborhoods, or they were placed in other types of public housing. The concerns of some families led to court challenges; however, for most low-income residents of public housing, the impact of HOPE VI was positive and dramatic.

The Baltimore experience with HOPE VI is a story that I am proud to report. I recognize that each city has had unique experiences under the program. But overall the positive developments represent a marked contrast to previous decades of indifference and failure. Policymakers should emphasize the accomplishments of HOPE VI, learn from its shortcomings, and design a renewed partnership that will benefit low-income communities throughout this great country.

Kurt L. Schmoke
Dean, Howard University School of Law

ACKNOWLEDGMENTS

Many people and institutions must be recognized for their help in making this book possible. First are the five organizations whose long-standing dedication to human and community development translated into financial support for this project: Bank of America, Annie E. Casey Foundation, Fannie Mae, Freddie Mac, and the John D. and Catherine T. MacArthur Foundation. They saw the value of telling the story of a transformative federal-urban partnership and the important and timely ideas still debated in its wake.

Second are the twelve contributors who shared their time, talent, and expertise to help tell the story. They gave great care and attention to their subjects and showed unflagging commitment to the arduous task of working with us to set their chapters into the greater narrative.

As we pulled the narrative together, we called on many outside experts to verify facts and test recollections and offer their insights, including current and former HUD officials, housing authority staff, and individuals with such key industry groups as the Council of Large Public Housing Authorities and the National Association of Housing and Redevelopment Officials. We are especially grateful to housing finance attorney Rod Solomon, our go-to guy on many issues, who was consistently reflective and responsive; Tony Hebert, who from his post within the HOPE VI program at HUD cheerfully answered our numerous requests for program data; and Tom Kingsley, who, as the author of the final chapter of the book, served as a sounding board for issues in pulling together the earlier chapters. Among the many others who also were generous with their time were Michael Reardon and Barbara Sard.

In this book, the images are a critical part of the story. In helping us tell it, our photo researcher, Hilary Mac Austin, was a true partner. She led us through the daunting world of image collection and reprint approvals and found some truly amazing photographs along the way. We came to depend on her keen instincts to select images and on her motivational coaching to forge through the problems that invariably arise in a project involving so many moving parts.

For taking all of the pieces and making it a book, we could have not been more fortunate in our choice of publisher, Brookings Institution Press. Bob Faherty, director, and Janet Walker, managing editor, bravely took on a project whose extensive images posed special challenges. Larry Converse, production manager, patiently guided us through the steps in bringing the project to fruition and wisely enlisted the services of a dynamic designer, Nancy Bratton, to help pull the text and images together. Her contributions, and those of the crack copy editor we were blessed to have on the crew, Eileen Hughes, are visible on every page of this book. The entire team's enthusiasm for the project sustained the momentum during the painstaking design and production process.

For their dexterity and resourcefulness in keeping the levers moving behind the scenes throughout this eighteen-month project, we thank Sylvia Arce-Garcia, Gloria Paniagua-Rodriguez, Yvette Solitaire, and Jessica Munoz with CityView and Choco Meza with American Sunrise. We know that invaluable organizational and administrative support was also provided by staff at our contributors' organizations.

These acknowledgments would be incomplete without recognizing that there have been individuals who were instrumental in our entry and growth in the housing and urban development field. While there have been too many to name here, we would like to thank, respectively, President Clinton and Mark Weinheimer.

Finally, with grateful hearts, we thank Mary Alice Cisneros, Jorge Bernardo, and our families. Without the steadfast support and encouragement of those closest to us, we would not be able to do the work that we do.

Henry Cisneros and Lora Engdahl

Program Origins and Defining Principles

HENRY CISNEROS

A New Moment for People and Cities

In the winter of 1993, early in my tenure as secretary of the Department of Housing and Urban Development (HUD) in the Clinton administration, I took a road trip to Baltimore that profoundly affected my aspirations for public housing and urban neighborhoods. I took the trip at the request of James Rouse, a lifelong community builder whom I knew from serving on the board of the Enterprise Foundation, which he founded. Jim thought I should see Enterprise's efforts to revitalize Baltimore's Sandtown-Winchester neighborhood.

Energized by Enterprise's comprehensive approach—pairing housing development with employment, training, drug rehabilitation, and schools— I joined Mayor Kurt Schmoke for a walk through the surrounding neighborhoods. The massive structure of the high-rise Lexington Terrace public housing development a few blocks away towered over the landscape. I had recently read a *Washington Post* article on conditions there, and I asked the mayor if we could take a quick walk through the buildings.

As we neared the entrance, we were approached by police officers from the Baltimore Housing Authority who told us that we should not enter the building because it had not been swept and secured. If we did, they warned, we might find ourselves in the cross-fire of a drug deal gone wrong. We went in anyway but restricted our tour to the lower floors.

The officers' warning stunned me. We expected mothers and children to make their way through the building every day but could not safely allow the U.S. secretary of housing and the mayor of the city to enter? In subsequent years, I visited many cities as HUD secretary, making a point to spend the night in public housing when I could. I met with residents who told distressing tales of long-delayed repairs, of living with the constant sound of gunshots and other horrors. But it was this Baltimore visit that first drove home the urgent need to improve conditions for public housing residents.

The opportunity lay in front of me. As I was touring Baltimore that brisk mid-winter afternoon, back on my desk in Washington sat legislation awaiting implementation. I returned to the office with a commitment to seeing

The Broadway-Overlook HOPE VI development (foreground) in Baltimore's Washington Hill neighborhood provides a bright new view of the city looking west toward downtown.

© 2005
J. Brough Schamp/
www.Schamp.com

On February 3, 1993, Mayor Kurt L. Schmoke of Baltimore (left) and Barbara Bostick of the Sandtown-Winchester Project (second from right) take the author (center) on a neighborhood tour that ends at Lexington Terrace, where the terrible conditions underscore the need to improve the environment for public housing residents.

The Baltimore Sun staff photograph/Amy Davis

that the legislation—the HOPE VI program—would enable fundamental and massive change.

Saving a Critical National Resource

HOPE VI posited drastic change as a way to save public housing, which had reached rock bottom in the court of public opinion. Headline events such as the 1991 publication of Alex Kotlowitz's book *There Are No Children Here* and the 1992 shooting of seven-year-old Dantrell Davis in Chicago's Cabrini-Green neighborhood seemed to tell the nation that with respect to public housing in its most troubled neighborhoods, it had failed: the projects were unlivable.

Change was brewing well before HOPE VI. Jack Kemp, my predecessor at HUD, had spent much of his tenure focusing on the idea of selling entire public housing complexes to their residents. While the plan drew a good deal of attention and resulted in a well-publicized conveyance of buildings in St. Louis, the idea did not catch on as the broad national solution to the public housing crisis.

The severe state of deterioration and the crushing costs of maintenance were among the chief roadblocks to Secretary Kemp's approach. Indeed, in 1992, the National Commission on Severely Distressed Public Housing, appointed by Kemp and members of Congress, concluded that upgrading or replacing the worst of the nation's public housing stock would require massive federal investment. Noting the commission's recommendations, Congress in late 1992 passed the Urban Revitalization Demonstration (URD) as part of Kemp's HOPE (Homeownership and Opportunity for People Everywhere) series of programs, the first of which were enacted in 1990. URD, which came to be known as HOPE VI, authorized a major new allocation of capital funds for the removal and replacement of the most blighted public housing.

That was the state of affairs in November 1992 when President Clinton asked me to serve as secretary of HUD. I had my own ideas about the imperative to address homelessness, about the importance of serving as liaison to the nation's mayors, and about the urban development component of the job. But I had no particular detailed plan for public housing reform, only a general belief in the importance of public housing and a strong commitment to reducing the concentrated poverty that drained the promise from once-proud communities.

My belief in the importance of public housing was formed early. I grew up in Prospect Hill, a central city neighborhood in San Antonio that was adjacent to three public housing developments: Alazán-Apache, Mirasol, and San Juan Homes. My family appreciated the importance of those developments, which were built to replace housing conditions so dire that a Jesuit priest from nearby Our Lady of Guadalupe Church had personally implored President Franklin Roosevelt to act.

But over the years the homes built on President Roosevelt's commitment to New Deal public housing in San Antonio deteriorated. Few efforts were made to maintain the densely packed, two-story, red-block buildings or to provide amenities or open space. When I became mayor of San Antonio in 1981, I worked with the San Antonio Housing Authority in its efforts to modernize the public housing stock. My wife and I spent time visiting with public housing families, and we gained a sense of what public housing meant to struggling families.

Developing a Public Housing Agenda

As secretary designate of HUD, I began to develop an agenda for public housing with the aid and resources of many partners. I reviewed the report of the National Commission on Severely Distressed Public Housing, which

Below left: In 1935, President Franklin D. Roosevelt speaks at Grant Field, on the campus of the Georgia Institute of Technology, during his visit to Atlanta to dedicate Techwood Homes, the nation's first public housing project.

Below right: Conditions in the Mexican quarter in west San Antonio, Texas, in the 1930s so distressed a Jesuit priest that he implored Roosevelt to bring public housing to the city.

San Antonio's first public housing project, Alazán Courts, opened in 1940 on the near west side, shown here in 1942. The subsequent decline of this and other public housing complexes deprived cities of an important resource for struggling families.

had as a member Lila Cockrell, my predecessor as mayor of San Antonio. I toured public housing projects with housing authority directors, attempting to understand better precisely how key capital programs interacted, learning of the urgency of remedying operating budget shortfalls, and listening to residents.

In January 1993, during my first trip as HUD secretary, I met with residents at a public housing project in Atlanta. Discussions about replacement and renovation were already under way there, and residents and Atlanta officials alike expressed hope that public housing improvements could be linked to the momentum generated by the revitalization of the surrounding near-downtown neighborhoods, including the largest economic generator in the area, the Georgia Institute of Technology.

The following month came my tour in Baltimore. There and in subsequent visits to public housing in Chicago and other cities, it became clearer and clearer that public housing in the form it took in many big cities was an unacceptable way to house the nation's most needy residents. It seemed, if anything, that the analysis of the National Commission on Severely Distressed Public Housing had understated the severity of the problem.

The Early Implementers

A core group of HUD staff, members of Congress, public housing authority directors, and private sector leaders shaped early HOPE VI rules with an eye to going beyond the first-order objective of the legislation. We knew that it was not enough to eliminate the most distressed public housing buildings—we needed to dramatically reorient the workings of public housing as a system.

The team included Bruce Katz, the HUD chief of staff, who, as a staff aide to the Senate Banking Committee, had been present for the drafting of the legislation, and Joe Shuldiner, assistant secretary of the Office of Public and Indian Housing at HUD, who had headed both the Los Angeles and New York City housing authorities.

We were fortunate to have the wisdom of important members of Congress, such as senators Donald Riegle of Michigan and Paul Sarbanes and Barbara Mikulski of Maryland, on the Democratic side, and senators Christopher Bond of Missouri and Alfonse D'Amato of New York, on the Republican side. Each had strong views about the way urban public housing could be improved in their states.

On the House side we consulted especially closely with representatives Louis Stokes of Cleveland, Henry B. Gonzalez of San Antonio, and Maxine Waters of Los Angeles, among the Democrats, and representatives Rick Lazio of Long Island and Jerry Lewis of Southern California, among the Republicans.

From the private sector we had the advice of people such as Richard Baron, of the private firm that is now McCormack Baron Salazar. In late 1993, he wrote a memorandum outlining how HOPE VI could be reshaped to attract meaningful private investment to public housing neighborhoods in the cities. And we had the advice of executives who were leading authorities on public housing at the time, prominent among them Richard Gentry from Richmond, Virginia, Sally Hernandez-Pinero from New York City, and Reneé Glover from Atlanta.

These leaders underscored the imperative that we had to do more than just replace the most distressed units. Simple replacement of units on the same sites, framed by the same concepts, and governed by the same regulations would certainly result in the same failures.

In our first iteration, we began requiring grant winners to pay attention to the economic and social needs of the residents as well as the physical condition of the housing. Further reforms were prompted by troubles with some of the early grants, which were made to the most distressed sites, which in some cases were managed by troubled public housing authorities with little experience in social service delivery or real estate development. Authorities were instructed to evaluate the welfare of displaced residents and to devise creative ways to enlist broader public and private sector investment in the new effort to change whole neighborhoods.

As HOPE VI matured, we designed new regulations, new operational practices, and new financial incentives to allow housing authorities across the nation to make changes on the scale necessary. We could drive their responses to the issues that cried for action: deterioration of the older stock, flawed physical designs that were overly dense, patchwork rules that were formulas for failure, lax administration, and the impossible dilemmas confronting residents who had to choose between work and housing assistance when their incomes increased just enough to make them ineligible for public housing but not enough to be truly self-sufficient.

HOPE VI Drives Broader Policy Change

HOPE VI was more than a housing or urban redevelopment program. It forced a dialogue on basic concepts concerning housing, redevelopment of cities, and generation of opportunities. Over time, as the program evolved and the ideas of many people were incorporated, the resulting debates and dilemmas forced working solutions, which became principles.

Among the working principles that emerged in the early years was the recognition that the physical design and density of the communities, in conjunction with rules that virtually expelled working families, were a significant part of the problem. As just one example, single mothers with children complained of being harassed by gang members as they carried groceries through unlit hallways that were hidden from view.

That recognition coincided with the emergence of an influential community-building movement called New Urbanism. A number of national architects were making serious progress in their advocacy of urban designs that featured "walkability" and encouraged social interaction by linking structures and streetscapes. They were espousing an architectural theory that understood "human scale" and incorporated shared amenities in practical ways. Our HOPE VI team invited New Urbanism leaders Peter Calthorpe, Andrés Duany, Ray Gindroz, Elizabeth Plater-Zyberk, and Dan Solomon to advise us on how we could apply community-building principles to the renovation of public housing. What emerged was an adaptation of New Urbanism through such practical concepts as "defensible space."

Lexington Terrace in Baltimore (shown here prior to demolition) was not designed to encourage residents to engage with one another or the surrounding neighborhood.

The HOPE VI strategy of constructing smaller-scale replacement buildings helped force the repeal of the "one-for-one" replacement rule, which required every public housing unit taken out of service to be replaced with a hard unit. Given the barriers to finding suitable sites for replacement units, that policy made meaningful redesign impossible because it required replacing high-rises and densely packed barracks-style buildings on essentially the same scale. Advocates for the homeless argued that no units should be sacrificed and that even the worst of the high-rise public housing was needed for the poorest of people on the streets. Advocates for redevelopment argued that significant numbers of the units in the worst buildings were already out of service: vacant, looted, and burned out.

The one-for-one rule was lifted by Congress in 1995, and HUD allowed the use of other forms of housing subsidies, such as Section 8 rental assistance vouchers, to house people who had previously lived in the worst units. It was my hope that residents who had lived in a development and wanted to return to the redeveloped site would be offered the first opportunity to do so. I personally insisted that without exception a housing authority had to be able to show that every resident who was in public housing before would be provided some form of housing, either a unit or a voucher.

In retrospect, given the lag in many cases between demolition and reconstruction as well as the unassisted use of Section 8 vouchers, my concerns were justified. While some cities, such as Chicago, eventually developed reliable organizations to help residents use Section 8 vouchers to find private market housing closer to jobs and educational opportunities, such "housing mobility" did not in effect exist in other cities. As was later discovered, some of the problems arose on the counseling end because of insufficient understanding of just how much effort was involved in helping people unfamiliar with the private market find housing. But at the time there was concern within HUD that people would not be able to use vouchers in part because suburban residents' opposition to relocating central city residents in the suburbs was so intense. At the same time, complaints from central city officials and landlords that new voucher recipients were concentrating in city neighborhoods fueled a push by leading advocates and researchers to expand the voucher program beyond high-poverty, high-minority areas.

HUD therefore changed its Section 8 regulations to make it easier for residents to use the program and for landlords to rent to voucher holders. For example, we changed the "take one, take all" regulation, which required a landlord who accepted one Section 8 resident to accept anyone with a Section 8 voucher. By lifting that requirement, we enabled participation in Section 8 by landlords who wanted to balance the mix of incomes in their properties.

Another key working principle that emerged was the need to attract private investment to the HOPE VI sites to create mixed-income communities with a seamless public housing component. Following a legal ruling by HUD general counsel Nelson Diaz that enabled HOPE VI grants to be used in conjunction with low-income housing tax credits and other private capital, we pushed through regulatory changes that sent a strong signal that HOPE VI was not going to operate by traditional public housing rules. With the commitment of real estate professionals and substantial private dollars, HOPE VI communities would be designed well and include socially beneficial amenities, and through the application of modern real estate management practices, they could be well maintained.

Creating opportunities for leveraging public housing grants with private sector equity and ultimately with other forms of private sector capital was transformative. It forced recognition of the need to modernize the management operations of the public housing authorities. Although in many cases the housing authority was the largest real estate manager in a city, few had the organizational structure and trained personnel to execute real estate transactions of the complexity required under HOPE VI, and they were not regarded by the municipal leadership or by the private sector as respected real estate enterprises. To capitalize on the full potential of private investment and enlist

Creating opportunities for leveraging public housing grants with private sector equity and ultimately with other forms of private sector capital was transformative.

the private sector in creative site planning and development, housing authorities needed to function in the bond and debt markets.

For HOPE VI to be a success, the authorities would have to retain the requisite talent, revamp their accounting systems, adopt less centralized operational models, and learn the techniques of site management. In turn, HUD needed to alter its public housing development processes to enable authorities' adoption of private sector practices and partners. To facilitate that on-the-ground transformation, HUD altered the way it did business. We assembled a mobile team from across the department to act as an incubator of change within public housing, staffed by some of the most creative civil servants, appointees, and consultants—David Sowell, Valerie Piper, George Latimer, Mindy Turbov, Paul Brophy, and others. It was their job to experiment and to expose the field—and HUD—to new ideas in design, planning, and finance. Thanks to the able leadership of Milan Ozdinec, who administered the HOPE VI program from the outset, HOPE VI became the "hot spot" where these new ideas came to fruition.

Solidifying the Core Program Principles

The contributions of creative and passionate staff continued when Andrew Cuomo succeeded me as secretary of HUD in 1997. Cuomo gave prominence to HOPE VI and encouraged the HUD team, working with its outside partners, to make the program's innovations a matter of course. Led by deputy assistant secretary Elinor Bacon, who had been working as a private real estate developer, HUD restructured HOPE VI administration to support the core program principles. Formerly separate HOPE VI and mixed-finance staff were merged into one working team to discourage straight public housing redevelopment and work projects through to completion. Leading real estate development consultants and practitioners were hired as "Expediters" on projects that were moving slowly. HUD standardized reporting requirements and began requiring housing authorities to evaluate their HOPE VI projects, generating a body of data enabling analysis of the program and communication with critical constituencies, from Congress to the public and the press.

The best minds in the public housing management, real estate development, architecture, legal, and finance sectors continued to apply their problem-solving skills to improving and expanding HOPE VI. Senators Mikulski and Bond and their staffs, as well as early partners from the private sector, remained engaged as informal advisors. Housing authority leaders and key executives with the Council of Large Public Housing Authorities, including Sunia Zaterman, CLPHA's executive director, and Gordon Cavanaugh, CLPHA's general counsel, helped HUD craft guidance that gave structure to the program while retaining flexibility at the local level. For example, cost guidelines were rewritten to allow for the high-quality design and construction needed to create communities that would attract market-rate buyers.

During the final four years of the Clinton administration, resident participation and supportive services came into sharper focus. To ease some of the tensions that had arisen during early development efforts, HUD met with resident leaders and held sessions in different regions training residents on real estate development and the opportunities and challenges of public housing redevelopment. The Community and Supportive Services division was established under the leadership of Ron Ashford, and HOPE VI began to require HOPE VI housing authorities to prepare clear, outcome-oriented CSS plans. Experts with the Urban Institute and other organizations were enlisted to research and disseminate community-building practices that centered on developing resident leaders and linking residents to resources.

The New Dynamics of Urban Opportunity

The HOPE VI solutions guided a substantial transformation of public housing—of physical sites, of the organization of housing authorities, and of the national system of rules and regulations. But they did more than that. The solutions also affirmed concepts concerning workable urban revitalization plans and increased confidence among urban leaders that change could occur.

We saw contemporary applications of the ideas of legendary urban writer and activist Jane Jacobs about the power of street-level vitality in urban neighborhoods. We were forced to think through the harnessing of metropolitan-wide opportunities as part of a focused revitalization strategy. We realized that public housing operations had to transcend "command and control" bureaucratic models and use market dynamics unleashed by proven real estate management practices. As we witnessed efforts to create mixed-income communities, we ventured beyond abstract conversations about urban design and came to understand how architecture that features human-scale solutions could be the impetus for better communities, worlds removed from the bleak environment of post–World War II superblocks.

Community-building design principles shaped the HOPE VI redevelopment of Baltimore's Lexington Terrace public housing project in the late 1990s.

Each of those realizations, which in theory seem obvious, emerged in physical form from the conundrums addressed and hard choices made in the actual building of HOPE VI communities. In turn these realizations expanded the realm of the possible in the nation's cities. Essentially, HOPE VI was a statement that public housing was important and that cities were important. That signature response to great needs by no means single-handedly saved cities, but it was one of the forces that effected a big change in outlook. HOPE VI not only helped spur new attitudes concerning the opportunities that ought to be available to public housing residents, it also reframed management concepts about how public authorities should operate. In measurable ways, HOPE VI sharpened the vision of what urban neighborhoods and cities could be. In many cities, substantial new investment has occurred immediately adjacent to HOPE VI redeveloped public housing. Sites that for decades had been off-limits to almost any kind of private investment suddenly have become magnets for new developments.

Today, city leaders are drawing confidence from and building on public-private investment as they nurture the growth industries of the New Economy—green building and renewable energy, higher education, health care, business and professional services, new media, international trade, biomedical research, telecommunications, and various other forms of technology. Public and private entities are investing in the anchor institutions that have chosen to stay and build up urban neighborhoods. Universities, medical centers, corporate headquarters, athletic facilities, convention centers, cultural and artistic venues, and church complexes are being tapped as the building blocks of employment growth, consumer spending, historic restoration, and newfound stability in urban neighborhoods.

Cities also are benefiting from a more entrepreneurial spirit of governance. Today mayors are the orchestrators of vast civic energies, drawn from the private and nonprofit sectors and applied to maximum effect. City administrators in many places have become non-ideological problem solvers, who, in a role akin to that of traffic cops, make sure that financial resources and the goodwill of community leaders flow to the most productive channels. They are joined in that effort by nonprofit community development corporations. These non-profits, formed in the 1960s and 1970s to give voice to raging anger over conditions in many minority communities, today have created sophisticated financial teams to build housing, construct neighborhood business districts, and launch commercial centers.

The new demographics of cities reinforces the potential of mixed-income communities. One of the most important dynamics in cities is the growth of the minority middle class—generating higher incomes, a pool of educated and skilled labor, and civic leaders intent on improving neighborhood schools and public facilities. Another major force is the growth of immigrant groups from many parts of the world whose members have flocked to inner-city urban neighborhoods, demonstrating the role of cities as a launching pad for upward mobility in U.S. society. Add to that the positive effects of new flows of urban residents, including suburban empty-nesters, tired of fighting traffic and ready for the stimulation of city life, and the creative class of young professionals so essential to the pool of urban talent and to the success of entertainment businesses.

There is good evidence in city after city of the market for infill housing and downtown residential construction to augment private housing investment in neighborhoods around HOPE VI sites. All of these trends toward stronger urban markets are likely to accelerate as the price of gasoline continues its long-term rise and makes it more expensive to commute to the only land available for traditional residential subdivisions—far in the urban hinterland, at distances that are increasingly prohibitive.

The new dynamics of urban opportunity reinforce the imperative to replace the most distressed public housing. But they also highlight the need to preserve homes for the most needy families in the nation's improving cities. Particularly in earlier years, when redevelopment took longer, HOPE VI was criticized for forcing people to move from their communities. Although even residents living in horrible conditions had mixed feelings about leaving neighborhoods where they had developed bonds of friendship and mutual support, it was our judgment that conditions in the most distressed public housing developments were so bad that replacement was the only reasonable course.

But it is imperative—indeed it is a moral obligation—that we provide housing for struggling families. Unfortunately, the new attractiveness of strategically located inner-city land has sparked calls from some real estate leaders to convert public housing sites to more commercial uses. As we go forward under HOPE VI and its successor programs, we must resist those calls and proceed from the core principle that when public housing residents are integrated into mixed-income communities, those communities can fulfill multiple roles that are crucial to the urban workforce, to the housing mission of cities, and to the metropolitan economy. Well-planned mixed-income communities can become the focal point for the essential social progress of our cities and our nation.

Public housing is an integral part of the housing policies under which families are provided safe and decent homes from which they can chart their path to personal advancement. HOPE VI has shown us that the public housing mission can be carried out with respect for the residents, with appreciation for the dynamic potential of our cities, and with confidence that wise public investments can support the values of our society.

City West, the HOPE VI redevelopment of Cincinnati's West End, is restoring economic vitality to a near-downtown neighborhood that is critical to the city's prosperity.

Steve Hall © Hedrich Blessing

BRUCE KATZ

The Origins of HOPE VI

HOPE VI is one of the most successful urban redevelopment initiatives of the past half-century. The program has had an impact on hundreds of distressed city neighborhoods, helping revitalize communities once characterized by lawlessness and decline. It has triggered a broader—though still incomplete—transformation of the public housing system from a rule-bound realm controlled by federal bureaucrats to an investment in the nation's future managed by market-savvy local leaders. Just as meaningful, in spite of its misses (and sometimes because of them), it has engendered a deep and abiding discussion on national housing policy with respect to the negative implications of concentrated poverty and the possibilities of broader economic integration and family mobility.

Broken windows in the homes of these children signify the appalling decades-long neglect of public housing that would finally prompt bold reform.

HOPE VI arose during a period of intense urban crisis in the United States that gave rise to the consensus that the extreme poverty in the inner cities and large public housing projects was intolerable. The prescription offered by HOPE VI (to reconstruct unlivable public housing, provide intensive support services, and allow for resident mobility) reflected the bold notion that public housing needed not merely to provide affordable shelter but also to generate broader community revival and to alleviate poverty.

Efforts of such reach and ambition rarely emerge fully formed. HOPE VI began with initial legislation molded by policymakers from a core set of principles. But as national leaders, working with visionary local partners, began to implement the legislation, they realized that they could go bigger and do more by drawing on the new opportunities and tools arising elsewhere in the real estate and policymaking environments.

Thus, new ideas regarding project design, mixed financing, and asset management transformed a program that initially focused on reconstruction and resident empowerment into one reaching for economic integration, deconcentration of poverty, and neighborhood revitalization. The shift was aided by government reinvention efforts, which emphasized the need for flexible rulemaking and new public-private partnerships, and by welfare reform, which stressed providing the services necessary to support low-income residents in the world of work. Further motivation was supplied by the promise of racial integration inspired by the Gautreaux experiment in Chicago. Future policymakers seeking insights on how such advances in public policy occur can learn much from the story of HOPE VI's origins.

The Urban Context for Reform

The HOPE VI program was conceived when many U.S. cities and urban neighborhoods were under extreme stress. During the 1980s, explosive sprawl at the periphery of metropolis after metropolis was matched by stagnation in the central cities and older suburbs. Population decline in older cities such as Chicago, Cleveland, Detroit, Philadelphia, and St. Louis was accompanied by the radical restructuring of the U.S. economy. Jobs grew in the service sector and shrank in manufacturing and production.[1] The overall city poverty rate rose from 17.2 percent in 1980 to 19 percent in 1990, reflecting the economic travails of the decade as well as the continued out-migration of the middle class from central cities.[2]

The rise of *concentrated poverty* and its racial composition was even more troubling. From 1980 to 1990, the number of people living in metropolitan neighborhoods of high poverty (those having a poverty rate of 40 percent or more) grew from 5.2 million to 8 million, a 54 percent increase. During that period almost 71 percent of the new high-poverty residents were either African American or Hispanic. Incredibly, by 1990 more than 42 percent of poor African American households lived in neighborhoods of high poverty.[3]

The profound repercussions of concentrated poverty were first captured by William Julius Wilson in his influential 1987 book, *The Truly Disadvantaged*. In that book and subsequent works, Wilson discussed how the limited economic opportunities available to residents in high-poverty urban neighborhoods translated into unemployment rates that were simply stunning. For example, during a typical week in 1990, only one in three people older than sixteen years of age living in Chicago's high-poverty neighborhoods held a job.[4]

Wilson also drew the connection between concentrated poverty and crime. Describing what he called "concentration effects"—the increasing social isolation of inner-city residents from "mainstream patterns of behavior"—he characterized the "communities of the underclass" as "plagued by . . . flagrant and open lawlessness."[5]

Statistical trends corroborated Wilson's conclusions. Violent crime reached exceedingly high levels in the 1980s, fueled by the introduction of crack cocaine into urban communities and the emergence of sophisticated and lucrative drug trafficking networks. On average, the rate of violent crime in central cities grew by 33 percent between 1979 and 1989. Chicago saw the most dramatic increase in violent crime during that period, 173 percent. By

By the 1990s, shrinking populations, job stagnation, and rising crime rates had placed many U.S. cities and urban neighborhoods under extreme stress, evident in this blighted neighborhood on the South Side of Chicago.

© Ralf-Finn Hestoft/ Corbis

1989, violent crime rates exceeded 3,000 per 100,000 residents in three cities: Atlanta; Newark, New Jersey; and St. Louis. In 1991, nineteen cities surpassed their previous homicide rates.[6]

Emblematic of these high-poverty, high-crime neighborhoods were the "federal enclaves" of concentrated poverty: public housing. Along with Wilson, such keen social observers as Nicholas Lemann, in his book *The Promised Land,* and Alex Kotlowitz, in *There Are No Children Here,* described the soul-crushing conditions in shoddily constructed, poorly maintained public housing projects with ubiquitous drug and gang problems and concentrations of profoundly poor families living on welfare.[7]

It wasn't always that way. Public housing was originally conceived during the Depression as temporary housing for people who needed assistance as they got back on their feet.[8] In following decades, however, federal policies altered the resident profile of public housing by restricting eligibility for admission to tenants under certain income levels and giving priority to exceedingly low-income families. Rent-setting policies discouraged work and penalized residents whose income increased.

Compounding these influences were the physical characteristics of the complexes themselves. As a consequence of neighborhood opposition and government decisions that often were racially motivated, many public housing developments had been constructed in the undesirable parts of a city, often isolated by natural barriers like rivers or artificial barriers like major highways.[9] Under the influence of post-war European modernist thought, the design of many of these large developments violated all notions of what architect and author

Oscar Newman labeled "defensible space."[10] Acres were consumed exclusively by ill-constructed high-rise buildings exposed to the elements and lacking any spaces toward which residents could feel a sense of ownership.

The passage of time took a physical toll. Dwindling federal funds for maintenance and modernization accelerated the physical deterioration. Many of the public housing authorities (PHAs) responsible for large numbers of troubled developments were themselves troubled—inefficient, unaccountable, and often penalized by HUD, which wouldn't dispense the full allocation of modernization funds to agencies it considered ill-equipped to make good use of them.

As public housing projects deteriorated, new federal policies prevented the sensible demolition and redevelopment of the most distressed projects. The "one-for-one" replacement law enacted in 1981 essentially prohibited any demolition by cash-strapped housing authorities by requiring that a new housing unit be built for every public housing unit demolished. Even housing

1940's

1940s

Above left: In 1942 War Department employee Edward Vaughn and his family relax in the living room of their new residence in Ida B. Wells Homes, a public housing development on the South Side of Chicago described in the 1945 book *Black Metropolis* as offering working families a step up to the lower middle class.

Above right: Ida B. Wells shown from above in 1942.

Right: Public housing projects like this one in North Philadelphia in 1973 were set on the path to decline by government decisions that placed them in undesirable, isolated parts of the city and restricted tenancy to exceedingly low-income families.

1970s

authorities that could afford to build new units faced serious barriers. Federal rules, for example, prohibited the construction of replacement units in neighborhoods that were racially segregated, but nonminority communities often opposed the introduction of any new public housing units. Also, small-scale properties at scattered sites were difficult to acquire and maintain.

As a result, many developments became nothing more than warehouses for the very poor. Between 1981 and 1991, the number of public housing households with incomes below 10 percent of local median income (a key indicator of extreme economic disadvantage) grew from 2.5 percent of the total public housing population to almost 20 percent. In the early 1990s, the average income in public housing was around $6,500; in many developments, literally no residents held full-time jobs or actively sought work. The absence of employed residents meant that children growing up in those environments had no appropriate role models.[11]

1940s

Left: A woman hangs clothes at the Denver Housing Authority's Curtis Park public housing project in Denver, Colorado, in 1941.

Below right: The ever-present piles of garbage outside the Arthur Capper public housing project in Washington, D.C., in 1981 symbolized the official neglect that accelerated the decline of public housing nationwide.

Right: The exodus from public housing of tenants who had other options was spurred by poor management and inadequate funds for maintenance, which created hazardous conditions for children such as these youngsters in front of Lincoln Heights Dwellings in far northeast Washington, D.C., in the 1970s.

1970s

1980s

By the 1990s, years of disinvestment and neglect of public housing had chased away all but the most vulnerable families and left overburdened housing authority police struggling to control the gangs that engaged in drug dealing from vacant apartments, corridors, and stairwells, such as this one at the Martin Luther King Plaza complex in South Philadelphia.

1990's

The population in many public housing developments also became heavily weighted toward female-headed households with children. By the late 1980s, approximately two-thirds of non-elderly families living in public housing operated by large PHAs were headed by single women. An even greater percentage of PHA families with *dependent* children were headed by single women: 85 percent on average and surpassing 95 percent in some cities.[12] The physical vulnerability and economic isolation of those residents were severe. As one analysis summarized:

> Poor design and decades of neglect permitted drug trafficking and gang activity to flourish, creating environments dominated by high levels of violence. Extreme racial and economic segregation isolated residents from the larger community, relegating them to failing schools, ineffective police protection, and poor city services. Families that were employed or had other options were largely driven out by the dreadful conditions, intensifying the economic segregation and isolation. Although some residents made heroic efforts to cope with their situation, forming strong networks of mutual support, there can be no doubt that these developments failed to meet even the most basic requirements for decent housing and that rehabilitation efforts alone were inadequate to address the myriad problems that had accumulated by the late 1980s.[13]

The Path to Legislation

The worsening conditions of inner cities and public housing during the 1980s—and the pervasive notion that federal policies had contributed to those conditions—emboldened policymakers to consider the most extensive reshaping of inner-city neighborhoods since the discrediting of urban renewal around the early 1970s.[14] The stakes were high. Public housing conditions had generated such widespread opprobrium that many feared that there would be a push for federal withdrawal from public housing programs altogether. Besieged policymakers seeking to "excise the cancer" and save the nation's cities needed a compelling plan.

Between 1987 and 1992, the reform effort was led by a small group of senators who held leadership positions in key congressional committees. Alan Cranston (D-Calif.) and Alfonse D'Amato (R-N.Y.) were the chair and ranking member respectively of the housing subcommittee of the Senate Banking, Housing, and Urban Affairs Committee. Barbara Mikulski (D-Md.) was the chair of the Senate Appropriations Subcommittee on Veteran Affairs, Housing and Urban Development, and Independent Agencies. Christopher S. Bond (R-Mo.) served on the Senate VA-HUD appropriations subcommittee (which he would come to chair later in the 1990s) and also was a senior member of the Senate Banking Committee's housing subcommittee. The leadership group was rounded out by two other senior members of the Senate Banking Committee, Don Riegle (D-Mich.), who was the committee chairman, and Paul Sarbanes (D-Md.).

These members—four Democrats, two Republicans—shared a commitment to pragmatic, evidence-based lawmaking. Keenly aware of the distressed condition of public housing in major cities and the options for redevelopment, they were fiercely committed to a bipartisan approach to housing policy. Senators Cranston and D'Amato, for example, initiated a rigorous three-year process led by Jim Rouse (the famed developer of festival marketplaces and head of the Enterprise Foundation) and David Maxwell (the CEO of Fannie Mae) that resulted in the pathbreaking National Affordable Housing Act of 1990.[15] Senators Mikulski and Bond routinely collaborated on appropriations laws. That level of collaboration was critical to the formation and enactment of HOPE VI. In developing HOPE VI, the senators and ultimately other members of Congress were influenced by several factors: the report of the National Commission on Severely Distressed Public Housing; Secretary Jack Kemp's push for resident ownership of public housing; mixed-income and mobility models of redevelopment; and devolution of authority and other policy trends.

THE NATIONAL COMMISSION ON SEVERELY DISTRESSED PUBLIC HOUSING

In 1989, Congress established the National Commission on Severely Distressed Public Housing, which was charged with developing a National Action Plan to eradicate severely distressed public housing by the year 2000.[16] The commission, which included eighteen members (an equal number of whom were appointed by the administration, the House of Representatives, and the Senate), was led by Bill Green, a former Republican member of the House, and Vincent Lane, the entrepreneurial chairman of the Chicago Housing Authority. The commission also included leading advocates for public housing reform in the private and public sector, including Richard Baron, a leading private developer in St. Louis; David Gilmore, the executive director of the San Francisco Housing Authority; and local elected officials such as the mayors of San Antonio, Texas, and Sacramento, California. It also included three highly respected resident leaders: Mildred Hailey, president of the Bromley-Heath Tenant Management Corporation in Boston; Irene Johnson, president of LeClaire Courts Resident Management Corporation in Chicago; and Lenwood Johnson, president of the Allen Parkway Village Tenant Council in Houston.

Over eighteen months, the commission and its staff visited public housing developments in twenty-five cities, held twenty public hearings, and talked extensively with a broad range of individuals and constituencies. The commission's final report to Congress, presented in August 1992, portrayed public housing residents as fearful and languishing in unhealthy, unsafe communities without access to jobs or programs designed to enable self-sufficiency.[17]

In keeping with one of its congressional mandates, the commission constructed a definition of "severely distressed public housing" that took into account the share of residents living in distress (as measured by such indicators as concentrated poverty), the incidence of crime, the nature and extent of management challenges, and the physical condition of the housing. The commission concluded that roughly 86,000 of the 1.3 million public housing units nationwide qualified as severely distressed and that the existing panoply of HUD programs and policies—including an early effort at redevelopment called MROP (Major Reconstruction of Obsolete Projects)—was insufficient to address the problems.

The commission therefore proposed a new and comprehensive approach for severely distressed public housing that encompassed increased funding for support services and new, coordinated systems for delivering those services; a new commitment to income mixing in public housing developments to alleviate the challenges associated with managing concentrations of extremely poor households; and increased funding (an estimated $7.5 billion over ten years) to rehabilitate or replace physically unsustainable housing.

The National Action Plan also recommended that HUD develop a special planning process for undertaking such complicated transactions, encouraged public housing authorities to pursue private and nonprofit management options, and proposed that Congress authorize a new partnership program for PHAs, nonprofit organizations, the private sector, and residents in order to attract additional resources.

SECRETARY KEMP'S PUSH FOR RESIDENT OWNERSHIP

Congressional action was also influenced by the intense ferment in housing policy in the late 1980s and early 1990s. In 1989, Representative Jack Kemp, a Republican representing Buffalo, New York, became secretary of the Department of Housing and Urban Development, ushering in an activist period of policymaking and intense competition of ideas between the administration and various factions within Congress.

Secretary Kemp, who had strong, controversial ideas about distressed public housing, advocated greater resident management and ownership of public housing. In 1990, he was able to persuade Congress to embrace several HOPE (Homeownership for People Everywhere) programs that aimed to transfer ownership of public and assisted housing to residents after extensive renovation of the dilapidated stock. While Kemp's ideas of resident ownership were radical, his acceptance of the reality of public housing—its location, its design, its racial and economic segregation—would have kept many public housing residents physically isolated from the economic mainstream. Kemp said that he did not want to be known as the "Secretary of Demolition," reflecting a widely shared belief that massive demolition was simply too charged an issue to contemplate.

MIXED-INCOME AND MOBILITY MODELS

While Kemp emphasized the benefits of resident management and ownership, other demonstration efforts stressed the need to rethink the social mix, project design, and neighborhood impact of public housing. In Boston, Chicago, and St. Louis, housing authorities and developers were using federal waivers and other tools to redevelop public housing sites and other subsidized housing at lower densities for households having a mix of incomes, under the assumption that economic integration was the only way to sustain successful projects and neighborhoods.

Emerging at the same time as the mixed-income pioneers was a growing cadre of housing mobility proponents. They drew their energy from mounting evidence that minority public housing households that moved to the Chicago suburbs under the court-ordered remedy in the *Gautreaux* v. *HUD* racial segregation case fared better than nonmovers on measures of employment and children's educational attainment.

The Gautreaux evidence (covered in chapter 5) coincided with another important evolution in the politics of housing, namely the growing embrace of housing vouchers by conservative thinkers and policymakers. The conservative embrace of vouchers as the most effective housing policy tool dated back to the beginning of the Reagan administration, when opponents of expensive project-based efforts like the Section 8 New Construction and Substantial Rehabilitation programs threw their support behind vouchers instead.

DEVOLUTION AND OTHER POLICY TRENDS

These new tools for public housing reform were gaining traction amid a broader shift toward devolution in housing policy and federal policy in general. For example, Congress enacted the Low-Income Housing Tax Credit Program in 1986 and the HOME program in 1990. Both programs gave state and local housing officials greater authority and responsibility for designing housing strategies tailored to their respective housing markets. Both programs rewarded partnerships between the public and private sectors and the leveraging of public resources with private capital. They offered a more trusting and flexible framework for developing federal-local partnerships on subsidized housing.

The late 1980s and early 1990s also saw the spread of the "reinventing government" movement, captured and promoted nationwide by reformers David Osborne and Ted Gaebler in their influential 1992 book of the same name.[18] The movement deemphasized top-down public management in favor of setting goals and allowing the parties responsible for meeting the goals the flexibility they needed to do so. In philosophical alignment were community policing and other evidence-based approaches to crime reduction that were proliferating nationwide. And in the wings were the early stirrings of welfare reform.

The Enactment of HOPE VI

By 1992, Senate leaders of both the authorizing and appropriations committees were ready and willing to move legislation on public housing redevelopment. Like the National Commission on Severely Distressed Public Housing, both committees agreed that a separate, distinct program was needed to address the varied social, management, and physical concerns of severely distressed public housing.

Both committees also agreed that the challenge was so urgent that legislation should be enacted in 1992. Normally, legislation authorizing a new federal program would precede appropriations for the program. In the case of HOPE VI, however, the sequencing was backward. Delays in passing and enacting federal housing legislation in 1992 (an election year) meant that the appropriations law (the Departments of Veterans Affairs and Housing and Urban Development and Independent Agencies 1993 Appropriations Act) was actually signed into law first.

THE BANKING COMMITTEE LAW

The Banking Committee legislation—the Housing and Community Development Act of 1992 (HR 5334), signed into law on October 28, 1992—drew many programmatic elements from the action plan of the National Commission on Severely Distressed Public Housing. The act authorized a federal grant program for local public housing agencies to revitalize "severely distressed public housing." As defined by the act, such housing exhibited the broad range of structural and social problems that afflicted high-poverty neighborhoods at the time. Public housing could qualify as "severely distressed" on the basis of the physical need for redesign, reconstruction, redevelopment, or demolition in order to correct for design deficiencies, obsolescence, or deterioration and deferred maintenance. The prevalence of unemployment, teenage pregnancy, single parenthood, poor academic achievement, long-term dependency on public aid, vandalism, drug-related crime, and other criminal activity could also distinguish severely distressed housing.

The act authorized HUD to administer grants for the physical revitalization of distressed projects, management improvements, and support services to promote residents' self-sufficiency. Eligible activities also included residents' involvement in redevelopment planning, job training, tenant relocation costs, and neighborhood economic development. HUD would evaluate applicants for grants by the quality of their proposals, the extent of local need, the extent to which the grantees were spread among different regions of the country, and the degree of resident and local public and private involvement in the project. Under the act, HUD would establish the Office of Severely Distressed Public Housing to administer the program.[19]

THE APPROPRIATIONS LAW

On October 6, 1992, several weeks before passage of HR 5334, Congress appropriated $300 million for the program that would become HOPE VI—an "urban revitalization demonstration" intended to facilitate the "major reconstruction of severely distressed or obsolete public housing projects." To encourage the administration's acceptance of HOPE VI, the program was positioned as part of a family of HOPE programs, including Secretary Kemp's reauthorized initiatives to sell off public housing to residents. Cities were eligible for funding of up to $50 million to reconstruct up to 500 units in as many as three separate areas "containing the community's most severely distressed projects." Local public housing authorities would apply for the grants after identifying severely distressed projects using criteria established by the National Commission on Severely Distressed Public Housing. On receipt of their grants, local PHAs were to use at least 80 percent of the federal funding for costs associated with reconstruction, rehabilitation, and physical improvements; the capital costs of replacement units; and technical purposes.

While both the authorization and appropriations laws reflected the influence of the National Commission on Severely Distressed Public Housing, the appropriations bill was also especially influenced by a 1992 report from the Cleveland Foundation's Commission on Poverty. The Cleveland Foundation's commission was headed by Art Naparstek, a respected academic in the fields of poverty and affordable housing. The report's call for "integrated programs for integrated lives" focused intensely on the need to join up the disparate health, education, skills training, and family development programs then under way in most inner-city communities.[20] The appropriations law therefore allowed up to 20 percent of the funding to be used for community service programs and such support services as job training, daycare, youth activities, and administrative expenses. The law also required participating cities to invest additional, nonfederal funds in support services in an amount equal to 15 percent of the federal funding for those services.[21]

Continued Evolution: The Implementation of HOPE VI

The enactment of HOPE VI in 1992 coincided with the election of President Bill Clinton and the appointment of Henry Cisneros, the former mayor of San Antonio, as secretary of HUD. It thus fell to Secretary Cisneros rather than

Secretary Kemp to implement the "urban revitalization demonstration" under the appropriations law as well as the HOPE VI program in general.[22]

Under a different administration or secretary, the transformative impact of HOPE VI might not have been fully realized. In fact, many of the initial proposals submitted to HUD under the 1992 appropriations law lacked creativity and focus. Most public housing agencies initially viewed HOPE VI as a kind of "souped up" reconstruction and support services program. To them, the program seemed to represent the next generation of public housing development rather than a transformative investment in urban revitalization. By the end of his tenure, Cisneros and his team had extended the objectives of the program, garnering bipartisan and industry support for an ambitious agenda that included

- tearing down rather than rehabilitating distressed public housing in order to enable substantial redevelopment of projects and sites[23]
- replacing some of the demolished housing with smaller-scale housing that was economically integrated and designed to promote greater public safety and social interaction within the neighborhood
- giving returning residents access to quality support services in order to promote self-sufficiency
- helping nonreturning residents to rent private housing with vouchers and offering them counseling and other support services
- requiring the insular public housing agencies to pursue these various reform efforts in concert with public, nonprofit, and for-profit entities.

All of these ideas, of course, had been present in the National Commission's report and in earlier efforts in some form or another. But Cisneros focused them and pushed them through the public housing system, using a variety of carrots and sticks (formal funding guidelines, large public forums, private briefings, technical assistance, the bully pulpit) to lift the aspirations and alter the practices of an entire industry.

As discussed in the following chapters, under the leadership of Cisneros the program evolved to place greater emphasis on some of the commission's recommendations. More attention was paid to using quality design to improve the quality of life in the complexes and their neighborhoods and to attract new residents and investment. HUD became a founding signatory to the Charter for New Urbanism (executed in Charleston, South Carolina, in 1996) and immediately engaged Andres Duany, Peter Calthorpe, Ray Gindroz, and other new urbanists in efforts to restore traditional neighborhood design to public housing communities. Ironically, a public housing system known for developing housing along standard institutional lines was soon, through the vehicle of HOPE VI, in the avant-garde of a new design movement.

In addition, as HUD and industry leaders grasped the potential of emerging financial innovations to recreate public housing, a program that once was financed almost exclusively by the federal government became sophisticated in leveraging private sector debt, private sector equity (raised through the federal low-income housing tax credit), and other federal and local public and private dollars, including philanthropic resources. Many of the financial innovations were made possible by opening up the redeveloped public housing communities to households that had a mix of incomes. In that respect, HOPE VI aligned with the National Commission's call for mixing families with diverse incomes on revitalized sites.

In turn, mixing incomes supported Cisneros's commitment to poverty deconcentration, which had been addressed in the Housing and Community Development Act of 1992, although not explicitly in HOPE VI. The 1992 act authorized the Moving to Opportunity (MTO) demonstration, which was designed to assess the impact of helping low-income residents move to lower-poverty areas, modeled after the Gautreaux initiative. In addition to calling for a quantum leap through the MTO demonstration, the Cisneros administration began making poverty deconcentration an explicit goal of HOPE VI in its Notices of Funding Availability (NOFAs) and in appropriations language a few years into the program.

At the same time, experiences in the field began to tell policymakers that HOPE VI's increased ambitions created a greater need to focus on displaced residents. Though the redevelopment of sites for households of varying incomes caused a loss of on-site public housing units that engendered a backlash in some areas (discussed in other chapters), it also created an opportunity to pursue poverty deconcentration more broadly. Congress and the administration realized that potential by permitting HOPE VI appropriations to be used for Section 8 rental vouchers, thus enabling recipients to relocate to areas of much less concentrated poverty.

Over time, Cisneros and his team began to understand that the successful implementation of HOPE VI was the first step in a more systemic transformation of public housing. By the close of 1995, the logic of public housing redevelopment had triggered a revolution in the basic laws governing public housing admissions, rent setting, and demolition and replacement as well as an enhanced commitment to vouchers as a means of expanding tenant choice and enabling mixed-income developments and neighborhoods. Many of the statutory changes, initially enacted as part of annual appropriations laws, received permanent authorization in the Quality Housing and Work Responsibility Act of 1998.[24] Thus by the late 1990s, what had started as an ambitious effort to revitalize the most distressed public housing had morphed into a full-scale overhaul of the public housing program.

Conclusion

The evolution of HOPE VI—from concept to research to law to implementation—is a textbook case of empirically grounded and outcome-driven

Experiences in the field began to tell policymakers that HOPE VI's increased ambitions created a greater need to focus on displaced residents.

policymaking. After some early stumbles by housing authorities that were learning how to run entirely new systems, the industry as a whole gained capacity and shed dysfunction. HOPE VI and other development innovations began to spread beyond the largest cities, with compelling results.[25] HUD and Congress engaged in a process of bipartisan cooperation that altered the program in real time, as early findings quickly informed appropriations, program competitions, and practice.

But the conversation continues. Currently, the debate over the future of HOPE VI and public housing in general ranges from sustaining the momentum to making the next leap—for example, with a more concerted effort to tie neighborhood redevelopment to school reform. In addition, recent controversies over concentrations of residents with Section 8 rental assistance will undoubtedly influence the design and implementation of future relocation efforts.[26] What is clear is that HOPE VI and public housing will continue to evolve and adapt to changing circumstances, as HOPE VI has since its inception.

····· Endnotes ·····

1. U.S.Bureau of the Census (www.census.gov/population/censusdata/c1008090pc.txt); U.S. Department of Labor, Bureau of Labor Statistics.

2. U.S. Bureau of the Census, "Characteristics of the Population below the Poverty Line," P-60 Series (Consumer Income), 1980 and 1990.

3. P. A. Jargowsky, *Poverty and Place: Ghettos, Barrios, and the American City* (New York: Russell Sage Foundation, 1997).

4. William Julius Wilson, *When Work Disappears: The World of the New Urban Poor* (New York: Knopf, 1996).

5. William Julius Wilson, *The Truly Disadvantaged: The Inner City, the Underclass, and Public Policy* (University of Chicago Press, 1987), p. 58.

6. John D. Kasarda, "Inner-City Poverty and Economic Access," in *Rediscovering Urban America, Perspectives on the 1980s* (HUD 1993).

7. Alex Kotlowitz, *There Are No Children Here: The Story of Two Boys Growing Up in the Other America* (New York: Anchor Books, 1992); Nicholas Lemann, *The Promised Land: The Great Black Migration and How It Changed America* (New York: Vintage Books, 1992).

8. Lawrence Vale, *From Puritans to the Projects: Public Housing and Public Neighbors* (Harvard University Press, 2000), p. 9.

9. The unconstitutional, discriminatory practices of the Chicago Housing Authority (CHA) and HUD in selecting sites for Chicago public housing were the basis of the Supreme Court case *Hills* v. *Gautreaux*, 425 U.S. 284 (1976), which affirmed broad federal court powers to provide equitable relief in such cases.

10. Oscar Newman, *Defensible Space* (New York: Macmillan, 1972).

11. *Final Report of the National Commission on Severely Distressed Public Housing: A Report to the Congress and the Secretary of Housing and Urban Development* (National Commission on Severely Distressed Public Housing, 1992), p. 48.

12. Ibid., p. 47.

13. Susan J. Popkin and others, "A Decade of HOPE VI: Research Findings and Policy Challenges," (Washington, D.C.: Urban Institute, 2004) (www.urban.org/UploadedPDF/411002_HOPEVI.pdf), pp. 47–48.

14. Beginning in 1949, the federal government enacted urban redevelopment programs that involved replacing structures in blighted areas with new residential and commercial development. The programs, which came to be known as "urban renewal," were active in the 1950s and 1960s but engendered criticism for displacing low-income people and neighborhoods, with a particular impact on African Americans. In 1974, remaining urban renewal–type programs were rolled into the new Community Development Block Grant Program. Source: Kent W. Colton, *Housing in the Twenty-First Century: Achieving Common Ground* (Harvard University, Wertheim Publications Committee, 2003), pp. 214–19.

15. The Cranston-Gonzalez National Affordable Housing Act, signed into law in November 1990, had provisions aimed at helping poor families achieve self-sufficiency. The act created the HOME Investment Partnerships (HOME) program, essentially a new affordable housing block grant, and the Homeownership for People Everywhere (HOPE) program initiatives, which sought to empower public housing residents through resident management and homeownership.

16. Department of Housing and Urban Development Reform Act of 1989 (P.L 101-235).

17. Report of the National Commission on Severely Distressed Public Housing.

18. David Osborne and Ted Gaebler, *Reinventing Government* (Reading, Mass.: Addison-Wesley, 1992).

19. Housing and Community Development Act of 1992; Public Law 102-550, 106 Stat. 3695-3701.

20. The Cleveland Community-Building Initiative, "Report and Recommendations of the Cleveland Foundation Commission on Poverty" (Case Western Reserve University, Mandel School of Applied Social Sciences, 1992).

21. The Departments of Veterans Affairs and Housing and Urban Development and Independent Agencies Appropriations Act, 1993 [P.L. 102-389 (1992)].

22. Since there was never an appropriation directly tied to the Banking Committee bill's provision for a severely distressed public housing program, HOPE VI is generally considered officially authorized only under appropriations until the passage of the Quality Housing and Work Responsibility Act of 1998. However, concepts in both bills shaped program requirements.

23. Paul S. Grogan and Tony Proscio, "The Fall (and Rise) of Public Housing," Harvard Joint Center for Housing Studies, 2000.

24. Quality Housing and Work Responsibility Act of 1998 (Title V of P.L. 105-276). For an extensive discussion of the myriad changes to public housing policy authorized by this act and in its wake, see Rod Solomon, "Public Housing Reform and Voucher Success: Progress and Challenges," Brookings Institution Metropolitan Policy Program, January 2005 (www.brookings.edu/metro/pubs/20050124_solomon.pdf).

25. In the beginning, only public housing authorities located in one of the nation's forty most populous cities or on HUD's Troubled Housing Authority list as of March 31, 1992, could apply for a HOPE VI grant. Source: Linda B. Fosburg, Susan J. Popkin, and Gretchen P. Locke, *An Historical and Baseline Assessment of HOPE VI*, vol. 1, *Cross-Site Report* (U.S. Department of Housing and Urban Development, Office of Policy Development and Research, July 1996), pp. 1–25. Eligibility was expanded to all public housing authorities in the fiscal 1996 NOFA.

26. Hanna Rosin, "American Murder Mystery," *Atlantic Monthly* (July-August 2008); Xavier de Souza Briggs and Peter Dreier, "Memphis Murder Mystery? No, Just Mistaken Identity," *Shelterforce*, July 22, 2008 (www.shelterforce.org/article/special/1043/ [October 1, 2008]).

RICHARD D. BARON

The Evolution of HOPE VI as a Development Program

Early in its implementation, the HOPE VI program took a significant turn that had far-reaching repercussions, not only for the program itself but also for the U.S. public housing system in general. As discussed in chapter 2, the National Commission for Severely Distressed Public Housing, created in 1989, called for redeveloping the worst of the sites, which comprised some 86,000 "severely distressed units."[1] The recommendations of the commission led to the 1992 enactment of the Urban Revitalization Demonstration (URD), the first iteration of today's HOPE VI program. By the end of 1993, more than $1 billion in fiscal year 1993 and 1994 grants had been pledged to dozens of public housing authorities serving the nation's larger cities.[2]

Renaissance Place in St. Louis is among the numerous mixed-income public housing redevelopments made possible by critical rule changes in the mid-1990s.

The program's initial guidelines called for housing authorities to replace severely distressed public housing with new and improved public housing with amenities and social services. My firm, McCormack Baron Salazar, argued for a shift in direction. Having worked in distressed urban areas for thirty years, we knew that concentrating low-income families in high-density developments created an untenable management situation. The extraordinary difficulty of sustaining housing restricted to occupants at the lower end of the income scale had been demonstrated repeatedly in large public housing sites.

In a memo to HUD in December 1993, I wrote: "URD does not go far enough in terms of transforming the basic approach to solving the conditions of conventional family sites. The net effect of a successful demonstration at a site may change its physical characteristics, and develop programs for the residents, but it will *not* change the demographic profile of the complex, nor will it integrate the site into the surrounding neighborhood."[3]

We proposed developing replacement public housing units within new mixed-income communities to create incentives for sustained investment in the communities as well as improved life chances for public housing residents. While before HOPE VI at least one federal public housing site had been redeveloped as true mixed-income housing—Boston's Columbia Point—it was done under waivers and with subsidies that were no longer available.[4]

Replicating mixed-income public housing redevelopment on a much broader scale required a standardized process for allowing public housing authorities (PHAs) to combine federal HUD funds with other public and private funds.

It is unlikely that anyone involved at the time fully appreciated the magnitude of the changes that would follow the adoption of the proposal. The policy innovations that arose from the exchange of ideas between the public and private sectors under HOPE VI created a new system of public housing development that broke from conventional concepts of design and management and brought in new capital and infrastructure. HUD rules and regulations that once prevented mixed-income communities now encourage them.

Why Mixed-Income Housing?

I had worked with more than a dozen public housing authorities in the late 1960s and early 1970s as a legal services attorney and consultant, and my observations of the deplorable conditions and dysfunction of many housing authorities stayed with me as I moved into development in the 1970s.[5] In fact, one of my first development efforts involved plans to redevelop the Pruitt-Igoe public housing complex, thirty-three high-rise buildings covering fifty-five acres on the north side of St. Louis. Built in the 1950s, this vast showcase of modernist architecture had become virtually uninhabitable and mostly vacant.

The rapid deterioration of the Pruitt-Igoe public housing development in St. Louis, which was demolished in the mid-1970s within two decades of its completion, came to symbolize the failure of high-rise, high-density public housing for families. (Photograph taken April 21, 1972)

AP Images/Fred Waters

Working with the housing authority and under the auspices of the St. Louis Civic Alliance for Housing, I and my business partner, Terry McCormack, won tentative approval for a plan to replace the development with a mixed-income community of low-rise garden and town house units. But George Romney, who was HUD secretary at the time, withdrew the approval. In March 1972, the St. Louis Housing Authority ignited the first of many explosives that brought the complex down into a widely televised cloud of debris. Postmodern architect Charles Jencks said the occasion marked "the day Modern Architecture died."[6] The buildings were fully torn down in 1975. Today what remains of the site is a wooded area of some thirty acres.[7]

Between Pruitt-Igoe's demolition and our second chance to redevelop public housing in St. Louis, my firm had gained decades of experience building and managing urban mixed-income communities, first by using project-based Section 8 subsidies and then low-income housing tax credits (LIHTCs).[8] By the early 1990s, we had developed a number of large-scale, mixed-income developments, such as Westminster Place in St. Louis; Phoenix Place and Hampton Place in Louisville; Lexington Village in Cleveland; and Crawford Square in Pittsburgh.

Our projects focused on the renewal of neighborhoods that had suffered a significant decline in their tax base, business activities, and employment. We learned that that the best way to restore such neighborhoods and improve the lives of residents was through a major transformation of the area that embraced thoughtful architecture, new infrastructure, and marketing efforts designed to attract higher-income families.

We knew first-hand that we had to attract a workforce by creating attractive housing that was competitive with other housing in the market. We understood that we were creating new incentives to maintain the housing, because if the market-rate tenants and homeowners found it lacking, they would leave the neighborhood. To create affordable, economically diverse "communities of choice," we encouraged neighborhood participation in the design of the communities, and to enhance residents' lifestyles, we insisted on higher standards for physical design and amenities than those typically accepted by public agencies.

Making the Argument for Change

In the fall of 1993, I had an opportunity to show one of these communities to a key appointee in the Department of Housing and Urban Development under Secretary Henry Cisneros. George Latimer, a former mayor of St. Paul, Minnesota, who had agreed to head a newly created special action office at HUD, was in Pittsburgh to make a speech. I took him to McCormack Baron's Crawford Square development in Pittsburgh's Hill District (whose police station inspired the name of the popular 1980s television program *Hill Street Blues*).

A visit in 1993 to the mixed-income, tax credit–financed Crawford Square development in Pittsburgh persuaded George Latimer, a top HUD appointee, to push for modification of the HOPE VI guidelines.

Latimer was amazed to learn that a number of the residents of Crawford Square's amenity-rich, tax credit units were former public housing tenants who were actually paying less at Crawford Square than they had been paying in the modernized but still poorly designed Pittsburgh Housing Authority development nearby.

Later, as Latimer, his assistant Valerie Piper, and Mindy Turbov with the Federal Housing Administration worked on strategies for using URD grants with other financial tools, Kevin McCormack and I drafted a policy memorandum to HUD outlining the possibilities for leveraging URD grant funds with state and local resources in order to create the kind of mixed-income communities that had revitalized distressed non–public housing communities.[9]

Chief among those potential resources were low-income housing tax credits. Designed to encourage investment in affordable rental housing, the ten-year tax credits are awarded by states to development projects that reserve units for families whose income is up to 60 percent of the area median income (AMI). The credits, which are activated when a sufficiently affordable development is placed in service, are usually sold before construction to investors or syndicators, generating cash to fund construction. Since the tax credit investor's primary return for investing comes from the tax credits themselves rather than any returns from tenant rents, rents remain affordable.[10] Because families making up to 80 percent of AMI are eligible to occupy public housing, it was clear that the same unit could theoretically be receiving both tax credit equity and public housing subsidies, leaving a far smaller gap in the financing needed for mixed-income development.

In our December 1993 memo we argued that by leveraging URD grant funds with tax credit equity and other state and local financing streams, HUD could double or triple the amount of affordable housing produced. We noted that a new approach to creating mixed-income developments could still accommodate the one-for-one replacement of low-income units that HUD then required by combining on-site development with development on available land in the adjoining neighborhood. We suggested that most of the conventional public housing sites were designed and built to an obsolete standard and that few were worth saving. We felt that most PHAs and their architects had become so accustomed to the emphasis on modernization that creating new communities of both market-rate and public housing units would require a very different mind-set.

Testing the Model

When HOPE VI was evolving, we recognized the opportunity to vastly expand the program's reach by leveraging tax credits, state resources, and other theretofore inaccessible sources of financing. We were in the unique position of being able to both present the argument and test the model.

While Bruce Katz, Cisneros's chief of staff, and other top HUD officials considered our proposal, we were drafting a plan for redeveloping the 658-unit George L. Vaughn public housing project, which was just down the street from the Pruitt-Igoe site, as a mixed-income development. Public housing development appropriations were not sufficient to fund the replacement of all units demolished, as then required by law. However, because of the degree of decay throughout the complex, Senator Kit Bond (R-Mo.) included in the Cranston-Gonzalez National Affordable Housing Act of 1990 a waiver of the one-for-one requirement.[11] The project was able to move forward leveraging later public housing development appropriations totaling $35 million.

The St. Louis Housing Authority was planning to redevelop Vaughn with all low-income public housing units until I asked Freeman Bosley, the newly elected mayor, to stop the design work and rethink the project. Our company, McCormack Baron Salazar, designed a financial package for Vaughn's redevelopment that would test a HOPE VI–like mixed-income model using $20 million of the $35 million set aside as the leveraging funds to create a 413-unit mixed-income rental community. More than half of the units would be public housing units, nearly a third would be market-rate units, and the remainder would be tax credit units only. Though the plan (shown in final form in table 3-1) was built on the tested tax credit model, it nevertheless hinged on some critical decisions to be made by state and federal policymakers.

The housing authority would lease the site to a private owner in the form of a limited partnership in which McCormack Baron would be the general partner and a tax credit investor would be the limited partner.[12] The benefit of the tax credits would go to that private entity.[13] The land would remain in perpetuity with the housing authority, which would have the option to purchase the "improvements" (the new development) at the end of the tax credit compliance period.

Existing capital funds for public housing were insufficient to address the degree of decay in the St. Louis Housing Authority's George L. Vaughn development.

Table 3-1. Murphy Park Financing

Type and source	Phase 1 (160 rental units)	Phase 2 (127 rental units)	Phase 3 (126 rental units)	Total (413 units)	Percent of development cost
First mortgage, from state housing authority funds	$2,180,000	$2,184,000	$2,800,000	$7,164,000	13
Second mortgage (and third mortgage in phase 2), from federal public housing funds	$9,153,000	$7,262,000	$7,210,000	$23,625,000	43
Equity capital, from LIHTCs	$3,720,000	$5,579,000	$6,501,000	$15,800,000	29
Community loan, from charitable contributions	$2,500,000	$350,000	$626,000	$3,476,000	6
Public improvement funds, from the city	$1,650,000	$1,000,000	$2,000,000	$4,650,000	8
Total	$19,203,000	$16,375,000	$19,137,000	$54,715,000	...

Source: McCormack Baron Salazar.

In addition to the equity raised through the sale of the tax credits, we needed debt financing for the project. Then as now, public housing funds can be used only to fund the public housing units. The Missouri Housing Development Commission had financed tax credit projects, but it had never financed a project involving public housing. After some persuasion, the agency's executive director, Dick Grose, agreed to finance Murphy Park—but only if the Federal Housing Administration (FHA) agreed to venture into new territory and provide mortgage insurance on a development that included public housing.

Though skeptical, the FHA signed on at the direction of the commissioner, Nicolas Retsinas. Andrew Craig and Doug Woodruff of Boatmen's Bank (now Bank of America) led the fund-raising effort that closed the last gap in the first phase, with $2.5 million from St. Louis's private and philanthropic sectors. The city of St. Louis committed up to $2 million for new streets and additional infrastructure.

The financing was arranged but by no means assured. The proposal for Murphy Park, as the development would be called, required the public housing units to be privately financed within the structure of an FHA-insured market-rate project and operating subsidies to be allowed to flow to a private entity that owned the improvements on the public housing site. Regulations governing public housing had never allowed so-called "privatization" of public housing.

Incorporating Mixed-Finance into HOPE VI and Public Housing Regulations

While we were pursuing the Vaughn redevelopment, we also were working with the Atlanta Housing Authority, which sought to use the URD grant that it received in 1993 to replace Techwood Homes with the mixed-income

Centennial Place community (see chapter 9). The legal opinions that enabled our progress encouraged the adoption of mixed financing as a program goal of HOPE VI and paved the way for a series of rulings and agreements that underpin the mixed-finance system operating in public housing today.

Recounting the pivotal sequence of events, Michael Reardon, who was HUD's assistant general counsel for assisted housing, noted that our proposals to HUD on behalf of Vaughn and Techwood were not the only ones then pending that asked HUD to approve private ownership of public housing by allowing operating subsidies and certain capital monies to go to entities other than public housing authorities. In Virginia, the Fairfax County Redevelopment and Housing Authority was requesting approval for an all–public housing redevelopment to be financed by a combination of public housing development funds and tax credit equity.[14]

An opinion issued in April 1994 ultimately transformed the public housing finance system. Called the Diaz opinion, after Nelson Diaz, HUD's general counsel, it argued that there was nothing in the U.S. Housing Act of 1937 that said that public housing had to be owned by a public housing authority as long as the private entity followed the rules that applied to public housing.[15] A few months later, a memo from Reardon regarding the Fairfax County proposal spelled out what safeguards a housing authority had to put in place in order to allow private ownership of public housing units that were still governed by public housing rules and still received operating subsidies.[16]

As our projects moved forward, the notion that mixed-income developments could buttress the public housing enterprise gained credence. In an interview in 1994, Joe Shuldiner, HUD assistant secretary for public and Indian housing, explained the need for an economic mix in public housing:

McCormack Baron Salazar's Murphy Park development in St. Louis, built in the mid-1990s to replace the high-rise George L. Vaughn public housing complex, launched a new model for public housing in which housing was provided as part of lower-density, mixed-income communities.

Above: Aware that stable communities need good schools, many of the corporate and philanthropic investors in the Murphy Park development led a successful effort to reform the neighborhood school, Jefferson Elementary.

Left: A Jefferson Elementary school teacher with her pupils. Students' rising proficiency in science far outpaced gains statewide, attesting to the benefits of making school reform a central component of public housing redevelopment and neighborhood revitalization efforts.

"The Robert Taylors [the notorious Robert Taylor Homes public housing project in Chicago] are so distasteful, we can't get the American public to ever fund any of it. So the real way to get housing for people is to have a product that the American public will be willing to pay for."[17]

Through its negotiations with Atlanta and St. Louis over their respective projects, HUD generated the prototype contracts and other legal documents necessary for entering into mixed-finance transactions. These documents enable mixed-income communities to be owned and managed by private firms while reserving a certain degree of oversight for public housing authorities in order to ensure that the firms comply with public housing rent rules and other regulations.[18] Chief among the safeguards is the Declaration of Restrictive Covenants, which records the number of public housing units originally funded with HOPE VI funds and requires that they remain public housing units for at least forty years.

Needless to say, mixed-finance public housing redevelopment required an adjustment in the thinking of real estate lenders, who normally expect an unfettered first mortgage position on property that they finance so that if all else fails, they can foreclose all other interests and take ownership of the property. Limits on lenders' recourse, designed to prevent the loss of public housing units, were not the only necessary variations from standard practice in residential development financing.[19]

The progress on the St. Louis and Atlanta mixed-income public housing redevelopments added fuel to a simultaneous but separate push to eliminate the one-for-one replacement law, which posed a major barrier to public housing redevelopment. Even with HOPE VI, most housing authorities did not have the funds to comply with the law by replacing each public housing unit demolished, including those long vacant.[20] And if they wanted to bring in a mix of incomes by reducing the number of on-site public housing units, it was difficult to find sites for replacement public housing elsewhere. HUD regulations largely prohibit building new public housing developments in neighborhoods that include large concentrations of minorities and low-income residents, but agencies found that nonminority communities often opposed public housing.[21] Congress suspended the one-for-one requirement beginning with 1995 appropriations (and permanently lifted it in 1998).[22]

At the same time, some members of the team that had been working out of Secretary Cisneros's office to mediate the negotiations creating the mixed-finance template were assigned to a special unit charged with pushing the approach more broadly throughout public housing—working especially closely with the Office of Distressed and Troubled Housing Recovery (ODTRH), which housed the HOPE VI office. Under deputy assistant secretary Kevin Marchman, ODTRH began to reshape HOPE VI, encouraging grantees to leverage funds and helping them work through the related issues.

By spring 1996, when the financing plans for Centennial Place and Murphy Park were approved, HUD had finalized a draft of the rule that would formalize the mixed-finance process[23] and created the new Office of Public Housing Investments, under Marchman's successor, Christopher Hornig, to further institutionalize mixed-finance public housing redevelopment. The office, which essentially replaced ODTRH, was headed by David Sowell. Sowell had played a critical advisory role in getting mixed finance off the ground as head of UDAG, the HUD neighborhood redevelopment program on which mixed-finance public housing was in many respects modeled.[24]

With the foundation in place, the number of mixed-finance and mixed-income HOPE VI projects expanded, spurred by the preference for mixed-finance development in HUD notices of funding availability (NOFAs), the use of FHA insurance "to 'pioneer' the market, and HUD's partnership with the Council of Large Public Housing Authorities to create a nonprofit Housing Research Foundation to share best practices."[25]

Expansion continued under Elinor Bacon, who came to HUD in 1997 to head the Office of Public Housing Investments under Andrew Cuomo, Cisneros's successor. One of Bacon's first tasks was to tackle the policy limits that made it hard to design and build communities that would blend into the surrounding neighborhoods and attract new residents. The HOPE VI team worked with new urbanist architects, housing authority officials, developers, and congressional staff to elevate the benchmarks for design and construction quality and to pass a new "total development cost" (TDC) policy. At the time, the TDC policy—which limits the amount of public housing development funds spent on any one project—was geared toward a standard of housing quality considered inadequate by HOPE VI developers who aimed to attract residents with a mix of incomes, leading to many applications for waivers. The new policy increased the cap on per-unit capital expenditures and exempted from that cap demolition expenses and extraordinary costs incurred when dealing with parcels that presented topographical and environmental problems.

The new TDC policy was among the policies and practices that emerged as mixed-finance deals went forward and that were enacted or ratified as part of the Quality Housing and Work Responsibility Act of 1998 (QHWRA). Both mixed-finance public housing development and HOPE VI were formally authorized under QHWRA.[26] The HOPE VI team worked with Rod Solomon, the HUD deputy assistant secretary who led the administration's participation in forming QHWRA, to retain flexibility and local control within the program. In addition to working with lawmakers to shape the HOPE VI and mixed-finance provisions in QHWRA, HUD further promoted mixed-financing in HOPE VI by restructuring staff, rewarding the leveraging of grant funds in HOPE VI NOFAs, and holding conferences on how to leverage public housing funds.[27]

Housing authorities grew increasingly adept at using the model. While some continued to engage firms such as McCormack Baron Salazar as lead developers, others assumed the lead development role themselves. Financing partners' comfort with mixed-finance deals grew as well, streamlining the process. For example, today state housing finance agencies regularly allocate tax credits to these deals and by and large no longer require FHA insurance on the mortgages. Banks and other private sector lenders now also regularly make loans to the projects. The approval process within HUD also is more routine, with applicants preparing term sheets (summaries of the key terms of a proposed mixed-finance deal) for review by loan committees and executing their plans with autonomy under certain new legal agreements—procedures initiated by Bacon's successor, Milan Ozdinec, and expanded by Dominique Blom, Ozdinec's successor.[28]

Mixed Financing Today

Most of the 240 public housing redevelopment projects funded under HOPE VI though 2007 have been funded with a range of variations on the mixed-finance model pioneered in St. Louis and Atlanta more than a decade ago.[29] As Orlando J. Cabrera, HUD assistant secretary of public and Indian housing, noted in June 2007 testimony to Congress, more than three-fourths (76 percent) of the 649 rental phases planned across HOPE VI developments by

Figure 3-1. **Financing of Selected HOPE VI Sites**

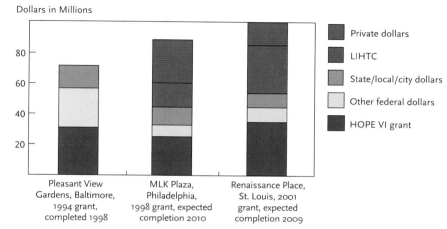

Dollars in Millions

Sources: Data on funding sources and unit mix were obtained from the Housing Authority of Baltimore City, the Philadelphia Housing Authority, and McCormack Baron Salazar, which is developing Renaissance Place for the St. Louis Housing Authority.

Figure 3-2. **On- and Off-Site Unit Mix of Selected HOPE VI Sites[a]**

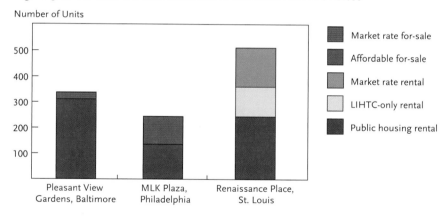

Number of Units

a. Many HOPE VI developments have units that are designated for public housing households but are also financed by tax credits. Tax credit units that are not also public housing are identified as "LIHTC-only rental."

2005 included LIHTCs.[30] HOPE VI developers in general have learned how to increase their leveraging of private and LIHTC dollars (figure 3-1) while aligning development goals with local market conditions (figure 3-2). Many cities have multiple mixed-income HOPE VI developments, and housing authorities continue to bring into these deals new leveraged funding sources, from tax increment financing in Chicago to new markets tax credits in Portland, Oregon, to name a couple of examples.

There also are a growing number of mixed-finance public housing revitalization projects leveraging LIHTC equity and other private funding with public housing capital funds other than HOPE VI, albeit usually on a smaller scale than HOPE VI. By August 2008, HUD had reported 643 public housing mixed-finance closings, 154 of which did not include HOPE VI.[31]

As the financing varies, so does the extent of income mixing. Some projects adhere to the fairly standard goal of one-third public housing units (usually serving households in the bottom-third income bracket), one-third tax credit units (usually serving folks in the middle third), and one-third market-rate units. Others have a different breakdown due to differences in local market conditions. (See appendix B.) While mixed financing is a critical tool in the development of mixed-income communities, mixed-finance developments can be built without market-rate units. However, such projects do not fulfill the real promise of mixed-income communities, which is to help create communities that serve households in a broader range of incomes and that do not lose working families that become ineligible for subsidized housing when their incomes rise.

Conclusion

With their compatible designs, mixed-income developments have clearly ended the isolation of public housing and reconnected the new communities with adjoining neighborhoods (see chapter 4 for more on the architectural changes ushered in under HOPE VI). Public housing residents of the new communities live in units of far better quality than before, and in some cases they have access to support services such as job training and placement and after-school and summer programs. Philanthropic organizations have become engaged in aiding these families and, more broadly, in the issue of affordable housing. Areas adjacent to the communities have seen new investment and an increased tax base. The new developments have focused policymakers' attention on the need for quality neighborhood schools; indeed, school reform, which was central to the Murphy Park development, has been a critical piece of the puzzle in such cities as Atlanta, Milwaukee, and Portland.[32]

Federal, state, and local leaders should work to sustain and expand these achievements. In recent years awareness has been growing of the importance of offering support services to help former public housing residents benefit from the changes under way. But funding those services after the HOPE VI grant funds expire remains a significant challenge—and HUD's sources of alternative funding for public housing revitalization do not dedicate resources for such services.

Financing also remains a great challenge. As I noted in March 2008, Congress can make low-income housing tax credits a more effective tool for financing mixed-income communities by boosting the number of credits going to the states, giving states "more authority to offer increases in basis for certain projects," and allowing households earning up to 100 percent of area median income to reside in the projects while retaining the requirement that the projects also serve very low-income households.[33] There also should be a new federal tax incentive for foundations that support affordable housing programs.

As Reneé Glover explores more fully in chapter 9, mixed-finance transactions are not easy to put together. The rules are complex, and although procedures have become somewhat standardized, any new twist requires new negotiations to ensure that checks and balances are in place that both enable private investment in the communities and protect the federal government's investment in them.[34] An agreement that gives private investors an acceptable level of risk while ensuring that the public housing units remain public housing is an achievable goal, but the process of achieving it is complicated. Further, HOPE VI developers must shoulder the risk that a shortfall in the federal budget for public housing operating subsidies might reduce the funds available to maintain the units.

Fortunately, there has emerged a group of lenders, credit enhancers, tax credit syndicators, architects, and local funding program administrators who recognize the tremendous value of these mixed-income developments to the community and who therefore are excited about participating in their expansion. In turn, the motivations of good HOPE VI developers extend beyond maximizing their long-term economic profits. A good HOPE VI developer seeks to maximize community impact while maintaining the development's economic viability. That means that we are including market-rate housing in neighborhoods where the near-term opportunity for market-rate rents is modest at best, leaving another gap in financing to fill.

Why do we include these unrestricted units in nearly all our HOPE VI developments when, contrary to conventional wisdom, they often do not cross-subsidize the affordable units?

Because it is the right thing for the community. Having unrestricted units in our development creates housing for working-class residents, retaining some of the strongest strands in the community's fabric. And it gives families with rising incomes an opportunity to stay in the community that they call home, rather than requiring them to abandon their neighbors the moment that they acquire the means to do so.

Not inconsequentially, a market-rate element also provides the right incentives for managing a development and gaining public support. When residents truly have housing options, the economic need to keep them in the development ensures a certain level of amenities, maintenance, and repair. Residents who can vote with their feet are going to demand adequate police protection and other public services and improved quality in area schools. One could argue that the difficulties of traditional public housing were caused largely by a failure of management. Market-rate units help ensure against that result.

> Residents who can vote with their feet are going to demand adequate police protection and other public services and improved quality in area schools.

····· Endnotes ·····

1. National Commission on Severely Distressed Public Housing, *Final Report* (Government Printing Office, August 1992), pp. 15–21.

2. HOPE VI Grant Program Status spreadsheet printed February 16, 2007, by the Office of Public Housing Investments, U.S. Department of Housing and Urban Development. HOPE VI grants for Fiscal 1993 and 1994 totaling $1,074,501,945 had been awarded to twenty-six housing authorities for twenty-seven projects (Baltimore received two awards) through November 19, 1993.

3. Richard D. Baron, McCormack Baron & Associates, Inc., memorandum regarding urban revitalization demonstration and mixed-income housing initiative to Bruce Katz, chief of staff; Joe Shuldiner, assistant secretary for public and Indian housing; and Michael Stegman, assistant secretary for policy development and research, at the Department of Housing and Urban Development, December 20, 1993.

4. In the 1980s, Boston's highly distressed and crime-ridden Columbia Point public housing project was transferred to a private developer, Corcoran, Mullins, Jennison, Inc., which partnered with a resident task force to redevelop the complex as a mixed-income community, using a range of private, state, and federal funding sources, including such since closed-out sources as federal urban development action grant funds. Under the financing strategy, the low-income units were no longer public housing but forty-year, project-based Section 8 housing. Now called Harbor Point, the community was modeled on King's Lynne, a mixed-income redevelopment of the state-owned America Park public housing complex in Lynn, Massachusetts, in the late 1970s—also developed by Corcoran, Mullins, Jennison, Inc. Lora Engdahl, interview with Rod Solomon, partner, Hawkins Delafield & Wood LLP, September 10, 2008; Michael F. Schubert and Alison Thresher, "Lessons from the Field: Three Case Studies of Mixed-Income Housing Development," Great Cities Institute, College of Urban Planning and Public Affairs, University of Illinois at Chicago, April 1996, pp. 8–13; and Urban Land Institute, ULI Development Case Studies/King's Lynne (http://casestudies.uli.org/Profile.aspx?j=8093&p=5&c=22 [November 7, 2008]).

5. McCormack Baron & Associates was founded in 1973 by Richard D. Baron and Terrance McCormack. Before founding the firm, Baron and McCormack partnered on a Pruitt-Igoe redevelopment proposal under the auspices of the St. Louis Civic Alliance for Housing, which was established to reconstitute the St. Louis Housing Authority in the wake of a public housing rent strike. McCormack Baron & Associates became McCormack Baron Salazar in 2002. Today Kevin McCormack, Terry McCormack's son, is president of McCormack Baron Salazar and Tony Salazar is president of West Coast operations.

6. Charles Jencks, *The Language of Post-Modern Architecture* (New York: Rizzoli, 1977), p. 9.

7. Since demolition of the public housing complex, twenty-five acres of the site has been used for a magnet school.

8. Project-based Section 8 contracts were essentially a pledge attached to certain units that those units would be leased only to certain low-income families for a set number of years and that the federal government would pay the landlord the difference between what the tenants paid—generally 30 percent of their income—and the market rent. The guaranteed income from the federal rent subsidies attached to the Section 8 units combined with the projected income from the rent or sale of the market units enabled McCormack Baron to obtain construction loans and, ultimately, mortgages on such properties. Congress eliminated new funding under the Section 8 new construction and substantial rehabilitation program in 1983 and enacted the LIHTC program in 1986. For a fact sheet on the tax credit program, see www.ncsha.org/uploads/20040311_HC_factsheet.pdf.

9. Baron memo to Katz, Shuldiner, and Stegman, December 20, 1993. Although the report of the National Commission on Severely Distressed Public Housing, on which I served, had considered the potential benefits of leveraging public housing funds with tax credits and other sources and had mentioned the option in its final report, neither the authorizing legislation nor the initial program Notice of Funding Availability included provisions encouraging or explicitly providing for such leveraging.

10. The units are subject to affordability restrictions for at least fifteen years.

11. Cranston-Gonzalez National Affordable Housing Act, P.L. 101–625.

12. To receive credits against their taxes, tax credit investors must have an ownership interest in the redevelopment. That interest is formally established through a partnership consisting of a general partner (a local sponsor who may be a private developer, the public housing authority, or a nonprofit) and a limited partner (consisting of the tax credit investors), which receives the distribution of tax credit benefits proportional to its percent of ownership of the property—usually 99.99 percent. The term "limited partner" does not refer to a diminished level of ownership interest in the partnership but to operational roles and responsibilities. The general partner assumes the main responsibility for development and management, as if the property were its own. The limited partner ensures that safeguards are in place to protect its investment interest.

13. The amount of tax credits that a project qualifies for is based in part on its "eligible basis," which roughly translates to depreciable basis. In order to keep the federal HOPE VI funds from reducing this basis proportionally, they must be loaned at a commercial interest rate (the applicable federal rate, set by the Treasury Department), complicating their repayment terms. However, because the HOPE VI funds enable additional construction, depreciable basis and therefore losses in these projects are typically higher, which can marginally improve the price an investor will pay for the credits and losses. On the other hand, it is now standard to offer the sponsoring housing authority an option to buy back the development at the end of the initial fifteen-year compliance period. That option can reduce the long-term sale value of the property to the investor, which will in turn reduce its available pricing.

14. Lora Engdahl, interview with Michael Reardon, partner, Nixon Peabody LLC, January 17, 2008.

15. Nelson A. Diaz, general counsel, Department of Housing and Urban Development, "Use of Public Housing Funds to Leverage Private Financing," memorandum to Joseph Shuldiner, assistant secretary for public and Indian housing, April 8, 1994. The memorandum mentions specific proposals from the Fairfax County Redevelopment and Housing Authority and McCormack Baron & Associates on behalf of the St. Louis Housing Authority as well as "other similar proposals." The memorandum is reprinted in Megan Glasheen and Julie McGovern, "Mixed-Finance Development: Privatizing Public Housing through Public/Private Partnerships," in *Privatizing Governmental Functions*, edited by Deborah Ballati (New York: Law Journal Seminars Press, April 2001), pp. 9-57–9-63.

16. Engdahl, interview with Reardon, January 17, 2008; Michael Reardon, assistant general counsel, Department of Housing and Urban Development, "Fairfax Tax Credit Proposal," memorandum to Raymond Hamilton, development division director, Department of Housing and Urban Development, July 29, 1994.

17. Chester Hartman, "Shelterforce Interview: Joseph Shuldiner, Assistant Secretary for Public and Indian Housing," *Shelterforce* 77 (September-October 1994).

18. Ensuring that the for-profit limited partnership that owned the mixed-finance project would operate it in accordance with public housing requirements called for revising standard HUD documents such as the amendment to the Annual Contributions Contract and approving

new documents such as the regulatory and operating agreement and the ground lease. The modifications in the documents allowed public housing units in mixed-finance projects to be treated differently from conventional public housing in terms of operating subsidies provided, site-based waiting lists, owner-managed tenant screening, and possible remedies in the event that the income from public housing was insufficient to cover public housing operating expenses. Michael Reardon, e-mail message to Lora Engdahl, December 2, 2008.

19. Although commercial debt can play a role in mixed-finance public housing redevelopments, the relative size of private mortgage monies in these developments is much lower than in traditional multifamily developments, given the diminished net operating income generated. Public housing units cannot generate an operating profit and therefore cannot contribute any debt service for the development. And affordable units will generate less— in some cases far less—operating income than a corresponding market-rate unit due to the restricted rents. Thus, where a developer might finance 70 percent or more of its construction costs for a market-rate multifamily development with private debt, mixed-income developments may support only 30 percent or less of construction costs with private debt.

20. According to Michael Reardon in an April 23, 2008, e-mail message to Lora Engdahl, initially housing authorities that received URD grants enjoyed some additional flexibility in meeting the one-for-one requirement because they could replace up to one-third of the units with Section 8 tenant-based certificates. However, Rod Solomon noted in a phone interview with Engdahl on October 24, 2008, that that flexibility did not stretch far enough to accommodate plans to demolish and rebuild entire sites.

21. The regulations governing the development of new public housing include "site and neighborhood standards" that outline a narrow set of circumstances under which public housing can be built in high-poverty, high-minority areas. These standards are published in the annually updated *Code of Federal Regulations* (CFR), title 24, §941.202, which can be found online at the Government Printing Office website (http://www.gpoaccess.gov/cfr/index.html). Of course, many existing distressed public housing complexes were located in such neighborhoods. An interim rule on mixed financing published in May 1996 (see note 24 below) essentially exempted mixed-finance redevelopment projects from the standards by clarifying that public housing units built to replace public housing units demolished as part of a mixed-finance project can be built on the original site or in the same neighborhood if the number of new units is significantly less than the number of units demolished.

22. Engdahl, interview with Reardon, January 17, 2008.

23. The rule, which is known as the mixed-finance rule, was published in the *Federal Register* on May 2, 1996, adding a new subpart F to title 24, part 941, of the *Code of Federal Regulations*. See "Public/Private Partnerships for the Mixed-Finance Development of Public Housing," 24 CFR §941.600.

24. The Urban Development Action Grant program, within the HUD Office of Community Planning and Development, had since the late 1970s awarded grants to distressed communities to leverage private sector investment in neighborhood revitalization projects that would lead to jobs.

25. A 2004 report from the Urban Institute and the Brookings Institution explains how the FHA insurance piece of the funding package was used to encourage private lending in investment-starved neighborhoods: "The goal was to make HOPE VI a flexible source of capital, thereby providing a catalyst for other investment in neighborhoods that had been redlined by conventional financial institutions." See Susan J. Popkin and others, "A Decade of HOPE VI: Research Findings and Policy Challenges" (Washington: Urban Institute and Brookings Institution, May 2004), p. 17. On page 14 of the report, the authors say that HUD began to encourage mixed-finance strategies with the 1996 NOFA.

26. The Quality Housing and Work Responsibility Act of 1998 was enacted October 21, 1998, as Title V of the fiscal 1999 appropriations bill for HUD, the Department of Veterans Affairs, and independent agencies (P.L. 105-276). The statutory provision relating to HOPE VI was in Section 535, which amended Section 24 of the U.S. Housing Act of 1937; the statutory provision related to mixed finance was in Section 539 of QHWRA, which added Section 35 to the Housing Act of 1937.

27. When HUD first began promoting mixed-finance HOPE VI development, it created a separate "HOPE VI-Plus" team to shepherd the mixed-finance HOPE VI projects through development. That team and HOPE VI staff working on straight public housing redevelopments operated separately but eventually were merged into one team.

28. HUD created a template term sheet for public housing authorities to complete when making an initial request for HUD's investment in a mixed-finance transaction. The term sheet enables PHAs to provide consistent and relevant information early on to speed the negotiations. See "Project Review Protocol," U.S. Department of Housing and Urban Development, April 9, 2003 (http://fhasecure.gov/offices/pih/programs/ph/hope6/mfph/project_review_panel.pdf). Ozdinec, who is mentioned in chapter 1 in connection with early HOPE VI implementation, is a career civil servant who was the program manager for URD/HOPE VI when it first began and who remained with the program until May 2005.

29. According to HUD, only 13 percent of HOPE VI grants involved plans to make all of the post-revitalization units public housing. See appendix A, table A-4.

30 "Improvements to Public Housing," statement of Orlando J. Cabrera, assistant secretary of public and Indian housing, Department of Housing and Urban Development, to Committee on House Financial Services Subcommittee on Housing and Community Opportunity, CQ Congressional Testimony, June 21, 2007.

31. Data provided to Lora Engdahl by the Office of Public Housing Investments, Office of Public and Indian Housing, U.S. Department of Housing and Urban Development, August 4, 2008.

32. A number of school reform efforts tied to mixed-income redevelopment are profiled in a report from Urban Strategies Inc., a nonprofit community-building partner of McCormack Baron Salazar. See Sandra M. Moore and Susan K. Glassman, "The Neighborhood and Its School in Community Revitalization: Tools for Developers of Mixed-Income Housing Communities," Urban Strategies.

33. "Industry Suggests Ideas for Change," Affordable Housing Finance, March 2008. The Housing and Economic Recovery Act (P.L. 110-289), enacted in July 2008, boosted the allocation of credits to the states for 2008 and 2009, but the allocations revert to prior amounts after 2009. From "Changes Affecting Low-Income Housing Tax Credits and Rehabilitation Tax Credits Resulting from H.R. 3221," Novogradac & Company LLP (www.novoco.com/low_income_housing/legislation/2008/hr_3221_novoco_summary.pdf [December 1, 2008]).

34. Even with the combination of HOPE VI, LIHTC equity, and private debt, gaps in project financing often remain. Although numerous local and federal programs can help fill those gaps, they have their own complexities. For example, cities can make community development block grant funds available but those funds can be used only for infrastructure work without significant legal restructuring. HOME funds can be used in LIHTC developments, but they require additional affordability restrictions and may require a commercial interest rate. The Federal Home Loan Banks' competitively awarded Affordable Housing Program funds can fill small gaps in a project's financing, as can city and state incentives for generating affordable housing. The challenge with all of these programs is to structure them without violating the regulations of any other program utilized and without running afoul of any tax rules.

PETER CALTHORPE

HOPE VI and New Urbanism

HOPE VI's goal of replacing enclaves of concentrated poverty with new mixed-income communities called for a revolutionary design approach as well as progressive social and economic programs. Fortunately, the creation of HOPE VI coincided with the emergence of New Urbanism, an alternative to the flawed design theories that had shaped architecture and urban design worldwide in the post–World War II era. At the behest of HUD, a group of new urbanists helped to apply their new design model to transforming public housing as well as other federal housing programs. Policymakers and practitioners began to harness the capacity of design to support many nonphysical goals of HOPE VI redevelopment—fostering safety, community, pride of place, and opportunity. By joining forces with HOPE VI, New Urbanism has helped change preconceptions of what urban neighborhoods and public housing should be.

To understand the design aspect of the HOPE VI program, it is important to review the philosophy and urban vision of the modern movement in architecture and planning. Public housing in America evolved directly from the urban design models and architecture developed by leading mid-century modernists. Embedded in their prescriptions were the underpinnings of the dysfunctionality that HOPE VI was to repair—the lack of diversity, human scale, connections, and identity that the "projects" came to embody.

The modernists advocated a complete break from traditional forms of architecture and urban design. Grounded in the socialist movements in Europe prior to World War II, they saw the historic city in its worst light, characterized by inequality, overcrowding, and disease. As a counterpoint, they envisioned a brave new world of machine-like high-rise buildings isolated from the street, surrounded by parks, segregated into single-use zones, and connected by grand new highways. Modern architecture and planning rejected what its adherents labeled the bourgeois building traditions and outdated urban forms of the historic city, applying instead a philosophy of industrialization to the building of communities. Standardization, mass production, and segregation of uses and

In Denver's Villages of Curtis Park, cottage homes with entries, windows, and balconies overlooking the back lanes discourage the illicit activities that once thrived there.

Le Corbusier's 1925 Plan Voisin for Paris (left) called for bulldozing the low-rise structures of the historic central city north of the Seine and erecting eighteen sixty-story cruciform towers on parkland. The failed plan's underlying ideas were manifest in such U.S. developments as the Pruitt-Igoe public housing project in St. Louis, designed by Minoru Yamasaki (shown above in 1955). The elevators in Pruitt-Igoe's thirty-three eleven-story buildings stopped only at every third floor, opening to "galleries" that became dangerous to traverse.

Standardization, mass production, and segregation of uses and people became Modernism's postulates.

people became Modernism's postulates. And paramount was modernists' love of the automobile, the symbol of modern technology and the new criteria for urban space. The contrast with the historic city, with its walkable neighborhoods and uniquely crafted buildings, was stark.

Perhaps the best example of the hubris of Modern design was Le Corbusier's 1925 proposal for the redevelopment of the Right Bank of Paris, the Plan Voisin, a photograph of which appears above left.[1] The Swiss-born architect's conception for imposing rationality and order amid rapid population growth in Paris was soundly rejected by French politicians. However, his vision of the wholesale destruction of the historic city tragically came to guide the rebuilding of many European cities after World War II and the redevelopment of many U.S. inner-city areas under the guise of urban renewal.[2]

Le Corbusier's model articulates many of the design flaws typical of the U.S. public housing projects built to house people displaced by urban renewal. Across the country, public housing towers set in superblocks destroyed the walkability and the human scale characteristic of traditional urban neighborhoods and critical to healthy communities. The remoteness of complexes from surrounding neighborhoods stigmatized their occupants and fueled an isolated and increasingly dysfunctional culture. The ubiquitous open space around towers became a no-man's land because its design precluded conducting the everyday activities seen on traditional urban streets and eliminated the natural opportunities for surveillance that they afforded. The lack of mixed uses and a one-size-fits-all building program led to communities that, without

In the spring of 1973, children play in the vast, unsecured areas between the high-rises of Stateway Gardens on the south side of Chicago (far left). Completed in 1958, the thirty-three-acre, eight-building public housing complex was set on superblocks created by razing structures of the kind visible in this view from Dearborn Street looking north to Stateway Gardens in 1959 (left).

a range of household types and incomes, offered few social or economic opportunities. Perhaps most egregiously, a lack of respect for the history and the cultural continuity of older neighborhoods led most urban renewal programs to wholesale demolition rather than to the sensitive restoration of existing community features. Much of what was best in urban centers and inner-city neighborhoods was lost in the process.

And there were deeper, more complex effects that grew from Modernism to compound the challenges of the inner-city poor. Modernism's advocacy of the automobile, freeways, and segregated land uses indirectly created the planning paradigm for sprawl and its negative effect on cities. The decay of the inner city and the lack of investment in the civic infrastructure of cities was fueled by a massive postwar middle-class exodus made possible by suburban sprawl, Veterans Administration home loans, and the Federal Aid Highway Act of 1956—and Modernism's fundamentally anti-city propositions.[3] While we destroyed what was best about our cities and urban neighborhoods, we simultaneously subsidized the alternative, the suburbs. In that context, it is no wonder that public housing failed.

New Urbanism and HOPE VI

As a counterpoint to the modernists, New Urbanism looked to what was best about the traditional American city and town. Its models of walkable, mixed-use neighborhoods had meaning in the city as well as the suburbs and applied across income groups. The new urbanists presented proposals for the city that were simple and concrete: instead of building isolated towers, they advocated bringing housing, complete with stoops and porches, back to the street. Instead of superblocks, they advocated a fine-grained street network designed for the pedestrian and connected to surrounding neighborhoods. Rejecting single-use zones, they proposed mixed-use areas with local shops, services, and civic institutions, all within walking distance. To replace towers and mid-rise slabs, they brought back a range of housing types—from bungalows to town houses and low-rise apartment buildings—that could accommodate a broader spectrum of households and their needs. Instead of a "project," they reasserted the simple idea of a traditional neighborhood.

New Urbanism began to take shape as a movement in the 1980s and was formalized in a series of congresses in the early 1990s. Its philosophy was greatly influenced by Jane Jacobs, a noted writer on urban planning and an activist whose seminal book, *The Death and Life of Great American Cities,* and other works rediscovered the simple truths of urbanism. But New Urbanism went beyond prescriptions for repairing the city and shaping the neighborhood. It structured its goals and techniques on three scales: those of the region, neighborhood, and building. It claimed that the three were interdependent and that to create healthier places each had to be redesigned. New Urbanism asserted that one could not create successful urban neighborhoods without a design approach that addressed its buildings, its street fabric, its open space, its civic places, its commercial opportunities, and the larger regional context.

On the regional scale, New Urbanism called for a fundamental alternative to sprawl by advocating transit-oriented development, regional open space systems, and, most significant for public housing, fair share housing policies across metropolitan areas. New Urbanism acknowledged that low-income housing should not and could not be considered just a problem of the inner city. As jobs and opportunities decentralized, the responsibility for affordable housing had to follow. New mixed-income communities in the city and within public housing sites needed to be matched by more affordable housing opportunities in the suburbs. In fact, the grand regional strategy of New Urbanism was to rebalance the city and its suburbs by bringing more middle-class families back to the city while creating more opportunity for affordable housing in the suburbs. The tactic was simply to create neighborhoods in both locations that included the broadest range of household incomes possible.

On the neighborhood scale, New Urbanism advanced principles that became the core of the HOPE VI design program—diversity, human scale, restoration, and continuity:

- Diversity is a core principle of New Urbanism and lies at the heart of the HOPE VI program, which promotes mixed-income and mixed-use redevelopment. In terms of urban design, diversity means mixing a variety of housing types to support a range of households of different incomes, integrating housing with local shops and safe public spaces, and providing social services.
- Human scale in design is achieved by such features as street- and pedestrian-oriented buildings; rich architectural detail; and a clear definition of public and private space. It implies foremost that the neighborhood and its streets should be walkable and safe. Security is reinforced by residents who

are able to keep an eye on the street because the streets are easily seen from their homes. Destinations should be close at hand, transit convenient, and community services easily accessible.

- Restoration entails preserving and in many cases reconstructing the positive social and physical infrastructure of the neighborhood. It often involves rebuilding some historic housing, restoring important civic buildings, respecting usable public space, and reconstructing the connections to surrounding neighborhoods.
- Continuity in the street network, architectural treatments, open space systems, and shared public spaces reconnects the "projects" with nearby neighborhoods and the city. They are linked at both the local and regional level, by safe pedestrian streets and transit systems. The building types and architecture of the new community also promote continuity by relating to the history and traditions of the place.

Urban renewal—and, in fact, suburban sprawl—ran counter to each of these four simple design principles. The typical single-use zoning and isolated housing of most urban renewal programs were the antithesis of the diverse and complex neighborhoods needed to vitalize inner-city public housing sites. The superblocks and towers (and, for that matter, the arterials and subdivisions of suburbia) were the opposite of the human-scale environments that had made most urban neighborhoods walkable and desirable. Lack of respect for the history and cultural continuity of older neighborhoods led most renewal programs to wholesale demolition rather than to sensitive restoration of key community elements and maintenance of continuity with the surrounding environment. Although each of New Urbanism's core principles may seem obvious, they were all radical in the world of planning and public housing.

On the third scale, that of the building, New Urbanism's ability to learn from historic and traditional building types proved equally significant to HOPE VI. The form of traditional housing throughout American cities offered important precedents: the stoop of a brownstone, the porch on a bungalow, or the secure courtyard of a small apartment building all offered ways to support safety in the public realm while providing identity for occupants. Rather than generic buildings, unique treatments and varied streetscapes could engender the kind of pride and sense of ownership so important to neighborhood stability. By tapping the architectural history of a place, New Urbanism could develop an architecture that related to what was unique about the place—its building materials, climate, and traditions.

The following case studies manifest the principles of diversity, human scale, restoration, and continuity in real ways and in real places. The differences created by the new urbanist design philosophy complemented many of the social and economic goals of the HOPE VI program. Under HOPE VI, these project sites were rebuilt in ways that diminished the historic isolation

Under Hope VI... project sites were rebuilt in ways that diminished the historic isolation of public housing blocks.

of public housing blocks, creating safer, socially diverse neighborhoods that, in the end, fostered the sense of pride, ownership, and community that had been missing before.

Martin Luther King Plaza, Philadelphia

Before redevelopment, the four high-rise towers of Martin Luther King Plaza in South Philadelphia cast a literal and figurative shadow on the working-class row house community around it. Built in 1960, with 594 units of public housing on six acres, this psychologically walled-off project only ten blocks from historic City Hall had fallen into serious disrepair by the mid-1990s. Two hundred units were continually uninhabited and uninhabitable, and a halo of blight radiated into the adjacent Hawthorne neighborhood.

Philadelphia's housing authority won a $25.2 million grant to redevelop the site in 1998. But despite substandard housing conditions (broken elevators, exposed pipes, and so forth) and rampant crime and drugs, MLK residents and community stakeholders were initially skeptical that redevelopment would make their lives or their community better. A seventy-person task force was formed that included city officials and staff, residents, politicians, clergy, and community leaders. Brought in to engage the community in the redesign process was the urban design firm Torti Gallas and Partners, based in Silver Spring, Maryland. Well-versed in New Urbanism's principles, Torti Gallas undertook door-to-door surveys and helped lead on-site community workshops and design charrettes to formulate the revitalization plan.

The design challenge thus produced was significant: to provide enough housing to rehouse existing MLK residents who wanted to return while dramatically reducing density. To respond, the developer, a joint venture between a local nonprofit community development corporation and a for-profit tax credit developer, formed a partnership with the city to acquire more than 100 vacant houses and lots in the surrounding Hawthorne neighborhood. The resulting comprehensive master plan and redevelopment replaced the dense, high-rise public housing with a new, mixed-use and mixed-income row house neighborhood that is woven into the existing urban fabric. The new housing—245 units—is equally divided between on-site reconstruction and off-site renovation and infill.

By the mid-1990s hundreds of units in Martin Luther King Plaza were unlivable. The defaced interior stairwells (page 20) were one sign of rampant crime and disorder.

One of the design goals was to make the new for-sale and rental homes similar to the existing Philadelphia-style row houses and to one another but not so indistinguishable that residents could not point to a house with pride and say, "That's my home." Torti Gallas addressed the challenge by matching the scale and materials of the existing homes—the red and orange brick, the front stoops—but adding the small architectural details that make homes distinctive—the color of a door, the details of a cornice, the color of the bricks and the mortar between the bricks. Also, 15 percent of

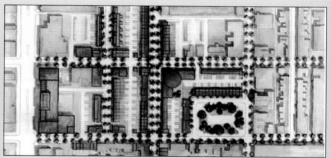

Torti Gallas and Partners' redesign of Martin Luther King Plaza replaced four towers situated on superblocks cut off from the street grid with smaller-scale residences and tree-lined through streets (above) more in sync with a traditional South Philadelphia neighborhood.

With their multicolored brick exteriors, detailed cornices, and other architectural features, the mixed-income rental homes on South 13th Street in South Philadelphia (above) are indistinguishable from the new for-sale row houses on nearby Juniper Street (right), also built as part of the redevelopment of the former Martin Luther King Plaza public housing project.

Photo above by Steve Hall © Hedrich Blessing

the on-site homes are handicapped accessible, but through use of creative façades, unity of design, and streetscaping, modifications are not evident from the street.

The Torti Gallas principal in charge, Tom Gallas, observes that of the more than thirty HOPE VI redevelopments that the firm has designed, MLK has likely done the best job of focusing on economic stability and support services for residents. A charter school and job training and placement center run by a nonprofit were built three blocks from the site. A program of extensive support services, including not only job and life-skills training but child care and transportation, was customized for each family and delivered through the center and other service providers, enhancing the community's human capital.

This comprehensive, neighborhood-wide revitalization has created a ripple effect throughout the entire neighborhood and its quadrant of the city. In early

Shown here in the late 1990s, the distressed, low-rise Broadway Homes project in east Baltimore looked much different from typical Baltimore townhomes and thus was easily identifiable as public housing. Rear yards were exposed to public areas, and front doors (not shown) opened up to unsecured interior walkways, leading to ill-defined public and private space.

2008, a *Philadelphia Daily News* article documented a 47 percent decrease in crime at MLK from 1999 to 2007 and the escalation of real estate prices, with private homes near the public housing town houses selling for roughly $700,000 in 2007.[4]

Broadway Overlook, Baltimore

Built in 1971, the Broadway Homes public housing project in east Baltimore housed 330 elderly residents in a tower of more than twenty stories and ninety-nine families in distressed, low-rise, barracks-like structures that were clustered around the base of the tower in a confusing pattern and connected by unsafe pedestrian lanes. Though the complex was adjacent to Johns Hopkins Medical Center, its location at the intersection of two major streets at the top of Washington Hill isolated it from the surrounding community, which had an excess of public housing and subsidized projects. Most important, it was only two roads from the edge of the historic Washington Hill neighborhood, which had maintained a mixed-income population through creative use of historic preservation guidelines and staunch resistance to the addition of public housing within its boundaries.

Winning the support of the Washington Hill neighborhood proved crucial to the site's redevelopment when a new opportunity arose between the time that the Housing Authority of Baltimore City submitted its HOPE VI application and received a $21.4 million grant, in 1999. The application had been based on reusing the existing site. But when the Church Home hospital across the major intersection announced that it would close, Johns Hopkins proposed purchasing it and donating it to the HOPE VI project in exchange for the original site, which was ideally suited for Hopkins's expansion. The move across the street into the Washington Hill neighborhood resulted in fierce opposition from the residents, who feared a negative impact on the community.

The intense process that followed focused considerable attention on the architectural character of the new development, responsibility for which fell to Pittsburgh-based Urban Design Associates. It was not enough, the community argued, to have "generic Baltimore traditional row houses"—this was, after all, Washington Hill, and it had its own distinctive interpretation of those traditional forms. Furthermore, the historic wing of the Church Home hospital dated back to the early nineteenth century and included the room in which Edgar Allen Poe had died. Its golden dome was a landmark visible all the way from Fells Point and the Inner Harbor. The design was developed and refined in dialogue with community members, who finally approved inclusion of the development in their neighborhood. Because of the land swap the Broadway Overlook HOPE VI project was not built on the footprint of a former public housing complex, but the same new urbanist principles were used to re-stitch the site into the urban fabric as were used with public housing sites, as illustrated in the sketches below.

The new Broadway Overlook community, developed by Landex Corporation of Linthicum, Maryland, was completed in 2005 at a cost of $54 million. It features a series of new streets lined with a variety of housing types and units:

Urban Design Associates (UDA) designed Baltimore's new Broadway Overlook community (right) to replace the Broadway Homes public housing development but on the Church Home hospital site (left). The large buildings on large lots that had visually separated the site from the community were razed, and the redesigned development took on a more human scale, with smaller structures placed closer together for pedestrian use. Streets were reattached to the street grid, providing for continuity with existing neighborhoods, while the redevelopment of the hospital wing (top center in before image at left) as a wing of a new apartment complex (L-shaped structure in after image) aligned with the new urbanist principle of restoration. In addition to conserving the urban architectural environment, the redesign incorporated trees planted throughout the site to restore the natural environment.

A mix of rental homes—including public, tax credit–assisted, and market-rate housing—lines a street of the Broadway Overlook community. The spire of the preserved historic wing of the Church Home hospital, now an apartment building, is just visible against the sky.

eighty-four public housing rental units, forty-eight non–public housing rental units, and thirty-four homes for sale at market rates.[5] The historic wing of the hospital has been restored on the exterior and modified inside to become an elevator apartment building. The new mid-rise wing attached to it has apartments with spectacular views of the harbor and downtown Baltimore. Two floors of the apartment complex operate as a short-stay hotel, with the remaining units serving market-rate renters, tax credit households, and elderly public housing residents.[6]

The streets within Broadway Overlook connect with Washington Hill through a shared park. An existing parking garage, which remains, is fronted by single-aspect town houses to create a congenial residential street. The parking garage for the elevator apartment building also is fronted by single-aspect units.[7] One of the new streets is aligned with an existing monument (to the founder of the Optimists Society of America!) in the middle of the median on Broadway, which was designed by Frederick Law Olmsted.

Broadway Overlook's architectural character and its location within the city has helped ensure its social success. The community—adjacent to a major medical facility, very close to downtown, included in a historic neighborhood, and perched on a hilltop that affords spectacular views from the upper floors of the apartment building—attracts residents with a wide variety of incomes. Rents range from $2,000 a year for the most deeply subsidized units to $2,000 a month for the most popular market-rate units. Broadway Overlook has reinforced the stability of adjacent neighborhoods, and it is playing an essential part in the East Baltimore revitalization program.

The Villages of Curtis Park, Denver

Set in a beautiful, historic, but decaying inner-city neighborhood near the center of Denver, Curtis Park and Arapahoe Courts Apartments did not suffer from the problems of high-rise development and high density common among public housing complexes. Its two-story buildings were somewhat in scale with the surrounding neighborhood of Victorian single-family homes and town houses. But the layout and design created many security and livability problems. The long, blocky residential buildings were more barrack-like than those in the surrounding neighborhood, creating a visual stigma. The building entrances did not face the surrounding streets; they faced inward, around unused open spaces and parking lots. Drug dealing and crime thrived in these central areas, hidden as they were from the street and surrounding community.

On winning a $25.8 million HOPE VI grant in 1998, the housing authority of the city and county of Denver and its private development partner, the Integral Group, hired Calthorpe Associates of Berkeley, California, which had helped prepare the original grant application, to create a master plan and architectural designs for the first phase.[8] The redevelopment replaced 286 public housing units with 135 public housing rental units, 94 tax-credit rental units, and 94 market-rate rental units, and an additional 257 for-sale homes, most of which could be purchased through a subordinate mortgage program. (Of the 580 units developed, 236 are off site.)

The redesign of the Villages of Curtis Park placed the entrances on the street side of the buildings and created a range of buildings of different styles for different uses. Lining the long side of each block are duplex homes that have the scale and massing of the neighborhood's single-family homes. Their front entries and porches serve to bring the life of the house back to the street and provide much-needed opportunities for casual surveillance. At the short ends of the blocks are live-work townhomes for occupants who operate home-based businesses and small corner stores to provide services to the community. Finally, the interiors of the blocks were redeveloped into a series of lanes lined by cottages. Today balconies, living room windows, and entries face the lanes, creating a safe place for kids to play that is frequented by pedestrians— not a no-man's land of anonymous parking lots.

The site is adjacent to a sizable city park and shares its space with a school, daycare center, and community center. With the addition of the community center and small tot lot, the site has become truly diverse in terms of housing types, public uses, and open space. Human scale was established by massing the buildings into duplex and cottage forms reminiscent of the historic architecture of the neighborhood. Walkability and safety were reinforced by simple design measures—streetside porches, entrances, and sidewalks; street trees; and parking spaces that line the streets and lanes. Historical continuity was established by the materials used and the architectural treatments of the homes. All of this has resulted in the reintegration of the public housing site into the surrounding neighborhood and has contributed to the revitalization of the area.

Conclusion

The marriage between New Urbanism and HOPE VI has been central to the mission of restoring public housing. The connections at the regional level, the seamless relationship between old and new and between traditional neighborhood and affordable community, and the reinvention of historic and place-specific housing types all have contributed to the success of the program.

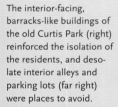
The interior-facing, barracks-like buildings of the old Curtis Park (right) reinforced the isolation of the residents, and desolate interior alleys and parking lots (far right) were places to avoid.

With their front porches and colorful street-oriented facades, the duplexes and single-family homes of the new Curtis Park (left) invite interaction with the surrounding neighborhood, while the balconies and large windows overlooking the interior lanes (above) create safe areas for pedestrians and children.

Although New Urbanism's respect for historic architecture and neighborhood form is evident in any new urbanist community, the case for this approach was strongest in redeveloping low-income communities. The visual and physical connections created by traditional architecture and human-scale street systems helped to break down the distinctions that had stigmatized projects and their occupants. Most public housing occupants disliked living in housing so remarkably different from traditional neighborhoods and endorsed traditional design features such as front porches and private yards with picket fences. In addition, the form of traditional neighborhoods helped resolve many of the most challenging problems of the projects: the lack of security and opportunities for resident surveillance of streets and parks, the lack of a clear definition of private and public domains, and the loss of civic focus.

The loss of units in most HOPE VI projects due to the addition of affordable and market-rate dwellings and the shift to lower densities was inevitable if HOPE VI was going to significantly change the character of the community, the mix of occupants, and ultimately the identity of the neighborhood. Using Section 8 vouchers for those who did not return had the hidden benefit of moving some families to new areas, perhaps richer in job and school opportunities. But many worried that in the long run, vouchers would be less dependable than government-owned housing. That ultimately was the trade-off—fewer public housing units in exchange for communities with more social integration.

As HOPE VI succeeded, there was a sense that the mix of incomes and overall neighborhood improvements brought about by the program would lead to some form of gentrification. Implicit in the notion of moving from segregated, dysfunctional public housing projects to mixed-income neighborhoods was the hope—not the fear—of an improved environment, neighborhoods that were safer and richer in social capital. Some displacement was inevitable given the time required for rebuilding, the addition of non–public housing units, and the lower densities implied by buildings of a more human scale. But ultimately many low-income households found their place in healthier, safer, and more opportunity-rich neighborhoods.

Moving forward, the next generation of public housing redevelopment projects can address some of the issues of density and gentrification. Some advocates have urged that the next iteration of the program include a new one-for-one replacement requirement for public housing units, which would result in denser site plans.[9] Such plans could be accommodated by mixing street-oriented townhomes with mid-rise structures and towers, as has been successfully accomplished in Vancouver over the last two decades. Although taller buildings intelligently designed can increase density, variety, and opportunity in a mixed-income neighborhood, care must be taken to avoid the mistakes of the past with respect to the design, maintenance, and security of public

Shallow swales that filter runoff after heavy rains and porous pavement sidewalks are among the components of the natural drainage system created in the High Point redevelopment.

housing. Replacing all units demolished while adding affordable and market-rate units could also be achieved by expanding the redevelopment area into adjacent neighborhoods. Doing so could help keep building densities down while restoring decaying or abandoned properties in the area.

Another potential improvement for a new wave of HOPE VI projects would be to employ green building and energy conservation measures. Reducing energy costs while mitigating the adverse environmental impact of construction should be an imperative for all government investments, especially affordable housing. With continuing funding shortfalls eating into their operating budgets, some housing authorities are exploring ways to incorporate green development features that can lower regular utility bills. At the same time, there is increasing pressure to marry public investment with sustainable principles, and indeed in some communities those features can be used to attract market-rate renters and homeowners to mixed-income communities. Many green strategies and models have emerged. For example, Boston's Maverick Landing was among the first LEED-certified apartment communities in the nation.[10] Seattle's High Point HOPE VI community features what is believed to be the first large natural drainage system developed within a dense urban neighborhood in the United States—a system whose improvements to water quality and flow help preserve the salmon spawning grounds in nearby Longfellow Creek.[11] Such strategies, along with efficient building footprints and insulation, climate-responsive design, natural ventilation, and daylighting, can reduce the carbon footprint of a project while potentially producing a healthier, more sustainable architecture.

Clearly design has played a key role in redefining public housing in the HOPE VI program. The program's fundamental postulate—creating mixed-income, mixed-use communities—depended on a new design paradigm as well as new public policy. New Urbanism's principles were a perfect fit: diversity and human scale in architecture helped create safer, more desirable places for all income groups. It helped end the isolation and stigma of the projects by restoring and preserving the best of the community, helping to maintain social identity and continuity, and creating more connections with surrounding neighborhoods. HOPE VI and the new urbanists created a new fusion of social policy and physical design, one that involved—symbolically and literally—a shift from the anonymity of high-rise flats to the human scale of town houses, from the fear of stairwells to the comfort of front porches, from dangerous open spaces to tree-lined sidewalks—and ultimately, from projects to neighborhoods.

····· Endnotes ·····

1. Le Corbusier's 1925 proposal for Paris was called the Plan Voisin because it was sponsored by Voisin, an automobile and aircraft cartel. From Kenneth Frampton, *Modern Architecture: A Critical History*, 3rd ed. (London: Thames and Hudson, 1992).

2. The Urban Redevelopment Program was created by the National Housing Act of 1949 (P.L. 81-71). The program funded slum clearance and redevelopment and the construction of public housing for those displaced by slum clearance. When those activities were expanded under the Housing Act of 1954, they were titled "urban renewal." Further expansion of urban renewal occurred with the passage of the Housing Act of 1959. Kent W. Colton, *Housing in the Twenty-First Century: Achieving Common Ground* (Harvard University Press, 2003), pp. 214–16.

3. In 1944, Congress passed the GI Bill which, among other things, authorized mortgage guarantees through the Veterans Administration, helping to fuel a housing boom. Although the interstate highway system began to form in the 1930s, the nationwide freeway construction boom began after Congress passed the Federal Aid Highway Act of 1956, which called for more than 41,000 miles of highways that would be 90 percent funded by the federal government. Colton, *Housing in the Twenty-First Century*, pp. 27–28; Michael Cabanatuan, "The Interstate Highway System at 50: America in the Fast Lane with No Exit," *San Francisco Chronicle*, June 17, 2006.

4. Julie Shaw, "Pride of PHA," *Philadelphia Daily News*, February 19, 2008.

5. Almost all of the for-sale units were reserved for buyers at 115 percent of area median income and thus were not purely market rate, but it is not certain that they would have sold for higher prices without the income restrictions. Two of the units were sold at a deeper discount to former public housing residents.

6. The short-term rental housing is provided through a program with the Marriott Corporation.

7. With single-aspect architecture, the windows face in one direction only—toward the street. These town house types are used as a "liner" in front of the parking garages in order to provide houses that face the street. Because they back up directly to the garage, they have to be designed with windows on one side only; so that daylight can fully penetrate the interior spaces, they are shallower than typical town houses.

8. The architects for the redevelopment were Abo Cervantes Loos Priebe Architects (phase I), Humphries Poli Architects (phases II and III), and Braun Yoshida Architects (phase IV).

9. At this writing, the House had passed a HOPE VI reauthorization bill that would add a one-for-one replacement requirement for all public housing units demolished under HOPE VI.

10. Bendix Anderson, "Boston Redevelopment Beats the Odds," *Affordable Housing Finance*, December 2006.

11. Elements of the drainage system include shallow grass-lined and deeper vegetated swales that filter water; two miles of porous concrete public sidewalks; reduced building footprints and pavement; and preservation of existing mature trees. Communication with Kathryn M. Gwilym and Peg Staeheli, SvR Design Company, January 8, 2009. SvR was the civil engineer and landscape architect on the project.

ALEXANDER POLIKOFF

CHAPTER

5

HOPE VI and the Deconcentration of Poverty

Serious study of urban poverty was ended for more than two decades by the fallout from Daniel Patrick Moynihan's controversial 1965 report on the problems of the black family.[1] In 1987, William Julius Wilson's examination of the "underclass," *The Truly Disadvantaged,* revived it.[2] Jump-started it, one might say. Within a few short years, Wilson's focus on the "concentration effects" of urban poverty had become conventional wisdom. It was not just poverty that moved so many inner-city neighborhoods into wretchedness; it was the *concentration* of poor urban African American families in geographic, economic, and social isolation that was the culprit.[3]

Scrutiny of the effects of concentrated poverty centered on public housing complexes such as the infamous Robert Taylor Homes. Completed in 1962, Taylor's twenty-eight buildings, which included over 4,000 units, stretched more than two miles along State Street on Chicago's South Side. In the late 1980s news media reported a litany of miseries facing the nearly 19,000 residents of the complex, which was largely under the control of drug-dealing gangs engaged in turf wars.[4] The social distress linked to concentrated poverty was evident in later data reported by the Chicago Housing Authority: $45,000 worth of drug transactions occurred at Robert Taylor Homes every day; the employment rate was 4 percent; and 95.5 percent of households were headed by women.[5]

Because urban public housing had become one of the most visible manifestations of concentrated poverty, the challenge of "distressed" public housing soon became a focus of national policy.[6] Two years after the appearance of *The Truly Disadvantaged,* Congress established the National Commission on Severely Distressed Public Housing to study the matter and propose a remedial plan. The commission's recommendations led to the enactment, in October 1992, of two seminal pieces of housing legislation that created a federal grant program that came to be called HOPE VI.[7]

Designed to foster, among other things, wide-ranging management improvements and services to promote residents' self-sufficiency, the new legislation

In the early 1990s, public housing complexes such as Chicago's Robert Taylor Homes (seen here in foreground, looking north toward the city, in 1996) were among the most visible manifestations of concentrated poverty.

AP Photo/Beth A. Keiser

also embodied a major policy shift. In undertaking to "revitalize" their worst buildings, housing authorities no longer would be limited (as for practical purposes most had been) to rehabilitating them—they could also tear them down and start over.[8]

Despite the Wilson-inspired learning, poverty deconcentration was not at the outset an explicit goal of the new laws—possibly because, as Bruce Katz describes in chapter 2, the multiple challenges of reshaping failed public housing were sufficient in themselves to fill HUD's administrative plate. Deconcentration made its first statutory appearance in a 1996 HOPE VI appropriations bill that set a goal of building replacement housing "which will avoid or lessen concentration of very low-income families."[9] That was enlarged by 1998's Quality Housing and Work Responsibility Act into a "purpose"—to provide housing "that will avoid or decrease the concentration of very low-income families."[10]

Still, Wilson's focus on concentrated poverty was not forgotten. In January 1993, three months after enactment of the legislation that created HOPE VI, Bill Clinton assumed the presidency and brought with him a new HUD secretary, Henry G. Cisneros, who describes in chapter 1 of this volume the dramatic reorientation of the public housing system that he believed was required. That reorientation very definitely included deconcentrating poverty.

A Passionate Crusade

In September 1994, the Cisneros-led HUD issued an Urban Policy Brief that pointed to two decades of "explosive growth" in areas of extreme poverty within many large cities, adding that minority households, for whom residential choice was constrained by racial segregation and housing discrimination, were "invariably overrepresented" in those areas (figures 5-1 and 5-2). Echoing Wilson, the policy brief said that the consequences of the interaction of "place and race" included urban neighborhoods with high levels of unemployment, public assistance, and female-headed households, plus poor schools, frayed social institutions, high crime, and crumbling infrastructure (figure 5-3).[11]

To "reduce concentrations of inner-city poverty," the policy brief continued, HUD had developed two "mobility" programs. The first, Choice in Residency, would provide grants for comprehensive housing counseling services to households seeking or receiving certificates that would pay a portion of their rent in private market housing under the federal Section 8 program. The second, Metropolitan Assisted Housing Strategies, would fund clearinghouses to coordinate information on the regional availability of housing and assistance, including the waiting lists for all assisted housing in a given metropolitan area.

The policy brief acknowledged that residential mobility programs were but one part of a larger poverty reduction strategy that included fair housing enforcement, welfare and health care reform, and other initiatives, as well as

Figure 5-1. **Growth in Extreme-Poverty Census Tracts, 100 Largest Central Cities, 1970–1990**[a]

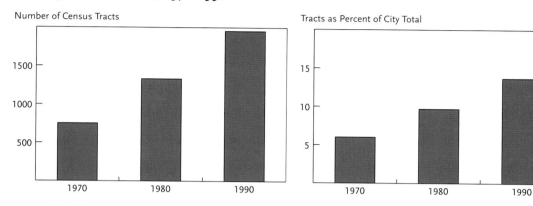

Number of Census Tracts

Tracts as Percent of City Total

Source: Adapted from John P. Kasarda, "Inner-City Concentrated Poverty and Neighborhood Distress: 1970 to 1990," *Housing Policy Debate 4*, no. 2 (1993), p. 258.

a. Extreme-poverty tracts are those in which at least 40 percent of residents live in poverty.

Figure 5-2. **Racial Composition of Extreme-Poverty Census Tracts, 100 Largest Cities, 1990**

Percent

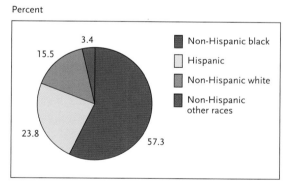

Source: Adapted from John P. Kasarda, "Inner-City Concentrated Poverty and Neighborhood Distress: 1970 to 1990," *Housing Policy Debate 4*, no. 2 (1993), pp. 263, 264.

Figure 5-3. **Population Characteristics, 100 Largest Central Cities, 1990**[a]

Percent

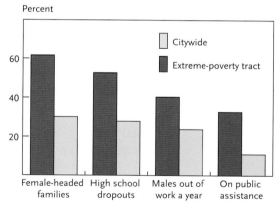

Source: Adapted from John P. Kasarda, "Inner-City Concentrated Poverty and Neighborhood Distress: 1970 to 1990," *Housing Policy Debate 4*, no. 2 (1993), pp. 271, 273, 275, 276, 278.

a. Specific characteristics measured by tract and city were percent of female-headed households with children under age eighteen, persons age twenty-five and over with less than a high school education, out-of-school males age sixteen to sixty-four who did not work in the previous year, and households receiving public assistance.

"place-based" programs such as those to revitalize distressed public housing. As a part of that larger strategy, residential mobility could make an "important contribution."

Also acknowledged was a debt to a long-running Chicago lawsuit, *Gautreaux* v. *Chicago Housing Authority,* which was described as the first and best-known attempt "to facilitate the movement of low-income African Americans from inner-city neighborhoods to predominantly white suburbs." *Gautreaux* began in 1966 in response to the racially discriminatory practices of the Chicago Housing Authority, carried on with HUD's knowledge, in siting and assigning tenants to Chicago's public housing. Practices aimed at keeping black public housing families away from white neighborhoods had led to a predominantly black public housing system that was located mostly in black neighborhoods, characteristics shared by the public housing systems of many other large cities. The first-named plaintiff in the case was Dorothy Gautreaux, a civil rights leader and resident of Chicago's Altgeld-Murray Homes public housing project.

A remedial approach, ultimately sanctioned by the U.S. Supreme Court in 1976,[12] aimed to give families access to housing in unsegregated neighborhoods throughout the Chicago metropolitan area—"breaching the jurisdictional wall," observed the policy brief, that had "historically insulated suburban communities from sharing responsibility for the segregation of the urban poor." Under the Gautreaux program, Section 8 certificates enabled eligible families to rent privately owned housing in neighborhoods that were no more than 30 percent black. Counselors aided families in searching for housing—identifying units, accompanying families to inspect units, and assisting with lease applications. Post-move counseling helped families adjust to their new environments.

At the time the *Urban Policy Brief* appeared, some 5,600 low-income black families had participated in the Gautreaux program. More than half had moved to predominantly white, middle-class suburbs, the balance to neighborhoods within Chicago. Studies of the experiences of the families had found that, on employment and education measures, the families that moved to the suburbs generally fared better than those that moved within the city and that—contrary to expectations—most families that relocated in the suburbs were not socially isolated. The policy brief concluded that Gautreaux and other smaller mobility programs "provide strong support for the assumptions underlying the residential mobility concept," noting also that some features of the Gautreaux program were replicated in Moving to Opportunity (MTO), a ten-year, five-city demonstration program, funding for which was first appropriated by Congress in 1991.[13] There was, however, a fundamental difference between Gautreaux and the MTO demonstration. The former was explicitly designed to remedy racial discrimination; MTO, eschewing racial criteria, permitted participants to move to any low-poverty area regardless of racial composition. With regard to that difference, the policy brief opined that "the high correlation between race and concentrated poverty in large metro-politan areas makes it likely that participant characteristics and destinations in the two programs will turn out to be substantially the same" (which—as noted later—proved not to be the case).

Thus, by mid-1994, HUD was readying an assault on the concentrated poverty of large urban centers. In his nationally syndicated column, David Broder called it "a mission to remake the face of Urban America." With Gautreaux as a "working model," the intention was "to break up the concen-trations of crime- and drug-ridden public housing by dispersing residents from the projects throughout the metropolitan area." Cisneros, Broder wrote, had become the Clinton administration's "passionate crusader against racial and economic segregation."[14]

Dorothy Gautreaux was the first-named plaintiff in the civil rights case that inspired housing mobility programs.

The results of the crusade have been mixed—there have been some achieve-ments and some disappointments. That tale begins with one of the biggest dis-appointments. In November 1994, just two months after the policy brief was issued, Republicans captured Congress in a political revolution that arose from Newt Gingrich's "Contract with America." The newly conservative Congress promptly went gunning for, among other targets, HUD itself. For a time the very existence of the agency was in doubt as proposals were floated to dismem-ber HUD and lodge its functions elsewhere within the executive branch. Only with much fancy footwork was Cisneros able to keep HUD alive, by dramatically reshaping its organization and programs. In the desperate jockeying of those months, potentially controversial, "liberal-sounding" initiatives such as Choice in Residency and Metropolitan Assisted Housing Strategies were stillborn.

In the garb of HOPE VI, however, a place-based deconcentration strategy did survive and quickly evolved into a major HUD endeavor that persists to this day. (In 2003, the George W. Bush administration began to try to elimi-nate HOPE VI and did succeed in reducing its funding substantially over the course of the Bush presidency.) The concept of Section 8 as an approach to residential mobility for families displaced by HOPE VI redevelopment also survived, although its potential in that respect has not been fully realized. The story of poverty deconcentration under HOPE VI thus has two principal parts, the physical revitalization of distressed public housing and the use of Section 8 as a vehicle for the residential mobility of displaced families.

HOPE VI Revitalization

In April 1994 HUD's general counsel ruled that public housing could be pri-vately owned as long as its operations complied with all the rules that applied to publicly owned housing.[15] Promptly moving to implement its counsel's rul-ing, HUD began to embrace what came to be called the "mixed-finance con-cept": public and nonpublic housing (and financing) could be combined in a single development, thereby opening the door to creating public housing that would no longer be an enclave exclusively of poor families. Although some early HOPE VI developments merely fixed up bad buildings that continued to house only public housing families, applicants for FY1995 HOPE VI funds were told that HUD intended to support strategies "that directly attack the isolation of public housing developments and residents by blending public housing units into economically integrated communities."[16]

As discussed in chapter 3, the inquiries that had led to the mixed-finance ruling sought permission to combine public housing in the same development with housing developed under the Low-Income Housing Tax Credit Program, a tax subsidy program that benefits renters who, while needy, generally have incomes somewhat higher than those typical of public housing residents—and much higher than the $5,350 median household income (1993 dollars) of families in the first set of HOPE VI sites.[17] Soon, the mixed-finance approach also began to include completely unsubsidized ("market rate") dwellings, resulting in developments that no longer housed only poor families but that could fairly be described as economically integrated. In a pattern employed in Chicago and elsewhere, approximately one-third of a replacement community consists of public housing, one-third of "affordable housing" using low-income housing tax credits, and one-third of unsubsidized market-rate housing. A study of some of the earliest mixed-income communities found significant differences in the median household incomes of market-rate renters, tax-credit renters, and public housing households (figure 5-4).[18] Market-rate homeowners, who were not included in the study, would likely have even higher incomes relative to those of public housing residents.

Over time, the scale of HOPE VI revitalization became considerable. The 240 revitalization grants made under HOPE VI through 2007 are projected to produce 111,059 new and rehabilitated residential units, 52,951 of them public housing rental units. Some 96,226 public housing units were to be demolished and well over 70,000 households relocated. Much of the work under these grants is now completed or well along; 87 percent have at least some mix of public and non–public housing units (see appendix A).[19]

Of course, tearing down distressed public housing and replacing it with economically integrated residential communities would perforce deconcentrate preexisting on-site poverty.[20] In addition, as Margery Turner explains in chapter 10 of this volume, because many public housing projects are large enough to affect a good-sized piece of geography, their replacement significantly reduces the concentration of poverty in the surrounding neighborhood. Her hypothetical (but realistic) numerical example drops a neighborhood's poverty rate from 47 to 20 percent. Indeed, Abt Associates Inc. and GAO studies of early HOPE VI neighborhoods found poverty rate declines in roughly three-fourths of the study sites. Declines ranged from the single digits to as high as 28 percent, with the declines in the Abt study far outstripping the citywide poverty declines against which they were measured (figure 5-5).[21] The consequences of high neighborhood poverty that Turner catalogues— among them blight and crime, which scare off prospective investment and residents; lower property values and tax revenues; higher costs of public services; and fuel for racial prejudice—make it unsurprising that a number of studies that she examines show dramatic improvements in neighborhoods surrounding some HOPE VI developments, including in market demand and investment activity.

It is too soon to know whether the new mixed-income developments will thrive as fully functioning communities and what the life trajectories of their public housing residents will be. Initial indications concerning the first question, however, are positive. Research thus far suggests that "mixed-income public housing developments can be successful in creating well-managed communities that attract higher-income tenants."[22] Yet no matter what the track records of the communities and their public housing residents turn out to be, the isolation of the black poor in enclaves of concentrated poverty—the focus of *The Truly Disadvantaged*—will have been done away with in scores of places across the country. HOPE VI may be said to be experiencing considerable success in deconcentrating a goodly portion of the poverty centered in distressed urban public housing and, to some extent, in adjacent neighborhoods.

Figure 5-4. **Unit and Income Mix of Five HOPE VI Communities**[a]

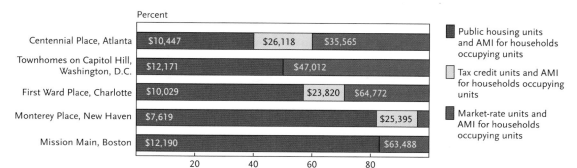

Source: Adapted from Mary Joel Holin and others, "Interim Assessment of the HOPE VI Program: Cross-Site Report," prepared by Abt Associates for the U.S. Department of Housing and Urban Development, September 19, 2003, pp. 41–44 (www.abtassociates.com/reports/20030_RETASK-XSITE_03.pdf).

a. Figures are in 2002 dollars. Homeownership units are excluded from the chart because most were not built at the time of the surveys on which the data are based. As a privately owned cooperative, the Townhomes on Capitol Hill has no public housing units, but units reserved for households with incomes below 50 percent of the area median income (AMI) were categorized as public housing by Abt Associates. The AMI for households occupying market-rate units in Monterey Place was not provided in the study.

Figure 5-5. Percent Change in Poverty Rate in 12 HOPE VI Neighborhoods and Citywide, 1990–2000

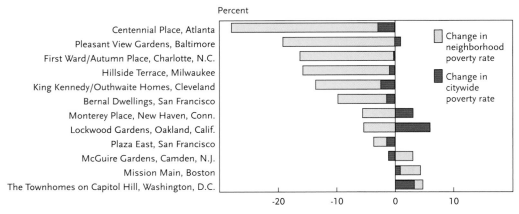

Source: Adapted from Mary Joel Holin and others, "Interim Assessment of the HOPE VI Program: Cross-Site Report," prepared by Abt Associates for the U.S. Department of Housing and Urban Development, September 19, 2003, pp. 114, 119, 124 (www.abtassociates.com /reports/20030_RETASK-XSITE_03.pdf).

a. The sites were selected from among the thirty-four HOPE VI grants made through August 1995 as those that represented the full range of physical, management, crime, and family distress, according to Abt Associates.

HOPE VI Residential Mobility

Relocating families involuntarily displaced in the tear-down process gives rise to HOPE VI's other principal opportunity to deconcentrate poverty. In the 1990s, as part of the poverty deconcentration agenda, changes were made to the Section 8 program "to make vouchers more acceptable to the private market," including the repeal of a provision requiring landlords who accepted one applicant with a Section 8 voucher to accept all qualified voucher applicants.[23] The number of HOPE VI households that have relocated under Section 8—about a third, studies show—is not insubstantial.[24] If the goal is to deconcentrate poverty and reduce racial and economic segregation, the race and poverty characteristics of the neighborhoods to which these households move is obviously of great import. If recipient neighborhoods themselves are (or become) racially segregated, high-poverty enclaves, the concentrated poverty of the demolished public housing is simply moved elsewhere. If, on the other hand, households relocate to unsegregated, low-poverty neighborhoods, the preexisting concentration of poverty is truly eliminated.[25]

This part of the HOPE VI tale is one of the proverbial glass seen as either half full or half empty. The half-full perspective begins with the reality that almost any move from the concentrated poverty of a public housing project is likely to be to an area of lower poverty. Although HUD has sadly not required data to be kept on the characteristics of recipient neighborhoods, evidence of poverty deconcentration surfaces from two studies of selected HOPE VI developments. The HOPE VI Resident Tracking Study provides a systematic look at what had happened to former residents of eight HOPE VI developments as of spring 2001, between two and seven years after their HOPE VI grant awards.[26] The HOPE VI Panel Study assembles data on former residents from five other HOPE VI sites for the period 2001–05.[27]

Both studies show an impressive reduction of poverty for very many displaced families. The resident tracking study data indicate that the average census tract poverty rate for displaced families moving under Section 8 dropped very substantially, from 61 percent in the families' former public housing developments to 27 percent in their new Section 8 locations. Although some 40 percent of tracking study households lived in census tracts with poverty rates of more than 30 percent, another 40 percent were living in tracts with poverty rates of less than 20 percent. In the panel study, about half of those renting in the private market were living in neighborhoods with poverty rates of less than 20 percent.

An initial move—even to a segregated, high-poverty neighborhood—may also be the first step on a journey to a better neighborhood. A consultant to HOPE VI developers speaks of "releasing" public housing families from the "captivity" of public housing. The reference is to the ills that beset many families who live in public housing generation after generation. In their book *The Hidden War*, Susan Popkin and colleagues describe a "substantial part" of a surveyed public housing population as traumatized by constant violence and suffering from a formidable array of health and other problems.[28] Being "released" from the public housing environment—having to cope, for example, with budgeting for utility bills formerly paid by the housing authority and with a private landlord impatient because of late rental payments—may for some families be the first, albeit painful, step toward self-sufficiency. Some housing authorities have "second mover" programs specifically designed to help families that have already moved under Section 8 to find better neighborhoods.

The reverse, of course, may also be true—families may move from unsegregated, low-poverty neighborhoods back to segregation and high poverty. Research on which of the two scenarios predominates among the HOPE VI Section 8 population is limited and inconclusive. Results would undoubtedly be influenced by the scope and nature of the housing authority's post-move counseling. Just as HUD's *Urban Policy Brief* said that intensive counseling was critical to effecting moves to better neighborhoods, so is intensive *post-move* counseling critical to enabling families that have moved into better neighborhoods to remain in them.[29]

Taking initial moves at face value leads to the conclusion that even though many moving families continue to reside in racially segregated neighborhoods of relatively high poverty, a considerable degree of poverty deconcentration has resulted from HOPE VI's Section 8 moves. This is the glass half full. From the half-empty perspective, the potential of HOPE VI Section 8 mobility has not been fully realized. As Susan Popkin and Mary Cunningham observe in chapter 11 in this volume, HOPE VI grantees did not generally provide mobility counseling to encourage and assist residents to move to low-poverty communities or to help them remain in such communities. Elizabeth Julian, who served in HUD in the early to mid-1990s, attributes the dearth of good mobility counseling under HOPE VI to an overriding focus on physical redevelopment. "Housing authorities were more interested in getting the dirt flying—and in a number of places filling up vacancies in other developments—than spending time and money to find housing in less segregated areas and prepare families for making those moves," she says.[30]

An independent review of the early years of HOPE VI relocation in Chicago concluded that no real effort was made to provide mobility counseling, with the result that "the vertical ghettos from which the families are being moved are being replaced with horizontal ghettos, located in well-defined, highly segregated neighborhoods on the west and south sides of Chicago."[31] Though the Chicago Housing Authority is attempting to correct this situation and has improved its relocation services, truly effective mobility and post-move counseling remain goals, not achievements.

Chicago's experience in this respect is not atypical. In Richmond, Virginia, for example, some 82 percent of voucher holders moved to job-poor census tracts containing less than 0.7 percent of metropolitan area jobs.[32] But neither is it universal. In Seattle, of 267 families that received Section 8 vouchers to relocate from the redeveloping Holly Park complex, more than half (147) moved to neighborhoods described as "non-poverty, non-minority concentrations areas."[33]

Though hard information is difficult to come by—housing authorities generally have not assembled data on the characteristics of the neighborhoods to which their Section 8 families moved—there is little doubt that helping families relocate with vouchers has been one of HOPE VI's weak spots. Yet families that lack experience in the private housing market—and therefore often have difficulty using their vouchers effectively—probably constitute a substantial portion of the HOPE VI–displaced families to whom vouchers are tendered.[34]

What about Race?

The discussion so far implicitly assumes that deconcentrating poverty through mixed-income revitalization and Section 8 mobility is desirable public policy. Not everyone agrees, and consideration of dissenting views necessarily involves the question of race.

University of Minnesota professor Edward Goetz, an articulate and thoughtful critic, mounts a host of counterarguments in his book, *Clearing the Way: Deconcentrating the Poor in Urban America.* Goetz argues not only that mobility is not likely to work well and will not in any event accomplish much deconcentration but also that deconcentration is *in principle* a flawed idea because it saps the political and civic will to improve the lives of poor people in the places where they traditionally have lived. According to Goetz, a focus on deconcentration directs efforts away from a declining housing stock in poor neighborhoods and toward "reducing services for lower-income families and attracting more middle-income home buyers."[35]

In fact, says Goetz, the greater the acceptance of deconcentration, the less support there will be for subsidized housing. Neighborhoods with such housing will oppose more of it because of the risk of increasing concentrated poverty. Neighborhoods without it will oppose any of it because social pathologies are linked through concentrated poverty to subsidized housing, and no neighborhood wants to invite trouble. While agreeing that approaches to reducing urban poverty "should include a program of voluntary mobility," Goetz contends that rather than focusing on poverty deconcentration, public policy should be based on a broad antipoverty agenda that includes revenue sharing, inclusionary zoning, eradicating housing discrimination, and ending exclusionary land use practices.[36]

The arguments that mobility can't or won't work—or in any event won't work on a meaningful scale—have been responded to elsewhere in the literature and will not be repeated here.[37] But the claim that poverty deconcentration is *in principle* a flawed idea calls for additional comment.

As HUD's 1994 *Urban Policy Brief* acknowledged, minorities' residential choices have been constrained by racial segregation and housing discrimination, with the result that minorities have been "invariably overrepresented" in urban areas of extreme poverty. Several studies have made clear that the high-poverty HOPE VI sites and their surrounding neighborhoods also were predominantly minority.[38] In this context, "race" should not be equated with "minority" in general; as a nearly limitless supply of statistics and studies clearly shows, the African American history of slavery, sharecropping, Jim Crow, and—their modern successor—the black ghetto, has been uniquely damaging. Some indications are as follows:

— For most other minorities, residential segregation diminishes as education levels rise. Not so for African Americans.[39] (In her chapter in this volume Margery Turner reminds us that the deck is stacked against even economically diverse predominantly black neighborhoods.)

— When the "minority achievement gap" is disaggregated by race in Chicago public schools, we find that black students perform less well than Latino students (though both perform well below the level of whites and Asians).[40]

— A recent study published by the National Academy of Sciences concludes that "exposure to concentrated disadvantage in Chicago appears to have had detrimental and long-lasting consequences for black children's cognitive ability." Notably, although white and Latino children were included in the

Minorities' residential choices have been constrained by racial segregation and housing discrimination.

study, the conclusion focuses on black children because concentrated disadvantage was a "treatment . . . experienced *almost solely by Chicago's black children*" [emphasis added].[41]

These and many other familiar findings show that the unique history of blacks in the United States has produced uniquely negative consequences. On the centennial of the Emancipation Proclamation, James Baldwin wrote that black ghettos were destroying hundreds of thousands of lives.[42] Two years later Kenneth Clark's classic, *Dark Ghetto,* provided the chilling details of the destruction.[43] In the ensuing decades, ghetto conditions did not improve. On the contrary, they deteriorated even further, and black ghettos today, worse than ever before, house more African Americans than ever before.[44]

Yet HOPE VI has made "minimal progress in helping families move to areas that are less racially concentrated."[45] Sue Popkin attributes HOPE VI's failure to improve the lives of many displaced families, at least in part, "to the political decision to avoid making racial desegregation an explicit goal of public housing transformation."[46] The use of poverty as a proxy for race did not work in MTO; though "experimental families" were required to move initially to low-poverty census tracts, some 60 percent were living in "heavily minority areas" at the time of HUD's MTO evaluation. Popkin's argument—that public housing transformation cannot achieve more than limited impact on the well-being of HOPE VI families without addressing race directly—is tellingly supported by the MTO experience, evaluation of which disclosed fewer significant beneficial effects than had been expected, particularly with regard to education and employment.[47]

Given the past and present realities of "place and race" in our society, would it profit us in the long run to emphasize building affordable housing and locating Section 8 families where the barriers are lowest—that is, where poor people, among whom minority households (frequently black) are "invariably overrepresented," already live? A "Faustian bargain," Elizabeth Julian calls it.[48] At bottom, that is the bargain Goetz proposes. The traumatic history and present travails of poor blacks in the United States weigh heavily against his counsel.

Conclusion

What would it mean to address race "directly," as Popkin urges, in the context of HOPE VI and Section 8? The answer includes using both racial and distance-from-poverty-area criteria to select destination or "opportunity" areas. A comprehensive outreach program that offered incentives to attract landlords in such areas would be essential. State-of-the-art mobility counseling for participating families would include a health assessment (with aid in accessing health providers and insurance when needed), credit repair and "financial literacy" training, unit showings (with free transportation) in opportunity neighborhoods, hands-on assistance in negotiating with landlords, and financial assistance with security deposits. Concurrently, HUD must address the administrative and financial headaches facing voucher administrators when holders of the vouchers that they issue want to move to a jurisdiction served by another agency. The present agency reimbursement system serves as a barrier to true "portability" of vouchers, particularly moves from lower- to higher-cost housing markets.

Post-move assistance would include driver education, automobile ownership, employment, and child care programs, as well as intensive school-related counseling, all by counselors trained in race issues and working in a whole-family, case-management mode. That would amount to a rich bundle of assistance designed to encourage and facilitate moves to new areas and to foster post-move stability by helping families to take full advantage of the resources available—and to "make it"—in their new neighborhoods.[49]

Concentrated urban poverty remains an enormous problem for the United States, a far larger problem than HOPE VI and subsidized housing can hope to solve. The statistical amelioration of poverty during the 1990s stemmed from the unprecedented economic boom of that decade, a boom that ended almost exactly at the conclusion—early 2000—of the period covered by the 2000 census. Concentrated urban poverty has undoubtedly increased since then.[50] Even as of 2000, although the proportion of the black population living in extreme poverty metropolitan areas decreased because of the growth in the total metropolitan black population, the absolute number of blacks and of poor blacks living in extreme poverty metropolitan areas was actually greater than it was in 1970, after the urban race riots of the preceding decade.[51]

Performing radical surgery on distressed public housing and fostering economic integration through HOPE VI mixed-income redevelopments is a hopeful and important step in the direction of deconcentrating poverty. It remains, however, to take a similar step toward implementing an effective mobility program for displaced families that would grasp the opportunity to address, at last, the persisting issue of race. That might help open the door to a still further step—comprehensive pre- and post-move mobility counseling, based on racial as well as poverty criteria, throughout the entirety of the Section 8 system, now the largest of HUD's assisted housing programs.[52]

William Julius Wilson reopened the door to the study of urban poverty and demonstrated that the worst of it was rooted in the nation's historic mistreatment of African Americans. With HOPE VI as one of his major tools, Henry Cisneros began to grapple with the public housing part of that mistreatment. It would be well if the limited but important success that HOPE VI has had in deconcentrating the public housing portion of urban poverty would whet U.S. society's appetite to do more. That would be a most satisfying part of HOPE VI's legacy.

····· Endnotes ·····

1. "The Negro Family: The Case for National Action," Office of Planning and Research, U.S. Department of Labor (March 1965). The report argued that it was not just the lack of jobs and other institutional factors but rather fatherlessness and other social pathologies tracing back to slavery and discrimination that were fueling the rise in minority urban neighborhoods dominated by single mothers and their children, and it maintained that efforts to address black-white inequality had to address the breakdown of the "Negro family." In the wake of vigorous—some would say erroneous—criticism that the report placed too much blame for then current conditions on blacks, leaving white racism and institutions off the hook, the report was essentially shelved by the Johnson administration.

2. William Julius Wilson, *The Truly Disadvantaged: The Inner City, the Underclass, and Public Policy* (University of Chicago Press, 1987).

3. Among the many discussions of the history of the creation of the nation's black ghettos, see Arnold R. Hirsch, *Making the Second Ghetto: Race and Housing in Chicago, 1940–1960* (Cambridge University Press, 1983); Douglas S. Massey and Nancy A. Denton, *American Apartheid: Segregation and the Making of the Underclass* (Harvard University Press, 1993); and Nicholas Lemann, *The Promised Land: The Great Black Migration and How It Changed America* (New York: Alfred A. Knopf, 1991).

4. See, for example, Jorge Casuso and Robert Blau, "Fear Lives in CHA's Taylor Homes," *Chicago Tribune,* June 18, 1989; and "Taylor Homes' Terrorized Children," *Chicago Tribune,* July 1, 1989. Casuso and Blau noted that exact figures for current residents were hard to come by but that there were 18,670 residents at the last count, in 1985.

5. Rick Kogan, "The Education of Miss Kelly; In the Shadow of the Projects, 'The Best Kids in the World,'" *Chicago Tribune Magazine,* April 18, 1999. It is not clear from the article when the data were tabulated, but a reference to census tract poverty data suggests 1990.

6. Within the larger ghetto-creating context, specific public housing policies—for example, giving preference for admission to the neediest families—contributed to making public housing the housing of last resort for poor urban black families. For one discussion of these policies, see "Racial Desegregation and Income Deconcentration in Public Housing," Cara Hendrickson, *Georgetown Journal on Poverty Law and Policy* 9 (Winter 2002).

7. Departments of Veterans Affairs and Housing and Urban Development and Independent Agencies 1993 Appropriations Act, P.L. 102-389 (October 6, 1992); Housing and Community Development Act of 1992, P.L. 102-550 (October 28, 1992).

8. As explained in earlier chapters, rules requiring one-for-one replacement of all public housing units demolished and restricting public housing construction to areas without high concentrations of poor, minority households essentially prohibited full-scale redevelopment.

9. Departments of Veterans Affairs and Housing and Urban Development and Independent Agencies 1996 Appropriations Act, P.L. 104-134, 110 Stat. 1321-269.

10. Quality Housing and Work Responsibility Act of 1998, P.L. 105-276, 112 Stat. 2581 (October 21, 1998).

11. U.S. Department of Housing and Urban Development, *Urban Policy Brief* 1 (September 1994).

12. *Hills* v. *Gautreaux,* 425 U.S. 284 (1976).

13. The Department of Veterans Affairs and Housing and Urban Development and Independent Agencies 1992 Appropriations Act (Public Law 102-139), which was enacted October 28, 1991, included a $20 million appropriation (Stat. 745) for a demonstration program. That program was authorized as the Moving to Opportunity Demonstration in the Housing and Community Development Act of 1992 (Public Law 102-550 Section 181).

14. David S. Broder, "For the Urban Poor, a Change of Venue," *Washington Post,* June 8, 1994.

15. Memorandum from Nelson A. Diaz, general counsel, to Joseph Shuldiner, assistant secretary for public and Indian housing, U.S. Department of Housing and Urban Development, April 8, 1994.

16. U.S. Department of Housing and Urban Development, "Further Information for Development of Proposals for FY 1995 HOPE VI Implementation Grants (1995)," pp. 6–7. See Mindy Turbov and Valerie Piper, "HOPE VI and Mixed-Finance Redevelopments: A Catalyst for Neighborhood Renewal," a discussion paper prepared for the Brookings Institution's Metropolitan Policy Program, September 2005. A few years later, particularly in the Quality Housing and Work Responsibility Act of 1998, other changes in public housing rules—for example, repealing federal preferences—further helped housing authorities move toward lessening concentrations of poverty.

17. Over fiscal years 1993 to 1995, a total of thirty-four HOPE VI implementation grants were awarded. For the median income across the grant sites, see Linda B. Fosburg, Susan J. Popkin, and Gretchen P. Locke, *An Historical and Baseline Assessment of HOPE VI,* vol. 1, *Cross-Site Report* (U.S. Department of Housing and Urban Development, Office of Policy Development and Research, July 1996), pp. 1-25.

18. Mary Joel Holin and others, "Interim Assessment of the HOPE VI Program: Cross-Site Report," prepared by Abt Associates for the U.S. Department of Housing and Urban Development, September 19, 2003, pp. 43–44 (www.abtassociates.com /reports/20030_RETASK-XSITE_03.pdf).

19. Although there are no comprehensive national data on the extent to which the mix of unit types mixes income levels, the HOPE VI interim assessment found that of five mixed-unit HOPE VI sites studied, three had a sufficiently broad range of incomes to be called truly mixed-income and a fourth came very close to that standard. See Holin and others, "Interim Assessment of the HOPE VI Program: Cross-Site Report," p. 43.

20. Poverty rates of the HOPE VI sites prior to redevelopment were extreme, according to several studies. Susan J. Popkin and others, "A Decade of HOPE VI: Research Findings and Policy Challenges" (Urban Institute and Brookings Institution, May 2004), p. 9.

21. Poverty rate declines in nine of twelve early HOPE VI sites were identified in Holin and others, "Interim Assessment of the HOPE VI Program: Cross-Site Report," pp. 114, 119, 124, and fourteen of twenty 1996 grant year HOPE VI neighborhoods were cited for declining poverty rates in General Accounting Office, "Public Housing: HOPE VI Resident Issues and Changes in Neighborhoods Surrounding Grant Sites," Report to the Ranking Minority Member, Subcommittee on Housing and Transportation, Committee on Banking, Housing, and Urban Affairs, U.S. Senate, November 2003, p. 25 (www.gao.gov/new.items/d04109.pdf [October 1, 2008]).

22. Susan J. Popkin and others, "A Decade of HOPE VI," p. 22.

23. Ibid., p. 15.

24. See General Accounting Office, "Public Housing: HOPE VI Resident Issues and Changes in Neighborhoods Surrounding Grant Sites," p. 3; Larry F. Buron and others, "HOPE VI Resident Tracking Study: A Snapshot of the Current Living Situation of Original Residents from Eight Sites" (Washington: Urban Institute, November 1, 2002) (www.urban.org/url.cfm?ID=410591[October 1, 2008]), p. ii.

25. Not all displaced families are moved through Section 8. An even larger number is expected to move to other traditional public housing developments. These may still be distressed places, especially if they receive an influx of relocating problem-plagued HOPE VI families. See Barbara Sard and Leah Staub, "House Bill Makes Significant Improvements in 'HOPE VI' Public Housing Revitalization Program" (Washington: Center on Budget and Policy Priorities, revised January 30, 2008) (www.cbpp.org/1-16-08hous.pdf [October 1, 2008]), p. 7 : "Concentrating households with multiple problems in traditional developments can quickly create the same sorts of problems as those in their previous developments. As a result,

families' living conditions can actually *worsen* after they are relocated." One of the failures of HOPE VI administration is that HUD has not required data to be kept on exactly where displaced families go, so it is not possible to say precisely how many families have moved to traditional (100 percent) public housing and how many into private housing under Section 8. Nor has HUD required data to be kept on the characteristics of the recipient Section 8 neighborhoods.

26. Buron and others, "HOPE VI Resident Tracking Study: A Snapshot of the Current Living Situation of Original Residents from Eight Sites".

27. Susan J. Popkin and others, "HOPE VI Panel Study: Baseline Report" (Washington: Urban Institute, September 1, 2002) (www.urban.org/url.cfm?ID=410590 [October 1, 2008]). The panel study is discussed in detail by Susan J. Popkin and Mary K Cunningham in chapter 11 of this volume.

28. Susan J. Popkin and others, *The Hidden War: Crime and the Tragedy of Public Housing in Chicago* (Rutgers University Press, 2000).

29. For a discussion of initiatives to help families take full advantage of new and better locations, see Xavier de Souza Briggs and Margery Austin Turner, "Assisted Housing Mobility and the Success of Low-Income Minority Families: Lessons for Policy, Practice, and Future Research," *Northwestern Journal of Law and Social Policy* 1, no. 1 (2006), p. 25 (www.law.northwestern.edu/journals/njlsp).

30. Personal communication from Elizabeth Julian, March 26, 2008. Julian served in HUD first as deputy general counsel for civil rights and litigation and then as assistant secretary for fair housing and equal opportunity. Since 2005, she has been the president of Inclusive Communities Project, a nonprofit in Dallas focused on fair housing and mobility.

31. Thomas P. Sullivan, "Independent Monitor's Report No. 5 to the Chicago Housing Authority and the Central Advisory Council," January 8, 2003, pp. 23–24. Page 24 of the report cites a study of 1,000 relocated families that found that the "overwhelming majority" lived in areas where the poverty level was not much different from that of the communities that they had come from and that close to 80 percent of the relocated families had moved to census tracts that were more than 90 percent African American. The monitor's report is available from Business and Professional People for the Public Interest of Chicago.

32. Sard and Staub, "House Bill Makes Significant Improvements in 'HOPE VI' Public Housing Revitalization Program," p. 8.

33. Seattle Housing Authority, "New Holly Redevelopment Plan: Relocation Results" (www.seattlehousing.org/Development/newholly/relocat.html [October 1, 2008]). The Seattle Department of Neighborhoods characterizes "non-minority concentrations areas" as those where the representation of any minority group is not more than 10 percent higher than the citywide average.

34. Sard and Staub, "House Bill Makes Significant Improvements in 'HOPE VI' Public Housing Revitalization Program," pp. 6–8.

35. Edward G. Goetz, *Clearing the Way: Deconcentrating the Poor in Urban America* (Washington: Urban Institute Press, 2003), p. 253.

36. Ibid., p. 255.

37. See Alexander Polikoff, *Waiting for Gautreaux: A Story of Segregation, Housing, and the Black Ghetto* (Northwestern University Press, 2006), pp. 369–89.

38. Popkin and others, "A Decade of HOPE VI," p. 8.

39. Massey and Denton, *American Apartheid*.

40. Consortium on Chicago School Research at the University of Chicago, "2006 ISAT Reading and Math Scores in Chicago and the Rest of the State," June 1007, pp. 6, 11–13.

41. Robert J. Sampson, Patrick Sharkey, and Stephen W. Raudenbush, "Durable Effects of Concentrated Disadvantage on Verbal Ability among African-American Children," National Academy of Sciences, 2007 (www.pnas.org/cgi/doi/10.1073/pnas.0710189104 [October 1, 2008]).

42. James Baldwin, *The Fire Next Time* (New York: Dial Press, 1963).

43. Kenneth B. Clark, *Dark Ghetto: Dilemmas of Social Power* (New York: Harper & Row, 1965).

44. Polikoff, *Waiting for Gautreaux*, pp. 336–47.

45. Sard and Staub, "House Bill Makes Significant Improvements in 'HOPE VI' Public Housing Revitalization Program."

46. Susan J. Popkin, "Race and Public Housing Transformation in the United States," paper presented at Symposium on Housing, Neighborhoods, and Communities in the U.K. and U.S., Urban Institute, Washington, June 2004.

47. For a description and discussion of the MTO interim results, see Polikoff, *Waiting for Gautreaux*, pp. 272–78.

48. Elizabeth Julian, "An Unfinished Agenda," *Shelterforce* (Winter 2007), p. 23.

49. See Briggs and Turner, "Assisted Housing Mobility and the Success of Low-Income Minority Families,"and Philip Tegeler, "Connecting Families to Opportunity: The Next Generation of Housing Mobility Policy," in *All Things Being Equal: Instigating Opportunity in an Inequitable Time*, edited by Brian Smedley and Alan Jenkins (New York: New Press, 2007). Mobility programs have long been described as enhancing choice and providing options. They do that, but Briggs and Turner and Tegeler describe and rightly propose an enhanced post-move case management system that would make it clear that the choice is not between one location and another but between one way of life and another. Some elements of such a program—financial literacy, security deposit assistance, and two years of some post-move services—are included in a housing mobility program in Baltimore operated by Quadel Consulting Corporation. The program resulted from a court order in a public housing deseg-regation case, *Thompson* v. *HUD*. At the end of 2007, some 1,100 families had moved from public housing and other inner-city areas of Baltimore to higher-opportunity areas in the city and surrounding region. Job training, driver education, and automobile purchase services are now being tested with the support of several national and local foundations. Health and educational counseling programs are to be added in 2008–09.

50. A Brookings Institution analysis of changes in the geographic distribution of low-income workers between 1999 and 2005 found that "trends suggest that the decline in concentrated poverty that occurred during the 1990s may be reversing over the course of this decade." Elizabeth Kneebone and Alan Berube, "Reversal of Fortune: A New Look at Concentrated Poverty in the 2000s," Brookings Institution, Metropolitan Policy Program, August 2008 (www.brookings.edu/~/media/Files/rc/papers/2008/08_concentrated_poverty_kneebone/concentrated_poverty.pdf [October 1, 2008]), p. 1.

51. Polikoff, *Waiting for Gautreaux*, pp. 338–39. The statistics do not, of course, capture the qualitative worsening of ghetto conditions following the entrance of crack cocaine on the inner-city stage in the early 1980s.

52. In "America's Murder Mystery," *The Atlantic* (July-August 2008), contributing editor Hanna Rosin attributes burgeoning crime in a number of Memphis, Tennessee, neighbor-hoods to recently arrived voucher families displaced by public housing redevelopment. The "noble" antipoverty experiment that Memphis had initiated with the demolition of its first public housing project in 1997 is said to be "bringing the city down." The data supporting her thesis are far from clear. It does appear that many if not most Section 8 families moved to predominantly black neighborhoods of relatively high poverty and that the moving fami-lies received little pre- and virtually no post-move counseling. The article therefore makes a strong case—probably not Rosin's intention—for state-of-the art mobility counseling.

Setting the Stage:
Early HOPE VI Redevelopments

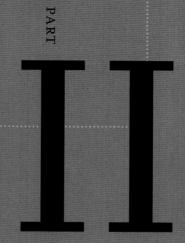

II

LORA ENGDAHL

An Overview of HOPE VI Revitalization Grant Projects

HOPE VI provides the seed capital and parameters for locally driven solutions to the problems that severely distressed public housing sites pose for residents, neighborhoods, and cities. At the end of 2008, HOPE VI Revitalization program grants had been awarded to 246 developments in more than 120 cities. Beneficiaries include large cities with multiple HOPE VI grants: Chicago had the most, with nine grants; Atlanta, Baltimore, and Washington, D.C., had received seven each. HOPE VI grants have also gone to dozens of smaller cities, such as Daytona Beach, Florida; Muncie, Indiana; and Wheeling, West Virginia.

The New Columbia HOPE VI in Portland, Oregon includes the award-winning Rosa Parks Elementary School, the nation's first public elementary school financed with new markets tax credits.

The HOPE VI redevelopment efforts undertaken by public housing authorities and their partners range widely in size. (See appendix B for a list of projects broken down by location, size, and unit type.) The largest HOPE VI redevelopments, involving the most units, are under way in Chicago, where the Chicago Housing Authority is two-thirds of the way through a 15-year plan to redevelop or rehabilitate 25,000 public housing units, nearly a third of which will be in mixed-income communities.[1] The thirty-one high-rises and a stretch of row houses that constituted the Cabrini-Green complex on the city's north side—which had over 2,600 units—are being replaced with more than 2,500 mixed-income condominiums and townhomes. On the city's near southwest side, the redevelopment of the 3,235-unit ABLA homes will create more than 3,100 mixed-income homes and apartments.[2] Nationwide, more than fifteen HOPE VI redevelopments have involved construction of more than 1,000 units, while upward of sixty have involved between 500 and 1,000 units.

The smaller HOPE VIs, which are redeveloping around 60 to 200 units, are not just in the smaller cities. For example, the Oakland Housing Authority replaced its 46-unit Westwood Gardens public housing development with a 168-unit mixed-income, mixed-use community called Mandela Gateway.

Promoting homeownership was a major goal of Wilmington, Delaware's HOPE VI, the New Village of Eastlake, which consists of ninety affordable and market-rate for-sale homes and seventy subsidized rental units.

While some HOPE VI redevelopments are all-rental housing, more than three-quarters offer at least some affordable or market-rate for-sale homes, with homeownership opportunities predominating in such developments as

Left: The market-rate rental units in Cascade Village, a half mile from downtown Akron, Ohio, have been leasing at a fast clip to employees of a nearby hospital and students at the University of Akron.

Above: The subsidized rentals and for-sale homes in Wheeling, West Virginia's HOPE VI serve families in a range of income levels.

the Village of Eastlake in Wilmington, Delaware; Jackson Parkway in Holyoke, Massachusetts; and the Townhomes on Capitol Hill in Washington, D.C.

Less than 15 percent of the new communities will include solely public housing. In more than a third of the redevelopments, less than half of the units will be public housing. Sixty percent of the redevelopments are projected to include non–income-restricted (market-rate) units. Moreover, inclusion of market-rate units is not solely the domain of redevelopments in what have been considered hot real estate markets, such as Boston and Chicago. The 249-unit Cascade Village HOPE VI in Akron, Ohio, has been leasing its market-rate apartments as fast as they have come on line, even through the economically turbulent second half of 2008.[3]

Although the inclusion of market-rate units (rental or for-sale) is one indicator of income mixing, subsidized for-sale homes also tend to serve households of low to moderate incomes, depending on the market. Three-quarters of the HOPE VI redevelopments are planned to include for-sale housing (either affordable or market-rate) or rental housing without income restrictions.

Other grantees are pursuing more limited income mixing by reserving subsidized rental units for households at different income levels within the low-income category (households making up to 80 percent of area median income). The HOPE VI project in Wheeling, West Virginia, which replaced a 330-unit complex with crime and gang problems, is taking a multipronged approach: it offers 122 new units that are a mix of such "income-tiered" public housing and tax-credit subsidized rentals as well as for-sale homes for first-time buyers under a lease-purchase program.[4]

Generally, HOPE VI redevelopments reduced the number of housing units per acre, but the redevelopments of some spread-out World War II–era public housing in the West and Pacific Northwest involved increasing their density. Higher densities have also appeared in transit-oriented HOPE VI developments such as Mandela Gateway and other projects in Oakland and North Beach Place in San Francisco. Boston's Maverick Landing was constructed under sustainable development principles that involved unusually high density for a HOPE VI project (forty-four housing units per acre). The density of the development enabled the replacement of nearly three-fourths of the public housing units demolished; in contrast, the average across HOPE VI was only 55 percent.[5]

HOPE VI developers have used their ability to tap additional local, state, and federal resources to develop new community and service facilities and retail stores along with the housing—in some cases acquiring and redeveloping sites adjacent to former public housing complexes. Gateway Crossing in Hagerstown, Maryland, has an award-winning community center constructed on a site expanded from fifteen to forty-five acres by acquiring adjacent underused industrial parcels. North Beach Place, near Fisherman's Wharf, has a Trader Joe's store in the middle of its public housing and senior rental units. Mandela Gateway and City West in Cincinnati each have 20,000 square feet of commercial space. Milwaukee's Parklawn HOPE VI community included construction of the new, high-tech Central City Cyberschool, a fully wired charter

Transit-oriented HOPE VI redevelopments, such as North Beach Place in San Francisco, tend to have higher densities; in this case, retail is included in the form of a Trader Joe's store at ground level.

school serving grades 1 through 8. New Columbia in Portland, Oregon, has the first public elementary school in the country built by using new markets tax credits.

Some of the new developments focus on serving populations with special health and care needs. JFK Apartments in Cambridge, Massachusetts, includes twenty-five assisted-living units offering daily personal care and meals and case management to residents. High Point in Seattle has sixty "breathe-easy" homes designed to high standards of air circulation and water quality to reduce allergens that may trigger asthma attacks, a health issue shown by studies to be prevalent among low-income children.[6] Finally, a number of HOPE VI redevelopments, such as Martin Luther King Jr. Plaza in Philadelphia and Manchester in Pittsburgh, involve infill development in adjacent neighborhoods to aid in the revitalization of those neighborhoods.

Given the variety of housing and amenities, selecting a "prototypical" HOPE VI redevelopment is difficult. Compounding the difficulty, references to "HOPE VI" by the industry and in the press today generally include mixed-finance public housing development using other public housing capital funds. However, some of the early HOPE VIs clearly set the stage for the redevelopments that came after, which is appropriate given that HOPE VI was established as a demonstration program. Authorized in annual appropriations acts, HOPE VI operated without formal regulations under program rules set by annual notices of funding availability as well as under the terms of the contracts that grantees entered into with HUD.[7] In chapter 1, Henry Cisneros explains how HUD used its flexibility to experiment and to expose the public housing sector to new ideas. The resulting exchange of ideas between housing authorities in the field and staff at HUD was also described in a 2004 Ph.D. dissertation by Yan Zhang. According to Zhang, housing authority leaders brought their redevelopment proposals to HOPE VI staff, who negotiated on their behalf "many of the program exceptions and waivers that have eventually come to define the HOPE VI program."[8]

In addition to the program-defining contributions made by leaders in St. Louis and Atlanta (see chapters 3 and 9), the early examples set by the housing authorities and their partners in cities such as Seattle and Louisville also greatly shaped the program.[9] Seattle's New Holly and Louisville's Villages of Park DuValle redevelopments were among the pathbreaking efforts that modeled best practices such as ending the isolation of public housing residents through thoughtful site reconfiguration and an "income-blind" approach to design; reducing concentrated poverty through income mixing with funds leveraged through public-private partnerships; creating sustainable neighborhoods through comprehensive redevelopments that included new health care facilities, schools, and other amenities; and protecting the investment in the new community by acquiring and redeveloping nearby troubled parcels. With

A floor of the JFK Apartments HOPE VI in Cambridge, Massachusetts, is devoted to assisted living units for residents who need help with daily personal care.

New Holly, the Seattle Housing Authority also showed that housing authorities could take the lead developer role at a time when other authorities were hiring mostly outside developers.

The best practices and lessons learned through HOPE VI spread informally through presentations at conferences, published case studies, and awards given by design and planning groups at local and national levels. In addition, the architect and developer partners engaged in the initiatives applied those practices to subsequent HOPE VI projects in other cities. At the same time, program shortcomings that emerged in the early HOPE VI projects—for example, inadequate tracking of relocated residents in the first HOPE VI project in Louisville and in other cities—led to new program rules.

Changes to HOPE VI and public housing program rules also resulted in part from the efforts of local leaders who called for rewriting the regulations that impeded their plans. For example, Mayor Jerry Abramson of Louisville and Mayor Bill Campbell of Atlanta were among those pressing Congress and HUD to develop new cost guidelines that would allow public housing units built in mixed-income communities to be of a quality comparable with that of the other units.[10] As recounted in chapter 3 of this volume, new total development cost guidelines were issued. The Louisville and Seattle housing authorities and their partners joined Kansas City and Washington, D.C., in lobbying for a rule change that would let them place HOPE VI funds in an endowment that would continue to fund support services after the end of the HOPE VI grant period.[11] The Quality Housing and Work Responsibility Act (QHWRA), enacted in 1998, included a provision allowing up to 15 percent of a HOPE VI grant awarded in fiscal 2000 or after to be deposited in an endowment trust for services for public housing residents.[12]

Yan Zhang's dissertation recounts more fully how the shaping of HOPE VI program requirements by HOPE VI developers during the program's initial phase was followed by standardization of best practices under Andrew Cuomo. But changes to the program continued. When Mel Martinez joined President George W. Bush's cabinet as HUD secretary in January 2001, the agency's focus shifted to expanding homeownership and ending chronic homelessness. HOPE VI award amounts were reduced and grantees had to line up their financing prior to winning a grant.

Concurrently, the scheduled sunset of HOPE VI in 2002 prompted a debate over the future of the program, which occurred against a backdrop of war spending and an escalating federal deficit.[13] While newly emerging studies showed positive impacts on neighborhoods and residents, long-standing complaints that projects took too long to come to fruition gained traction. (Indeed, a subsequent report from GAO in 2003 showed that many housing authorities had not yet dug their way out of the production deficit that they had gotten into in the early years.)[14] Other sources countered that lengthy development timelines

Changes to HOPE VI and public housing program rules also resulted in part from the efforts of local leaders who called for rewriting the regulations that impeded their plans.

were the by-product of the process of packaging the multiple financing sources needed for mixed-income redevelopment.[15]

Deciding that the slowness with which many HOPE VI grants were being spent argued against any new funds for the program, President George W. Bush eliminated funding for HOPE VI in his fiscal 2003 budget. Attempts to cut the program altogether failed, but funding, which hovered around $575 million from fiscal years 2000 to 2003, was cut to $150 million in FY 2004. Alphonso Jackson, who was HUD secretary from March 2004 to June 2008 (followed by Steve Preston) presided over a much smaller program, funding for which remained at or below $100 million, despite the progress HOPE VI grantees have made in "catching up" on both spending and production (see appendix A).

Nevertheless, the public housing redevelopments under way had long since begun to have an impact on residents, neighborhoods, cities, public housing authorities, and the public housing system in many ways. The following two chapters explore in depth two of the landscape-altering HOPE VI developments. The broader outcomes are surveyed in the second half of the book.

····· Endnotes ·····

1. The Plan for Transformation is the plan that the Chicago Housing Authority (CHA) created to participate in the federal Moving to Work (MTW) demonstration, a program that loosens certain rules and regulations for participating public housing authorities so that they can combine HUD funding streams, impose time limits on housing assistance, and pursue other initiatives toward MTW's statutory goal of increasing the housing choices of and self-sufficiency among residents (see chapters 9 and 12 for details on MTW). Under the plan, the CHA, working with private and nonprofit partners, is transforming sixteen family public housing complexes (fourteen of which are being demolished and redeveloped and two of which are being substantially rehabilitated) into numerous mixed-income communities, both on and off site. Within the new mixed-income communities will be nearly 7,700 public housing units. Another 17,300 public housing units in other family complexes, seniors' complexes, and scattered low-rise developments also are being rehabilitated under the plan. By the end of 2007, the eighth year of the plan, more than $1.1 billion in federal public housing capital dollars had been invested in the plan. In addition to the federal housing dollars, the plan is being funded by a mix of other public and private financing, including tax credit equity, bonds, tax increment financing, and construction loans and mortgages from private lenders. The plan has received a high level of local political and philanthropic support, but it also has been highly controversial because many former tenants of the razed projects have been unable to pass the credit or criminal record checks and other stringent requirements for eligibility for the public housing units in the new mixed-income communities. From "FY2008 Moving to Work Annual Plan," Chicago Housing Authority Plan for Transformation Year 9, December 28, 2007 (www.thecha.org/transformplan/files/1_Cover_030108.pdf and www.thecha.org/transformplan/files/2_MTW_030108.pdf); "Tearing Down Cabrini-Green," CBS News, July 23, 2003; "Two Tales of One City," Good magazine, March 6, 2008.

2. The description of the Cabrini-Green complex prior to redevelopment comes from "Two Tales of One City;" prior unit counts for Cabrini-Green and ABLA come from "FY2008 Moving to Work Annual Plan;" and the rough count of post-development units for the two developments comes from "FY2008 Moving to Work Annual Plan" and appendix B, whose numbers

differ slightly due to the different reporting times. The count of post-development units reported to HUD under HOPE VI for Cabrini-Green and, thus, in appendix B may differ from the total post-development units because not all the phases of the Cabrini-Green redevelopment are necessarily funded by HOPE VI.

3. Author's conversation with Lou Mitsch, a vice president of Community Builders which is developing the project, on December 19, 2008. According to Mitsch, of the fifty-one affordable and twenty-nine market-rate rentals offered in the second half of 2008, only one affordable rental remains unoccupied. But, Mitsch said, the downturn in the housing market did put a halt to the homeownership component of the development after seven of twenty-seven planned for-sale homes had been constructed (six of which sold). More for-sale units are planned as reflected in the Elizabeth Park grant data in appendix B.

4. Author's conversation with Lisa Zukoff, former executive director, Wheeling Housing Authority, December 19, 2007; e-mail communication with Rick Synowiec, director of operations, Wheeling Housing Authority, January 31, 2008.

5. Bendix Anderson, "Boston Redevelopment Beats the Odds," *Affordable Housing Finance*, December 2006. Public housing replacement figures come from appendix A.

6. See for example, "Poverty May Aggravate Asthma," *U.S. News and World Report*, November 10, 2008 (http://health.usnews.com/articles/health/healthday/2008/11/10/poverty-may-aggravate-asthma.html).

7. E-mail to author from Michael Reardon, partner, Nixon Peabody LLC, December 2, 2008. Reardon was HUD's assistant general counsel for assisted housing in the mid-1990s.

8. Yan Zhang, "Wills and Ways: Policy Dynamics of HOPE VI from 1992 to 2002," Ph.D. dissertation, Massachusetts Institute of Technology, September 2004, p. 130.

9. As well-managed agencies, the Louisville and Seattle housing authorities were better equipped to administer HOPE VI than many other early grantees. As many studies have noted, the program's focus on eradicating the most severely distressed public housing complexes meant large grants went first to some of the most ineffective agencies, whose management problems were often compounded by high leadership turnover, local politics, and resident distrust of public housing authorities. See, for example, Linda B. Fosburg, Susan J. Popkin, and Gretchen P. Locke, *An Historical and Baseline Assessment of HOPE VI*, vol. 1, *Cross-Site Report* (U.S. Department of Housing and Urban Development, Office of Policy Development and Research, July 1996), pp. 2–4 to 2–18.

10. Zhang, "Wills and Ways," pp.156–157.

11. Ibid, p. 155

12. Quality Housing and Work Responsibility Act of 1998, P.L. 105-276, 112 Stat. 2562-2563, 2583-2584.

13. A provision in QHWRA had HOPE VI expiring after fiscal 2002 unless it was reauthorized; however, Congress funded HOPE VI for fiscal 2003 through appropriations and in 2003 reauthorized it through 2006. Center for Community Change, A Hope Unseen: Voices from the Other Side of Hope VI (Washington: 2003), p. 3; "HOPE VI," National Low-Income Housing Coalition, March 1, 2007.

14. According to the report, as of December 31, 2002, grantees had completed 27 percent of the units slated for construction under their plans and spent roughly $2.7 billion of $4.5 billion in funds awarded. U.S. General Accounting Office, "HUD's Oversight of HOPE VI Sites Needs to Be More Consistent" (GAO-03-555), May 2003, p. 3.

15. Sean Zielenbach, "The Financing of HOPE VI Developments: Findings and Recommendations" (Washington: Housing Research Foundation, 2003).

LORA ENGDAHL

New Holly, Seattle

The author visited Seattle December 10-11, 2007, to tour New Holly, interview Seattle Housing Authority officials and other partners and observers, and review planning and evaluation documents. This case study is based in part on that visit.

Recent immigrants to this country perceive the community in which they live and the United States as one and the same. For the many immigrants residing in Seattle's Holly Park public housing project in the early 1990s, the United States must have seemed far from a land of opportunity.

The multilingual offerings of a busy branch of the Seattle Public Library and many other services make the New Holly neighborhood campus a central gathering place.

Built with haste during World War II as temporary housing for shipyard workers, the barracks-style Holly Park community was largely falling apart by the early 1990s. A disheartening degree of physical decrepitude, socioeconomic distress, and crime was borne resolutely by inhabitants, many of whom had experienced far worse in the refugee camps, political prisons, and desperately poor countries from which they came.

To be sure, Holly Park was not nearly as bad as such notorious public housing high-rises as Cabrini Green in Chicago and Lafayette Courts in Baltimore, where children learned young to hit the floor at the sound of gunshots.[1] But, with one of the highest homicide rates in the city, Holly Park was a place where residents locked their doors and windows, pulled the drapes, and avoided the streets after sundown.[2]

The American Dream was a remote notion for the more than eight in ten heads of household in Holly Park who, although they were able to work, were unemployed, cut off from job opportunities by their physical isolation from the surrounding neighborhoods, their lack of social connections outside their own ethnic group, and, often, their limited grasp of English. Life prospects also appeared dim for the more than six in ten Holly Park children living in poverty.

Holly Park's transformation into a stable working community that offers opportunities for a better future was enabled by the $48 million HOPE VI grant awarded the Seattle Housing Authority (SHA) in 1995. The housing authority was among the handful of early HOPE VI grantees to spot the potential for leveraging redevelopment resources by building mixed-income housing and thereby deconcentrating poverty. By some accounts, early opposition and obstacles almost derailed the effort. However, leaders' handling of such issues as resident displacement and replacement housing created a model of mixed-income public housing redevelopment that spread through the Pacific Northwest. The successful redevelopment of Holly Park into New Holly led in turn to the transformation of the housing authority as financing and management approaches first tested at New Holly spread throughout the agency.

The Need for a New Holly Park

In early 1993, HUD issued the first notice of funding availability (NOFA) for the Urban Revitalization Demonstration, later known as HOPE VI. The NOFA invited public housing authorities in the forty most populous U.S. cities or on HUD's list of troubled housing authorities to apply for a total of $300 million in grants to plan or implement a public housing revitalization effort.[3] Implementation grants could cover no more than 500 units in no more than three areas of the city, although grantees were welcome to undertake the redevelopment of sites with more than 500 units as long as the additional units were funded from other sources.

The Seattle Housing Authority—not on HUD's troubled list but serving one of the forty biggest U.S. cities—had been frustrated by limitations in existing funding programs, which essentially allowed only piecemeal patch-ups of what it considered unsustainable housing stock.[4] In the new program, the authority saw the opportunity to undertake the kind of comprehensive overhaul of both housing and services that previously had been out of financial reach.[5] Holly Park, in southeast Seattle, was selected for the first application for funds because it was the SHA's most distressed complex and because it was not very densely developed, allowing for a net gain of housing units on the development site.[6]

To be eligible for funding under the program, a development had to exhibit one of four indicators of severe distress: concentrated poverty; serious crime; lack of management control of the development or failure of the development to meet residents' needs; and physical deterioration.[7]

In 1993, Holly Park met the definition. The 102-acre complex was the "choice of last resort" for public housing residents,[8] sheltering well over 800 households in one- and two-story frame houses that were so depressing, a resident leader said, that occupants wondered why they should bother to get out of bed.[9] There was dry rot in porches, utility rooms, and bathroom floors. Lead-based paint was peeling off the wood siding. Insecure windows and doors were easily broken into. Ventilation problems caused mold and mildew in the units, and lead-based paint on some interior surfaces posed an additional health threat. Heating and electrical systems were at the end of their

useful lives, leaving buildings too hot in summer, too cold in the winter, and subject to blackouts.[10]

In addition to the poor conditions, the units were poorly arranged. Residents in the upper west section of Holly Park were cut off from those in the upper and lower east sections by a high voltage power transmission line. The 200-foot-wide right-of-way, owned by the city power department, had become a dumping ground for garbage and an unpatrolled gathering spot for miscreants. Residents in the upper and lower sections also were separated by South Othello, a major east-west arterial road. All of Holly Park was severed from the surrounding neighborhoods of Beacon Hill and the Rainier Valley (so-called for its views of Mount Rainier to the south) by winding roads and cul-de-sacs largely disconnected from the city grid. No single units had ownership of the rear yards, which had no barriers and abutted parkland and the right-of-way, creating indefensible spaces that aggravated safety concerns.

Residents also were linguistically isolated, often speaking only one of the nineteen languages spoken in the community, though seven languages were predominant—English, Cambodian, Laotian, Vietnamese, Amharic, Oromo, and Tigrinya. The separate ethnic groups had little interaction.[11]

Limited fluency in English was just one of the challenges that residents faced. According to the Seattle Housing Authority's annual population report for 1993, well over half (58.4 percent) of Holly Park households were headed by a single parent, and 1993 median family income was $7,012—86 percent below the Seattle median family income of $48,000.[12] Sixty-three percent of Holly Park children under the age of eighteen were living in poverty, while the figure for same age group was only 16.2 percent citywide.[13] Only 19 percent of households had some income from employment.[14]

When gang-fueled violent crime surged throughout Seattle's public housing in mid-1993, sources told the *Seattle Post-Intelligencer* that SHA's

Above left: Rotting porches, peeling lead-based paint, and mold and mildew caused by poor ventilation were just some of the problems plaguing the World War II–era Holly Park public housing complex by the early 1990s.

Above right: Holly Park, in southeast Seattle, lay east of Boeing Field, whose workers occupied the complex during World War II. Holly Park stretched 102 acres, into Beacon Hill at the northwest end and into the Rainier Valley to the east and south, both low-income areas of high ethnic diversity.

Map reprinted with permission of the *Seattle Times.*

stepped-up drug-related evictions were having minimal impact because of the poor physical design of the housing site, inadequate social services and tenant screening procedures, and residents' fear of involvement.[15] Some suspected gang involvement when an eleven-year-old Holly Park resident was fatally shot by his fourteen-year-old friend while the boys were playing with a gun.[16] Responding to bad press about gang activity in its developments, the Seattle Housing Authority said that it was spending about $1 million a year on youth programs and other crime reduction activities—but that, by and large, resources were consumed by the ever-expanding maintenance backlog at authority properties, which never were built to last as long as they had.[17] "In many ways, we've abandoned the public housing developments to the criminals," said newly appointed SHA executive director David Gilmore to reporters in 1993.[18]

Plan Proposes Bold New Direction

The Seattle Housing Authority won a $500,000 planning grant for Holly Park in 1993 and a $48 million revitalization grant in 2005.[19] The redevelopment planning process, which lasted for more than three years, was exhaustive and at times very difficult. There were town meetings, resident surveys, focus groups, design workshops, and consultant studies of market needs and regulatory barriers that might have to be waived to address the more systemic factors contributing to the distress in Holly Park. Governing the process was a steering committee consisting of a dozen "stakeholder citizens"—residents, city officials, local developers and architects serving on city of Seattle planning boards, and the dean of the local community college.[20] The steering committee served as a conduit to and from a large advisory committee of about fifty community members, residents, service providers, local business people, city officials, and others. Translators had to be hired to ensure that residents attending meetings or reading planning materials could understand the proceedings.

Early on in the process, Seattle distinguished itself by planning the total physical and socioeconomic transformation of Holly Park. In the first NOFA, HUD challenged housing authorities to "incorporate boldness and creativity in addressing difficult issues such as high density, crime, poor structural design, and oppressive social and economic conditions."[21] Grantees were invited to apply for waivers from departmental regulations, such as the prohibition of site-based waiting lists. In keeping with the 1993 Appropriations Act, the long-standing requirement that all public housing units demolished be replaced one-for-one was eased by giving grantees the option of substituting Section 8 rental assistance vouchers for one-third of the units.[22] HUD also encouraged grantees to open the redeveloped public housing units to households with a broader range of incomes by exempting grantees from federal public housing preferences that gave priority to the most disadvantaged families.[23]

Yet despite the call for innovation and some flexibility, other initial program guidelines, such as the directive to provide "modestly designed housing for low-income persons" seemed to suggest business as usual.[24] More important, housing authorities' general capacity to envision new responses to housing problems had atrophied over decades of being told what to do by HUD rather than being asked to propose solutions. As a result, the first set of HOPE VI plans resembled souped-up modernization efforts rather than a new direction for public housing.[25]

In contrast, the plan for Holly Park that began to take shape in 1994 under executive director David Gilmore called for total demolition, dramatic reconfiguration of the site, and income mixing to draw in working families and thus end the isolation of the poor. The commitment to income mixing went well beyond what most grantees were suggesting at the time—broadening the range of household income levels served within public housing (income tiering)—by proposing to develop more shallowly subsidized housing and completely unsubsidized units, including for-sale homes.[26] The steering committee visited successful mixed-income developments in Boston and Lynn, Massachusetts, which were well known to Gilmore, who had held senior positions at the Boston Housing Authority throughout the 1980s.[27]

The Holly Park redevelopment plan was submitted to HUD in early 1995.[28] It had strong support from Mayor Norm Rice, who thought that the comprehensive redevelopment of Holly Park would improve conditions for public housing residents and the neighborhood while supporting the city's goal of sustainable development. The state's Growth Management Act required the city to develop a long-range plan for managing an expected population increase of 60,000 by 2000.[29] To handle that increase without adding to urban sprawl, city leaders wanted to direct growth to mixed-use, pedestrian- and transit-friendly centers in already developed areas. Holly Park was positioned as an experiment in smart growth, with plans for its redevelopment slated to include a neighborhood shuttle service to get people to and from transit stops.[30]

In May 1995 HUD awarded $48 million to the Seattle Housing Authority to redevelop Holly Park according to the plan outlined in the grant application submitted in January. Under the plan, all 893 public housing units on the site (some of which were vacant) would be torn down and replaced with 1,200 new units, divided equally among public housing, subsidized units for low- to moderate-income households, and market-rate units (mostly for-sale units). Nearly 500 more units for very low-income families would be developed off site.[31]

Early Challenges to the Plan

Challenges to the plan erupted after Congress rescinded the one-for-one rule in July 1995, allowing HOPE VI grantees to demolish units without replacing them. For the Seattle Housing Authority, which had been planning to create a mixed-income community on site by creating some of the replacement housing off site, the rule change presented a dilemma. The same bill that lifted the one-for-one replacement requirement rescinded the 1994 appropriation for public housing development funds, which had been awarded competitively to housing authorities seeking to replace obsolete public housing. The SHA had been relying on using the now-rescinded funds for replacement housing.[32] Stories about resident displacement in Chicago prompted the Seattle Displacement Coalition to organize residents, who feared that the SHA would be unable to raise the necessary funds for replacement housing, against the Holly Park redevelopment. The city, in turn, was not going to greenlight the plan, giving it the necessary land use approvals and funds for infrastructure, without resident support.

Complicating matters further, nonprofit housing developers worried that the redevelopment would soak up all available local resources, including monies in the city general fund, Seattle housing levy dollars, and housing tax credits for their projects. Some housing advocates went to the city council to argue for simply rehabilitating Holly Park at a sliver of the cost. Some council members were already skeptical of the Holly Park financing plan, which counted in part on proceeds from the sale of market-rate homes in what outsiders viewed as a dicey area.

The negotiations that ensued in the wake of the conflicts that emerged were led, on the housing authority side, by Doris Koo, the SHA's director of development, and on the city side by Tom Tierney, then head of the city's urban planning and budget office, who answered the critics and helped broker the deals that moved the project forward.

Koo, now the president and CEO of Enterprise Community Partners, recalls asking residents to decide whether they would meet the housing authority halfway by brainstorming plan amendments that would bring the costs down in exchange for the SHA's pledge to create replacement housing for all the units demolished. Residents held fast to such amenities as a library, teen center, and playgrounds, but gave up other features, such as individual garages and square footage in the units, Koo said.[33] The authority pledged one-for-one replacement housing, defined as hard units reserved for low-income households for a minimum of forty years. Some of the replacement units would be created off site to allow the addition of fewer subsidized and nonsubsidized units on the original site.

SHA also assembled an advisory panel to decide whether it could manage the redevelopment itself rather than contract with a major national developer, as many of the other HOPE VI grantees were doing. Residents were concerned that an out-of-town developer would be too far removed from their interests, and the housing authority, deeming the cost of hiring outside too high, wanted the option to take the developer fee itself and plow it back into the project.[34] The panel determined that the authority, though unschooled in such a large undertaking, would have sufficient local expertise to tap for assistance. In March 1996, the SHA hired a private local developer, Henry Popkin, to help it undertake its new role as developer by handling the management tasks that a developer usually handles, but without the risk entailed or ownership of the project.

Doris Morgan, who was president of the Holly Park residents' council at the time and who served on numerous committees and subcommittees, cites the veto of plans to hire a national developer as one of many examples of residents' influence on the redevelopment.[35] In turn, the residents' vote of confidence in having the housing authority act as the developer may have been the turning point for New Holly, says Tierney, who is the SHA's current executive director.

"When the residents under Doris Morgan said, 'Yes, we want this, and we trust the housing authority enough to do it,' that changed the city's sense of the project dramatically," Tierney says. "The city would have had a hard time blessing the project, putting money into it, and issuing the necessary land approvals if the residents had been fighting it."

To address the concerns of the city's nonprofit housing community, city officials pledged to limit the use of general fund and housing levy monies for New Holly and instead use primarily funds from the utilities budget and other capital fund sources. The pledge assuaged the nonprofit community's concerns that New Holly would consume too large a share of city resources, thereby gaining its acceptance of the project. In turn, the housing authority said that it would finance subsidized rental units not with highly sought-after 9 percent low-income housing tax credits but with the less competitive 4 percent low-income housing tax credits, combined with bond funds.[36]

Nonprofit developers were incorporated in the plan to build replacement housing for extremely low-income households in mixed-income settings around the city. Since the on-site housing would be serving some of the households with incomes of 30 to 60 percent of area median income (AMI)—the households customarily served by nonprofits—the SHA offered the nonprofits the opportunity to incorporate in their projects units for the 0 to 30 percent AMI households usually served in public housing. Specifically, the authority pledged that it would use part of its HOPE VI developer fees or donate land to lower the cost of nonprofit development projects and commit annual public housing operating subsidies or project-based Section 8 vouchers to cover the costs of operating the units reserved for extremely low-income households.[37]

Residents were concerned that an out-of-town developer would be too far removed from their interests.

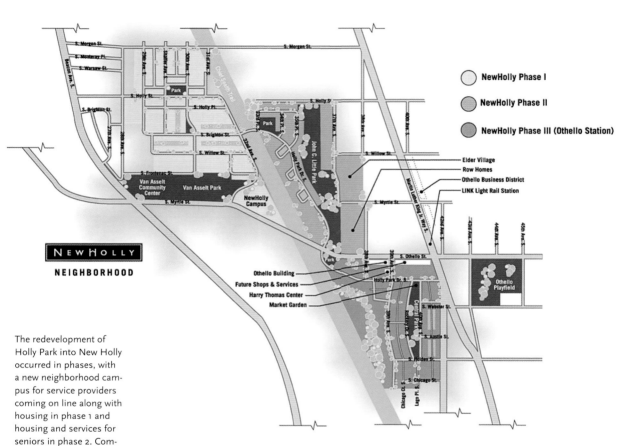

The redevelopment of Holly Park into New Holly occurred in phases, with a new neighborhood campus for service providers coming on line along with housing in phase 1 and housing and services for seniors in phase 2. Commercial development is sought for phase 3, which was marketed as Othello Station because of its proximity to the light-rail stop scheduled to open in 2009.

Phased Relocation and Redevelopment

In the spring of 1996, when planning was still under way, the SHA launched an extensive, site-wide counseling effort to prepare residents for relocation. Relocation and redevelopment would occur in phases, beginning in upper Holly Park, to minimize the need for temporary off-site relocation of those residents who wanted to live in the redeveloped community. To empty on-site units for the first relocation, residents who did not want to move back to the redeveloped community were required to move before demolition began in July 1997. Nearly half (382) of the 832 households living in Holly Park when the grant award was made elected to move permanently from Holly Park before redevelopment began, with the majority choosing Section 8 vouchers to rent homes in the private market. Families that wanted to move from Holly Park and buy homes of their own with homebuyer assistance from the SHA and other sources had to stay on site to undergo homeownership counseling. (Ultimately, more than fifty residents bought homes, mostly off site).[38]

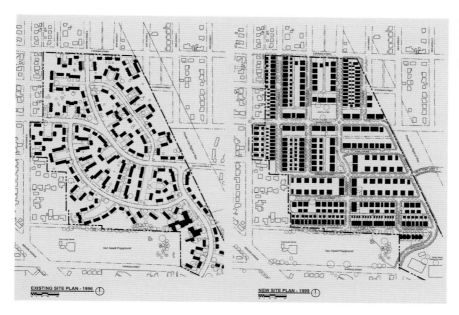

The site plans of upper New Holly in 1996 and 1999 show how the street grid was redrawn.

Amid the phased relocation, a total reconfiguration of the site took place, in keeping with the goal of reconnecting residents to one another and the broader neighborhood. Serpentine streets were replaced with a conventional street grid and stitched to adjacent areas so that homes, parks, and recreation amenities would be accessible for people within and outside the development.

Construction of rental housing, primarily paired duplex homes and town-homes, got under way first.[39] For the public housing units, the SHA spent the maximum allowable grant amount per unit to expunge doubts that the redevelopment represented real change. Although the rental and homeownership components of New Holly would be financed separately, the SHA knew that homeowners would be leery of buying in an untested market without visible proof that the housing would be of high quality.

It was also important to make the rental units—all of which were subsidized—as indistinguishable as possible from the for-sale homes. Edward Weinstein of Weinstein A/U Architects + Urban Design who led his firm's work planning and designing the first two phases of New Holly followed what he calls a "kit-of-parts" strategy for the duplexes that also would apply to the single-family homes. The kit included three variations of the same floor plan for the three- and four-bedroom first floors, over which would be set one of several interchangeable upper floors, each of which yielded a different roof configuration, or "hat."[40]

The SHA began to build and market the first for-sale homes (by itself, given the untested state of the market) based on initial studies projecting sale prices averaging around $140,000.[41] Aided greatly by the increasingly hot housing market in Seattle at the time, the homes in phase 1 sold for $167,000 to $306,000 (or $294,000, if homes with carriage house rental units are excluded). Thirteen percent of the homes sold for less than $200,000.[42] Such success enabled the SHA to move from building the for-sale housing under the guidance of the architect and freelance project manager to assuming the full role of master developer itself. Midway through phase 2, the authority began selling developable sites to private for-sale homebuilders under a profit-sharing arrangement that funneled funds back to the development of low-income housing.

Around the same time, a city auditor's report giving high marks to the relocation of Holly Park residents dispelled some of the lingering resistance to the redevelopment among housing advocates. According to the report, the relocation process, which was completed in 2002, provided sufficient advance notice, multilingual relocation counseling, moving assistance, and compensation for moving expenses. About 70 percent of the Holly Park households eligible for relocation benefits relocated to their first preference for housing. Another 15 percent did not relocate to their first preference only because they bought homes (even though buying was not their first preference), returned to New Holly rental units when they were unable to buy homes, or had health issues that required them to move into a supportive living environment.[43] Almost 90 percent (227) of those who had said that they wanted to return to the redeveloped community had moved back to New Holly.[44] Another study found that those who did not return were very satisfied with their new homes and neighborhoods.[45]

A "kit-of-parts" design strategy under which finished residences were assembled from a set of standardized elements produced homes that blended well together without looking totally alike, as shown in the image of subsidized rental duplexes (below) and for-sale single-family homes (below right).

Boys rest astride their bikes on one of New Holly's many sidewalks, alongside which residents park their cars instead of in parking lots. The homes in the background are town houses for public housing assisted families.

By the summer of 2005, New Holly was substantially developed and gaining widespread attention, with homes selling for just over $300,000 to as high as $450,000. At one point buyers literally camped overnight to buy a home in New Holly.[46]

Building a Self-Sufficient Community

Today, New Holly is a community of 1,414 residences on 118 acres funded by a total of $340 million in public and private investment.[47] It is home to families in a broad range of incomes, with some homeowners having paid more than $450,000 for their homes and public housing residents paying an average of $262 a month in rent.[48] (Table 7-1 shows the financing for New Holly and table 7-2 shows the on-site unit mix). Rental and for-sale residences have front porches and private back yards bordered by low cedar fences that afford a sense of ownership while still allowing neighbors to see and converse with one another. Parking is provided next to units, not in parking lots. Parks, playgrounds, and basketball courts abound, and there are community gardens. The formerly bleak power line right-of-way that bisects the neighborhood has been transformed into the Chief Sealth trail, a bike and pedestrian path that connects to a regional trail system. The trail, which was created using excavated soil and concrete from the Link Light Rail project along Martin Luther King Jr. Way, will access the new rail stations along MLK Way.[49]

At the same time, the inadequate model of service provision at Holly Park— services scattered throughout the site in former public housing units, limiting their scope, coordination, and accessibility—has been overhauled. Services are co-located at the neighborhood campus, a cluster of three buildings linked by pathways, anchored by a busy branch of the Seattle Public Library, and sited along an east-west arterial road that is served by a bus line and connects to two major north-south arterials and the freeway.

The low cedar fences that enclose back yards create private space but encourage interaction among neighbors. The housing shown is of New Holly phase three, designed by WRT/Solomon E.T.C.

While there are more Caucasians, Chinese, and East Africans in New Holly than before and proportionately fwer African Americans and Southeast Asians, the community is still incredibly diverse, with residents representing more than twenty different languages and cultures.[50] While most New Holly residences have two, three, or four bedrooms and therefore serve families rather than individuals, housing for senior residents is provided in New Holly's Elder Village. Developed in partnership with the Retirement Housing Foundation and Providence Health Systems, the village includes 318 units for elderly and disabled residents of all income levels, some living independently and others in assisted living environments.[51]

New and returning residents are by and large very satisfied with the community, praising it for being quiet, clean, safe, well maintained, and well laid out, with larger and more amenity-rich living spaces and access to community amenities.[52] Census crime data suggest that the new sense of safety is justified. In 1996, there were 112 violent crimes per 1,000 people in the census tract that coincides with Holly Park; in 2007, the rate had fallen to 41 crimes per 1,000.[53]

However, feelings of satisfaction and safety are insufficient indicators of success for the Seattle Housing Authority's "bold and risky experiment to create an ideal urban community" where people of different races and classes interact equally.[54] Indeed, housing authority officials say that many of the pioneers who purchased homes in New Holly were attracted as much by the opportunity to support the goals of social interaction and economic integration as by its affordability and amenities.

To help realize those goals, self-sufficiency and community-building features were built into the New Holly plan early on. First—under requirements created with resident input—nonelderly, nondisabled public housing heads

Table 7-1. New Holly Financing[a]

Source of funds	Amount in $ millions
HOPE VI grant	$50.12
Other federal funds	31.43
State/city government	18.57
(includes federal HOME funds awarded by city)	
Tax-exempt borrowing	56.00
LIHTC equity	40.38
Private investment	144.01
(includes $105 million SHA and private homebuilder investment in homes for sale)	
Total	$340.51

Source: Seattle Housing Authority.

a. In addition to the planning grant and implementation grant, the SHA received a 2001 demolition grant of $1.8 million for phase III.

Table 7-2. **New Holly On-Site Unit Mix**

Housing type	Income category	Units
Public housing	Extremely low-income[a]	400
For-sale housing	Any income level	364
Affordable rental housing	Low-income[b]	288
Affordable for-sale housing	Low-income	112
Senior housing	Extremely low-income	80
Senior housing, assisted living	Any income level	54
Senior housing, assisted living	Extremely low-income	50
Senior housing, assisted living	Low-income	50
Rental housing	Any income level	16
Total		1,414[c]

Source: Seattle Housing Authority.

a. "Extremely low-income" defines households with incomes at or below 30 percent of area median income.

b. "Low-income" defines households with incomes at or below 80 percent of area median income.

c. Another 471 units for extremely low-income residents were created off site; the Seattle Housing Authority also received an additional 250 housing assistance vouchers for relocated households.

of households who are not working must commit themselves to seeking out and obtaining employment. On-site employment services are offered to all community members at the New Holly job connection center. To support residents seeking work, the authority and its property management company have hired public housing residents for many management and maintenance jobs at New Holly.[55] The public housing lease addendum also commits tenants to sharing their children's school attendance record with management if requested to do so.[56]

Residents of all income levels have access to the comprehensive self-sufficiency services offered by partner agencies working out of the neighborhood campus.[57] The campus includes a building jointly owned by the SHA, the Seattle Public Library, and South Seattle Community College, each of which uses space in the building; the library, for example, maintains a branch there, and the community college maintains a satellite center. Other agencies lease the remaining space, together providing numerous services, including Head Start, youth tutoring, an employment center, a computer lab, ESL (English as a second language) and GED (general equivalency diploma) training, college admissions counseling, and family support services. While a significant investment from the original HOPE VI grant was used to provide initial service delivery, to ensure continuity of service provision over the long haul, the SHA partnered with agencies with solid independent funding that pledged to maintain a long-term presence in the community. Viewing the entire southeast neighborhood as their service area, the partner agencies formed a collaborative and have begun writing grant applications together and conducting joint programming.

And, in a model that has drawn attention from housing leaders nationwide, the property management budget for New Holly includes the salary of

In May 2007, New Holly residents gather for a potluck, one of the communitywide events held to foster cross-cultural interaction.

Thomas James Hurst/ the *Seattle Times*

a full-time "community builder" charged with getting residents of all socioeconomic and ethnic backgrounds involved in common activities and communicating across cultural divides.[58] New Holly's community builder, Joy Bryngelson, was the first person to hold that position for the SHA, which now has six community builders on staff throughout the agency's communities. Bryngelson trains community leaders and supports them to organize block groups and committees, plan potlucks and other community events, and advocate for community resources. She also brokers relationships among the service providers to meet newly identified needs.[59] Some clubs and committees, such as the garden club and the traffic committee, aim to bring residents together around common interests. Community-wide events such as the multicultural New Year's celebration and community potlucks aim to introduce residents to one another's cultures.

The operative principle behind the community services provided is empowerment—giving residents the tools to engage effectively with local government—explains John Forsyth, community services administrator for the SHA. For example, when residents grew concerned about youth hanging out in the public park at night, Bryngelson prepared community representatives for a meeting with senior parks staff by helping them go beyond voicing their complaints to presenting possible solutions. As a result, the city lowered the curfew.

The city and service providers outside New Holly contribute to community building by sponsoring additional activities. Thanks to the city's public-private "P-patch program," five community gardens incorporated throughout all three portions of the development are tended by residents, some of whom sell greens and produce weekly while others grow food for their families. The city sponsors programs at the John C. Little Park for the broader community, such as movies at the park, community cookouts, and dance contests.[60]

Harmony and Barriers

The community-building and self-sufficiency policies of New Holly have helped produce a solid community whose members live in relative harmony and engage in some cross-cultural exchange—a community much more aligned with the American ideals of inclusivity and opportunity than the old Holly Park.

Except for senior residents and persons with disabilities (of whom there are few outside Elder Village), New Holly is largely a working community. Although current statistics on the entire New Holly community will not be available until the next census, the portion of working-age public housing families with income from employment increased from 19 percent in 1993 to around 87 percent in 2008.[61] It is hard to determine how much of the change is attributable to new public housing residents moving in under the new work requirement, to general economic trends, and to Washington state's relatively strict interpretation of federal law ending public assistance after five years.[62] Nevertheless, Holly Park residents who remained at New Holly appear to have benefited from income and job gains. A 2003 evaluation by the Daniel J. Evans School of Public Affairs at the University of Washington found that residents who stayed at New Holly increased their incomes more than those who relocated, despite the fact that few differences marked the two groups prior to redevelopment. Average annual household income for former Holly Park residents who remained at New Holly increased from $7,479 before redevelopment (in 1996) to $17,340 after redevelopment (in 2003). Average annual income for relocatees increased from $6,108 before redevelopment to $11,765 after redevelopment. The authors speculated that the difference might be due to the work requirements of the new development.[63] The study also showed that public housing residents were making use of the self-sufficiency services.[64]

New Holly residents told Evans School researchers that they generally get along, and that they do come together at the library and at certain events, such as community meetings and potlucks. Children of families living in public housing, for-sale homes, and tax-credit subsidized rental units are all using the library and Central Park. But many amenities or events tend to attract only certain groups, and non–English speakers say that they participate less in events because they are busy or embarrassed by their inability to communicate.[65]

The Evans study also showed that people tend to socialize only with others of the same ethnicity and education level, noting that some public housing residents feel less involved in shaping the community because the old resident councils, organized along ethnic lines, have been disbanded.[66] Indeed, as Bryngelson notes, committees to tend to be staffed by homeowners because committees are a "Eurocentric" form of organization.

The lack of extensive, comfortable interaction across ethnic and economic lines has been explored in news reports on New Holly. A 2007 *Seattle Times* article observed a persistent "clannishness," with community residents saying that language barriers were a greater divider than income differences.[67] The *Seattle Post-Intelligencer* reported in 2008 that class and cultural divides appeared especially difficult for youth, some of whom had a hard time making friends, and that some homeowners were keeping their children and teens away from the neighborhood campus and places where youth hang out.[68]

The mixed results on social interaction at New Holly—which has been documented in HOPE VI redevelopments in other cities—may derive more from the ambitious goals of the housing authority than from any flaws in the model of development or its implementation.[69]

"People did expect a utopia. Where has that happened in the world?" asks Joy Bryngelson. Maybe it is sufficient that, given the responsibilities and pressures in their lives, neighbors greet one another in the street or occasionally stop to chat and attend periodic events that build awareness of other cultures and dispel stereotypes. All of that occurs at New Holly.[70] Staff have hopes that a sense of community will continue to strengthen as programs expand beyond such pursuits as adult education and ESL to culinary arts and other interests that are more likely to attract participation across income levels.

Goals Reached and Yet to Be Achieved

While New Holly may not have turned into a utopia, it has achieved many of the initial goals set back in the mid-1990s: ending the isolation of the community from the neighborhoods around it; reducing the stigma of public housing by creating attractive homes, whether subsidized or market-rate, that blend together; creating a safe place for families to live; and offering residents opportunities to become more self-sufficient.

However, the redevelopment is lagging on the goal of becoming a thriving, transit-oriented community of shops and housing. In 2001, when Sound Transit announced that it would run the first light-rail line in the region down Martin Luther King Jr. Way, the Seattle Housing Authority recast its plans for the third phase of New Holly to take advantage of the stop slated for MLK and South Othello. Prime parcels on the corners were saved for last in the expectation that rail-spurred development would increase the value of land for development. A 2002 Housing Research Foundation evaluation noted that while the commercial and retail market around New Holly was still fairly weak, local developers and real estate professionals concurred with the housing authority's expectation of new investment with the rail line—a positive forecast reinforced by decreasing crime and unemployment rates in the area and rising residential loan rates.[71]

And indeed, in early 2008 prospects looked good, with the *Seattle Times* reporting that the long-predicted "redevelopment boom in one of Seattle's poorest, most neglected, most ethnically diverse corridors" was starting to take shape and that proposals had been made to build more than 1,500 condo and apartment units near the rail stations to be built along MLK.[72] In addition to light rail, Rainier Valley was benefiting from its status as a close-in but still "relatively affordable" real estate market, the redevelopment of the Holly Park and Rainier Vista public housing projects into new mixed-income communities, and the renewed popularity of the Columbia City neighborhood to the north and slightly east of New Holly, which is noted for its art galleries and cultural attractions.

A major issue of concern was how to retain the rich ethnic flavor created by the many immigrant-owned stores and restaurants facing rent increases that threatened to force them out of business. Many already had suffered big drops in business from the disruptive light-rail construction process. Owners of mom-and-pop stores could tap a $50 million remediation fund set up by the city to help displaced businesses, but some said that the funds did not make up for the loss of customers.[73]

As the light-rail line got closer to opening, developer interest in constructing projects around Othello Station, New Holly's third phase, peaked. But by later in 2008, trouble in the national economy and credit markets had put projects on hold, dimming hopes for any big near-term boost in commercial activity, although officials expect the projects to move forward when credit markets loosen. Without the hoped-for level of commercial investment, socioeconomic improvements, though critical, have been incomplete. Housing authority officials confirm that while crime has fallen, there is still crime, some gang issues, and problems with domestic violence. Concentrated poverty has decreased, but a large population of low-income people remains. The in-flux state of the Rainier Valley, in which New Holly sits, has led to contrasting points of view, with some residents complaining of gentrification while others say that southeast Seattle still has too much low-income housing.[74]

The growing socioeconomic diversity of New Holly, exhibited in the spike in for-sale home prices mentioned earlier, may have added to the conflict. With the development of Othello Station, some critics have charged the authority with breaking from the uniformity of earlier phases and building homes that are distinguishable by the incomes of their occupants—citing in particular the placement of the fanciest homes up on the hill, above the lower-income homes below.

Without the hoped-for level of commercial investment, socioeconomic improvements, though critical, have been incomplete.

Authority officials say that all the homes do not have to look alike for residents to coexist peacefully. But there is a segment of the housing advocacy community that has remained critical of what it views as the shortcomings of the public-private partnership model and its sometimes precarious balance between the needs of residents and the dictates of the broader market. Likewise, there may never be full reconciliation of opposing views of what constitutes acceptable replacement housing. Authority officials say that they have been fighting persistent doubts that the SHA has fulfilled its commitment to replace, one for one, all public housing units demolished at Holly Park.

What exactly has replaced the 871 public housing units that were in service prior to redevelopment? According to the Seattle Housing Authority, the New Holly redevelopment produced 993 apartments for people with incomes below 30 percent of the area median income. That includes 530 on-site public housing and senior housing units and 471 off-site units created with SHA assistance, although they are not necessarily owned by the SHA (see table 7-2). Of those 993 units, the 400 on-site public housing units and the 471 off-site SHA-subsidized units are counted, technically, as replacement units. Critics say that the off-site units that are not public housing (not governed by the ACC contract between the SHA and HUD) but are funded by project-based Section 8 subsidies should not count.[75] Authority officials say that what matters is not what mechanism ensures long-term affordability but the fact that a mechanism is in place, ensuring affordability for forty years. Further, says Tom Tierney, any discussion about whether new units are sufficient to replace those demolished should acknowledge that new units with many decades of service ahead of them better preserve affordable housing opportunities than those that had only a few years of useful life left.

The debate is joined at the national level by experts in federal housing policy who argue that the advances that the housing authorities in Seattle and other cities have made since HOPE VI began may, in the long run, better safeguard housing opportunities for the lowest-income households than would maintaining communities that are 100 percent public housing (see chapters 12 and 15).

The Evolution of the Housing Authority

Proof, through New Holly, that Seattle residents were willing to live in mixed-income settings enabled the Seattle Housing Authority to evolve from an inexperienced developer to a sought-after partner in promoting mixed-income developments around the city. By 2001, the SHA had begun demolition on Rainier Vista, a denser, 55-acre complex just northeast of New Holly, followed in 2003 by demolition at High Point, a 120-acre complex atop a bluff in west Seattle. Emulating New Holly, the new communities feature a mix of townhomes, row houses, single-family homes, and small apartment buildings, with specialized housing for seniors and people with disabilities and a neighborhood hub where a mix of services, including job services, can be obtained.[76]

The basic financing plan is the same: to leverage the HOPE VI grant with tax-exempt bond issues that generate 4 percent tax credit equity and front-load as much of the HOPE VI grant as allowed into the first phases to show homebuyers what the new community would look and feel like. Later, proceeds from home sales in the early phases are used and developable land is sold to make up for shortfalls in HOPE VI funds for developing the public housing units. The authority fills gaps in financing by using tools that increase the amount of money that lenders will offer to the project, such as interest rate swaps attached to bond issues and replacement of ACC units with units subsidized by project-based vouchers.

This strategy has worked in Seattle because the market-rate component of the developments has been valuable enough to leverage real private investment. Part of Rainer Vista's appeal for middle-income renters and homebuyers is its proximity to the services and amenities of the Columbia City business district, while High Point is an award-winning "green" community with some of the best views in the city.[77] The SHA protects its investment in the rental component of these communities by creating a homeowners' association that enforces covenants regarding such things as design guidelines to maintain curb appeal and by acquiring and renovating nearby known drug houses and other troubled parcels that would scare off prospective renters and homebuyers.

Green features and good views attract middle-income households to Seattle's mixed-income High Point HOPE VI.

On all the developments, the authority brings to bear new management practices and financing innovations piloted at New Holly and since applied throughout the agency. They include on-site property management with site-based waiting lists; on-site rent collection (to maintain interpersonal contacts with residents); hiring of public housing residents as maintenance staff; rent ceilings to discourage working families from moving out of the community; utility allowances that require high users to pay for excess use; quarterly asset management reviews; establishment of reserve funds; a line item for community building in the property management budget; new leasing rules, including requirements that nonworking heads of household participate in self-sufficiency programs and that residents observe housekeeping standards in order to maintain the curb appeal of their homes; and a more flexible staff of "universal maintenance mechanics," who can be deployed to do a range of repairs at different SHA sites. The implementation of these best practices has generated cost savings for the SHA as well as created an "upwardly mobile mindset" among officials about families receiving SHA housing assistance and among the families themselves, says Willard Brown, property management administrator for the authority.

The SHA is planning a mixed-income redevelopment of 582-unit Yesler Terrace, which overlooks south downtown, with seed funding coming not from HOPE VI but from the value of the land. It also is partnering with nonprofit and private entities on two mixed-income developments that do not involve public housing. In addition, the authority was selected by the city to be the master developer of the Fort Lawton Army Reserve base, which was closed under the BRAC (Base Realignment and Closure) program. Plans call for building a mixed-income community on eighteen acres of the base, with 40 percent of the units reserved for formerly homeless families and seniors.

A New Direction for the Region

As the Pacific Northwest's first HOPE VI redevelopment project, New Holly influenced housing authorities from Portland, Oregon, to Tacoma, Washington, which followed with public housing redevelopments that adopted New Holly's core principles, such as one-for-one replacement, community-building services, and assisted housing for seniors. These agencies are undertaking some of the nation's most forward-looking redevelopments. For HOPE VI communities like New Columbia in Portland, quality public education is a centerpiece of the redevelopment effort. The Housing Authority of Portland partnered with the city, the school board, and private donors, businesses, and foundations to replace an aging K-6 school with the new Rosa Parks Elementary School. The school, which was designed as part of a community campus whose partners share space and costs, recently won the 2007 Richard Riley Award for Schools as Centers of Community.

Salishan, in Tacoma, has a new elementary school as well as a health and service-oriented focus, with a planned medical-dental clinic and service-enriched units for homeless families. Greenbridge, in the unincorporated King County, Washington, community of White Center, seeks to tackle the historical lack of access its low-income residents have had to economic opportunities. The redevelopment involves improved access to White Center's business district, new storefronts for different businesses, live-work units for microbusiness owners, and an array of adult education and other services offered through multiple community partners. Greenbridge also has a new on-site elementary school. Salishan, Greenbridge, and Seattle's High Point all are pursuing sustainable development through green building. [78]

With its track record of mixed-income redevelopment and its ethnically diverse population, the region could provide lessons for tackling other next-generation public housing and urban development challenges, from improving residents' self-sufficiency through improved service coordination to accommodating the growing senior population to forming relationships across racial and ethnic divides. And, of course, in tougher economic times, to building and sustaining mixed-income communities.

····· Endnotes ·····

1. National Public Radio, on *All Things Considered,* January 2, 2004, aired a segment on housing problems regarding racial segregation in Baltimore, in which former Lafayette Courts resident Isaac Neal described how he had to teach his two sons "to fall on the floor and stay there," referring to one son as "my baby boy."

2. Doris Koo, director of development of the Seattle Housing Authority during planning for Holly Park's redevelopment, had an office on site. She shared memories of anxious residents telling her to lock her doors, pull her drapes, and leave the site at night. Washington State Housing Finance Commission newsletter, June 2008, p. 9.

3. "HOPE VI Program Authority and Funding History," U.S. Department of Housing and Urban Development, March 2007 (www.hud.gov/offices/pih/programs/ph/hope6/about/fundinghistory.pdf).

4. Agencies on HUD's troubled housing authority list were those that had indicators of mismanagement, such as high vacancy rates and rental payment delinquencies. Of the thirty-two housing authorities that received HOPE VI implementation grants in fiscal years 1993 to 1995, twelve were on the list. The Seattle Housing Authority was one of only six considered "high-performing." (Thirty-four grants were awarded but Detroit and San Antonio got two grants apiece.) Linda B. Fosburg, Susan J. Popkin, and Gretchen P. Locke, *An Historical and Baseline Assessment of HOPE VI,* vol. 1, *Cross-Site Report* (U.S. Department of Housing and Urban Development, Office of Policy Development and Research, July 1996), pp.1-10, 1-14, 1-18 (www.huduser.org/Publications/pdf/hopevi_vol1.pdf).

5. In 1989, the realization that some public housing projects had "severe modernization needs" that could not be handled through the existing formula-based grant program for routine modernization led to the enactment of the Major Reconstruction of Obsolete Projects (MROP) program. But with its limited funds and low cap on per-unit expenditures, the program was not very helpful. In 1990, Congress authorized the Comprehensive Grant Program, a new formula-based modernization grant program for public housing authorities with more than 500 units. While the program offered PHAs a reliable, flexible source of modernization funding, the formula did not cover the extraordinary costs of revitalizing severely distressed public housing. Further, housing authorities could not just demolish severely distressed public housing because federal regulations required that they be fully replaced and the public housing development program that provided grants to PHAs to develop new public housing was historically underfunded and was terminated after 1994. See Yan Zhang, "Wills and Ways: Policy Dynamics of HOPE VI from 1992 to 2002," Ph.D. dissertation, Massachusetts Institute of Technology, September 2004, p. 77; and Susan J. Popkin and others, *A Decade of HOPE VI: Research Findings and Policy Challenges* (Washington: Urban Institute and Brookings Institution, May 2004), p. 13. Information about the public housing development program came from HUD's website and a conversation between the author and Rod Solomon, partner, Hawkins Delafield & Wood LLP, November 24, 2008.

6. The site had a density of nine units per acre but was zoned for up to fifteen units per acre. Holly Park HOPE VI Revitalization Plan, Seattle Housing Authority, January 1995, p. 2-2.

7. *Federal Register* 58, no. 2 (January 5, 1993). Sites selected also had to be among the housing authority's most severely distressed sites.

8. Holly Park HOPE VI Revitalization Plan, p. 1-2.

9. The plan said that Holly Park had 893 units, 21 of which were taken offline permanently for use by service providers, and 813 occupied units as of December 31, 1993. Holly Park HOPE VI Revitalization Plan, p. 2-1, 2-12; Fosburg, Popkin, and Locke, *An Historical and Baseline Assessment of HOPE VI,* p. 1-25, cites a December 1993 extract of data from the Multi-Family Tenant Characteristic System for New Holly's 858 households.

10. Holly Park HOPE VI Revitalization Plan, January 1995, pp. 2-1 to 2-14.

11. Ibid., p. 2-12

12. Ibid., pp. 2-12 to 2-13.

13. Ibid., p. 1-1. While it is not entirely clear whether the statistic regarding children in poverty pertains to 1993 it is likely, because 1994 data on tenant characteristics may not have been tabulated by the time the plan was submitted in January 1995.

14. Fosburg, Popkin, and Locke, *An Historical and Baseline Assessment of HOPE VI,* p. 1-25.

15. Eric Houston, "High Point Cries for Help; Gunfire at Night, Drugs, and Violence," *Seattle Post-Intelligencer,* October 20, 1993, p. A1. According to the article, between May and October 1993, nearly 100 assaults were reported at the Holly Park and Rainier Vista public housing complexes in the South End, with another 87 at the authority's High Point development in west Seattle.

16. Newspaper accounts of the shooting characterized it as an accident, but according to Doris Morgan, in her testimonial in the June 2008 newsletter of the Washington State Housing Finance Commission, the boys were playing Russian roulette. A 2002 study that included a case study of the Holly Park redevelopment called the shooting a gang initiation rite. Sean Zielenbach, *The Economic Impact of HOPE VI on Neighborhoods* (Washington: Housing Research Foundation, 2002), p. 43.

17. Houston, "High Point Cries for Help."

18. Ibid. The article quotes David Gilmore, then the director of the Seattle Housing Authority, who left the SHA in summer 1995 to take the post of court-appointed receiver for the District of Columbia's highly troubled housing authority.

19. "HOPE VI Program Authority and Funding History," pp. 1–2 (www.hud.gov/offices/pih/programs/ph/hope6/about/fundinghistory.pdf). Information on the requirement to fund prior years' planning grantees comes from Fosburg, Popkin, and Locke, *An Historical and Baseline Assessment of HOPE VI,* pp. 1–13.

20. E-mail communication from Scott Jepsen, partner, EJP Consulting Group, December 5, 2008. Jepsen was the HOPE VI redevelopment manager for the Seattle Housing Authority from 1993 to 1997.

21. Department of Housing and Urban Development, Office of the Assistant Secretary for Public and Indian Housing (Docket No. N-93-3557; FR-3412-N-1), Funding Availability (NOFA) for Urban Revitalization Demonstration, Tuesday, January 5, 1993, in *Federal Register* 58, p. 436 (hereafter referred to as 1993 NOFA).

22. They also could also replace units with for-sale units meeting the guidelines of certain HUD homeownership programs. 1993 NOFA.

23. Although households making up to 80 percent of area median income are eligible for public housing, most households living in the public housing sites slated for redevelopment fell below 50 percent of AMI, partly due to federal preferences introduced in 1980 that give priority to homeless persons, households paying more than 50 percent of their income for housing, and people who have been displaced or who are living in substandard housing, noted Gayle Epp, design consultant to the National Commission on Severely Distressed Public Housing. See Gayle Epp, "Emerging Strategies for Revitalizing Public Housing Communities," *Housing Policy Debate* 7, no. 3 (1996): 576–77.

24. In her 2004 dissertation, Yan Zhang notes that the 1993 NOFA may have psychologically encouraged limited creativity by requiring grant applicants to adhere to eight existing regulations regarding public housing, leaving them some flexibility only in meeting one-for-one replacement requirements and establishing site-based waiting lists. Zhang, "Wills and Ways," p. 91. Also see 1993 NOFA, p. 2.

25. See "The HOPE VI Program," National Association of Housing and Redevelopment Officials (www.nahro.org/programs/phousing/hopeVI/index.cfm).

26. On February 14, 1994, the steering committee for the Holly Park redevelopment project established a set of overarching principles to guide planning, among which was a commitment to pursue income mixing through housing that served a range of incomes and included market-rate housing. Holly Park HOPE VI Revitalization Plan.

27. As explained in chapter 3, note 4, in the 1980s the Boston Housing Authority's highly distressed Columbia Point public housing project was redeveloped as a mixed-income community including subsidized and market-rate units through a financing strategy that called for replacing public housing with low-income units subsidized by the project-based Section 8 program.

28. At the behest of Congress, the eight housing authorities that had received planning grants in 1993 and 1994 were automatically eligible for implementation grants as long as they submitted an acceptable plan. See "HOPE VI Program Authority and Funding History."

29. Holly Park HOPE VI Revitalization Plan, January 1995, p. 4-4.

30. Ibid., pp. 1-3 to 1-7.

31. Ibid., pp. 1-3, 4-17, and Epp, "Emerging Strategies for Revitalizing Public Housing Communities," p. 580.

32. E-mail to the author from Ann-Marie Lindboe, SHA asset management director, December 15, 2008.

33. Koo joined the Seattle Housing Authority as director of development in 1994 and was named deputy executive director in 1999. By the time she left the SHA in 2001, all of the authority's HOPE VI grants had been secured. Author's conversation with Doris Koo, July 14, 2008.

34. The developer's fee is an allowable use of HUD grant funds to compensate for the time and risk involved in developing the project. It typically is based on the size of the project, the total development cost, and the risk associated with the project. From the website of the U.S. Department of Housing and Urban Development (www.hud.gov). Prior to deciding to act as the developer itself, the SHA had received an initial bid from a prospective developer, McCormack Baron in Saint Louis.

35. Washington State Housing Finance Commission newsletter, June 2008, p. 6.

36. Before the nation's economic woes lessened the value of tax credits (reflecting the much lower corporate profits against which tax credits are applied), the 9 percent LIHTCs, which are allocated on a competitive basis by state housing finance agencies, were always in high demand. Historically there has been less demand among affordable housing developers for the 4 percent credits, which are allocated in conjunction with tax-exempt bonds, because the credits are not as valuable and thus generate less equity.

37. Author's conversation with Doris Koo, July 14, 2008.

38. Office of City Auditor, "Seattle Housing Authority's Holly Park Relocation Efforts," April 1, 2003, pp 5, 6. According to the report, another fifty-six residents either did not make a choice, lost relocation eligibility due to lease violations, or died. Different published SHA materials have the number of households purchasing homes at either fifty-one or fifty-two. In an e-mail communication on January 24, 2008, SHA communications director Virginia Felton said that most of the residents who bought homes did not buy them in New Holly.

39. About two dozen 800-square-foot coach houses were built atop garages in some of the alleys. About half a dozen single-family rental homes were built. Bill Kossen, "New Holly: Holly Park Went Up to Help Fight a War; New Holly Goes Up in the Name of Harmony," *Seattle Times*, September 25, 1999.

40. The design won numerous awards, including a 2005 John M. Clancy Award for Socially Responsible Housing.

41. In an e-mail communication with the author on December 8, 2008, Ann-Marie Lindboe recalled that initial studies predicted that homes would sell around $140,000 on average. Her recollections track with the $114,000 to $180,000 sale price range reported in the news right before launch of home construction. See Jerry Large, "Holly Park to Rise Again," *Seattle Times*, May 6, 1997.

42. Author's communication with Ann-Marie Lindboe, December 8, 2008.

43. Office of City Auditor, "Seattle Housing Authority's Holly Park Relocation Efforts," pp. 1-8. According to the report, only two formal complaints were filed during the redevelopment and relocation process. While the phased-construction approach minimized the number of moves for most households, households electing to return to New Holly moved more than once within the community during construction, the report said.

44. Another 267 households obtained a rental voucher; 137 households had moved to another SHA community; 52 households purchased homes; 59 households moved to other, non-SHA housing; 28 residents moved into supportive housing; and 62 were evicted, abandoned their apartments, moved out of state, died, or did not apprise the SHA of their whereabouts. Seattle Housing Authority, "New Holly Redevelopment Plan: Relocation Results" (www.seattlehousing.org/redevelopment/newholly/replacement/ [December 19, 2008]).

45. Unsurprisingly, the study, a 2003 evaluation by the Daniel J. Evans School of Public Affairs at the University of Washington, also found that residents who relocated outside New Holly were not as well connected to services but also not disappointed in that regard, perhaps because they were less likely than returnees to have used services prior to redevelopment. Rachel Garshick Kleit, Daniel Carlson, and Tam Kutzmark, "Holly Park and Roxbury HOPE VI Redevelopments: Evaluation Report," Daniel J. Evans School of Public Affairs, University of Washington, December 2003, pp. ii–iv, 158–59 (http://evans.washington.edu/files/NHR_Entire.pdf).

46. Nina Shapiro, "Rich House, Poor House," *Seattle Weekly*, July 13–19, 2005.

47. By summer 2008, construction was almost complete, with a few dozen for-sale homes pending construction. During redevelopment some parcels were added to the original site, bringing the acreage up to 118.

48. As of December 2008, the highest price paid for an original home sale at New Holly was $468,000 while a home resold by an original owner went for more than $500,000. The average public housing tenant rent of $262 is for November 2008. Author's communication with Ann-Marie Lindboe, December 12, 2008.

49. Seattle Department of Transportation, press release, "Chief Sealth Trail Grand Opening!" May 12, 2007 (www.seattle.gov).

50. Author's conversation with Joy Bryngelson, New Holly community builder, December 10, 2007. According to Bryngelson, many of the new homeowners are Caucasian, boosting their share of the population, while the Southeast Asians who formed an earlier wave of immigrants have moved up and out of public housing and a new wave of immigrants from East African nations have moved in.

51. The Elder Village includes Holly Court, a public housing community for elderly and disabled persons; Peter Claver House, an assisted-living facility financed by the HUD 202 program and operated by Providence Health Systems; Esperanza Apartments, an affordable senior housing residence sponsored by Retirement Housing Foundation; and Park Place, a market-rate assisted-living senior community also sponsored by Retirement Housing Foundation. The total number of units comes from Seattle Housing Authority, "Report to the Community," September 2008.

52. Kleit, Carlson, and Kutzmark, "Holly Park and Roxbury HOPE VI Redevelopments: Evaluation Report," pp. 44, 51, 95. As noted on page 44, only 6 percent of public housing tenants and tax credit renters surveyed said that they considered New Holly "not very safe," with no homeowners feeling "not very safe."

53. Source for 1996 crime rate is Kleit, Carlson, and Kutzmark, "Holly Park and Roxbury HOPE VI Redevelopments: Evaluation Report," p. 93. Crime data were reported for Part I Index crimes (murder, robbery, and so forth) for census tract 110, which encompasses New Holly phase 1. Source for number of 2007 Part I crimes in census tract 110 (325 crimes) is Seattle Police Department, "Offenses Reported by Census Tract of Occurrence," January 2007–December 2007 (www.seattle.gov/police/crime/stats/pur170/200712y.htm [July 22, 2008]); the 2007 population estimate for census tract 110 (7,836 residents) comes from "Census Tract Estimates of Housing Units, Households, and Population: 2007," Puget Sound Regional Council (http://psrc.org/data/dem/pophsgdata.htm [July 22, 2008]).

54. Stuart Eskenazi, "A New Neighborhood Built to Tear Down Old Barriers," *Seattle Times,* May 13, 2007.

55. A private company, Quantum Management, managed the property until the SHA turned property management over to its subsidiary property manager, Impact Property Management. E-mail communication from Joy Bryngelson to author, July 25, 2008.

56. Author's conversation with Willard Brown, New Holly property management administrator, December 10, 2007.

57. The development cost for the New Holly Campus of Learners was $9.1 million, funded by the Seattle Housing Authority ($2.8 million), federal and local governments ($4 million), donations from various greater Seattle businesses and foundations, including the Seattle Library Foundation, Boeing, and Microsoft ($1.5 million); and other sources. E-mail communication to the author from Virginia Felton, SHA communications director, August 8, 2008.

58. Initially funded by the HOPE VI grant, the community builder's salary is now paid from property revenues, a testament to the perceived value of community building to New Holly's success as a real estate venture, according to John Forsyth, SHA community services administrator.

59. For example, to help lessen the isolation of the Somali Muslim women in the community, the Atlantic Street Center, in partnership with Seattle Parks and Recreation, sponsors a "Women of the World" swim class for women only at the Rainier Beach pool.

60. Office of Seattle mayor Greg Nickels, press release, "Mayor Nickels Announces Summer Programs for Central District," June 17, 2008.

61. Information on current workforce participation comes from author's communication with Willard Brown, New Holly property management administrator with the Seattle Housing Authority, July 22, 2008. According to Brown, the information for the percentage of public housing households with some income from employment as of 2008 comes from Seattle Housing Authority reports from year-end 2007. Only households with working-age members, not elderly or disabled households, are included in the count. The shift from a community where residents rarely worked to one where most residents worked is attributable not just to the Family Self-Sufficiency program (FSS) lease addendum but also to time limits on welfare assistance, says Brown.

62. According to an April 2008 MDRC (formerly Manpower Demonstration Research Corporation) report, the final regulations for the Temporary Assistance for Needy Families (TANF) program that replaced welfare in the wake of the Personal Responsibility and Work Opportunity Reconciliation Act of 1996 "gave states considerable flexibility in terms of how they could structure their TANF programs to meet state goals as well as the requirements established by PRWORA." As a result, the extent to which families receiving assistance are

affected by the sixty-month time limit set for TANF at the federal level varies greatly across the states. While Washington state—which implemented TANF time limits in late July 1997, as did many other states—grants hardship exemptions to extend benefits beyond the sixtieth month, caseworkers emphasize the time limits and the need to move to self-sufficiency and do not discuss the possibility of extensions ahead of time. Also, Washington state requires all eligible clients to participate in work activities or face a 40 percent reduction in benefits. Mary Farrell and others, "Welfare Time Limits: An Update on State Policies, Implementation, and Effects on Families," prepared by the Lewin Group and MDRC for the Office of Planning, Research, and Evaluation, Administration for Children and Families, U.S. Department of Health and Human Services, April 2008, pp. ES-2, 171–72.

63. Kleit, Carlson, and Kutzmark, "Holly Park and Roxbury HOPE VI Redevelopments: Evaluation Report," pp. iv, 139, 144, 160. Comparisons of pre-and post-redevelopment incomes are in 1996 dollars. Although the study assessed the experiences of residents affected by the redevelopment of Holly Park and the much smaller HOPE VI redevelopment of Roxbury Village, which began in 1998, the study broke out some findings by development. Data for Holly Park residents who stayed at New Holly came from current New Holly certification records and include former Holly Park residents who were still public housing residents as well as those who were tax credit renters. Information on the increase in their income comes from table 18, p. 160. Data for Holly Park relocatees were not pulled from table 18 but table 16, because one of the study authors said that the numbers in table 16 were correct. The study authors caution that the figures for the increase in relocatee income may be overstated "as those who are no longer in SHA housing or whose records are incomplete are omitted from these figures" (p. 144). Note that researchers were able to compare changes in income by source only for relocatees; they found that income earned from wages had increased while welfare dependence had decreased.

64. Ibid., pp. 74–75. According to the report, 57 percent of public housing residents used the computer lab, 43 percent used the continuing education center, and 38 percent used the career development center, which also was used by 32 percent of tax credit renters.

65. For example, children living in public housing and tax credit rentals used the teen center whereas homeowners' children largely did not. Kleit, Carlson, and Kutzmark, "Holly Park and Roxbury HOPE VI Redevelopments: Evaluation Report, pp. 62, 64, 70, 71, 78.

66. Ibid., pp. 47, 64, 68.

67. Eskenazi, "New Neighborhood Built to Tear Down Old Barriers."

68. Ambreen Ali and Kathy Mulady, "Diverse New Holly Still Struggling to Break Down the Cultural Divide; Vision for Community Misses the Mark for Many Youths," *Seattle Post-Intelligencer,* May 13, 2008, p. B1.

69. For example, limited resident interaction was noted in Mark L. Joseph, "Early Resident Experiences at a New Mixed-Income Development in Chicago," *Journal of Urban Affairs* 30, no. 3 (August 2008): 229–57.

70. Kleit, Carlson, and Kutzmark, "Holly Park and Roxbury HOPE VI Redevelopments: Evaluation Report," p. 158; author's conversation with Joy Bryngelson, December 10, 2007.

71. Sean Zielenbach, *The Economic Impact of HOPE VI on Neighborhoods* (Washington: Housing Research Foundation, 2002), p. 44–45.

72. Eric Pryne, "New Light Rail Clears Way for an MLK Makeover," *Seattle Times,* April 21, 2008.

73. Ibid.

74. See, for example, Mark D. Fefer, "The Intersection of Gentrification and Neglect," *Seattle Weekly,* May 14, 2008; Debera Carlton Harrell, "Visions for the City: Mistrust of City Ideas

Evident in Rainier Valley," *Seattle Post-Intelligencer,* July 6, 2007; and Debera Carlton Harrell, "Neighbor Groups Split over Density Disputes: In Southeast, Lake Union, Residents' Visions Clash," *Seattle Post-Intelligencer,* July 20, 2008.

75. Plus, they say, some of the off-site units are in other public housing properties that were slated to come back into service anyway.

76. About a quarter of the units at High Point and well over a third of the units at Rainier will serve people with very low incomes; public housing units not replaced on site are built elsewhere, either by the SHA or nonprofit developers using project-based vouchers or other SHA assistance.

77. All thirty-four blocks of the project have been turned into a state-of-the art natural drainage system, capturing rainwater runoff to preserve nearby Longfellow Creek, a salmon-bearing stream. The drainage system consists of streets that are narrower than usual in order to reduce runoff and that slant slightly to direct rainwater into shallow swales planted with shrubs and grasses. Most of the streets and sidewalks are made of porous concrete. Sixty of the rental units will be Breathe Easy® homes, designed to relieve asthma. High Point is also the nation's first Energy Star–rated rental housing development, according to the EPA 2007 National Award for Smart Growth Achievement. In addition to the EPA smart growth award, High Point won an Urban Land Institute Global Award for Excellence in 2007, a 2007 Rudy Bruner Award (silver medal), and many others.

78. Information on the developments cited in this paragraph comes from the Washington State Housing Finance commission newsletter, June 2008.

LORA ENGDAHL

The Villages of Park DuValle, Louisville

The author visited Louisville December 3–4, 2007, to tour Park DuValle, interview officials of the Housing Authority of Louisville and other partners and observers, and review planning and evaluation documents. This case study is based in part on that visit.

It is hard to believe that a pretty yellow house with a basket of pink flowers suspended between its porch columns now sits at 32nd Street and Young Avenue, once the "the meanest street corner in Louisville."[1] On a weekday afternoon in December 2007, the green chairs on the front porch are empty and all is quiet. Similarly well-tended homes up and down the block also are quiet—although the sight of a school bus rounding the corner a few blocks away suggests that the scene may soon get livelier.

According to the *Louisville Courier-Journal,* on any given day in the mid-1980s you would have been likely to see as many as 200 people at this intersection, mostly men gathered in and around a trash-covered lot by Thirty-Second Street Liquors. The older folks would be sipping whiskey out of paper bags as they warily eyed the younger men cutting deals or fencing stolen property. In the first half of 1986, city emergency medical services crews made sixty-one runs to this corner, nine times for stabbings.[2]

In fact, the entire Park DuValle neighborhood, at the southeastern edge of Louisville's West End, was a crime zone. Although there were churches, community centers, and some decent residential areas in the vicinity, residents of the dingy barracks that were the Cotter Homes and Lang Homes public housing projects told *Courier-Journal* reporters stories of sleeping under their beds to avoid gunshots and finding toddlers playing with bloody hypodermic needles.

But in the mid- to late 1990s, under the federal HOPE VI program, the liquor store, Cotter and Lang Homes, and other distressed properties spanning 125 acres were demolished and replaced by a stable mixed-income neighborhood that includes public housing. With its tree-lined streets, wide boulevards, and homes in a variety of sizes and styles, the Villages of Park DuValle

A yellow house now sits as what was once Louisville's most notorious intersection.

As part of the HOPE VI redevelopment of Park DuValle, a liquor store and lot dubbed "the meanest street corner in Louisville" because of frequent stabbings and other violent crimes has been replaced with single-family homes on a quiet residential street.

Photo at right,
© *The Courier-Journal*

has the same slightly suburban feel of other, older Louisville neighborhoods. As this case study shows, the physical transformation of the site has been accompanied by a striking drop in crime and poverty and a spike in income, employment, homeownership, and home values. New housing, stores, and community services have come to the surrounding areas for the first time in years.

The redevelopment demonstrated the potential of HOPE VI to spur comprehensive community revitalization. It also showed how a new urbanist–style community erected in a part of town that had seen little new residential development of any kind in fifty years could uncover a "hidden market for housing."[3] The well-publicized success of the Villages of Park DuValle, with home sales that have exceeded expectations and confounded skeptics, helped fuel the trend for urban infill projects that draw people back to city living.

An Opportunity for West Louisville

HOPE VI provided Louisville with the opportunity to eradicate the dire conditions at Cotter and Lang and to bring homeownership and stability back to its historically strong but threatened western section. Six miles from downtown, West Louisville had significant assets, befitting its status as a home to working-class African Americans. Among those assets were some healthy residential areas; pockets of strong commercial activity; proximity to Jefferson Riverport International, one of the fastest-growing employment areas; and parks and parkways that linked to the citywide parkway system, which was designed by Frederick Law Olmsted, the famed nineteenth-century landscape architect.[4]

But the area was suffering from the crime and blight spreading out from the Park DuValle neighborhood at its southeastern edge. Park DuValle was dominated by the Cotter and Lang public housing projects, 118 barracks-like structures built in the 1950s that included 1,116 units and spanned seventy-five contiguous acres. Surrounding the site were liquor stores, a pricey convenience store, vacant or underused industrial buildings, unused school land, and—astride Algonquin Parkway, one of Olmsted's grand boulevards—a private apartment complex that was in many respects the biggest evil in the neighborhood. Developed in the early 1960s, FHA-insured Algonquin Manor had 374 units in eighty-seven buildings that were subsequently divided into individual properties and sold to multiple parties. Over time the complex fell into disrepair, suffering heavily from vandalism, illegal dumping, increasing vacancies, and drug dealing, much of which occurred in the abandoned units.[5]

In 1994, there were 1,036 criminal offenses in Cotter and Lang Homes alone, pushing the crime rate in the Park DuValle neighborhood to 137 percent above the city average; furthermore, about nine of every ten criminal offenses in the neighborhood were violent crimes.[6] Single women headed 91 percent of the families in the two developments, and 82.5 percent of Cotter and 78 percent of Lang residents reported no earned income.[7] Census data from 1990 complete the picture of distress. Nearly eight of every ten Park DuValle residents were living in poverty (78 percent), and the unemployment rate was 34 percent. The median household income was $5,338; 52 percent of households were receiving some form of public assistance.[8]

The Redevelopment Plan

The HOPE VI redevelopment of Park DuValle is a testament to determination, having sprung as it did from the city's failure to win federal empowerment zone (EZ) status for West Louisville in 1994. Launched by the Clinton administration in 1993, the empowerment zone program allowed economically distressed communities nationwide to compete for a special designation that would funnel $100 million in federal grants as well as various tax benefits their way. In Louisville, a planning committee of more than 100 government representatives, business leaders, community activists, and regular citizens developed a strategic plan for creating jobs and opportunities in the West Louisville district that encompassed Cotter and Lang.

When West Louisville was not selected for empowerment zone status, Jerry Abramson, Louisville's mayor, Andrea Duncan, executive director of the Housing Authority of Louisville, and other supporters forged ahead, eyeing the newly sizable public housing redevelopment funds offered under HOPE VI as a resource to help transform the area. Using the momentum generated and the community engagement apparatus developed during the public planning process for the EZ, the city and the housing authority worked with public housing residents and other stakeholders on a comprehensive plan to draw people of different income levels to this Louisville neighborhood, where many

By the early 1990s, the squalor and crime of the Cotter Homes (above right) and Lang Homes public housing projects—coupled with the drug dealing at the private Algonquin Manor apartments (above)—had made Park DuValle one of Louisville's most feared and bypassed neighborhoods.

The Park DuValle redevelopment site, in the southern part of Louisville's West End—an area six miles from downtown—stood astride Algonquin Parkway, one of the grand boulevards linked to the citywide parkway system designed by famed landscape architect Frederick Law Olmsted. To the west, the I-264 expressway connected Park DuValle with job centers elsewhere in the city.

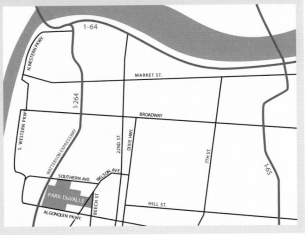

had very deep roots. The strategy was to remove the blighted properties and link the successful parts of the community together with new neighborhood streets and public spaces and a mix of housing types and styles.[9] Signing onto the plan with support and resources were many of the same partners that had been a critical part of the empowerment zone drive, not the least of which was Jefferson County Public Schools, which pledged to reopen a school in the neighborhood.

This time around the city and the housing authority did succeed in their objective, securing HUD redevelopment funds totaling more than $50 million, which at the time was at the top end of funds being awarded under HOPE VI.[10] That included $31.4 million in special housing development funds secured in 1995, followed by a $20 million HOPE VI grant in 2006.[11] Other funds that became part of the overall package (coming in at different times for different phases, as is the case with all such projects) were $12 million from the city in federal community development block grant (CDBG) funds over five years

Table 8-1. **Financing Chart**

Source of funds	Amount in $ millions
HOPE VI grant	$20.00
Public housing development funds	46.26
(includes $14.86 million in prior funds and $31.4 million in new HUD approved funds)	
Other federal funds	14.65
City government	13.87
(pass-through of CDBG funds awarded to city)	
LIHTC equity	37.24
Private investment	65.86
(includes housing authority and private home builder investment in homes for sale)	
Total	$197.88

Source: Louisville Metro Housing Authority.

for infrastructure and another $1.9 million in CDBG funds for development; $14.8 million in public housing development funds that the housing authority already had on hand; a comprehensive revitalization grant of $9.9 million; and $4.6 million in HUD economic development initiative funds.[12] With those federal monies, the authority and its partners were able to start lining up the tax credit equity (to total $37.2 million by the time the project was finished) and debt financing ($56.3 million in total) needed to complete the financing. Overall about $200 million was spent on what was then and most likely still is one of the most ambitious public housing redevelopment projects of its kind. Although HOPE VI funds did not constitute the bulk of the federal investment, the public housing development financing reforms spurred by HOPE VI (discussed in chapter 3) allowed public and private funds to come together at a scale sufficient for a redevelopment of this magnitude. The final financing structure is presented in table 8-1.

The initiative involved expanding the footprint of the public housing sites to include nearby land owned by the school board, the 21.7-acre Algonquin Manor site, and other vacant or underutilized contiguous land to create a development area of approximately 125 acres. With the additional acreage, purchased in part with HOPE VI funds, the authority and its partners planned to preserve the number of housing units while decreasing the concentration of the poorest families. Some replacement housing also would be built elsewhere in the city and county.

The centerpiece of the plan was an effort to create a homeownership market where none existed by getting higher-income buyers to invest first and thereby create confidence in the neighborhood. After the market was primed by the construction of new high-quality rental homes, model for-sale homes would be constructed and marketing would begin in earnest, with home purchase assistance in the form of a forgivable second mortgage offered as an incentive to potential urban pioneers. From there, sales would build, with amenities created along with the housing serving as an additional attraction.

And that is largely what occurred, with the added twist that the initial demand from homebuyers outpaced expectations. The Algonquin Manor buildings and properties such as the liquor store, a convenience store, and an auto body shop were acquired or conveyed with negotiating assistance from the mayor's special liaison to the housing authority, Tim Barry, who later became the authority's executive director.[13] Demolition on Cotter and Lang began in June 1996, and construction began on the first phase, the Oaks at Park DuValle, in October; the housing authority, acting through an affiliate, was the developer.[14] The mixed-income complex, which included 100 rental single-family residences, town houses, and apartments situated around a clubhouse and swimming pool, was completed in the spring of 1998 and fully leased within a few months.

Pattern Book and Subsidies Were Key to Homeownership

When the first rental phase of the Park DuValle redevelopment was well under way, the authority and its partners moved forward on the for-sale component, where the ambitious aspirations for this community would be tested. By the time construction began on the Oaks, the authority had brought in Community Builders, Inc., a nonprofit national affordable housing developer, to oversee infrastructure development and design planning for the rest of the project and to develop the remainder of the rental phases. Louisville Real Estate Development Company (LREDC), a for-profit subsidiary of the Louisville Community Development Bank, was engaged as the developer of the for-sale housing component.[15] Urban Design Associates (UDA) of Pittsburgh was hired to work with Community Builders to develop the master plan for the rest of the phases and a pattern book that would govern the architectural styles and design features of both the for-sale and rental homes to come.[16]

To create the pattern book, UDA architects toured the city, surveying people to determine which architectural styles and features had enjoyed long-lasting popularity and were associated with sustained home values. Renderings were presented to public housing residents for their input. People understood the concept of "defensible space" and embraced such features as raised front porches and large windows, with the result that those features were integral to the design of both for-sale and rental units.[17] The designs ultimately chosen align with Victorian, Arts and Crafts, and Colonial Revival styles. To further ensure consistency with Louisville's traditional neighborhoods, the pattern book also called for mixing lots of different sizes on any given block, with the lot type determining how far a structure is set back from the front and side property lines, the types of plantings, garage placement, and other features.

Fortuitously, the design of the Oaks rental community, which already had been built, aligned fairly well with the housing arising around it. With the remaining rental and affordable for-sale homes, the clever use of pitched roofs on multifamily structures and other architectural sleights of hand allowed the more affordable multifamily for-sale and rental residences to coexist seamlessly with their single-family brethren.

The brick colonial six-flat apartment house (left), like the Villages of Park DuValle's three- and four-flat residences, is designed to blend in with the single-family homes in the development, including the for-sale home below.

The pattern book was a critical piece of the homeownership strategy. Despite a market analysis projecting thirty-nine home sales in the first year, builders were too skeptical to build on speculation.[18] So, with Algonquin Manor gone, six model homes were built on a new street just north of Algonquin Parkway and aggressively marketed; those homes were followed by a handful of larger "Estate Homes" lining the parkway. The remaining homes would be built to order by homebuyers choosing a parcel, a house type from the pattern book, and a partner builder, thereby ensuring a cohesive and yet varied look.[19]

The housing authority and its partners did not want to depress the potential of this brand new housing market by offering homes at below-market prices. They also knew that many of the buyers that they initially were wooing earned enough to afford nice homes in established neighborhoods. Hence came the plan to sell homes priced at market rates and to subsidize the buyers through the creative use of HOPE VI funds with broader economic development resources.

All buyers of the first batch of homes were offered a second mortgage loan to cover 18 percent of the cost of the home, regardless of their income, as an incentive to take a chance on the neighborhood (an incrementally declining subsidy was offered to subsequent buyers as confidence in the local market grew). The authority and its partners were able to do that by setting up two similar but separate subsidy programs. Higher-income buyers were assisted with funds from HUD's economic development initiative (EDI), which was aimed at stimulating job creation, with subsidies as high as $27,000 for initial buyers. As a community-based development organization, the LREDC had the flexibility to use some of the EDI funds for soft second mortgages that were not linked to income eligibility.[20] HOPE VI funds went toward soft second mortgages of up to $18,000 in the initial phase, mostly for households eligible for public housing.[21] For both programs, the loans were fully forgivable after the buyer had spent ten years in the home.[22]

Once the model village opened in June 1999, the buyers came. Within three and a half months, there were sales contracts on thirty-eight homes and another fifty-two were pending.[23] By the fall of 1999, the first group of homeowners began to move in, and all 150 homes of the first for-sale phase were occupied or under contract by the summer of 2003. Among the first wave of homeowners were a pediatrician, two bank vice presidents, lawyers, and other professionals, extending the range of incomes represented by homebuyers from less than 80 percent of area median income to as high as 411 percent. Despite expectations to the contrary, fully 65 percent of the homes sold for $100,000 or more, with one going for more than $217,000.[24] As LREDC president Kim Burse said at the time, people were proving "willing to bet their net worth on a neighborhood with decades of bad headlines."[25]

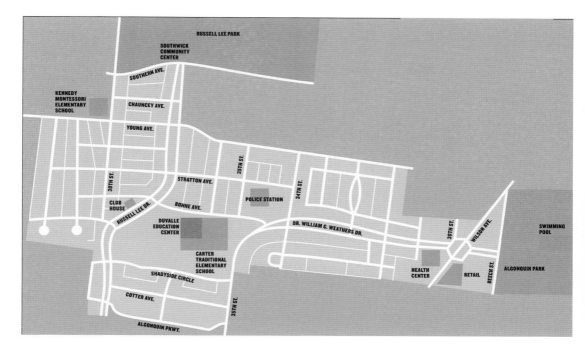

Educational and Health Services Come to the Community

As subsequent rental and homeownership phases were completed, demand continued to be strong, with waiting lists for the rental homes. The diverse mix of owners and renters held up as amenities came into fruition—amenities that anchor the new community, both literally and figuratively.

At the eastern end of the development is the Town Centre, consisting of a rental complex for low-income seniors and rental town houses, both with ground-floor retail space, and duplex, triplex, and fourplex rental homes. The capstone of Town Centre is the 43,000 square-foot, two-story Park DuValle Neighborhood Health Center. Built at a cost of $6.6 million, the center replaced another much smaller center that was once housed in two of the barracks-like buildings of the old Cotter Homes. With the new facility, the center, which serves roughly 20,000 pediatric, dental, and other patients annually, has gained new standing in the community. The environment now matches the quality of services. Programming, which has always addressed the particular health concerns of the community, has expanded to include enhanced prescription assistance, living-well workshops and chronic disease management, tutoring to help teens make better health choices, smoking cessation, and more screenings to help detect conditions such as cognitive decline in seniors earlier.[26]

This site map of the Villages of Park DuValle does not include the first phase of the development, the Oaks at Park DuValle, which occupies the space south of Russell Lee Park and east of Russell Lee Drive.

Rental homes for public housing, tax credit–assisted, and market-rate households line the streets near the elementary school (background) and community center that make up the new DuValle Education Center.

At the center of the development is the 164,775-square-foot Carter-Duvalle Education Center, a new multipurpose community center and elementary school, built on the site of a historic school building erected in 1956. Elements of the original school facility, which ceased functioning as a school in 1986, were retained in the $16 million rehabilitation project, which was spearheaded by Jefferson County Public Schools. The award-winning complex includes the K-6 Carter Traditional Elementary School, with classrooms wired for Internet access; science, art, music, and computer labs; a media center; and a gymnasium and kitchen/cafeteria that are used for after-hours community events.[27] Attached to the school is the DuValle Education Center, which offers meeting space for community programs, before- and after-school programs, and classrooms for the Head Start Program. The old gymnasium was converted to the Ujima Neighborhood Place, a one-stop health and human services center run by the Louisville metro government that includes space for workforce development programs.

The neighborhood also features a police and fire department substation; two spruced-up parks, Russell Lee Park and Algonquin Park; two clubhouse and swimming pool complexes; the Southwick Community Center, which benefited from $1.1 million in renovations by Metro Parks; and the John F. Kennedy Montessori/Magnet Elementary School.

The Neighborhood and Community Today

Once strictly an extremely low-income community, the Villages of Park DuValle today is a thriving mixed-income community, home to 613 renter households and 345 homeowner households, with all 400 planned for-sale homes expected to be built and occupied by spring 2009.[28] The rental units range in price and size from $530 a month for a 600-square-foot, one-bedroom flat in the seniors complex to $808 a month for a 1,590-square-foot, four-bedroom rental home. Roughly two-thirds of the units are occupied by families with incomes at or below 60 percent of area median income (AMI); the remaining units are considered market rate since market-rate rents in Louisville's very affordable rental market are accessible to families making at or above 60 percent of AMI.[29] (Median income in Louisville is just shy of $60,000). The monthly rents on the market-rate units have increased 19 percent to 25 percent since initial lease-up and now are competitive with market-rate developments in the region.[30]

Prices for the for-sale homes also have had strong growth since initial development, when prices started in the mid-$70,000s and topped out at around $217,000.[31] Currently, at the more affordable end are town houses and single-family homes with three bedrooms, ranging from just over 1,100 to 1,300 square feet and selling for about $100,000 to $141,000. At the pricier end are the Estate Homes, which exceed 2,300 square feet and are priced at about $278,000; one custom-built home that has such features as a hot tub in the master bathroom cost $325,000.[32] The initial buyers of the for-sale homes purchased to date are of varying incomes, with roughly 55 percent having incomes of less than 80 percent of AMI, 27 percent having incomes of 80 percent to 115 percent of AMI, and 18 percent having incomes greater than 115 percent of AMI. Fully three-quarters were first-time homebuyers.[33]

Income levels, labor force participation, and other indicators of neighborhood strength have risen sharply along with income integration—and at rates well outpacing citywide gains. Between 1989 and 1999, household median income in the census tract coinciding with the redevelopment site nearly quadrupled, to $21,023, while the poverty rate fell nearly 50 percent, to 28.5 percent (however, it was still above the overall city poverty rate of 21.6 percent, even though the city poverty rate fell less than 2 percent over the decade). Unemployment dropped from 35 percent to 7.2 percent (the citywide decline was only from 8 percent to 7.4 percent); the percent of households receiving public assistance fell from 52 percent to 10.1 percent; and the percent of adults twenty-five years of age or older without a high school diploma fell from 51 percent to 22.4 percent.[34] The median home value increased 127 percent. Home appreciation took an even sharper upswing since the 2000 census. According to a University of Louisville study, home values in the Park DuValle neighborhood increased 241 percent between 2000 and 2006, more than in any other city neighborhood. The median home value reached $90,500 in 2006, up from $26,540 in 2000.[35] And crime plummeted—82 percent over roughly a decade, from an annual average of 541 reported crimes from 1990 to 1996 to an average of sixty-four a year from 1997 to 2002.[36]

John Vahaly, an associate professor of economics at the University of Louisville hired by the housing authority to evaluate the one-time (versus

The Villages of Park DuValle has the appearance of a community that developed over a long period of time. Homes on some streets come in a mix of styles and are located close to the street (above); busier thoroughfares are lined with set-back residences that come for the most part in one of the three Park DuValle styles, such as these mostly Craftsman-style rental homes (right).

ongoing) impact of the project, found that the redevelopment has had a significant economic impact. According to Vahaly, as of 2004, 3,261 jobs were created, $94 million in total wages were produced, $9.3 million in state and local taxes were generated, and the net "total value added" was $133 million (in goods and services produced).

Sources say the effects of the site's redevelopment have rippled throughout West Louisville. After suffering from disinvestment since the riots of the 1960s, West Louisville got its first real investment in decades in the form of the HOPE VI and EDI funds. That show of confidence reinforced the city's focus on investing CDBG, HOME, and other public funds in the needy neighborhoods surrounding Park DuValle—Russell, Portland, and Shawnee—and now developers are reporting success building unsubsidized housing there.[37] Investors are paying attention. A massive redevelopment under way in Park Hill, just east of Park DuValle, seeks to transform an abandoned Phillip Morris plant into a huge retail mall.

The Villages of Park DuValle also has helped shape subsequent development in the Louisville metro area along smart-growth lines by creating the municipal government's best example of how to create new, compact, traditional neighborhoods that include many different but compatible types of housing. The Urban Neighborhood Zoning District was revised to enable

Multi-family rental buildings ring the town square, giving the area a more urban flair.

small-lot and zero lot line development for town homes, duplexes, and tri-plexes, allowing for greater usable yard space and more development flexibility within the single-family detached house model. Learning from Park DuValle, Louisville has since created the Planned Development (PD) District, in which developers can mix uses and structures to create livable, diverse communities without obtaining multiple special permits. The PD District is coming into broader acceptance by the development community in Louisville, and such zoning tools are being used increasingly in cities across the United States to enable the development of urban villages.[38]

Lessons of Achievements and Shortcomings
Sources attribute the pathbreaking success of the Villages of Park DuValle to numerous factors, not the least of which was the strong involvement of Mayor Abramson and Dave Armstrong, who served as mayor from January 1999 through January 2003. (In 2003, when the city of Louisville and Jefferson County merged to form one metro government, Abramson became mayor again, this time as mayor of Louisville Metro.) During the phases of intense development, Mayor Abramson had key staffers from critical city agencies meet weekly to discuss and resolve issues such as relaxing easement requirements for gas and electric hookups; meetings were held monthly during construction.[39]

Mayoral leadership also helped draw other key players to the table. For example, Abramson helped persuade the Kentucky Housing Finance Authority to make an unusual multiyear commitment of tax credits to the project.

Significant technical support from the local HUD office also was a boon to the project, as was the multifaceted role played by strong community-based institutions, such as the LREDC and Housing Partnership Inc., which developed and marketed the first for-sale homes. Individuals too made a difference—for example, such long-time Park DuValle residents as Marshall Gazaway, who, as a member of the DuValle neighborhood advisory group, helped engage residents in planning for the revitalization and actively recruited people to the new neighborhood.[40]

But the revitalization of Park DuValle, which has won national accolades, has had its disappointments and its detractors.[41] It has not been successful in attracting stores and businesses to the town center—and certainly not the big-name store envisioned as an anchor back in the planning stages. However, as of June 2008, there were promising although not yet reportable developments in the effort to bring retail and commercial development to areas adjacent to the development, which would help the town center, according to the LREDC.[42]

Housing authority officials also say that while the subsidies used to attract homebuyers have declined substantially, plans to eliminate homebuyer subsidies have been foiled by the decline of the housing market nationwide.

Also problematic to some observers is the unchanged racial composition of Park DuValle. In 2000, African Americans accounted for 96.5 percent of the population, a slight decrease from the figure of virtually 100 percent in 1990.[43] Although Community Builders officials say that the next census will likely show a slight uptick in Hispanic and other immigrant families, the community is still almost all African American. On one hand, Park DuValle has been praised for creating a strong new African American community in the heart of Louisville. But some African American community leaders interviewed by *Louisville Magazine* suggested that the redevelopment has inadvertently supported segregation. When middle-class, highly educated blacks began to leave the community after enactment of the 1968 Kentucky Open Housing Law, which paved the way for African Americans to move to communities theretofore closed to them, it left a leadership vacuum, said former state senator Georgia Powers. Now, with efforts to lure them back to West Louisville, the area is not becoming appreciably less segregated as it becomes higher income, noted Blaine Hudson, a professor of Pan-African Studies at the University of Louisville.[44]

Views on the fate of former Cotter and Lang residents also are mixed. Of the households initially in Cotter and Lang Homes, less than 5 percent returned to the redeveloped Villages of Park DuValle. In the initial relocation process, most went to other public housing sites, and officials lost track of hundreds.[45] According to John Gilderbloom, director of the Center for Sustainable Urban Neighborhoods at the University of Louisville, and Michael Brazley, an assistant professor in the School of Architecture and Interior Design at Southern Illinois University–Carbondale, the outcomes raise serious questions about the welfare of the relocated residents.[46] They cite in particular the disappointingly low percentage of residents moving back to the redeveloped community.

But housing authority officials note the preference among relocatees for moving with the aid of Section 8 vouchers, and indeed about a quarter of residents did so. Housing authority officials note also that most of the 62 percent of relocating families that moved to other family public housing went to their first relocation choice, the Beecher Terrace public housing complex, which is closer to employment and to hospitals than Cotter and Lang was. Moreover, because Beecher Terrace underwent modernization while relocation was proceeding, it is a definite improvement over their former public housing (although the neighborhood is still very high poverty).[47] Thanks to subsequent opportunities to relocate, by early 2001 nearly half of the original residents surveyed by Abt Associates and the Urban Institute were living in private housing using vouchers, and—despite the fact that most were in high-poverty neighborhoods—85 percent said that they were satisfied with their current housing. Overall, most former residents—71 percent—were satisfied with their current housing.[48]

The work requirement and other criteria for returning to the Villages of Park DuValle were strict, but residents and neighborhood leaders determined the criteria.[49] The housing authority has pledged to work with former residents who currently are ineligible to return but who wish to do so in order to help them meet the criteria.

Still, authority officials acknowledge that they would have done some things differently with regard to resident tracking and services. They are applying the lessons that they have learned to the Clarksdale HOPE VI project, just east of downtown, for which the authority received HOPE VI grants totaling $40 million in 2003. In transforming the 725-unit, 1940s-era Clarksdale public housing site into a new mixed-use community, Liberty Green, the housing authority and its partners are taking advantage of the site's proximity to nearby medical and educational institutions to develop it at an urban density. Rather than single-family homes, the community will feature apartments and town houses built in an almost modular fashion, so that homeowners could opt to buy one, two, or three floors, depending on their budget.

The authority has committed itself to doing one-for-one replacement, with replacement public housing units on and off site. Its commitment has been reinforced by the 2003 merger of the Housing Authority of Louisville and the Housing Authority of Jefferson County as part of the broader merger of the

Louisville is taking advantage of the proximity to nearby medical and educational institutions of its second HOPE VI redevelopment, Liberty Green, to develop the project at an urban density.

city and county governments. The expansion of the service area to encompass former suburbs enhances the authority's existing scattered-site program, which consists of buying a portion of units in buildings put up for sale and purchasing stand-alone units in various locations.[50]

Learning from the loose tracking of and lack of support services for relocated Cotter and Lang residents, the authority has implemented a much more sophisticated tracking system for relocating Clarksdale residents, whom it will provide with a comprehensive array of case management services to help them move toward self-sufficiency. The authority also reconnected with 565 former Cotter and Lang residents and offered to provide them with case management and support services under the Family Self-Sufficiency Program (FSS), but many did not accept the offer.[51]

The authority's partner, developer Community Builders, has also applied the lessons learned from the Villages of Park DuValle, its first HOPE VI redevelopment, to the fourteen subsequent HOPE VIs it has developed in nine other cities. Knowing the importance of design to returning and new residents, the developer has carefully planned the other communities to include unit layouts and square footage that meet assessed needs, exteriors and yards that have high curb appeal, and streets that are easy to navigate. City governments and other partners are cultivated to help create or upgrade critical neighborhood amenities such as community centers and commercial facilities. Finally, according to Willie Jones, senior vice president and director of Community Builders, the developer is working with service partners on ways to help residents who grew up in the public housing system become more comfortable with the perceived risks of achieving financial independence and moving to market-rate housing. Jones notes that families in the new mixed-income communities who have tenuous work situations move in and out of the public housing system, and he says that service providers must recognize that fact.[52]

> The redevelopment destigmatized public housing by creating a neighborhood where families of different income levels can coexist in attractive homes whose exteriors reveal no clues about the income level of their occupants.

As for the current public housing residents in the Villages of Park DuValle, they are enjoying an enhanced quality of life, with approximately 80 percent of public housing and non–public housing residents reporting satisfaction with the housing, location, safety, and recreation programs of the neighborhood.[53]

Clearly, the redevelopment destigmatized public housing by creating a neighborhood where families of different income levels can coexist in attractive homes whose exteriors reveal no clues about the income level of their occupants. The homes must be indistinguishable because they "float," perhaps serving a public housing–assisted family one year and a household paying market rates the next. The developers reinforce income integration by refusing to identify homes by occupant status. That little yellow house at the corner where the liquor store once stood? Without consulting a file somewhere, housing authority officials touring the neighborhood could not necessarily identify the status of the residents; that the family belongs to the community is all that they need to know.

····· Endnotes ·····

1. Hunt Helm, "The Meanest Street Corner in Louisville," *Louisville Courier-Journal,* October 5, 1986, p. 1.

2. Ibid., pp. 1, 12.

3. "Hidden Markets for Urban Homes" and "Growth in TND Steady, but Slower; Neotraditional Home Sales Strong," *New Urban News,* September-October 1999.

4. "Park DuValle Neighborhood Transformation: An Application for HOPE VI Funding," Housing Authority of Louisville, September 10, 1996, pp. 7,9.

5. Ibid., p. 13.

6. Ibid., p. 7, and Housing Authority of Louisville Application for Demolition of Public Housing Projects Cotter Homes (KY 1-6) and Lang Homes (KY 1-9), February 14, 1995, p. 1. According to housing authority officials, the statistics are for police district 2, whose boundaries have changed since the merger of the city and county governments in 2003. The figure for violent crimes includes domestic violence.

7. "Park DuValle Neighborhood Transformation," p. 7.

8. U.S. Census Bureau, American FactFinder, 1990 Summary Tape File 3 (STF-3): Sample data, Tract 14, Jefferson County, Kentucky. All figures in the paragraph are for 1989, except for employment status, which is as of 1990.

9. "Park DuValle Neighborhood Transformation," p. 9.

10. HOPE VI grants for program years 1993 to 1995 ranged from $18,000 to $50,000, with a good number in the $45,000–$50,000 range. From 1996 to 2001, the largest grants were $35,000; after that, the largest grants were for $20,000.

11. As explained in the Housing Authority of Louisville's "Board Resolution for Submission of HOPE VI Application," August 20, 1996, the authority had begun preparing an application for HOPE VI funding in 1994 but was informed that it was not yet eligible to apply because HOPE VI was limited to the forty largest U.S. cities. HUD encouraged the authority to submit instead an application for demolition or disposition of Cotter and Lang and to apply for HUD Development Program funds. HUD had a surplus of appropriated funds, which was awarded to Louisville after the mayor made the case for Louisville's need in the face of the failed empowerment zone application.

12. In 1993, the Housing Authority of Louisville had begun planning for the rehabilitation of Cotter Homes through the comprehensive grant program, which was then HUD's primary source of modernization funds for physical improvements to public housing units. When the opportunity arose to compete for a HOPE VI grant, housing authority leaders decided that the overall goal for revitalizing the area could not succeed with Cotter and Lang Homes in their existing form.

13. The housing authority has power of eminent domain but did not need to invoke it; the authority was able to acquire the properties through negotiations.

14. The Oaks development was financed by a portion of the $31.4 million in public housing development funds and low-income housing tax credit equity. The Housing Authority of Louisville had decided to develop the phase itself (through a subsidiary), having already redeveloped two former public housing projects into townhomes for first-time buyers under the 5(h) program, which allowed conversion of public housing to owner-occupied housing. Roughly a third of the units are public housing, a third are middle-income tax credit housing (for households making up to 60 percent of area median income), and a third are leased at market rates. The same formula was followed in all subsequent rental phases.

15. The Louisville Real Estate Development Company is a for-profit subsidiary of the Louisville Community Development Bank. LREDC is a certified community-based development

organization and therefore is eligible to arrange the Section 108 loans (loans collateralized by a city's future federal CDBG allotment) for construction financing.

16. The pattern book also establishes such requirements as minimum sizes for porches and heights of windows. For-sale homes created off site did not need to comply with pattern book requirements.

17. Designing for public safety involves creating internal and external spaces that someone is accountable for instead of a lot of common space that no one really controls. Features such as raised front porches played a dual role, creating a grander effect for modest housing and enhancing the feeling of community safety when residents sit outside, observing passers-by and activity on their street.

18. "Hidden Markets for Urban Homes," *New Urban News,* September-October 1999, p. 2.

19. Each buyer chose his or her own builder and was encouraged but not required to select from a set of partner builders. The housing authority would grant the builder the legal right to construct on the lot; the Louisville Real Estate Development Company would obtain construction financing for the builder and then help the buyer obtain a first mortgage. Only after the home was built would the title be transferred from the housing authority to the buyer. Initial plans called for 125 for-sale homes, but LREDC delivered 150 under the financing scenario described.

20. As HUD's website explains, the homeownership zone initiative was an EDI demonstration program aimed at creating new neighborhoods of mixed-income, single-family homes in a concentrated target area near major employment centers. There were two competitive funding rounds, in fiscal years 1996 and 1997. As one of the six winning applicants for 1996, Louisville was awarded a $4.6 million EDI grant coupled with a $5 million Section 108 loan guarantee, a guarantee that allowed the city to advance loans backed by the future federal commitment of community development block grant funds. The Section 108 loan funds went toward construction financing while the EDI funds were used to provide second mortgages.

21. Prior to the passage of the Quality Housing and Work Responsibility Act (QHWRA) of 1998, HOPE VI was authorized under appropriations acts as an "urban revitalization demonstration program," with language allowing some of the replacement units funded by the program to be for-sale housing subject to the same eligibility requirements as certain other existing HUD homeownership programs. The Villages of Park DuValle homeownership program was modeled on and approved as a Nehemiah Homeownership Program, which allowed buyers to have household incomes of up to 100 percent of area median income, with 15 percent of households served earning up to 115 percent of AMI if that would promote neighborhood stability. With QHWRA, HOPE VI was folded into the same authorizing statute as the public housing program and subject to the eligibility requirements—that is, eligible households could make up to 80 percent of AMI.

22. Homebuyers were not required to make monthly payments on the notes, which charged no interest, and each year that the original buyer remained in the home from years six through ten, 20 percent of the outstanding debt on the loan would be written off; thus buyers who remained in their homes ten years or more owed nothing.

23. "Growth in TND Steady, but Slower; Neotraditional Home Sales Strong," p. 5.

24. Forty-three percent of the buyers in the first phase were households making less than 80 percent of AMI, another 27 percent were households making 81 to 115 percent of AMI, and 30 percent were families with incomes of more than 115 percent of AMI. Mindy Turbov and Valerie Piper, "HOPE VI and Mixed-Finance Redevelopments: A Catalyst for Neighborhood Renewal," Brookings Institution Metropolitan Policy Program, September 2005, p. 35 (www. brookings.edu/~/media/Files/rc/reports/2005/09metropolitanpolicy_piper/20050913_ hopevi.pdf [July 4, 2008]).

25. Michael L. Jones, "The Rebirth of Park DuValle," *Louisville Magazine*, November 1999, p. 54.

26. Author's conversation with Ann Hagan-Grigsby, administrator, Park DuValle Community Health Center, Inc., September 11, 2008.

27. The description of the school comes from "The Heart and Soul of a Revitalized Neighborhood: Park DuValle," an article in the newsletter *Central Kentucky Architect* (AIA Central Kentucky Chapter), April 2002, pp. 2, 4. "Award-winning" refers to the center's designation as a semifinalist in the 2004 Richard W. Riley Award program honoring "community learning centers for the 21st century." The school was lauded for its function as a neighborhood hub, and the design of the complex was praised for its three facades, each of which is different, letting visitors know whether they are approaching the elementary school, health clinic, or preschool. "Carter-DuValle Education Center: Historic School Building Finds New Role as Center of Community" (www.richardrileyaward.org/en/School.asp?intSchoolID=1 [May 8, 2008]).

28. Another 150 affordable rental opportunities and forty-four affordable home-purchase opportunities were created off site as part of the redevelopment plan, with six more home-purchase opportunities in the works. In both cases, the authority and its partners worked predominantly with developers to subsidize units in existing buildings or to provide assistance to buyers selecting from existing inventory, rather than constructing new units.

29. Well over half of the rental units (350 units, or 57 percent) are in the public housing program; about a quarter (160, or 26 percent) are subsidized only through the tax credit program (thus commonly referred to as tax credit–only units); and 103 are market rate.

30. Figures for current rental sizes and rates come from the author's conversation with Wavid Wray, deputy executive director, Finance Cabinet, Louisville Metro Housing Authority, and with Darnell Jackson, senior project manager, Community Builders, Inc., June 5, 2008. The percent increase is determined by comparing current rental rates with initial lease-up rates of $425–$680, provided by Turbov and Piper in "HOPE VI and Mixed-Finance Redevelopments," p. 34. The percent increase in rental rates is skewed low because the least expensive, smallest units (the senior units) were not completed when the initial lease-up rates were determined.

31. Source for first-phase home sale prices is Turbov and Piper, "HOPE VI and Mixed-Finance Redevelopments," p. 35.

32. Author's conversation with Steve Ward, development manager with the Louisville Real Estate Development Company, June 24, 2008. The homes for which Ward gave 2008 sales figures were three-bedroom homes with one and one-half to two and one-half baths, with finished or unfinished basements.

33. These figures pertain to all of the 389 existing for-sale households, 345 on site and 44 off site.

34. U.S. Census Bureau, American FactFinder, Census 2000 Summary File 3 and 1990 Summary Tape File 3 for Census Tract 14, Jefferson County, Kentucky, and for city of Louisville.

35. Marcus Green, "Urban Areas See Biggest Gains in Property Value," *Courier-Journal*, June 5, 2007. According to Michael Price, Kentucky state demographer with the Urban Studies Institute at the University of Louisville, the university's data on median home values were much more inclusive than census data because the university looked at the tax assessment universe, which incudes vacant properties.

36. For the crime drop of 82 percent and the time periods covered, see Turbov and Piper, "HOPE VI and Mixed-Finance Redevelopments," pp. 27–28. For clarification on the numbers of crimes that informed Turbov and Piper's findings, see Patrick E. Clancy, "Public Housing in the Competitive Market Place: Do Affordable and Public Housing Developments Benefit from Private Market and Other Financial Tools?" testimony before the House Government Reform

Subcommittee on Federalism and the Census, May 23, 2006. See www.tcbinc.org/whats_new/Pat_Clancy_Congressional_Testimony.pdf and www.brookings.edu/~media/Files/rc/reports/2005/09metropolitanpolicy_piper/20050913_hopevi.pdf.

37. Green, "Urban Areas See Biggest Gains in Property Value." According to the Green article, the city invested more than $26 million from such sources as community development block grants and direct budget appropriations in the Russell neighborhood. Residential builder Argie Dale was quoted as saying that he used to build tax credit housing in Russell but had since developed five properties without tax credits.

38. Author's communication with Charles C. Cash Jr., director, Louisville Metro Planning and Design Services of the Louisville Metro government, July 3, 2008.

39. Staff involved in the regular Park DuValle redevelopment meetings included officials such as the attorney for the city department of housing, someone from the redevelopment authority (charged with ushering the project through zoning approvals), and others; periodically public works and building permits staff would attend. According to Willie Jones, senior vice president and director of Community Builders, and Darnell Jackson of Community Builders, there were as many as 100 permits in the works at any one time and it took strong leadership at the top to keep things moving.

40. Jones, "The Rebirth of Park DuValle," pp. 53, 57.

41. Park DuValle has won numerous local and national awards, including a 2000 Urban Design Honor Award from the American Institute of Architects and a 2002 designation as "One of the World's Great Planned Communities" from the Urban Land Institute; in 2005 it was *Affordable Housing Finance's* "Readers' Choice Finalist" in the master-planned community category.

42. Author's conversation with Steve Ward, June 27, 2008.

43. U.S. Census Bureau, 1990 Summary Tape File 1, Tract 14, Jefferson County, Kentucky; Census 2000 Summary File 1, Census Tract 14, Jefferson County, Kentucky.

44. Comments by Powers and Hudson are from Jones, "The Rebirth of Park DuValle," p. 56.

45. Of the 1,304 households initially in Cotter and Lang Homes, 428 left prior to relocation; 204 were unaccounted for; 138 left for nonpayment of rent; 59 moved without notice; and 27 left for better housing. Of the remaining 876, 62 percent (546) went to other family public housing sites, with a majority (339) of the 546 relocating to the recently renovated Beecher Terrace complex. About a quarter (211 families) relocated with Section 8 vouchers, and five percent (47) returned to the redeveloped Park DuValle. Thirty-four families went to housing authority scattered-site housing, and 15 moved into senior housing. Twenty-three households were unaccounted for. Data provided by Janice Burns, Louisville Metro Housing Authority, June 25, 2008.

46. Michael Brazley and John I. Gilderbloom, "HOPE VI Housing Program: Was It Effective?" *American Journal of Economics and Sociology,* April 1, 2007 (www.encyclopedia.com/doc/1G1-164949331.html). Although the numbers that Brazley and Gilderbloom based their conclusions on differed from the numbers provided in note 45 above (according to the housing authority, Brazley and Gilderbloom used numbers from earlier in the relocation data collection process), both sets of numbers showed similar patterns; most important were the small shares of residents who returned to the redeveloped site.

47. Larry Buron and others, *The HOPE VI Resident Tracking Study: A Snapshot of the Current Living Situation of Original Residents from Eight Sites* (Cambridge, Mass.: Abt Associates and Urban Institute, 2002) p. 41. According to the authors, Beecher Terrace "is in a census tract with a poverty rate that, at 84 percent, is even higher than the 1990 poverty rate for Cotter and Lang."

48. Ibid., pp. 37, 39, 41.

49. Among the criteria for public housing residency is that heads of household who are able to work must be employed or participating in a job training program or the authority's self-sufficiency program; have a record of timely rent payments and a clean police report; and pass housekeeping inspections and credit checks. At the time of the Abt Associates and Urban Institute study, nearly 150 former residents who had applied did not succeed in returning. Buron and others, *The HOPE VI Resident Tracking Study,* p. 38.

50. As part of its deconcentration effort, the housing authority purchases only about 10 percent or so of the units in any one complex. The scattered-site strategy works because there is still a large number of reasonably priced apartments available in the Louisville metro area.

51. At one point, the number of former Cotter and Lang residents and new residents in Park DuValle who were enrolled in the Family Self-Sufficiency Program totaled 296.

52. Personal communication to the author from Willie Jones, December 16, 2008.

53. Brazley and Gilderbloom, "HOPE VI Housing Program: Was It Effective?"

Author's general note: In the early stages of the HOPE VI redevelopment in Park DuValle, when the housing authority and its partners were still planning to give each development phase a different name, the Villages of Park DuValle referred to phase two of the development, in contrast to phase one, called the Oaks at Park DuValle. After the plan to assign each phase a name was dropped, the Villages of Park DuValle generally came to be used to refer to the entire HOPE VI redevelopment, a convention followed in this chapter.

Broader Impacts
of the Model

III

RENÉE LEWIS GLOVER

The Atlanta Blueprint: Transforming Public Housing Citywide

Public housing in Atlanta has undergone a remarkable transformation over the past fifteen years, and along with it, so have many once-broken urban neighborhoods and the marginalized families living in them. Changes of such significance were possible only through a radical rethinking of how to improve housing and housing options for families living below the poverty line—a rethinking enabled in great part by HOPE VI.

West Highlands, Atlanta's largest residential redevelopment, opened in northwest Atlanta in 2003.

Before that transformation began, the Atlanta Housing Authority (AHA) consigned approximately 70 percent of the extremely low-income households that it served to living in forty-three public housing projects, many of which were highly distressed, obsolete, and crime ridden and nearly all of which were economically and racially segregated. Today, AHA is assisting 19,500 households (approximately 6,000 more than in 1994) in a much broader array of healthier, safer, and opportunity-enhancing housing, from private apartments rented with Section 8 vouchers to nine new mixed-use, mixed-income communities; five mixed-income communities; and more than thirty-five project-based rental assistance mixed-income arrangements with private owners.[1] Moreover, AHA is implementing plans under its Moving to Work agreement with the U.S. Department of Housing and Urban Development to relocate affected households by using Section 8 vouchers and to close and demolish by the end of 2010 its remaining distressed and obsolete family public housing projects and two projects for senior citizens and disabled individuals.

AHA is seen nationally as a leader and innovator in providing great housing opportunities in healthy, mixed-income communities. As a result of the authority's initiatives, tens of thousands of Atlantans are living in now-thriving neighborhoods that were once urban war zones with crumbling infrastructure, high crime rates, failing schools, and declining property values. As those housing projects have been razed and redeveloped as market-quality, mixed-use, mixed-income communities, Atlanta has flourished. Affluent and middle-class residents are moving in, and the city's population recently topped 500,000. Crime decreased by at least 44 percent over the last decade, and billions of private dollars have been invested in the city.[2]

However, it has not been easy to provide more people with better options—and better serve the neighborhoods within which AHA operates—while dealing with continuing cuts in federal operating subsidies.

Getting Ready for the Spotlight

In the early 1990s, Atlanta was very much a city on the brink of change. In 1990, we had won an improbable bid to host the 1996 Centennial Olympic Games, beating Athens and other big-name cities that boasted the kind of international cachet that Atlanta's civic leaders had always coveted. It was a heady time, marked by the expectation that the Olympics would catapult Atlanta into the echelon of world-class cities. Very few people swept up in the Olympic fervor had heard of HOPE VI, but that too would soon change.

Although the Olympic announcement initially sent spirits soaring, the warm-and-fuzzy afterglow was congealing into cold reality. Behind the scenes, city and business leaders were nervously wondering whether we would be able to "fix" several major problems that had eluded sustainable solutions. In 1992, Atlanta had the nation's second-highest poverty rate, with more than 27 percent of the population living below the federal poverty line. It had the country's highest rate of violent crime and one of the highest unemployment rates for African Americans. The public schools were failing, and middle-class residents—black and white—had been fleeing the city in droves for at least three decades.[3]

Many intractable problems could be traced back to the Atlanta Housing Authority, a lumbering and ineffectual bureaucracy that federal officials had deemed one of the worst in the country. AHA was facing receivership, and most city leaders had dismissed it as a lost cause. Nonetheless, the agency was responsible for serving more than 50,000 residents (approximately 13 percent of Atlanta's population), mostly young children and their mothers. Atlanta had more public housing per capita than any other large city in the United States. Not surprisingly, about 40 percent of Atlanta public school students resided in public housing.

More often than not, AHA did not fulfill even its most basic mandate—to provide "safe and decent" housing. Its forty-three properties were in deplorable condition. At any given time, 5,000 of its roughly 14,000 units were vacant and uninhabitable. Audits of AHA had produced hundreds of adverse findings, and the agency was a defendant in several class-action lawsuits arising from its woefully ineffective management practices. It should have been obvious to anyone who was paying attention that the practice of concentrating poor people in public housing was not working. The public housing projects were going downhill fast and dragging everything else in the city along with them.

Far more was at stake than the condition of the housing projects. AHA's tenants were effectively locked out of the mainstream; they were economically marginalized, politically disenfranchised, and systematically being destroyed. Moreover, although they were living in Atlanta's most dangerous and desperate communities, many were openly hostile to change. Fearful about the future, residents had been misinformed by advocates and persuaded to believe that their only recourse was to protect the status quo—even if it meant continuing to imprison themselves and their children in substandard housing and failing schools.

As a matter of conscience and sound public policy, the stalemate that consigned thousands of Atlantans to abject hopelessness could no longer be tolerated. The only lasting solution was to permanently close those warehouses of crushing poverty by moving residents into improved environments and better housing in a thoughtful, careful manner and then beginning in earnest the longer-term process of integrating them into the economic and social mainstream. Fortunately for Atlanta, HOPE VI—and the regulatory freedom that came with it—proved to be the right program at the right time, giving us the tools that we needed to make the deep structural changes that our circumstances demanded.

Leadership of AHA

In March 1994, while I was chair of the AHA board, the executive director left abruptly. I remember thinking that the seriousness of the situation that we faced was, at once, extremely intimidating and oddly liberating. The agency was in such a deep hole, there was nowhere for us to go but up.

A national CEO search, hampered by AHA's less-than-stellar reputation, proved unsuccessful. The board, HUD, and the mayor turned to me, believing that I was the best candidate for the job. In September 1994, I accepted the position, in part because of a meeting that I had attended in Washington, D.C., that centered on HOPE VI.

Senator Barbara Mikulski (D-Md.) and HUD secretary Henry Cisneros convened the meeting to share their passion about the possibilities that HOPE VI (then called the Urban Revitalization Demonstration) represented. They agreed that public housing was failing and challenged local housing authorities to use HOPE VI to dramatically alter their outdated approaches to serving residents. For his part, Secretary Cisneros stated that he would be willing to "toss the rule books" to reform public housing and replace it with a new model. I realized then that although I was not the prototypical public housing "professional," my training and unique background would be an asset. As a corporate finance attorney from the private sector, I was familiar with complex problems and with market-based strategies and solutions. And, unlike many housing industry professionals who were resigned to the glacial pace of the public sector, I was accustomed to getting things done in a timely fashion.

In addition to my legal credentials and corporate experience, there were intangibles that would prove invaluable to me, including my experiences growing up during the Jim Crow era in Jacksonville, Florida. Notwithstanding the insidious design and destructive nature of segregation, I was blessed to have been raised in an economically integrated neighborhood in which youngsters were taught to believe that, because they were children of God, all things were possible and that they were destined to be the future leaders of our nation. With that future in mind, my siblings and I were nurtured and protected by our parents, our schools, our churches, and our neighbors. We were imbued with a strong work ethic and taught to study diligently. As people of color, we knew that we had to be better prepared than everyone else in order to succeed.

Racial segregation was a painful part of my past. But my family and my social network did not allow it to define my life, limit my prospects, crush my character, or hinder my dreams. As a consequence of my upbringing, when I interact with Atlanta public housing tenants who are confined by the modern-day version of racial and economic segregation, I see children of God, who are blessed with unlimited human potential and are destined to become the next leaders of our nation. In order to realize their potential, these families and individuals must be nurtured and protected from the pathologies that have become endemic to poverty-stricken communities. Dr. Martin Luther King Jr. said it best:

> This is why segregation has wreaked havoc with the Negro. It is sometimes difficult to determine which are the deepest—the physical wounds or the psychological wounds. Only a Negro can understand the social leprosy that segregation inflicts upon him. The suppressed fears and resentments, and the expressed anxieties and sensitivities make each day of life a turmoil. Every confrontation with the restrictions imposed is another emotional battle in a never-ending war. He is shackled in his waking moments to tiptoe stance, never quite knowing what to expect next, and in his subconscious he wrestles with this added demon.[4]

In some ways, economic segregation can be crueler than racial segregation, because if a person is poor, it often is assumed that he or she is incapable of doing better.

The Atlanta Blueprint

In real terms, the conventional approach to public housing in large cities had degenerated into warehousing as many poor people as possible—as cheaply as possible—away from mainstream society. Typically a captive, failing elementary school rounded out the model. As a matter of practical application, the laws and regulations governing public housing institutionalized low expectations and virtually guaranteed chronic failure. The public debate was driven by a small number of vocal advocates of traditional public housing strategies whose argument generally went as follows: "Since poor people can't reach the bar, just keep it as low as possible." As a consequence, many families and individuals locked into this self-defeating system never adopted the coping skills that they needed to overcome obstacles and failure became a self-fulfilling prophecy.

The Atlanta Housing Authority was determined to use HOPE VI to break away from that flawed social design and reverse the cycle of low expectations and poor outcomes. We were convinced that effective community building would require a sustained investment by the public and private sectors and the active participation of affected public housing residents in rebuilding their lives. Therefore, we rejected the idea of creating a new and improved version of traditional public housing—a product of what we viewed as a failed strategy. Instead, we set out to replace isolated public housing projects with economically integrated, market-quality mixed-income communities that are developed, owned, and managed by private sector real estate professionals. Each community would include critical amenities, such as good schools.

Our plan was to begin with the revitalization of Techwood–Clark Howell Homes before the start of the Centennial Olympic Games.[5] Techwood Homes, dedicated by President Franklin Roosevelt in 1935, was the oldest public housing development in the country; Clark Howell Homes was constructed in 1938 as an expansion of Techwood on an adjacent site.[6] Situated near the downtown

In 1994, with a vacancy rate of about 50 percent and a high incidence of crime, Techwood Homes was not the symbol of optimism that it was in 1935 when it was dedicated by Franklin D. Roosevelt as the nation's first public housing development.

commercial corridor, these complexes, totaling almost 1,100 row house and two-story walk-up apartments, were adjacent to the Georgia Institute of Technology. Techwood–Clark Howell was a grievous example of public housing failure and disenfranchisement. For example, in 1993 the crime rate was 69 percent more than the citywide rate; annual median household income was $3,960; and only 14 percent of the 998 households there had any earned income.[7]

In the summer of 1994, while I was still chair of the board of directors, we began meeting with some tenant leaders, hoping that they would embrace the new vision. At one early session, we shared pictures of market-rate rental communities. To our surprise, several residents literally turned their chairs around and sat with their backs to the table. When we asked why, they replied that the housing authority was "lying to us" because the communities shown in the pictures were "too nice." They also could not believe that tenants who could pay market-rate rents would ever choose to be their neighbors. Their comments were stunning, and they broke my heart. They confirmed the extent of the damage that had been inflicted on the residents' spirit.

After several additional and sometimes contentious meetings from May to August 1994, we finally negotiated an agreement, which AHA and the Techwood–Clark Howell Resident Association signed in August 1994. The agreement enabled AHA to proceed with the process to select a qualified program manager and developer to create a mixed-income community on the site where Techwood–Clark Howell had stood since the Great Depression. AHA also agreed that two members of the tenants' planning group would participate on the five-member evaluation committee. Despite some other concessions, I demanded veto power over the process since the fiduciary responsibility for the project ultimately rested with me, as the chief executive officer. When the dust settled, the evaluation committee made its unanimous choice: the Integral Partnership of Atlanta (TIPA), a joint venture between the Integral Group, a local urban development firm, and McCormack Baron, an urban development team based in St. Louis, Missouri.

The type of mixed-income community that we envisioned did not exist anywhere. The financial, legal, and regulatory model for this public-private hybrid had to be created from scratch, all while we were working with a hodgepodge of state and local agencies, and, of course, HUD. During a nine-month period, we met with numerous HUD officials to work through the myriad policy and regulatory issues that were involved in the deal. Many of them were flying blind because HUD had never granted permission for an entity other than a local housing authority to own public housing units.

With the countdown for the Olympics getting louder, we closed on the initial phase of Centennial Place on March 8, 1996. With that financial closing, we had created the legal, regulatory, and financial framework for the first

Centennial Place, the mixed-use, mixed-income community that opened in 1996 on the site of Techwood and Clark Howell Homes, includes rental homes (shown here in a later photograph) and for-sale homes, Centennial Place Elementary School, a YMCA, an early childhood development center, and retail and commercial buildings.

mixed-income community in the nation developed with public and private resources that included public housing–assisted (financed) units.[8]

The Centennial Place Model

By the time Muhammad Ali lit the Olympic torch during the opening ceremonies on July 19, 1996, the first buildings of phase I of the multifamily rental apartments at Centennial Place were constructed and a model unit had been furnished. Today, many years after the Olympics, Centennial Place remains a showplace. Owned by a public-private partnership, it is a market-rate, top-quality residential community with a seamless, long-term, affordable component built in. Forty percent of the 738 apartments are reserved for public housing–assisted families; 20 percent are reserved for families that qualify under the Low-Income Housing Tax Credit Program; and 40 percent are reserved for families that pay market rents. The relative percentages must be maintained at all times, but all of the units are built to the same high standards and with the same amenities, with no sections reserved for any economic segment.

Proof of the success of the concept is reflected in the fact that families earning $7,000 a year live next door to households whose annual income exceeds $100,000. Success also is evident in spin-off investment. The $42.5 million 1993 HOPE VI grant for the revitalization of Techwood–Clark Howell has been leveraged into approximately $150 million in new investment on that site. Other components of the Centennial Place master plan include the elementary school, the YMCA, a Sheltering Arms Early Education and Family Center, a branch of SunTrust Bank, and a mini city police precinct. Most recently, for-sale townhomes, as envisioned in the Centennial Place master plan, were sold for prices ranging from $200,000 to $800,000. Other retail and commercial uses and additional market-rate residential housing will be developed in later unsubsidized phases of the Centennial Place master plan. Today, approximately $1 billion of private investment has flowed into the surrounding neighborhood.

Producing such results requires a comprehensive change management process that anticipates, mentally tests, and refines the systems and structures that support program goals. AHA has had to overhaul its policies, operations, business processes and systems, and personnel with the new model in mind. AHA has repositioned itself as a diversified real estate company with a public mission and purpose.

OWNERSHIP STRUCTURE

AHA decided that in order to be successful, the mixed-income community had to be developed, owned, and managed by private sector developers. During and after the development phase, AHA takes the role of sponsor of the revitalization. That is, AHA assumes the role of facilitator and problem solver with HUD and other public bodies and of traditional asset manager with respect to its investments.

As has become standard in Atlanta with mixed-income revitalization of public housing, each of the various phases of multifamily rental at Centennial Place is owned by individual limited partnerships ("owner entities"). At Centennial Place, the owner entities are limited partnerships made up of an affiliate of TIPA as the managing general partner and an affiliate of AHA as a limited partner of the managing general partner.[9] The limited partners are investors in the 9 percent low-income housing tax credits; they typically own at least 97 percent of the limited partner interests. For each phase of multifamily rental development, the AHA retains ownership of the land under the buildings but leases it to the owner entity under a long-term ground lease, typically of fifty to sixty years. When the lease is up, the land and all improvements revert to AHA. A declaration of trust or declaration of restrictive covenants is recorded so that the obligation to provide the agreed number of units to public housing–assisted families will survive any foreclosure proceeding. The federal government will not fund a project and commit operating subsidies to it without

> The innovation of the Centennial Place financing model was that for the first time, public housing–assisted units were incorporated into a development that otherwise was underwritten and financed by the market.

some assurance that the asset in which HUD funds are being invested will remain affordable. The for-sale townhomes and condominiums are sold with a fee interest in the land. The commercial and retail uses involve either a long-term ground lease or sale of the fee interest.

FINANCIAL STRUCTURE

The financial model has many moving parts. It is an innovative mix of private sector market principles and practices and public sector safeguards that have become standard but remain a stretch for many stakeholders; tenant advocates and financiers alike must venture out of their comfort zone and modify their requirements in order to achieve consensus among all parties. Creating a successful mixed-income, mixed-finance community requires a financial structure that allows families earning well below 60 percent of area median income to afford the rents without any reduction in the quality of construction or the community's long-term financial viability. In order to compete for market-rate renters, private developers build and manage the development to appeal to the high end of the market, with first-class amenities. The community must be a "value" proposition to all residents. The private market governs the quality of the housing, the financial feasibility of the property, the management of the property, and its long-term sustainability, because the disposable income of the market-rate renters dictates the number and quality of services that the communities can attract and sustain.

The innovation of the Centennial Place financing model was that for the first time, public housing–assisted units (which provide no financial return on investment) were incorporated into a development that otherwise was underwritten and financed by the market. A substantial portion of the development costs for the public housing–assisted units is covered by HOPE VI funds. Indeed, HOPE VI funds can be used only toward the development of public housing–assisted units (often referred to as ACC units) because the operating subsidy is provided pursuant to the Consolidated Annual Combined Contributions Contract (ACC) between a housing authority and HUD. Furthermore, the federal government issues guidelines regarding total development costs for ACC units.

Since ACC units cannot, by law, generate any net operating income, they cannot be used to obtain construction loans. HOPE VI essentially buys down the costs of the ACC units, so that the units can be constructed without incurring any debt and can be afforded by public housing–assisted families using the same rent formula as used for conventional public housing. HOPE VI, however, is not sufficient to fund all the construction costs of the required low-income units. Developments with a certain portion of low-income units can compete for 9 percent low-income housing tax credits based on the overall development cost. Since a grant of HOPE VI funds would reduce the eligible basis of a tax credit property and thus reduce its tax credit equity, HOPE VI funds are lent by AHA to the owner entity on a subordinated basis.

All of these nuances were addressed in the mixed-income, mixed-finance model for Centennial Place. Through its 221(d) (4) mortgage program, the FHA insured the first mortgage loan, providing assurances to lenders unaccustomed to making construction loans on a project in which a percentage of the units cannot, by law, provide net operating income or be foreclosed on. Before the closing of phase I of Centennial Place, FHA had never provided mortgage insurance on a project that included ACC units.[10] AHA provided the HOPE VI funds to the owner entity as a soft second loan and a small grant. Proceeds from the sale of 9 percent low-income housing tax credits provided the much-needed equity for the financing.

An operating subsidy is provided by AHA to ensure affordability for families earning much less than 60 percent of the area median income. The subsidy is in keeping with a regulatory and operating agreement between AHA and the owner entity that states that the public housing–assisted units will be operated on a break-even basis (that is, rents collected and subsidy must cover the operating costs). No net operating income is generated on the public housing–assisted units. TIPA and AHA earned a development fee, and AHA and the owner entity participate in the net operating income from the non-subsidized units, based on their negotiated deal. Tax credit investors received certain agreed-upon returns on their investments.

The city of Atlanta contributed $12 million to pay for infrastructure improvements in the public right-of-way at Centennial Place. The city and Fulton County agreed to provide tax relief to the property for the first ten years by designating it a housing enterprise zone and tax relief for the public housing–assisted apartments for the life of the property.

PROPERTY MANAGEMENT

Because mixed-income communities compete with market-rate properties for market-rate tenants, the key to making the communities work is consistent implementation of proven management practices and enforcement of high standards. Consistent with the Atlanta Blueprint, an affiliate of TIPA manages Centennial Place. It simply makes sense to give property oversight to the entity that ultimately is responsible for the property's performance. TIPA has the underwriting and performance risk for the first mortgage debt, and TIPA's principals have provided performance guarantees to the investors in 9 percent low-income housing tax credits. Allowing the owner entity to manage the property and to establish and manage a site-based waiting list for its public housing–assisted units was a critically important change allowed under the HOPE VI grant agreement. Historically, all public housing–assisted units were leased by using a process that was centrally managed by a housing authority. Given the strategic importance of these changes to the long-term success of the model and the political sensitivity of the policy decision, we decided to request approval up front for all future mixed-income, mixed-finance communities. Fortunately, HUD approved the request, which would prove essential for mixed-income deals leveraging non–HOPE VI public housing development funds.

The public housing–assisted families are required to sign a lease addendum that requires, among other things, that able-bodied, non-elderly adults work and that all school-aged children attend school. The residents agreed to this additional requirement because counseling, education, job training, and other services were provided to the affected Techwood–Clark Howell residents for the five-year period during which the real estate was undergoing revitalization.

EDUCATION AND COMMUNITY STRATEGY

No less important to the long-term sustainability of a mixed-income community is the sociology of the community and the "quality-of-life infrastructure," which includes high-achieving neighborhood schools; excellent child care; recreational facilities; retail and commercial services; and access to public transportation. All of these amenities address the needs of the community, regardless of income.

When the plans for Centennial Place were coming together, Norman Johnson, former assistant to the president of the Georgia Institute of Technology and erstwhile member of the Atlanta School Board, correctly observed that

Figure 9-1. **Scores of Centennial Place Students Compared with Those of All City and State Elementary Students**

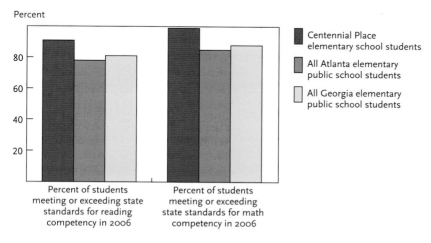

no child from Techwood–Clark Howell Homes had ever crossed the street to attend Georgia Tech. Given that reality, the master plan for Centennial Place proposed a new elementary school to serve the community. Since TIPA and AHA had committed to building communities—not just rental properties— that decision was a no-brainer. Working with Egbert Perry, founder and CEO of The Integral Group, and with me, Johnson galvanized other school board members, Georgia Tech, and Coca Cola—whose world headquarters is across the street from Centennial Place—to partner to create Centennial Place elementary school. Centennial Place elementary today is in the top tier of elementary schools in Atlanta and the state of Georgia. In 2006, we received news that one of the public housing–assisted residents of Centennial Place (who also graduated from Centennial Place elementary) had been admitted to Georgia Tech. Figure 9-1 shows Centennial Place students' performance on state reading and math tests, which is better on average than that of other public school students in the city and the state.

Another major stakeholder, the YMCA (under the leadership of Milton Jones, a senior executive at Bank of America and then the chair of the YMCA Metropolitan Board), had its original home office near the old Techwood– Clark Howell site and expressed an interest in being part of the community under the master plan.[11] Sheltering Arms Early Education and Family Centers developed and operates an early childhood development facility.

In 1995, more than 60 percent of the 650 units in the East Lake Meadows public housing project in southeast Atlanta were substandard, and the project's crime rate was eighteen times the national average.

The Villages of East Lake, a mixed-use, mixed-income community completed in 2000 to replace East Lake Meadows, is one of Atlanta's most desirable addresses. The master-planned community includes rental homes, the eighteen-hole Charlie Yates golf course, Drew Charter Elementary School, a YMCA, an early childhood development center, and retail and commercial facilities. The adjacent East Lake Golf course is currently the host of the PGA FedEx Cup.

RELOCATION OF THE TECHWOOD–CLARK HOWELL FAMILIES

During our discussions with the Techwood–Clark Howell residents regarding their willingness to support a new model, the single biggest issue was how the relocation process would work. The residents insisted on receiving Section 8 vouchers instead of moving to another public housing project because, simply put, they did not want to leave the "hell" that they knew for one that they did not know. Consequently, AHA applied for and received additional vouchers, enabling all of the affected households who elected to take vouchers as their relocation resource to seek better housing opportunities.[12] Approximately 75 percent of the affected households chose the voucher; of those, 95 percent were successful in finding a new housing opportunity—for most, in a better environment. The households that did not choose a voucher or were unsuccessful in obtaining housing with the voucher were relocated to other public housing developments, other subsidized housing, or private housing.[13]

Critics of AHA's strategic revitalization program have said that Section 8 vouchers are not a stable resource for low-income families and that voucher families are not moving to better living environments. Thomas D. Boston, a professor of economics at the Georgia Institute of Technology, has researched those questions. He found that families that moved from the housing projects using the vouchers were doing substantially better on measures of workforce participation, children's school performance, and family income.[14]

Above: Built in 1940 under FDR's New Deal, John Hope Homes experienced decades of neglect and high crime rates before it was demolished in 1996.

Right: The mixed-use, mixed-income Village at Castleberry Hill was completed in 2000 on the site of the former John Hope Homes. Located near the Georgia Dome and the Atlanta University Center, the master-planned development has spurred revitalization along Atlanta's Northside Drive, including a busy arts, entertainment, and residential district.

One unanticipated outcome is that most of the families affected by the HOPE VI revitalization in Atlanta that elected vouchers as their relocation option often chose to keep the vouchers rather than return to the newly revitalized mixed-income communities.[15]

The Olympic Legacy Program

By the opening of the Olympic Games, we wanted to send a clear and powerful message that AHA had made a sea change in providing housing for low-income families. When teams from 197 nations converged on Atlanta in the summer of 1996, AHA and TIPA unveiled to the world Centennial Place—the first mixed-income, mixed-finance community in the United States that included ACC units. We also announced the launching of the Olympic Legacy Program.

"Olympic Legacy Program" is the name that we created to brand our effort to take mixed-income community development in Atlanta to scale. We aimed to use the political and corporate will generated by the Centennial Olympic Games to fast-track the remaining redevelopment phases of Centennial Place and to revitalize three additional notorious, distressed public housing developments using the Centennial Place model. Those housing projects—East Lake Meadows, John Hope Homes, and John Eagan Homes—had been funded and slated for comprehensive modernization, work that we halted when I joined AHA because we did not want to waste any precious resources.

Each development had tens of millions of dollars in modernization grant funds that could be used only for renovation. The law was changed in 1996 to allow the funds to be used for mixed-income development, as if they were HOPE VI funds.[16] There were many early critics of the Olympic Legacy Program (from both the private and the public sector) who were concerned that AHA was overly ambitious and that it was moving too fast and too soon with an unproven model. I believed that mixed-income development was the only strategy that would work. We were not going to waste the millions of dollars in grant funds that AHA had on hand or squander the opportunity to use them. Implementing the mixed-income, mixed-finance revitalization program at scale was the only way to answer the critics and satisfy the skeptics. By taking the program to scale, AHA also was able to improve markedly our financial and operational performance and resolve hundreds of long-standing disputes and problems—all while meeting the needs of low-income Atlanta families in substantially healthier living environments.

In order to leverage the Centennial Place mixed-income, mixed-finance model further, AHA sought and was granted a waiver by HUD to procure TIPA, on a sole-source basis, to act as program manager for the revitalization of the three additional housing projects. Hiring TIPA as program manager, one of the AHA's most strategic decisions ever, saved AHA millions of dollars in grant funds, streamlined the predevelopment processes, and fast-tracked the development

timelines.[17] In addition to granting the waiver, HUD placed the Centennial Place blueprint for mixed-income community development on its website to encourage housing authorities around the country to adopt the model.[18]

PROOF OF MIXED-INCOME CONCEPT

Since the conclusion of the 1996 Olympics, the Olympic Legacy Program has been expanded to include additional highly distressed and dysfunctional public housing family projects.[19] Since 1996, leveraging both HOPE VI and non–HOPE VI grant funds, AHA has undertaken the demolition and mixed-income revitalization of thirteen of its most distressed and obsolete public housing family projects, all of which are in various stages of revitalization using the Centennial Place mixed-income, mixed-finance model.

With each of the mixed-income revitalization projects, crime has fallen in the redeveloped communities and surrounding neighborhoods by approximately 90 percent, surrounding property values have risen, new homeowners have moved into the adjacent neighborhoods, and additional private investments have been made in those areas.[20] Table 9-1 illustrates the scope and economic impact of the strategy.

AHA's strategic revitalization has had a ripple effect that has produced substantial results for our neighbors as well. The projects in the master plan are at various stages of ongoing development; when they are completed, approximately $400 million of various HOPE VI and non–HOPE VI public housing development funds will have leveraged approximately $4 billion in private investment. So far, about $220 million in various HOPE VI and non–HOPE VI public housing development funds has leveraged approximately $3 billion in private investment at the affected sites and in areas adjacent to AHA developments.

AHA earns a range of negotiated transaction fees related to the various phases of the mixed-income transactions. These fees are based on the value-added services, such as asset management and loan underwriting, provided to

Above left: In 2000, the last residents were relocated from the forty-year-old Perry Homes public housing project, some 944 units in shabby barracks on the grassy slopes of a forgotten area five miles west of downtown Atlanta.

Above right: Multifamily rental and single-family, detached for-sale homes encircle a neighborhood park and pond in West Highlands, Atlanta's largest residential redevelopment. The master plan for the mixed-use, mixed-income community, built on the site of the old Perry Homes, also calls for an elementary school, an early childhood development center, and retail and commercial structures.

Table 9-1. Atlanta Housing Authority Olympic Legacy Program
Scope and Economic Impact Matrix

Type of community developed	Community name and size	Family public housing project that occupied the development site	For-sale unit mix (number)	
			Market rate	Affordable
Mixed-use/mixed-income communities (built on the footprint of a former all–public housing site, under master plans that include commercial, recreational, and educational facilities)	Centennial Place (60 acres)	Techwood–Clark Howell	108	27
	Villages of East Lake (175 acres)	East Lake Meadows	...	...
	College Town at West End[c] (42 acres)	Harris Homes	290	99
	Village at Castleberry Hills (28 acres)	John Hope Homes	...	...
	Villages at Carver (111 acres)	Carver Homes	184	67
	West Highlands (209 acres)	Perry Homes	456	141
	Capitol Gateway (34 acres)	Capitol Homes	229	141
	Auburn Pointe[d] (30 acres)	Grady Homes	37	32
	Mechanicsville[e] (41 acres)	McDaniel Glenn	230	67
	Community in predevelopment, to be named	University Homes	TBD[f]	TBD
On-site mixed-income rental communities (built on the footprint of a former public housing site)	Magnolia Park (28 acres)	...	...	...
	Ashley Courts at Cascade[g] (35 acres)	...	...	...
Off-site mixed-income rental communities (built on sites not owned by the Atlanta Housing Authority	Ashley Terrace at West End (12 acres)	...	...	...
	Columbia Village (14 acres)	...	...	...
	Columbia Commons (11 acres)	...	...	...
TOTALS	...	...	**1,534**	**574**

Source: Atlanta Housing Authority.

a. PBRA stands for *project-based rental assistance,* whereby rental assistance vouchers that have been converted by the housing authority to project-based vouchers enable the authority to lease units in market-rate buildings for low-income families that are eligible for public housing.

b. New investment in properties surrounding the redeveloped site.
c. The John O. Chiles senior public housing buildings, which were within the Harris family public housing site, have been added to the Harris revitalization plan and are under development.

Rental unit mix (number)				Federal funding (HOPE VI grant/ other capital funds, in millions)	Total on-site investment (millions)	Surrounding area investment[b] (millions)
Market rate	Tax credit	Tax credit with public housing assistance	Tax credit with PBRA[a]			
311	126	301	0	$42.6/0	$150.0	$1,000.00
271	0	271	0	0/$28.8	$64.9	$61.00
189	65	246	175	$39.3/0	$234.1	$102.5
180	90	180	0	0/$17.0	$44.1	$304.0
207	165	329	150	$44.4/0	$218.9	$168.2
259	89	228	124	$25.1/$21.8	$250.1	$290.8
168	100	138	233	$35.0/0	$155.9	$201.5
180	70	196	297	$24.2/$23.6	$155.8	$103.8
180	48	247	181	$20.6/$18.5	$184.5	$64.2
TBD	TBD	TBD	TBD	TBD	TBD	TBD
160	80	160	0	$0/$17.7	$38.2	$160.8
101	167	116	0	$0/$8.0	$42.3	...
44	34	34	0	$0/$2.7	$7.2	...
0	70	30	0	$0/$2.2	$8.8	...
79	31	48	0	$0/$3.3	$14.3	...
2,329	**1,135**	**2,524**	**1,160**	**$231.2/$143.6**	**$1,569.1**	**$2,456.8**

d. The Antoine Graves and Graves Annex senior public housing buildings, which were within the Grady Homes family public housing site, have been added to the Grady revitalization plan and are in pre-development; in addition, some of the housing built on the old University Homes site will serve as off-site replacement units for the Grady revitalization plan.

e. MLK Towers senior public housing building and the McDaniel Glenn Annex family public housing building have been added to the McDaniel Glenn revitalization plan and are in pre-development.

f. TBD = To be determined.

g. Some of the housing built on the old Kimberly Courts public housing site serves as off-site housing for the Techwood–Clark Howell revitalization plan.

the revitalization projects by AHA. AHA also participates in the net cash flow from the mixed-income communities. Such fees and entrepreneurial income are treated as program income and used by AHA to further its revitalization efforts and provide additional housing for low-income families.

Impact of the Citywide Public Housing Transformation on Affected Households

To date, more than 10,000 households have successfully relocated, primarily by using Section 8 vouchers.[21] The true intent of the work, of course, was never to make mere brick-and-mortar improvements. The overarching goal was to create holistic environments that encouraged and inspired public housing residents to unlock their God-given human potential.

As mentioned, Thomas D. Boston has studied the effects of revitalization on affected public housing families. His research concluded that "using Atlanta as a case study, we found strong evidence that the neighborhood environment contributes significantly to the socioeconomic mobility of families." Specifically, the study found that

- revitalization did not cause a statistically significant loss of housing assistance for affected residents
- families whose communities were affected by revitalization primarily chose vouchers
- greater improvement in socioeconomic status occurred among families affected by revitalization than among those not affected
- the socioeconomic status of families that used vouchers or lived in mixed-income communities was superior to that of families that lived in public housing projects
- families that moved from public housing projects to voucher-subsidized housing were 1.5 times more likely to be employed in the long term than were those who remained in the projects
- families that moved to mixed-income communities were 2.1 times more likely to be employed in the long run than those who remained in the projects.[22]

Moving to Work

Following the success of its strategic revitalization program, AHA was designated a Moving to Work (MTW) agency in 2001, a status granted to only thirty housing authorities in the country. AHA applied for that designation in order to leverage the best practices and lessons learned from the Olympic Legacy Program. After protracted negotiations with HUD, AHA signed its Moving to Work agreement on September 25, 2003. The agreement provides substantial statutory and regulatory relief from all of the provisions of the U.S. Housing Act of 1937, as amended, with certain exceptions, and most provisions of the ACC, thereby empowering AHA to apply private sector real estate principles and to implement local strategies to address the affordable housing needs of low-income families in the city of Atlanta.

Under AHA's MTW agreement, operating funds for low-income housing, Section 8 budget authority, and capital funds are treated as a "single block grant fund," eliminating the artificial barriers among them. Therefore, the funds may be reprogrammed and spent on eligible MTW activities in accordance with the MTW objectives of increasing cost-effectiveness, residents' self-sufficiency, and housing choices for low-income families.[23]

AHA has implemented sweeping changes to all of its programs. In 2004, AHA implemented a work requirement for all non-elderly, nondisabled adults as a condition of receiving housing assistance, either in the form of a public housing unit or a housing voucher. In 2004, when the policy change was adopted, only 24 percent of the affected adults in the public housing projects were working. Because of the single-fund approach to financing, AHA has

Rashon Mitchell, with one-year-old India Simmons, looks out over her apartment balcony at the Villages of Carver in June 2002. The masterplanned, mixed-use community in south Atlanta replaced drug-infested Carver Homes, which was razed in 1998.

AP Photo/Ric Feld.

been able to partner with the city's local workforce development agency and other local stakeholders to provide job training, child care, and family counseling. As of December 31, 2007, more than 80 percent of the households were in compliance with the work requirement.[24]

Building on Success

Civic, business, and housing authority leaders agree that none of the investment, none of the increased choice for families, and none of the new focus on self-sufficiency would have been possible if Techwood–Clark Howell Homes had not been fundamentally transformed. Our experience has solidified many key lessons for success—for us going forward, for other housing authorities, and for policymakers in Washington:

- Most residents do not desire to return to the revitalized community, because they are leaving behind a painful time in their lives. The Section 8 voucher represents choice and better opportunities.[25]
- Long-term individualized family coaching and counseling must be provided by professional firms during relocation and for at least three years afterward. Place-based strategies are much less effective.[26]
- A long-term investment in the affected households yields huge dividends; God-given human potential is infinite.
- Community revitalization must be holistic and comprehensive to be sustainable over the long term.
- Public housing, as it evolved historically, is the product of a failed social design. Concentrating low-income families in isolated projects is bad public policy. An economically diverse living environment is a necessary and essential step to ending structural poverty.
- Isolating poor families from mainstream society to solve housing problems is the wrong approach; the cost (financial, human, social, and other) is staggering.
- We must have the political courage and the corporate will to adopt high expectations and implement high standards for assisted families. Income dictates opportunities, not values or human potential.
- Housing policy is education policy and education policy is housing policy.
- The success of the HOPE VI Program should be measured by its outcomes—improvements in the life prospects of the affected residents and improvements in and impact on communities, neighborhoods, and cities.
- HUD must recognize the sea change that mixed-income community revitalization represents and adapt its systems, processes, and subsidy programs to support ACC-assisted units after development is completed. The low-income operating subsidy is inadequate, and HUD should consider subsidizing the assisted units with Section 8 project-based rental assistance.

····· Endnotes ·····

1. Under a project-based rental assistance arrangement, a Section 8 tenant-based voucher is converted to a ten-year renewable rent subsidy that closes the affordability gap for households that earn between minimum wage and 60 percent of the metropolitan area median income. The rent subsidy remains with the property, not the tenant. These arrangements with private owners create additional mixed-income communities throughout the city of Atlanta by leveraging ongoing development activity by private owners.

2. In 1995, the city of Atlanta recorded 69,011 crimes; in 2006, it recorded 39,779 crimes. During the same period, the city's population increased from 404,337 to 485,804 persons, causing the crime index per 10,000 persons to decrease from 1,707 to 818, or by 52 percent. Crime statistics were derived from the Federal Bureau of Investigation, Uniform Crime Reports (www.fbi.gov/ucr/ucr.htm).

3. Frederick Allen, *Atlanta Rising: The Invention of an International City 1946–1996* (Marietta, Ga.: Longstreet Press, 1996), p. 232

4. James M. Washington, *A Testament of Hope: The Essential Writings and Speeches of Martin Luther King Jr.* (New York: HarperCollins, 1991), p. 121.

5. Approximately two acres of the Techwood site had been sold to the Georgia State Board of Regents in 1992 to construct the Olympic dormitories, which later were used as dormitories for Georgia State University and then for Georgia Tech. Fields slated to host some of the Olympic events also were nearby.

6. Charles F. Palmer, *Adventures of a Slum Fighter* (New York: Van Rees Press, 1955), pp. 136, 237.

7. Crime rate information comes from Thomas D. Boston, "Environment Matters: The Effect of Mixed-Income Revitalization on the Socioeconomic Status of Public Housing Residents, A Case Study of Atlanta," Working Paper 1 (Georgia Institute of Technology, School of Economics, January 2005), p. 13 (www.econ.gatech.edu/faculty/thomas-boston/). Information on median household income comes from Jerry J. Salama, "The Redevelopment of Distressed Public Housing: Early Results from HOPE VI Projects in Atlanta, Chicago, and San Antonio," *Housing Policy Debate* 10, no. 1 (1999), pp. 102, 104. (www.fanniemaefoundation. org/progams/hpd/pdf/hpd_1001_salama.pdf).

8. During the same period, as discussed in the chapter by Richard Baron, negotiations with HUD were under way to transform Vaughn Homes, a severely distressed public housing project in St. Louis, into a mixed-income community. The negotiations regarding the St. Louis revitalization project proved to be very helpful, because the HUD funds being used were public housing development dollars rather than HOPE VI funds. Moreover, the intersection of these negotiations helped to convince HUD that a new model for providing HUD-subsidized affordable housing was possible and perhaps could be taken to scale. The financial closing for the first phase of Murphy Park was in April, 1996, a few weeks after the closing for the first phase of Centennial Place. As Baron's chapter explains, there was an earlier mixed-income redevelopment of Boston's Columbia Point public housing complex, but the redevelopment involved converting the public housing units to units assisted under the project-based Section 8 program.

9. AHA supported this structure so that the private sector development partner would lead the development process. AHA and our private sector development partners were seeking to develop a market-rate community with a seamless affordable component, thereby providing a housing opportunity for households that needed a subsidy to pay their rent.

10. Several financial power players—the late Terrence Duvernay, a former deputy secretary of HUD; Nicolas Retsinas, then the assistant secretary of the Federal Housing Administration; and Carl Riedy, an investment banker—worked with AHA and TIPA to make FHA mortgage insurance work in this context.

11. The YMCA raised all of the capital and operating subsidies needed to develop and build a state-of-the-art facility.

12. Section 8 vouchers empower families to choose where they would like to live in the private real estate market. Using the voucher, families generally pay 30 percent of their monthly adjusted gross income toward rent and utilities, just as they did when they lived in public housing. If a family has to pay for electricity, gas, or any other utilities, the portion of the rent that the family pays (the tenant portion) is reduced by the amount of the AHA utility allowance. The family pays the tenant portion to the landlord, and AHA pays the landlord the difference between the tenant portion and the total contract rent for the housing unit.

13. Of the families that chose vouchers, approximately 75 percent chose to stay in the city of Atlanta and the balance chose to move to locations in other parts of metropolitan Atlanta. A handful of families moved out of Georgia, primarily back to their hometowns and family.

14. Thomas D. Boston, "The Net Social Benefit of Transforming Public Housing Projects into Mixed-Income Communities: A Case Study," paper prepared for the MacArthur Foundation Cost-Benefit Analysis Planning Seminar, Chicago, October 2007. Also, Thomas D. Boston, *Benchmarking Family Socioeconomic Progress under MTW: A Case Study of the Atlanta Housing Authority*, report prepared for the Atlanta Housing Authority and the U.S. Department of Housing and Urban Development, March 2006, pp. 88 (www.econ.gatech.edu/faculty/thomas-boston/).

15. The preference for retaining vouchers has had no adverse effect on the revitalization program. In fact, it is an important asset in that it enables families to make their own choices, based on their needs and interests. Moreover, the voucher allows low-income families to rent market-rate units that they would not otherwise be able to afford.

16. East Lake Meadows had been awarded a $33.5 million grant from the Major Reconstruction of Obsolete Projects Program (MROP), which funded major reconstruction of existing public housing or the acquisition and rehabilitation of existing rental projects. John Hope Homes and John Eagan Homes had been awarded smaller MROP grants, but when added to available funds from the Comprehensive Improvements Assistance Program (CIAP), each had about $25 million in capital grant funds that could be leveraged. The fiscal 1996 appropriations act for HUD (the Omnibus Consolidated Rescissions and Appropriations Act of 1996, P.L. 104-134), enacted April 26, 1996, included a provision in Section 201(a) allowing non–HOPE VI public housing development funds to be used for replacement housing, not just modernization, thus enabling the expansion of mixed-finance, mixed-income public housing redevelopment beyond HOPE VI.

17. The program manager arrangement provided AHA much-needed development expertise. TIPA, primarily through the Integral Group, facilitated the revitalization of East Lake Meadows, John Hope Homes, and John Eagan Homes by bringing private sector know-how and discipline to the process of procuring master planners and developers, overseeing the demolition and site work, and assisting with the negotiation of the business deals for the new development.

18. Today, hundreds of phases of mixed-income communities based on the Centennial Place model have been completed across the country.

19. Public housing includes family projects and housing for seniors and young disabled residents, which have their own set of issues.

20. Thomas D. Boston, "The Benefits and Costs of Reducing Concentrated Poverty: A Case Study of the Villages of East Lake," Working Paper 3 (Georgia Institute of Technology, School of Economics, 2005); Boston, "The Net Social Benefit of Transforming Public Housing Projects into Mixed-Income Communities."

21. Since September 1994, AHA has razed 8,402 obsolete and distressed units; received HUD approval to raze an additional 1,288 distressed and obsolete units; and applied for approval to raze an additional 2,368 obsolete and distressed units, for a total of 12,058 obsolete and distressed units.

22. Boston, "Environment Matters: The Effect of Mixed-Income Revitalization on the Socioeconomic Status of Public Housing Residents."

23. The statutory goals and objectives of MTW are to reduce federal costs and improve the cost effectiveness of federal expenditures; to encourage and assist adult family members to obtain employment and become economically self-sufficient; and to increase housing options for low-income families.

24. AHA has hired social workers to work with each noncompliant household to determine why it is not in compliance. If AHA determines that additional services are needed, it facilitates referral to another agency. If a household refuses to comply with the work requirement, it may, after a deliberative process, lose its subsidy. Very few households have chosen not to comply with the requirement and lose the subsidy.

25. Based on our experience with HOPE VI revitalization since late 1994, I would strongly suggest to HUD and Congress that the correct measure of whether a HOPE VI revitalization has been successful is not how many of the original families have returned to the new community but how many of the affected families have improved their lives in substantial and sustainable ways since the revitalization activities began.

26. A major lesson that AHA and the Integral Group learned over the years resulted in a mid-term course correction in our approach to human development. Initially, TIPA proposed and AHA embraced the Work Force Enterprise Program (WFEP), which was a place-based comprehensive job training and education program housed in the Centennial Place community center and managed by the YMCA. We had not anticipated that the families, when given a choice, would relocate all over the metro Atlanta area. They did not choose to return to the site for those services. More important, we had not anticipated the variety and depth of the problems and challenges facing the affected families. After an assessment of the effectiveness of WFEP, in 1998 the Integral Group proposed and AHA embraced an individual, family-centered approach that calls for assigning a professionally trained family counselor to each affected family to coach and counsel the family over a five-year period. The goals are family self-sufficiency and financial independence. Since that change in strategy was implemented, the improvement in outcomes for affected families has been outstanding.

MARGERY AUSTIN TURNER

HOPE VI, Neighborhood Recovery, and the Health of Cities

In Atlanta, Louisville, Seattle, and other cities across the country, thriving neighborhoods are now emerging, replacing the pervasive blight that surrounded public housing projects little more than a decade ago. In these cities, the contribution of HOPE VI to the revitalization of long-distressed neighborhoods seems undeniable. And the neighborhood benefits appear to spill over, enhancing the cities' social and fiscal health. But are these isolated examples, or has HOPE VI proven to be an effective tool for neighborhood and city transformation elsewhere?[1] What does experience suggest about the conditions necessary to catalyze change at the neighborhood and city level? And are the gains sustainable over the long term?

Evidence on those questions reveals that while redevelopment of public housing clearly can contribute to the health and vitality of neighborhoods and cities, success is not guaranteed. It takes careful planning, sustained leadership, and effective implementation to achieve good outcomes for public housing residents, neighborhoods, and a city as a whole. Moreover, the new, mixed-income communities created by HOPE VI may need ongoing support to ensure their sustainability as "communities of opportunity." And where the housing market is hot, the loss of deeply subsidized housing units may undermine a city's ability to maintain economically diverse neighborhoods. Future policy and practice should build on the experience to date to ensure that the transformation of distressed public housing achieves its full potential as one component of cities' strategies for achieving broader neighborhood revitalization and ensuring an adequate supply of affordable housing.

Distressed Public Housing Blights Neighborhoods and Undermines City Health

From the outset, public housing was intended not only to provide decent and affordable housing for low-income families but also to eliminate slums and blight, thereby helping to revitalize ailing central cities. During the 1950s

Coordinated investment by city government, the city housing authority, and the private sector is bringing transformed public housing (opposite), workforce housing, retail space, and office buildings to a once desolate area of southeast Washington, D.C.

When run-down, mostly black neighborhoods south of the U.S. Capitol (top left, shown in the late 1940s) were razed in the 1950s and 1960s for new development and freeways, many residents were relocated to public housing projects, including distant ones such as Valley Green (top right, in 1969) east of the Anacostia River in Washington, D.C. Within a decade of its completion in 1961, Valley Green was already suffering from crime and neglect and contributing to the blight of the neighborhood, as evident in a row of boarded-up stores blocks away in 1971 (bottom).

and 1960s, construction of public housing in many cities went hand in hand with slum clearance and "urban renewal." Large tracts of run-down housing (mostly in black neighborhoods) were demolished and displaced residents were relocated to new public housing projects, often in distant neighborhoods. For example, the "renewal" of Washington, D.C.'s southwest waterfront district replaced a low-income, mostly black neighborhood with office buildings (including HUD's headquarters) and new, higher-density housing, relocating many of the original residents to huge blocks of public and assisted housing east of the Anacostia River.

These policies had the effect of geographically isolating poor families—particularly poor minorities. Their isolation was intensified by federal policies that reserved scarce public housing resources for the neediest households on the waiting list, significantly reducing the number of moderate-income working families living in public housing. Ultimately, some public housing projects themselves came to blight the neighborhoods in which they were located, contributing to city distress. Large public housing projects, earmarked exclusively for occupancy by low-income families, exacerbated prevailing patterns of racial segregation, redlining, and white flight. And as years passed, poor management, physical deterioration, and runaway crime fed a downward spiral of disinvestment and distress in the adjacent neighborhoods.

In such troubled projects and the neighborhoods that surround them, crime and violence are common, jobs are scarce, schools often are ineffective, and young people see few opportunities for success. Living in such severe conditions undermines the life chances of both adults and children. But the damage these projects cause extends further. High concentrations of poverty increase the costs of delivering local public services, particularly police protection. Pockets of severe poverty, blight, and crime scare off prospective city residents, businesses, and investment, thereby undermining property values and hence, local tax revenues. And the concentration of minority poverty and distress fuels racial prejudice and polarization, slowing progress toward a healthy diversity of residents of all races, ethnicities, and incomes.[2] For all these reasons, tackling the problem of severely distressed public housing is essential to the revitalization of central cities.

HOPE VI Removes Major Deficits

Simply demolishing a distressed public housing property constitutes a critical first step, because it significantly reduces the concentration of poverty that does such terrible damage to people and their communities. Public housing projects often account for a large share of a neighborhood's poor population, pushing poverty rates in the whole area to 50 or 60 percent. To illustrate, suppose that a 750-unit project—with perhaps 2,000 poor residents—is located in a census tract of 6,000, where 20 percent of the other residents are poor. Demolishing the project will by definition reduce the tract's total poverty rate from 47 percent to 20 percent (and its original residents can be relocated to safe, vibrant neighborhoods where they can thrive).

Over time, the poverty rate among non–public housing residents probably will decline too, given statistical evidence suggesting that concentrations of distressed public housing discourage moderate- and middle-income families from living nearby and therefore increase the proportion of people in the surrounding neighborhood who are poor. Specifically, a ten-point drop in the percentage of public housing households in a census tract is associated with a 4.5 point reduction in the non–public housing household poverty rate.[3] Simulations predict that demolition and mixed-income redevelopment will roughly halve neighborhood poverty rates.[4]

Given the damage caused by very high concentrations of poverty, this change alone may remove a major barrier to private investment and redevelopment.

In addition, before-and-after studies of HOPE VI developments have documented dramatic reductions in crime when distressed public housing is

Before-and-after studies of HOPE VI developments have documented dramatic reductions in crime when distressed public housing is demolished.

Figure 10-1. Reduction in Type I and Other Crimes in the Park DuValle Neighborhood, 1990–2002[a]

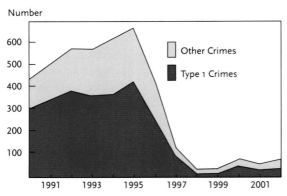

Number

Source: City of Louisville Police Department, in Mindy Turbov and Valerie Piper, "HOPE VI and Mixed-Finance Redevelopments: A Catalyst for Neighborhood Renewal," Metropolitan Policy Program, Brookings Institution, September, 2005, p. 28.

a. Type 1 crime is violent crime.

demolished. The Housing Research Foundation (HRF) found that violent crime rates in eight HOPE VI neighborhoods dropped 30 percent faster than in their cities overall.[5] Similarly, in its assessment of eleven HOPE VI sites, Abt Associates reported declining crime rates in all the neighborhoods for which they had data; in three cities (Charlotte, Milwaukee, and Boston) the declines substantially exceeded the declines in the neighborhoods with which the HOPE VI neighborhoods were compared.[6] Turbov and Piper's in-depth examination of neighborhood impacts in four seasoned mixed-income developments also shows impressive reductions in crime. To illustrate, in the neighborhood surrounding Park DuValle in Louisville, the number of crimes plummeted from close to 700 a year in 1995, prior to demolition, to fewer than 100 a year between 1998 and 2002, when the first two phases of redevelopment were nearing completion (figure 10-1).[7]

The impact of such reductions in crime—like the reductions in neighborhood poverty rates—can be profound. Crime and violence put neighborhood residents at constant risk of harm, with far-reaching consequences, including persistent anxiety and emotional trauma. Moreover, serious crime and the accompanying social disorder deter neighborhood investment by both homebuyers and businesses. In some market conditions, cutting neighborhood poverty and crime may be all it takes to trigger significant new private sector development.

New Assets Attract People and Investment

But HOPE VI has done more than just remove blight. It has replaced distressed projects with new housing—applying an entirely different set of standards for design, financing, and occupancy. Where traditional public housing maximized the number of units on a site, either in high-rise towers or barracks-style rows, HOPE VI developments have generally reduced densities, building houses and apartments that are more harmonious with the architecture in surrounding neighborhoods. Where older public housing often was cut off from the surrounding neighborhood by a separate street grid or forbidding open spaces, many new developments have adopted the new urbanist principles discussed by Peter Calthorpe in chapter 4. And whereas traditional public housing was financed entirely by HUD and occupied exclusively by low-income residents, HOPE VI communities typically serve a mix of families at various income levels, compete for tenants in the marketplace, and rely on multiple funding sources.

Not every HOPE VI project has successfully implemented all these innovations. Some simply replaced obsolete buildings with better housing, still occupied exclusively by public housing families. But over the life of the program, an increasing share of HOPE VI developments have reflected new standards for design, financing, and occupancy. As illustrated by the case studies in this volume, these innovations completely change the face of public housing, integrating it into attractive, marketable developments that enhance the surrounding neighborhood. Although precise measurement remains elusive, there seems little doubt that some HOPE VI projects have unleashed an impressive market turnaround in their broader communities.

Three studies have assessed the neighborhood effects associated with HOPE VI investment.[8]

The Housing Research Foundation's study of eight sites compared census data from 1990 and 2000 in eight HOPE VI neighborhoods with city averages.

The Boston Housing Authority received a HOPE VI grant in 1996 to redevelop the Orchard Park public housing complex (shown at left in photo above). Demolition, which began in 1997, was followed by a 74 percent drop in violent crime by the end of 1999 (see "Orchard Gardens," Boston Housing Authority, at www.bostonhousing.org/detpages/deptinfo155.html [November 14, 2008]).

The redevelopment of Orchard Park into Orchard Gardens—which was accompanied by a reconnection of the street grid and a reduction of on-site density—is credited with aiding the ongoing revitalization of Boston's Dudley Square neighborhood.

Peter Vanderwarker, photographer

HRF found that the average per capita income of neighborhood residents rose 57 percent faster than citywide average income and that unemployment fell by an average of 10 percentage points although there was no significant net change at the city level. The number of private sector mortgage originations in HOPE VI neighborhoods also was higher—and increased faster—than the average for their respective counties, indicating that the neighborhoods were experiencing increasing rates of economic activity.

Similarly, Abt Associates' interim assessment of outcomes in eleven HOPE VI sites found that key indicators of well-being in most HOPE VI neighborhoods improved faster than in the city as a whole.[9] And a clear majority of people living both inside and outside public housing rated their neighborhoods as better places to live after HOPE VI.[10]

Turbov and Piper focus more explicitly on market changes in the neighborhoods surrounding four highly regarded public housing redevelopment projects: Centennial Place in Atlanta; Park DuValle in Louisville; Manchester in Pittsburgh; and Murphy Park in St. Louis.[11] Median household incomes (figure 10-2) and workforce participation rates rose dramatically in these neighborhoods, reflecting an influx of higher-income, working people. The market-rate housing has succeeded in attracting and retaining both renters and homebuyers who have a choice of housing, and increases in rents over time indicate that market demand is robust. As a result, new unsubsidized investment is now under way in the surrounding neighborhoods. For example, once Atlanta's Centennial Place succeeded in attracting market-rate renters, developers began investing in loft conversions and condominium developments nearby, significantly increasing homeownership in the neighborhood.

Diverse Stakeholders Learn to Work Together

In many cities, the targeted infusion of federal resources has motivated city and state governments and private investors to focus on public housing communities, engage with local housing authorities, and align resources in

Applying new financing and design standards, the Charlotte Housing Authority transformed the Earle Village public housing project (right) into First Ward Place, a mixed-income community of apartments (bottom, foreground) and for-sale homes. Between 1990 and 2000, the neighborhood poverty rate fell 16 percent faster than the citywide average, the high school dropout rate fell 24 percent faster, and homeownership increased 20 percent more, according to Abt Associates' 2003 study.

Figure 10-2. Income Changes in Four HOPE VI Neighborhoods, 1990–2000

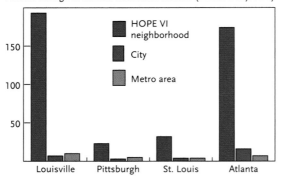

Percent change in median household income (inflation-adjusted)

Source: U.S. Census data, reported in Mindy Turbov and Valerie Piper, "HOPE VI and Mixed Finance Redevelopments: A Catalyst for Neighborhood Renewal" (Brookings, 2005).

new ways. Prior to HOPE VI, many public housing agencies were isolated from other city housing and community development institutions. Mayors and redevelopment directors tended to think of distressed public housing as "HUD's problem," one over which they had no influence and for which they bore no responsibility. But as other chapters in this volume illustrate, the redevelopment of public housing in many cities has engaged mayors, community development officials, state housing agencies, and private sector investors in sustained partnerships.

For example, Louisville's Park DuValle and St. Louis's Murphy Park both had active mayoral leadership from the outset, leveraged funding from numerous sources, and ultimately engaged private investors as well as multiple city agencies in the reconfiguration of streets; redevelopment of parks, playgrounds, and community centers; reconstitution of public schools; and development of new retail shopping facilities.[12] Pittsburgh's Manchester development arose from a partnership between the public housing agency and a community-based organization that included—but extended beyond—the public housing project. Redevelopment was guided by a comprehensive neighborhood plan developed by community residents, and the neighborhood organization remains deeply involved in management and marketing of both the public housing and market-rate units developed with HOPE VI resources.

In some cities, new institutional partnerships have extended beyond and outlasted individual HOPE VI projects. In the District of Columbia, for example, the city government is working with the housing authority to launch its own public housing redevelopment projects, financed in part by a local affordable housing trust fund. San Francisco also is pursuing HOPE VI–like projects with local bond financing. Chicago is replacing or rehabilitating virtually all of its public housing as part of its comprehensive Plan for Transformation, tapping federal public housing capital and HOPE VI funds but also such local sources as tax increment financing.[13] And Atlanta's redevelopment of public housing represents an integral part of the city's larger housing and neighborhood development strategy. In these and other cities, public housing agencies are no longer isolated from larger housing and community development institutions, and public housing communities are seen as inextricably linked to neighborhood health and city vitality.

Public Housing and Public Schools Can Sometimes Be Transformed Together

HOPE VI projects in at least fourteen cities have explicitly included investments in neighborhood public schools in order to improve school quality for poor kids as well as for their new, higher-income neighbors.[14] One of the best-known examples is Atlanta's Centennial Place. Prior to HOPE VI, the neighborhood elementary school served children from the public housing project almost exclusively, and its performance was dismal. In conjunction with HOPE VI, the school got a new building, a new principal, new teachers, and an updated curriculum (developed with assistance from faculty and students at the Georgia Institute of Technology, one of Centennial Place's neighbors). The children of all original residents were entitled to attend the new school, even if they did not move back to the new public housing units. For the most part, the school still serves black children from low-income families, but test scores have climbed to be among the highest in the Atlanta school district, meeting or exceeding state performance standards.[15]

Jefferson Elementary School, located near the Murphy Park housing project, was among the worst in St. Louis, but most of the children in the project did not attend it. Under a court-ordered desegregation plan, three-quarters of the neighborhood children were bused to schools elsewhere in the county. After the public housing was demolished and replaced, Jefferson Elementary reopened as a neighborhood-based school with a community advisory board that had the authority to hire the principal. It has seen significant gains in test scores and is now the school of choice for most children living in the surrounding neighborhood, including those in the redeveloped public housing. It also serves as a neighborhood learning center, offering classes and activities for adults as well as children during evenings and weekends.[16]

Linking school improvements with public housing redevelopment offers tremendous promise. High-quality schools can significantly enhance the life chances of children living in public housing and in the surrounding neighborhood, potentially breaking the cycle of poverty for families that have been cut off from mainstream opportunities. In addition, the quality of a neighborhood's elementary school can be a key factor in attracting middle- and upper-income residents. However, improving local public schools while redeveloping public housing—which requires an additional set of institutional partners, priorities, and constraints—also makes the whole undertaking more complex. And to respond to varied local circumstances, different communities may need to adopt quite different strategies for linking the redevelopment of public housing projects and the improvement of schools.[17]

Rising Property Values Strengthen City Fiscal Health

By removing a major source of blight and jump-starting new investments, HOPE VI projects have the potential to increase property values in their neighborhoods and property tax revenues for their cities.[18] For example, Bair and Fitzgerald found that home values increased roughly 8 to 10 percent for every quarter-mile closer a property was to a HOPE VI site,[19] and an analysis of six Philadelphia HOPE VI sites estimates that between 1995 and 2004, prices of nearby homes increased by an annual average of 9 percent while the average annual rate for the city as a whole was only 6.5 percent. The Philadelphia study concludes that the HOPE VI redevelopment projects raised area home values by more than $200 million, generating more than $4 million in additional property taxes for the city.[20]

Building on those findings, the Urban Institute estimated that demolishing and replacing a prototypical (700-unit) distressed public housing project still remaining in the inventory could boost local tax revenues by $6.5 million over a twenty-year period. Smaller projects, projects developed in weak markets, and projects in locations far from a city's economic "action" would likely generate smaller gains. But even under those circumstances, the anticipated contribution to a city's fiscal health is substantial.[21] New research similarly concludes that HOPE VI redevelopment has often resulted in substantial increases in surrounding house values—and local property tax revenues. A forthcoming study by Zielenbach and Voith finds that variations in impacts on property values reflect both the size of the redevelopment projects and the market potential of their location.[22]

If the demolition of public housing simply shifted the concentration of poverty and distress from one city neighborhood to another, property value gains would be undermined. But HOPE VI redevelopments generally do not involve the construction of large subsidized projects in new locations, nor does relocating low-income families with vouchers significantly affect property values in the receiving neighborhood as long as all of the families are not relocated to the same place. The arrival of a voucher family actually triggers a slight increase in sales prices for homes within a 500-foot radius and has no effect on prices farther away.[23]

Effective Redevelopment Saves Taxpayer Dollars

Not only does HOPE VI have the potential to increase city tax revenues, but it also can save taxpayer dollars by reducing the costs of public programs. Investing in demolition and mixed-income redevelopment can be expected to yield dramatically better outcomes for public housing projects and their residents than leaving distressed public housing in place, with significant cost implications for the public sector.

More specifically, mixed-income redevelopment has been shown to result in markedly improved physical conditions and substantial reductions in crime; in addition, vacancy rates have been much lower than in the original projects. As a consequence, the new public housing developed on HOPE VI sites can be expected to have much lower annual operating and capital costs per unit, and its higher occupancy rates are likely to yield higher tenant rent contributions. Replacing a severely distressed 700-unit project with new mixed-income housing (and using vouchers to help some residents relocate elsewhere) could save an estimated $3.9 million a year in federal housing subsidies while serving the same number of very low-income families.[24]

As Popkin and Cunningham note in chapter 11, most residents of severely distressed public housing redeveloped under HOPE VI have ended up in better-quality housing and safer neighborhoods whether they used vouchers to relocate permanently or returned to the new development. Such changes can contribute to lower rates of obesity and better mental health, which can translate into lower costs to the criminal justice system and lower Medicaid spending, saving the public sector an estimated $248,000 a year in the prototypical, 700-unit HOPE VI project.[25] Over twenty years, the reduced costs of operating public housing and meeting resident needs plus the increased property tax

Table 10-1. Long-Term Public Costs of HOPE VI Demolition and Redevelopment[a]

Twenty-year net present value	No intervention	Demolition and mixed-income redevelopment
Estimated public cost		
Public development cost	0.0	45.6
Project operating/subsidy cost	105.1	46.5
Public cost of resident needs	73.0	70.5
Estimated revenue		
Resident income taxes	0.5	0.5
New property tax revenue	0.0	6.5
Total	177.6	155.6
Net cost	. . .	-22.0

Source: Margery Austin Turner and others, *Estimating the Public Costs and Benefits of HOPE VI Investments: A Methodological Report* (Washington: Urban Institute, 2007).

a. In millions of dollars.

revenues more than pay for the initial public investment in redevelopment. In fact, HOPE VI could actually save the public sector $22 million over a twenty-year period for a typical distressed project still standing in the public housing inventory (see table 10-1).

In fact, the forthcoming study by Zielenbach and Voith of the economic costs and benefits of eight HOPE VI projects in six cities confirms that the investment in the projects often generated significant net gains for their localities and regions. More specifically, redevelopment has reduced crime (and its attendant costs), sparked regional economic growth, increased the local tax base, and enhanced local tax revenues. Net public welfare benefits over the thirty-year life of a HOPE VI project—the net aggregate wealth created for society—are estimated to be in the tens of millions of dollars. And the estimated economic benefits (total indirect and induced spending in the region) are even higher. [26]

Market Context Matters

HOPE VI has the potential to transform neighborhoods and strengthen cities. But it would be unrealistic to expect the same dramatic effects in every neighborhood and every city. Certainly, the quality of a project's design and execution makes a big difference; not every HOPE VI project to date has been well conceived or effectively implemented. But market conditions also matter. Attracting market-rate renters and homebuyers to a previously distressed neighborhood is far more difficult in a city with a weak housing market than in one where housing demand is robust. If a project is unable to trigger new market demand, its spillover effects—for returning residents, the surrounding neighborhood, and the city's fiscal health—will be far more limited.

For example, little change has occurred in the neighborhood surrounding the McGuire Gardens project in Camden, New Jersey, a severely distressed central city with low average income, high unemployment, and a weak housing market. Market conditions there are so weak that HOPE VI redevelopment alone is unlikely to spur significant revitalization.[27] Even in more economically vibrant cities, some public housing projects may be located too far from centers of economic activity to generate significant market demand, at least in the near term. Under such circumstances, a HOPE VI investment may substantially improve housing quality and neighborhood conditions, but it is less likely to result in significant market or fiscal effects.

Therefore, while the revitalization of public housing can have a sizable impact on the revitalization of surrounding neighborhoods, dramatic turnarounds are not likely to be achieved—and should not be expected—everywhere. Moreover, where neighborhood transformation has occurred, questions remain about the extent to which the HOPE VI investment caused the improvements. In many cases, other public sector investments—some of

Washington, D.C.'s Wheeler Creek Estates replaced the Valley Green complex, shown earlier, and an adjacent private property called Skytower. Although mixed-income public housing redevelopments far from economic centers improve housing quality and neighborhood conditions, they may not attract significant new private investment, at least in the near term.

which were launched earlier or in adjacent neighborhoods—may have helped trigger the market turnaround. Or strong local market forces may already have been under way, creating a wave of new demand and investment on which the HOPE VI development and its surrounding neighborhood could capitalize.

Few, if any, HOPE VI projects can claim full credit for the resurgence of market activity in their neighborhoods. Successful revitalization of severely distressed and disinvested communities is almost always the product of a combination of strategies, often pursued over a decade or more, and it is subject to larger economic and demographic forces. For example, in the District of Columbia, a HOPE VI project currently is under way in a long-distressed neighborhood between Capitol Hill and the Anacostia River, where decades of planning for riverfront redevelopment are finally coming to fruition and a new baseball park has just opened, at a time when the city's population is growing and the housing market is hot.[28] There can be no doubt that the distressed public housing contributed to the decline of the neighborhood and that revitalization probably would have been stymied if it had remained in place. But trying to pinpoint the independent contribution of the HOPE VI project to the area's transformation not only is very difficult, it also misses the point. It makes far more sense to think of public housing redevelopment as an essential ingredient of a larger revitalization strategy than to try to differentiate impacts that would not have occurred "but for" HOPE VI.

Neighborhood Recovery May Be Fragile

The benefits of public housing redevelopment—when thoughtfully planned and effectively implemented—can spill over to help turn around long-neglected neighborhoods, attracting new residents and new investments that strengthen a city's social and fiscal health. But it is still too soon to render a final verdict about the sustainability of the new mixed-income communities and the central city revitalization that they are helping to fuel. In particular, the persistence of racial segregation could undermine HOPE VI's long-term benefits to cities.

The concentrated poverty and social isolation of severely distressed public housing developments resulted from policies that explicitly and implicitly promoted racial segregation.[29] Consequently, most severely distressed public housing developments are predominantly African American and typically are located in predominantly black neighborhoods.[30] When the projects are redeveloped, it is considerably easier to attract middle- and high-income black residents than significant numbers of whites, and the evidence to date suggests that the neighborhoods surrounding most HOPE VI sites remain majority black.[31]

Some argue that racial integration is not essential to neighborhood revitalization as long as meaningful income mixing is achieved. They point to successful HOPE VI sites, like Louisville's Park DuValle, that are almost exclusively

African American and have attracted substantial numbers of high-income residents. But for decades, black communities, both rich and poor, have been starved of essential resources, and majority-black communities today still suffer from significant deficits in both public and private investment, even when they are middle-class or affluent.[32] Unfortunately, the three key factors on which the sustainability of HOPE VI neighborhoods hinges—continued private sector investment, quality public sector services, and safety—historically have been denied to black neighborhoods.

Many minority communities—including affluent suburbs like Prince George's County, Maryland—still lack the department stores, sit-down restaurants, specialty stores, and other retail amenities of comparable white communities.[33] If markets were truly color blind, one would expect more retail development to flow to these underserved communities, but research suggests that many business owners still perceive black communities to be unacceptably high risk. They may fear, for example, that even if residents have high disposable incomes, customers and employees will be more likely to shoplift and white employees will not be willing to work there.[34] Lenders have also been less willing to invest in predominantly black communities, or they have offered predatory loans and loan terms that strip wealth from black homeowners rather than help them build wealth.[35]

Public sector agencies also have a history of neglecting or underserving predominantly black communities, raising questions about whether schools and other public services will receive the investment that they need to meet high standards of performance. In majority-black jurisdictions, it is possible that middle- and upper-income African Americans now wield sufficient clout to demand quality public services. But again, the Prince George's County example raises concerns; despite the county's overall affluence, its school system is struggling with low achievement levels and problems in attracting and retaining qualified teachers and administrators.[36] Finally, research indicates that middle-class black neighborhoods are more vulnerable to social disorder and distress than comparable white neighborhoods, both because of their proximity to distressed neighborhoods and because they lack wealth and political clout.[37]

In sum, policymakers and practitioners must recognize that racial prejudice and inequality may still stack the decks against black neighborhoods, even those that are economically diverse. Enhancing the vitality of predominantly black communities constitutes an important goal, but HOPE VI alone cannot reverse long-standing patterns of residential segregation. Public officials must acknowledge that the persistence of racial segregation poses ongoing challenges, they must monitor the health of HOPE VI neighborhoods over time, and they must to be prepared to make additional investments to ensure the neighborhoods' long-term sustainability.

Majority-black communities today still suffer from significant deficits in both public and private investment, even when they are middle-class or affluent.

Cities Need Affordable Housing

If one potential threat to the sustainability of HOPE VI revitalization is insufficient market activity in the surrounding neighborhood, the flip side is the possibility of runaway gentrification and the loss of affordable housing options citywide. When the housing market is hot—with low vacancy rates and rapidly rising rents—the loss of deeply subsidized public housing units that is typically associated with HOPE VI may undermine a city's ability to address the problem of affordable housing. In fact, most redevelopment projects involve "de-densification," building fewer units on the new site than there were in the original public housing project. And in order to achieve income mixing, only a fraction of the new units have the deep subsidies needed to make them affordable for very low-income families.[38]

Estimates suggest that HOPE VI will replace only about two-thirds of all the original public housing units in the affected properties.[39] However, roughly one-third of all the original units were unoccupied at the time of redevelopment, and of those, some were uninhabitable. Thus, the number of replacement units may come close to the original number of occupied units. In most market environments, housing vouchers do a good job of making up the difference.[40] But in cities like Seattle, San Francisco, and Washington, D.C., where HOPE VI redevelopment has coincided with renewed demand for central city living, voucher recipients may have difficulty using their assistance.[41] Rents in previously affordable neighborhoods have shot out of reach for all but the most affluent, and opportunities to achieve meaningful income mixing by preserving deeply subsidized housing have been lost.

The consequence is not just increased hardship for individual households, but a larger threat to the city's capacity to accommodate a mix of residents at different income levels. Although cities should certainly welcome the return of middle- and upper-income families, their long-term social and economic health will be compromised if they become completely unaffordable for low-wage workers, the elderly, and people with disabilities. Therefore, if HOPE VI is to achieve its full potential as a contributor to city health and vitality, some markets may require additional investment in truly affordable rental housing.

Looking to the Future

HOPE VI has proven the potential of public housing redevelopment as a tool for restoring neighborhoods, catalyzing revitalization, and strengthening the health of cities. To date, HOPE VI projects have significantly reduced concentrations of poverty and crime in surrounding neighborhoods, replaced poorly designed and obsolete structures with high-quality housing that harmonizes with local architecture, and created communities that serve a mix of households of different income levels. In many instances, HOPE VI has been creatively linked with other public and private sector investments, so that redevelopment extends beyond the immediate public housing site to the surrounding area, upgrading streets and sidewalks, parks, community centers, recreational facilities, and public schools.

Such investments appear to have helped catalyze real market turnarounds in central city neighborhoods that had long been given up as hopelessly distressed. Middle- and high-income households—including homebuyers—are moving in, market rents and sale prices are rising, and new, private sector investment in both homes and retail businesses is taking root. A successful HOPE VI project can significantly enhance property values in the surrounding neighborhood, substantially increasing city tax revenues over time.

As part of a long-planned revitalization of the neighborhood just southeast of the U.S. Capitol, the twenty-three-acre Arthur Capper and Carrollsburg public housing sites are being redeveloped as a mixed-income community of apartment buildings, including senior housing (right) and soon townhomes, a community center, and retail and office space. Blocks away, fans lingering outside the new Washington Nationals ballpark well after the last pitch was thrown (below) suggest that the city's efforts to coordinate investment in the once-desolate area are beginning to have an impact.

The magnitude of neighborhood improvements varies widely across sites, and not enough research has rigorously addressed the issue of neighborhood impacts to try to pinpoint the determinants of success. Nonetheless, the evidence strongly suggests that a visionary plan, durable partnerships among public and private actors, high-quality project design, and a commitment to income mixing are all essential ingredients. When a HOPE VI project is viewed narrowly as a single development deal, is planned and implemented primarily by the public housing agency, and is designed exclusively to provide decent housing for tenants with few other affordable options, it is unlikely to change the market dynamics in the surrounding neighborhood, attract residents who can afford other options, or catalyze new private sector investment.

In order to maximize positive impacts on neighborhoods and cities—and avoid unintended, negative impacts—HOPE VI projects should not be treated as stand-alone investments, managed primarily by the local housing authority and HUD. Instead, they should be considered a critical component in a city's larger neighborhood revitalization and affordable housing strategies. Only then can they fully realize their potential to catalyze neighborhood revitalization, reverse old patterns of racial segregation and poverty, and provide affordable housing in communities of choice and opportunity.

Four key principles should guide efforts to integrate public housing redevelopment into cities' larger, "place conscious" revitalization and affordable housing strategies:

— First, cities should choose sites where the blighting effect of distressed public housing is substantial and where conditions seem ripe for achieving spillover benefits.

— Second, public housing redevelopment should be implemented in conjunction with other city investments to capitalize on locational and market assets and opportunities.

— Third, cities should link the redevelopment of public housing with a larger affordable housing strategy that expands the availability of affordable options in healthy neighborhoods throughout the city, using tools such as inclusionary zoning, low-income housing tax credits, federal block grants, resources from local affordable housing trust funds, project-based vouchers, and voucher mobility counseling.

— Fourth, cities must remain committed to redeveloped neighborhoods over the long haul to ensure that their turnaround is both equitable and sustainable. That means monitoring the market response over time and stepping in with supplemental investments to protect neighborhood vitality or preserve affordable housing options.

When HOPE VI was launched, most people thought that the future of distressed central city neighborhoods was bleak. The notion that public housing redevelopment could help turn around whole neighborhoods and strengthen cities' fiscal health seemed naively optimistic. But in a significant number of cities, HOPE VI investments—imaginatively planned, well designed, and competently implemented—have coincided with positive market and demographic forces to accomplish just that.

····· Endnotes ·····

1. Note that HUD did not explicitly require housing authorities to tie their HOPE VI redevelopment plans to neighborhood revitalization until 1996.

2. For further discussion of the ill effects of concentrated minority poverty, see Douglas S. Massey and Nancy Denton, *American Apartheid: Segregation and the Making of the Underclass* (Harvard University Press, 1993); Ingrid Gould Ellen and Margery Austin Turner, "Does Neighborhood Matter? Assessing Recent Evidence," *Housing Policy Debate* 8, no. 4 (1997): 833–66; and Janet R. Pack, "Poverty and Urban Public Expenditures," *Urban Studies* 35, no. 11 (1998): 1995–2019.

3. See Margery Austin Turner and others, *Estimating the Public Costs and Benefits of HOPE VI Investments: A Methodological Report* (Washington: Urban Institute, 2007). This analysis was conducted for 6,414 census tracts in metropolitan areas that had some public housing, at least 100 non–public housing households, and non-missing values for key analytical variables. Chicago, New York City, and Puerto Rico were excluded from this analysis because some developments operated by these three entities extended to entire census tracts and not just single public housing developments within a tract.

4. Turner, *Estimating the Public Costs and Benefits of HOPE VI Investments*.

5. Techwood (Atlanta); Orchard Park (Boston); Earle Village (Charlotte); Quigg Newton (Denver); Kennedy Brothers (El Paso); Hillside Terrace (Milwaukee); Richard Allen Homes (Philadelphia); and Holly Park (Seattle). Sean Zielenbach, *The Economic Impact of HOPE VI on Neighborhoods* (Washington: Housing Research Foundation, 2002).

6. The study focused on eleven sites but thirteen developments (in two cities two separate public housing complexes were being redeveloped under the same HOPE VI grant). The sites, listed by the name of the public housing complexes replaced, were McGuire Gardens (Camden); King Kennedy Estates and Outhwaite Homes (Cleveland); Hillside Terrace (Milwaukee); Lockwood Gardens (Oakland); Bernal Dwellings and Plaza East (San Francisco); Lafayette Homes (Baltimore); Mission Main (Boston); Elm Haven (New Haven); Earle Village (Charlotte); Ellen Wilson (Washington, D.C.); Techwood–Clark Howell (Atlanta). Mary Joel Holin and others, "Interim Assessment of the HOPE VI Program: Cross-Site Report," prepared by Abt Associates for the U.S. Department of Housing and Urban Development, September 19, 2003, pp. iii, 103 (www.abtassociates.com/reports/20030_RETASK-XSITE_03.pdf).

7. Centennial Place (formerly Techwood, Atlanta); Park DuValle (Louisville); Manchester (Pittsburgh); and Murphy Park (St. Louis). Mindy Turbov and Valerie Piper, "HOPE VI and Mixed-Finance Redevelopments: A Catalyst for Neighborhood Renewal" (Brookings, 2005).

8. These studies are discussed more extensively in G. Thomas Kingsley and others, *Lessons from HOPE VI for the Future of Public Housing* (Washington: Urban Institute, 2004).

9. Holin and others, "Interim Assessment of the HOPE VI Program."

10. These figures are based on surveys of residents in and around the HOPE VI sites; they exclude results from Boston and Atlanta.

11. Turbov and Piper, "HOPE VI and Mixed-Finance Redevelopments."

12. Though technically the Murphy Park redevelopment received no HOPE VI funding, it is considered among the family of HOPE VI redevelopments because it served as a prototype for HOPE VI, as explained by Richard Baron in chapter 3.

13. Under the Plan for Transformation, 25,000 units of public housing will be rehabilitated or replaced as the Chicago Housing Authority and its partners demolish and redevelop former high-rise public housing sites as mixed-income communities and rehabilitate senior and low-rise family public housing sites. Nine HOPE VI grants are helping fund the initiative. For details see chapter 6.

14. See Martin D. Abravanel, Robin E. Smith, and Elizabeth C. Cove, *Linking Public Housing Revitalization to Neighborhood School Improvement* (Washington: Urban Institute, 2006).

15. Turbov and Piper, "HOPE VI and Mixed-Finance Redevelopments."

16. Ibid.

17. Although conventional wisdom may suggest that schools serving deeply distressed neighborhoods typically are failing the children who live in those communities, a single school does not always serve the majority of children in the neighborhood; moreover, targeted school improvements may already be in place, or families may already have been offered better options under local desegregation or choice plans. See Abravanel, Smith, and Cove, *Linking Public Housing Revitalization to Neighborhood School Improvement.*

18. Previous research examining the impacts of subsidized housing on neighborhood property values has found small effects, sometimes negative and sometimes positive. See Chang-Moo Lee, Dennis P. Culhane, and Susan M. Wachter, "The Differential Impacts of Federally Assisted Housing Programs on Nearby Property Values: A Philadelphia Case Study," *Housing Policy Debate 10,* no. 1 (1999): 75–93; Robert A. Simons and David S. Sharkey, "Jump-Starting Cleveland's New Urban Housing Markets: Do the Potential Fiscal Benefits Justify the Public Subsidy Costs?" *Housing Policy Debate 8,* no. 1 (1997): 143–71.

19. Edward Bair and John M. Fitzgerald, "Hedonic Estimation and Policy Significance of the Impact of HOPE VI on Neighborhood Property Values," *Review of Policy Research 22,* no. 6 (2005): 771–86. This study used decennial census data to estimate residential property values using a hedonic real estate price model; the results apply to properties within a radius of 1.5 miles of the development. Zielenbach and Turbov and Piper also find evidence that HOPE VI developments increase property values in the surrounding neighborhoods, although neither of these studies controls rigorously for other factors that might have contributed to neighborhood changes. See Zielenbach, *The Economic Impact of HOPE VI on Neighborhoods,* and Turbov and Piper, "HOPE VI and Mixed-Finance Redevelopments."

20. Because other public sector investments occurred in these neighborhoods at the same time, the authors attribute only a fraction of the estimated property value gains to the HOPE VI investments. See Philadelphia Housing Authority and Econsult Corporation, "Economic Impacts of PHA Housing Redevelopments on Adjacent Neighborhoods" (Philadelphia Housing Authority, 2005).

21. These estimates represent the present discounted value of annual increases in residential property tax revenues, based on average effective tax rates for a national sample of central cities and intermediate estimates of the property value gains attributable to HOPE VI redevelopment. For details, see Turner and others, *Estimating the Public Costs and Benefits of HOPE VI Investments.*

22. Sean Zielenbach and Richard Voith, "Assessing the Economic Spillover of Major Public Housing Redevelopment: An Economic Cost-Benefit Analysis of HOPE VI Developments" (2008 draft undergoing review by the MacArthur Foundation, which sponsored the study). The HOPE VI developments included in the study are First Ward (Charlotte), Guinotte Manor

and Villa del Sol (Kansas City), Mission Main and Orchard Gardens (Boston), New Holly (Seattle), North Beach (San Francisco), and Town Homes and Wheeler Creek (Washington, D.C.).

23. On the other hand, when a large number of apartments in the same immediate vicinity were occupied by voucher recipients, nearby sales prices declined. These negative price effects occurred in minority neighborhoods and moderate- to low-value neighborhoods with already declining values. See George Galster and Anne Zobel, "Will Dispersed Housing Programmes Reduce Social Problems in the U.S.?" *Housing Studies 13*, no. 5 (September 1998): 605–22; and George C. Galster, "A Review of the Existing Research on the Effects of Federally Assisted Housing Programs on Neighboring Residential Property Values" (National Association of Realtors, September 2002).

24. Simulations assume that 63 percent of 701 units in the original, distressed project were occupied and that the project is replaced with a lower-density, mixed-income development. One hundred fifty-six units in the new development receive deep public housing subsidies, and an additional 285 families receive housing vouchers. Rents from market-rate units in the mixed-income development are assumed to cover operating costs and debt service. For detailed calculations, see Turner and others, *Estimating the Public Costs and Benefits of HOPE VI Investments.*

25. For detailed calculations, see Turner and others, *Estimating the Public Costs and Benefits of HOPE VI Investments.*

26. Zielenbach and Voith, "Assessing the Economic Spillover of Major Public Housing Redevelopment." The study defines public welfare benefits as the net additional aggregate wealth created for society, including property value appreciation accruing to owners, additional "implied" rental subsidies received by public housing tenants as a result of increased market rents, and savings to society from crimes not committed. Economic benefits are defined as the total indirect and induced spending in the region associated with the HOPE VI redevelopment, including spending on construction and ongoing maintenance as well as increased consumer spending resulting from rising neighborhood household incomes.

27. Holin and others, "Interim Assessment of the HOPE VI Program."

28. The D.C. Housing Authority was awarded a $35 million HOPE VI grant in 2001 to replace the Arthur Capper and Carrollsburg public housing complexes, which together had 707 units, with a new mixed-income community of nearly 2,000 units, at least 707 of which will be public housing.

29. Because public housing so explicitly segregated on the basis of race and because most distressed public housing developments are predominantly African American, our focus here is on black-white issues. See Massey and Denton, *American Apartheid.*

30. See Linda Fosburg, Susan J. Popkin, and Gretchen Locke, *An Historical and Baseline Assessment of HOPE VI*, vol. 1 (U.S. Department of Housing and Urban Development, 1996); John Goering and Ali Kamely, "Recent Research on Racial Segregation and Poverty Concentration in Public Housing in the United States," *Urban Affairs Review* 32, no. 5 (1997): 723–45; Susan J. Popkin and others, *HOPE VI Panel Study: Baseline Report* (Washington: Urban Institute, 2002).

31. Holin and others, "Interim Assessment of the HOPE VI Program." Moreover, as Susan Popkin and Mary Cunningham discuss in chapter 11 of this volume, most of the original residents of HOPE VI developments who relocated with vouchers still live in majority-minority neighborhoods.

32. Mary Pattillo, "Black Middle-Class Neighborhoods," *Annual Review of Sociology* 31 (2005): 305–29.

33. Sheryll Cashin, *The Failures of Integration: How Race and Class Are Undermining the American Dream* (New York: PublicAffairs, 2004).

34. Amy Helling and David S. Sawicki, "Race and Residential Accessibility to Shopping and Services," *Housing Policy Debate* 14 (2003): 69–101.

35. See Melvin L. Oliver and Thomas M. Shapiro. *Black Wealth/White Wealth: A New Perspective on Racial Inequality* (New York: Routledge, 1997); U.S. Department of Housing and Urban Development, *New Standards for a New Century: The Transformation of HUD's Systems for Monitoring and Enforcing the Quality of HUD-Assisted Housing* (2000); James H. Carr and Lopa Kolluri, "Predatory Lending: An Overview," in *Financial Services in Distressed Communities: Issues and Answers* (Washington: Fannie Mae Foundation, 2001); and Paul S. Calem, Kevin Gillen, and Susan Wachter, "The Neighborhood Distribution of Subprime Mortgage Lending," *Journal of Real Estate Finance and Economics* 29, no. 4 (December 2004): 393–410.

36. Cashin, *The Failures of Integration.*

37. See Pattillo, "Black Middle-Class Neighborhoods"; Robert D. Crutchfield, Ross L. Matsueda, and Kevin Drakulich, "Race, Labor Markets, and Neighborhood Violence," in *The Many Colors of Crime: Inequalities of Race, Ethnicity, and Crime in America,* edited by Ruth D. Peterson, Lauren J. Krivo, and John Hagan (New York University Press, 2006). However, other scholars argue that socioeconomic factors other than race explain disparities in crime rates. See Robert J. Sampson, Stephen W. Raudenbush, and Felton Earls, "Neighborhoods and Violent Crime: A Multilevel Study of Collective Efficacy," *Science* 277, no. 5328 (1997): 918–24; and Edward Shihadeh and Wesley Shrum, "Serious Crime in Urban Neighborhoods: Is There a Race Effect?" *Sociological Spectrum* 24, no. 4 (July–August 2004): 507–33.

38. As Popkin and Cunningham discuss in chapter 11, most households that lived in properties that were later redeveloped were given housing vouchers to find replacement housing, although some were moved into other public housing developments.

39. Orlando Cabrera, assistant secretary for public and Indian housing, U.S. Department of Housing and Urban Development, in testimony before the Financial Services Subcommittee of the U.S. House of Representatives, *Reauthorization of the HOPE VI Program,* 110 Cong. 1 sess., June 21, 2007.

40. This assumes that the total number of housing vouchers available in the community increased in response to the HOPE VI demolition and that the federal voucher program is sustained and adequately funded over time.

41. For example, see Margery Austin Turner and others, *Housing in the Nation's Capital: 2005* (Washington: Urban Institute, 2005).

SUSAN J. POPKIN AND
MARY K. CUNNINGHAM

Has HOPE VI Transformed Residents' Lives?

When Chicago's Ida B. Wells Homes became a HOPE VI site, it was like a war zone, plagued by sporadic episodes of gang violence, random shootings, and overwhelming drug trafficking. Adding to the pervasive disorder were the many vacant units and the hundreds of squatters who slept in the stairwells. The public housing development, which was located on the south side of the city, was in desperate need of repair: the heat was unreliable, elevators rarely worked, toilets overflowed, apartments were overrun with cockroaches and vermin, and buildings were scarred with graffiti. Few Wells residents had full-time jobs, only half had graduated from high school, and most had never lived anywhere but in public housing. Carla, who was 14 and lived in Wells before HOPE VI, talked of her fears: "I don't really like the neighborhood. There's too many shootings and killings going on. A lot of the little kids are starting to come out and play because it's the summer, and it's really not safe enough, because you never know when they're going to shoot or, you know, drive by. You never know."[1]

Phyllis Williams (second from right) holds the hand of her grandson Rea-Sean Camphor as she and her family, son DeAndre Williams and great-nieces Arlisa and Felecia Payton, walk through their new neighborhood on the South Side of Chicago.

Severely distressed public housing developments like Ida B. Wells circa 2000 are among the most troubled communities in the nation. Families living in these communities are likely to suffer some of the most severe consequences of concentrated poverty—most devastating, the profound and lingering effects of constant violence and disorder. HOPE VI was designed to improve the life chances of public housing residents trapped in such adversity. Taking note of research on the Gautreaux program, which found that helping families move to better neighborhoods dramatically improved their lives (see chapter 5), policymakers hoped to create healthier, less economically and racially isolated communities for these families.[2]

The HOPE VI Panel Study, the only national study of whether life improved for the former residents of public housing transformed under HOPE VI, found a more mixed picture. According to the study, whose findings are explored in this chapter, there were dramatic improvements in quality of housing, neighborhood safety, community poverty rates, and other indicators of well-being

Because of the gangs at the Ida B. Wells housing development in Chicago in the 1990s, the Chicago Housing Authority tenant patrol escorted school-children to and from the elevators.

© Ralf-Finn Hestoft/ Corbis.

for those who moved to private market housing or back to the redeveloped communities.[3] Critics' worst fears—that large numbers of residents would become homeless as a result of HOPE VI or end up without assistance—were not realized.[4] Still, movers reported new challenges, particularly being able to pay increased utility costs, and while they moved to lower-poverty communities, their new neighborhoods still were predominantly minority.

Further, the substantial minority of residents who stayed behind in traditional public housing—many of whom had problems that made them hard to house—did not experience any improvements. Finally, because of the low rates of return of former residents to redeveloped sites, even this comprehensive study leaves important questions about the potential for mixed-income developments unanswered. The study does suggest new directions for policy development and research and areas for renewed attention, in particular the sustainability of mixed-income housing and whether its potential to improve the lives of low-income public housing families can be fully realized.

Relocation under HOPE VI

The primary goals of the HOPE VI program are to "improve the living conditions for residents living in severely distressed public housing" and to "provide housing that will avoid or decrease the concentration of very poor families."⁵ Initially, the architects of the program envisioned temporarily relocating original residents in order to allow for demolition and reconstruction; once reconstruction was complete, residents were to move back to new apartments in a revitalized development. However, as the program matured and policymakers began to see creating mixed-income communities as the best strategy for improving neighborhoods, it became clear that not all residents would be able to return. Shifting to the mixed-income model meant that generally the new development would have fewer deeply subsidized units for the lowest-income households and that many residents would need to find other housing. Permanently relocating residents and ensuring that they are provided with housing options that support the program's goals has been the most challenging aspect of the HOPE VI program.

As are any federal agencies that displace residents, housing authorities are required by the federal Uniform Relocation Act to provide affected residents with a "comparable unit" and to cover moving expenses.⁶ Typical relocation services include moving expenses and assistance in finding a new public housing or voucher unit. Generally, housing agencies have gone further, assisting with the actual move. Residents typically are offered two choices: to rent a private unit with a voucher or to move to another public housing unit. Some residents also are offered the option of returning to the revitalized HOPE VI site when it is complete, although eligibility requirements (proof of employment, drug testing, criminal background check) could preclude them from being admitted.⁷ Relocation services and policies vary considerably across sites and even within the same city, as housing authorities with multiple HOPE VI sites learn from experience and redefine their services.

For children living in public housing, barren or restricted play areas (Ida B. Wells below right and Robert Taylor Homes below left) have long been a product of the physical isolation and high crime that HOPE VI sought to address.

The most recent HUD figures indicate that more than 72,000 households have been relocated under HOPE VI.[8] The sheer magnitude of the undertaking has made it extremely challenging; moreover, few housing authorities have had any previous experience in conducting large-scale relocations or providing needy households with adequate services and support.[9] During the early years of the HOPE VI program, HUD provided relatively little oversight of relocation services; as a result, some residents ended up little better off—if at all—than they were in their original distressed housing.[10] Early on, the failure to track resident outcomes led to a number of critical questions about what was happening to residents.[11]

To answer those questions, the Urban Institute launched the HOPE VI Panel Study, the only national study that focused on relocation over the longer term, surveying neighborhood conditions, physical and mental health, and socioeconomic outcomes for original residents of five HOPE VI housing projects that underwent redevelopment beginning in mid- to late 2001. The five projects were Shore Park/Shore Terrace in Atlantic City, New Jersey; Ida B. Wells Homes/Wells Extension/Madden Park Homes in Chicago; Few Gardens in Durham, North Carolina; Easter Hill in Richmond, California; and East Capitol Dwellings in Washington, D.C. Three waves of survey data were collected from 887 heads of household from 2001 to 2005; in addition to the quantitative data collected, the research team conducted in-depth interviews with a subsample of adults and children.[12]

By 2005, redevelopment was under way at all of the sites, although it had not been completed at any of them. A minority (16 percent) of the families in the HOPE VI Panel Study were still living in their original housing; those respondents were from either Atlantic City's Shore Park or Chicago's Wells Homes, where the housing authorities were relocating residents in stages. The majority (84 percent) of the families in the panel study had relocated from the five original housing projects. The largest number of families—43 percent—had received vouchers and moved to private market housing, and 22 percent had moved into other traditional public housing developments. Another 10 percent were renting private market units with no assistance, 5 percent were living in the new HOPE VI redevelopment, and 4 percent had become homeowners. Approximately 1 percent of the HOPE VI Panel Study respondents were either homeless or in prison.

The slow pace of redevelopment means that it can take years before former residents are able to return to new housing; therefore it is not surprising that only 5 percent of panel study respondents had moved into a newly remodeled HOPE VI unit by the 2005 follow-up. The greatest share of former residents who had moved back into redeveloped units (14 percent) was found in Atlantic City's Shore Park, where the housing authority was building a revitalized unit for every household that wanted one. Other research suggests that resident return rates to HOPE VI sites overall have varied considerably, from less than 10 percent to 75 percent, with the largest share of residents returning to housing that was rehabilitated rather than demolished and rebuilt. Based on that evidence, it seems likely that the final figures for returning residents for the study sites will increase somewhat over time but remain relatively low. Thus, for most original residents of HOPE VI sites overall, HOPE VI has meant relocation, not living in a new, mixed-income community.

Vouchers and Private Market Housing

Not returning to a site did not necessarily indicate a poor outcome—many panel study respondents viewed vouchers as an opportunity to move to a better neighborhood and showed little interest in returning.[13] Although most residents had not—and likely will not—move back, the majority had experienced meaningful improvement in their quality of life as a result of relocation under HOPE VI. Respondents who moved to the private market or to mixed-income developments reported substantial improvement in the quality of their housing. At baseline, in 2001, respondents from all five sites reported intolerable and hazardous housing conditions; in 2005, circumstances had improved significantly for those respondents who had moved to the private market. For example, while slightly more than half of respondents who ultimately moved to the private market reported having two or more housing problems—such as mold, broken plumbing, or cockroach infestations—at baseline, just a quarter of voucher holders and unassisted renters reported two or more problems in 2005. In contrast, those who remained in traditional public housing— either their original development or a different one—experienced virtually no improvement in housing quality over time. About 40 percent of those who had moved to other public housing and about 60 percent of those who were living in their original public housing units reported having two or more problems at baseline and at the 2005 follow-up.[14]

Phyllis Williams and her family walk through their neighborhood on Chicago's South Side. They moved with the help of mobility counseling when the public housing in which they had lived was redeveloped.

Beyond improvements in basic housing quality, relocation had a profound impact on residents' life circumstances. While most respondents were not living in new, mixed-income developments, those who had left traditional public housing were living in communities that were much less poor. All five of the HOPE VI Panel Study developments were located in extremely high-poverty communities, with poverty rates of more than 40 percent. After relocation, half of those renting in the private market were living in neighborhoods that had poverty rates below 20 percent—despite the fact that the HOPE VI program did not provide mobility counseling to encourage and assist residents to move to low-poverty communities. Another indicator of improved neighborhood quality was that private market relocatees were living in communities with lower unemployment rates—about 5 percentage points lower than rates in their original public housing neighborhoods.[15]

However, while relocatees were living in less poor neighborhoods, there was little change in racial segregation—nearly all HOPE VI Panel Study families moved into predominantly minority neighborhoods. And, while private market movers were living in less distressed communities, residents who relocated to other public housing developments had not experienced the same benefits— they were living in communities only slightly less poor and no less racially segregated than those in which they were living in 2001, at baseline.[16]

The "Safety Benefit" of Relocation

Fear of crime has profound implications, creating stress and social isolation among people. The proportion of panel study respondents overall reporting "big problems" with drug sales in their community dropped from 78 percent at baseline to 47 percent in 2003 and declined even further, to 33 percent, in 2005—a drop of 45 percentage points. The trends for virtually every measure of neighborhood safety showed the same dramatic decline.[17]

The trends for respondents who had moved to mixed-income developments or to the private market (with vouchers or on their own) were even more striking. In 2005, Nicole, a voucher holder from Richmond's Easter Hill, described the best things about her new neighborhood: "There's no gun violence. There's no drugs. There is no alcohol. There's no bottles, broken glass, and everything and everywhere."[18] Figure 11-1, which shows the trends in respondent reports of "big problems" with drug trafficking by housing assistance status, dramatically illustrates the "safety benefit" that relocatees gained from moving out of distressed public housing. Respondents reported extraordinary improvements in their conditions. For example, while about 80 percent of voucher holders and HOPE VI movers (those who moved into the new, mixed-income communities) had reported big problems with drug trafficking in their original

Figure 11-1. **HOPE VI Panel Study Respondents Reporting That Drug Selling in Their Neighborhood Is a "Big Problem," by Type of Housing**

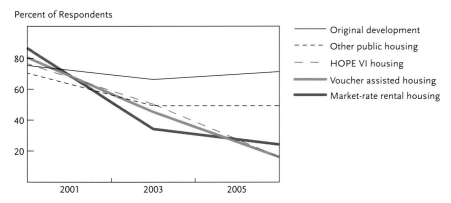

Percent of Respondents

——— Original development
– – – – Other public housing
— – — HOPE VI housing
——— Voucher assisted housing
——— Market-rate rental housing

neighborhoods at baseline, only 16 percent reported the same problems in their new neighborhoods in 2005.

Employment Expectations

In addition to providing residents with an improved environment, the HOPE VI program sought to help them attain self-sufficiency. However, while the panel study results document dramatic improvements in quality of life for many respondents, there were no changes in employment or self-sufficiency for private market movers, the few HOPE VI movers, or those who remained in traditional public housing.[19] At baseline, 48 percent of the working-age respondents were not working, even part-time—the same share as at the 2003 and the 2005 follow-ups. Findings from the panel study suggest that standard HOPE VI relocation and community support services are unlikely to affect employment or address the many factors that keep extremely disadvantaged residents out of the labor force. Most such residents probably will require more intensive employment support and other services to be able to address the complex problems that have made it difficult for them to maintain steady employment.

A major factor affecting employment status is health, and HOPE VI Panel Study respondents were in extremely poor health. In 2005, two of every five respondents (41 percent) rated their overall health as either "fair" or "poor."[20] At every age level, respondents were much more likely to describe their health as fair or poor than other adults overall, and they even were more likely to do so than black women, a group with higher-than-average rates of poor health. Further, respondents reported high rates of a range of chronic, debilitating conditions, including arthritis, asthma, obesity, depression, diabetes, hypertension, and stroke. When residents had such conditions, because of poor health care or living in a stressful environment, they were severely debilitated by them—for example, while many people have diabetes, many of the diabetic respondents suffered from complications like heart disease and circulatory problems. Underscoring the debility caused by illnesses, 40 percent of respondents reported moderate or severe difficulty with mobility (being able to climb a flight of stairs, walk four blocks, or stand on their feet for two hours).

Mental health also was a very serious problem for respondents. Not only depression, but reported rates of anxiety and other indicators were very high: overall, 29 percent of HOPE VI Panel Study respondents indicated poor mental health. Relocation seems to have reduced anxiety and perhaps depression for private market movers, but it had no impact on any other health condition.

Analysis of the panel data shows that health problems are by far the biggest barrier to employment—and that moving to the private market or mixed-income housing made no difference in employment outcomes. Among working-age respondents, nearly a third (32 percent) reported poor health, and

Figure 11-2. **Employment Barriers and Employment Status among Working Age HOPE VI Panel Respondents**

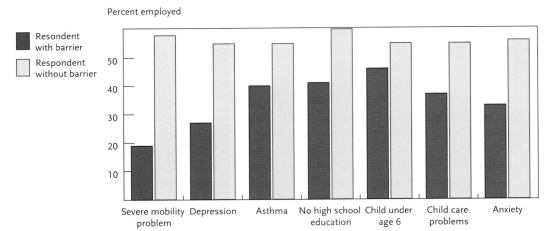

Source: 2005 HOPE VI Panel Study.

most of them (62 percent) were unemployed. As figure 11-2 shows, the strongest predictor of not working was having severe difficulty with physical mobility: less than half of the residents with any mobility problems (38 percent) and less than a quarter of those with severe problems were employed in 2005. In fact, a typical respondent with no employment barriers had a roughly 82 percent chance of being employed; severe mobility problems lowered the probability by 40 percentage points.

Depression also substantially reduced the probability of being employed, as did having been diagnosed with asthma. While health was clearly the biggest obstacle to obtaining and keeping a job for HOPE VI Panel Study respondents, other factors affected employment as well. Specifically, not having a high school diploma, having children under the age of six, and having problems obtaining child care also reduced the probability of employment for working-age respondents.

Making Ends Meet

While HOPE VI residents who moved to private market housing with vouchers were doing well in many ways, findings from the panel study show that many were having difficulty making ends meet.[21] Moving out of public housing presents new financial management challenges: private market property managers can be less forgiving of late rent payments than public housing managers, making it imperative to pay the rent on time. Also, since utilities are generally included in the rent in public housing, many former public housing residents are unused to paying utility bills. They may find coping with the seasonal variation in utility costs, particularly the high cost of heating in winter, or spikes in the cost of natural gas very daunting.

At the 2005 follow-up, voucher holders were significantly more likely than public housing movers to report financial hardships related to paying utilities and providing adequate food for their family. Nearly half (45 percent) of voucher holders reported trouble paying their utility bills, compared with just 8 percent of residents in public housing. Likewise, voucher holders (62 percent) were more likely than public housing households (47 percent) to report financial hardship in paying for food. However, voucher holders were significantly less likely than public housing residents to be late paying their rent. These findings suggest that, when faced with the trade-offs, most voucher holders chose to pay their rent on time to avoid risking their housing and instead delayed paying their utility bills and cut back on food or other items.

Comments from Shenice, a voucher holder from Chicago's Wells Homes, illustrate the financial challenges facing private market relocatees: "We really had to use our gas—and it was high—and got behind, and I was at risk . . . I did end up getting on the payment plan. But this is the school season, so what am I going to do about uniforms and everything? My kids have school fees, my high school kids, and it's hard on me right now."[22] This problem is likely to also affect residents who move to mixed-income developments where utilities are not included in the rent.

"Hard-to-House" Residents

The HOPE VI Panel Study results show that "hard-to-house" residents—families coping with multiple, complex problems, such as mental illness, severe physical illness, substance abuse, large numbers of young children, weak employment histories, and criminal records—were less likely than other residents to realize significant improvements in their quality of life as a result of HOPE VI revitalization. Findings from the panel study baseline showed that such residents made up a substantial proportion of the population at all five sites and more than two-thirds of the households in Chicago's Wells Homes and Washington's East Capitol Dwellings. In 2005, analysis showed that at every site, hard-to-house families were more likely to end up in traditional public housing than in the private market; they therefore ended up little better off than they were at baseline. Placing them in other traditional developments—or, as in Atlantic City's Shore Park and Chicago's Wells Homes, leaving them in parts of the development that were awaiting revitalization—may well have kept them from becoming homeless. But concentrating families with multiple problems in a few traditional public housing projects may well mean that those projects rapidly become as distressed as—or even more distressed than—the developments from which the families came.

Most interview respondents who moved into other public housing said that their new developments still had substantial problems with crime and disorder, and they described feeling unsafe because of pervasive drug trafficking, gambling, and sporadic shootings in neighborhood streets. As figure 11-1 shows, the proportion of those who reported "big problems" with drug sales declined from 70 percent at baseline to just under 50 percent in 2005, after they had moved to other public housing. Although that change represents a statistical improvement, it nonetheless means that residents are still living in communities that are dominated by drug trafficking and violent crime and only slightly less dangerous than their original developments. Further, figure 11-1 shows that the 16 percent of respondents who had not been relocated by 2005 were living in conditions that were just as bad as those at baseline in 2001. Most of those residents were from Chicago, where conditions seemed to be getting even worse as vacancy rates increased and physical structures deteriorated. Families from the Ida B. Wells development described increasing disorder, including problems with squatters and nonresidents sleeping in vacant units and hallways, locks and lights not being repaired, and trash collecting in hallways and stairwells.

Conclusion

After tracking residents through the relocation process, the HOPE VI Panel Study was able to address the question of whether HOPE VI had succeeded in its goal of improving residents' life circumstances or whether the critics' dire predictions had been realized. For the most part, the long-term results show tremendous improvements in quality of life for former residents: most were living in neighborhoods that were dramatically safer and that offered far healthier environments for residents and their children. Carla, who was fourteen years old and living at Wells at the beginning of the study, was eighteen during the last study follow-up. She told researchers that she no longer had to worry about violence: "Up here it's quieter. I can get more peace up here than I would have gotten in the Wells. I can sit out on the porch and just sit there all night, without having to worry about somebody coming up and messing with [me]. You don't have to worry about no shooting—anything like that."[23]

Most of the adults and children who moved with vouchers had the same outlook as Carla's—the rate of crime and violence in their new neighborhood was dramatically lower. However, some were struggling with the challenges of living in the private market, and a substantial minority of respondents continued to live in traditional public housing developments that were only marginally better than the distressed developments that they had left. For them, the promise of HOPE VI remained unfulfilled, underscoring the need to continue to seek solutions for the problems that have kept too many from being

In August 2003, a man walks through Ida B. Wells, where residents remaining in buildings not yet demolished for redevelopment experienced worsening physical deterioration and disorder.

© David Schalliol, 2003.

able to take advantage of new opportunities. Truly improving the life circumstances of the most vulnerable families may require strategies such as providing housing with on-site social services, long-term intensive case management services, and transitional jobs. None of those approaches is simple, and all will require a significant long-term investment.[24]

However, the HOPE VI Panel Study also leaves several key questions unanswered. First, we do not know whether the improvements that voucher movers experienced will be sustained, especially as former residents grapple with the challenges of the private market. Second, we do not know how much of the lack of impact on self-sufficiency is attributable to residents' own problems, such as poor health, and how much is due to the fact that residents did not move to neighborhoods that truly offered new economic opportunity. The communities to which residents moved were substantially less poor than their original public housing developments, but they still had moderately high poverty rates (20 to 30 percent on average), and they still were predominantly African American. As Alex Polikoff discusses in his chapter in this volume, policymakers may need to reconsider the difficult question of whether—given the role that race may play in disinvestment—residents in predominantly African American communities can access the same kinds of opportunities offered to those in white communities in the United States.[25]

Finally, because so few panel study respondents had moved into new mixed-income communities by the end of the study, we do not know whether living in such developments will help to truly transform residents' lives. Will those who live in the developments gain more than the general improvements in neighborhood and quality of life that voucher holders experienced? Can developers provide effective employment and support services to help residents improve their economic circumstances? Will residents and higher-income neighbors truly interact, thereby helping to create a strong community? Answering these critical questions requires a new, comprehensive research agenda that both tracks the long-range outcomes for all former residents—HOPE VI movers, voucher holders, public housing movers, and those who no longer receive assistance—and also focuses specifically on the long-term experiences of those who move into mixed-income communities.

····· Endnotes ·····

1. Quote is from the final round of data collection for the HOPE VI Panel Study, an Urban Institute study that collected survey data in three waves from 2001 to 2005 and conducted in-depth interviews with a subsample of adults and children.

2. Susan J. Popkin and others, "The Gautreaux Legacy: What Might Mixed-Income and Dispersal Strategies Mean for the Poorest Public Housing Tenants?" *Housing Policy Debate* 11, no. 4 (2000), pp. 911–42.

3. Susan J. Popkin and others, "The HOPE VI Program: What about the Residents?" *Housing Policy Debate* 15, no. 2 (2004), pp. 385–414.

4. Debi McInnis, Larry Buron, and Susan J. Popkin, "Did Many HOPE VI Original Residents Become Homeless?" in *HOPE VI: Where Do We Go From Here?* Brief 7 (Washington: Urban Institute, 2007).

5. Susan J. Popkin and others, *A Decade of HOPE VI: Research Findings and Policy Challenges* (Washington: Urban Institute, 2004) (www.urban.org/publications/411002.html).

6. The Uniform Relocation Assistance and Real Property Acquisition Policies Act of 1970 was enacted to ensure "that people whose real property is acquired, or who move as a direct result of projects receiving Federal funds, are treated fairly and equitably and receive assistance in moving from the property they occupy." The objectives of the act are to ensure that "relocation assistance is provided to displaced persons to lessen the emotional and financial impact of displacement; and to ensure that no individual or family is displaced unless decent, safe, and sanitary (DSS) housing is available within the displaced person's financial means" (www.hud.gov/offices/cpd/affordablehousing/training/web/relocation/overview.cfm).

7. Popkin and others, *A Decade of HOPE VI*, p. 35.

8. Information on the number of relocated households and other summary data on HOPE VI redevelopments to date come from the U.S. Department of Housing and Urban Development and are summarized in appendix A of this book.

9. Popkin and others, *A Decade of HOPE VI*, pp. 33–40.

10. Ibid.

11. National Housing Law Project, *False Hope: A Critical Assessment of the HOPE VI Public Housing Redevelopment Program* (Washington: Center for Community Change, 2002) (www.nhlp.org/html/pubhsg/FalseHOPE.pdf).

12. For a complete description of the study methods, see Popkin and others, "The HOPE VI Program: What about the Residents?"

13. Mary K. Cunningham, "An Improved Living Environment? Relocation Outcomes for HOPE VI Relocatees," *A Roof over Their Heads*, Policy Brief 1 (Washington: Urban Institute, 2004) (www.urban.org/url.cfm?ID=311057).

14. Larry Buron, Diane Levy, and Megan Gallagher, "Housing Choice Vouchers: How HOPE VI Families Fared in the Private Market," *HOPE VI: Where Do We Go from Here?* Brief 3 (Washington: Urban Institute, June 2007) (www.urban.org/UploadedPDF/311487_HOPEVI_Vouchers.pdf).

15. Jennifer Comey, "HOPE VI'ed and On the Move: Mobility, Neighborhoods, and Housing." *HOPE VI: Where Do We Go from Here?* Brief 1 (Washington: Urban Institute, June 2007) (www.urban.org/UploadedPDF/311485_HOPEVI_Mobility.pdf).

16. Ibid.

17. Susan J. Popkin and Elizabeth Cove, "Safety Is the Most Important Thing: How HOPE VI Helped Families," *HOPE VI: Where Do We Go from Here?* Brief 2 (Washington: Urban Institute, 2007) (www.urban.org/UploadedPDF/311486_HOPEVI_Safety.pdf).

18. Quote is from the final round of data collection for the HOPE VI Panel Study in 2005.

19. Diane K. Levy and Mark Woolley, "Employment Barriers among HOPE VI Families," *HOPE VI: Where Do We Go from Here?* Brief 6 (Washington: Urban Institute, 2007) (www.urban.org/UploadedPDF/311491_HOPEVI_Employment.pdf).

20. Carlos Manjarrez, Susan J. Popkin, and Elizabeth Guernsey, "Poor Health: Adding Insult to Injury for HOPE VI Families," *HOPE VI: Where Do We Go from Here?* Brief 5 (Washington: Urban Institute, June 2007) (www.urban.org/UploadedPDF/311489_HOPEVI_Health.pdf).

21. Buron, Levy, and Gallagher, "Housing Choice Vouchers: How HOPE VI Families Fared in the Private Market."

22. Quote is from the final round of data collection for the HOPE VI Panel Study in 2005.

23. Ibid.

24. Susan J. Popkin, "No Simple Solutions: Housing CHA's Most Vulnerable Families," *Journal of Law and Social Policy* 1, no. 1 (2006) (www.law.northwestern.edu/journals/njlsp/v1/n1/index.html).

25. See Margery Austin Turner, Susan J. Popkin, and Lynette Rawlings, *Public Housing and the Legacy of Segregation* (Washington: Urban Institute Press, 2008).

RICHARD C. GENTRY

How HOPE VI Has Helped Reshape Public Housing

The world of public housing is currently undergoing a great deal of change. Much of the shift is due to draconian reductions in federal funding that have created great challenges for the more than 3,100 local housing authorities that administer the traditional public housing program and its nearly 1.2 million housing units.[1] Years of funding shortfalls have left housing authorities struggling to simply maintain their properties, let alone chip away at long-deferred needs for repair and replacement.[2]

But in an industry seemingly awash in bad news, there is good news. The ongoing quest to do more with less coincides with an emerging paradigm that will transform the public housing industry and equip local housing authorities to weather today's challenges better than the old top-down, process-oriented system did. This new way of being has its roots, in great part, in HOPE VI:

- By requiring the public housing industry to focus on projects as real estate, HOPE VI forced it to rethink its basics and move toward a more effective system of management.
- By opening the door to leveraging federal public housing funds with private capital, the program gave local housing authorities, which manage public housing, greater control of their own destinies.
- By introducing local housing authorities to new tools and partnerships, the program changed their perceptions about what they could be.
- By reintroducing a generally long-absent mix of incomes in public housing communities, the program spurred housing leaders to reexamine what public housing should look like and whom it should serve.

That HOPE VI would serve as "the laboratory for the reinvention of public housing" and produce "models for ending the isolation of the public housing agency" was expressly spelled out by HUD in one of the early funding notices for the program.[3] But although HOPE VI did lead to a real revolution in thinking within the world of public housing, the new operating model has not yet been adopted and institutionalized across the public housing industry. If the industry

The unrepaired kitchen ceiling in Inez Davis's apartment in Lincoln Heights Dwellings in 1971 attested to the severe dysfunction afflicting the District of Columbia's public housing authority, which, like many big city PHAs, was just as troubled in the early 1990s.

hopes to maintain the critical resources that it offers U.S. communities, it must continue on its positive trajectory.

Dysfunction Begets Distress

In 1990, when I was CEO of the Redevelopment and Housing Authority of Richmond, Virginia, I testified before the National Commission on Severely Distressed Public Housing. I told the commission that distressed sites were not the only entities needing an overhaul: the terrible conditions at some sites were in many respects the physical manifestation of fundamental design flaws in the public housing system itself.

At the time, running a local housing authority was akin to being an East German business manager. One had to learn how to make do in an overly centralized, top-down system in which program control was vested in Congress and HUD, leaving almost no autonomy to local housing authorities. Due to an odd provision in the Annual Contribution Contract (ACC), which sets the terms by which local authorities receive funds for operating public housing units, the unilateral right to call the shots rested with the federal government. The ACC stipulates that a local housing authority must accept any change to the ACC made by the federal government (that is, adhere to future HUD regulations, notices, and directives).

HUD tended to operate by issuing rigid, uniform directives and evaluating housing authorities on how well they complied with the one-size-fits-all program rules. Furthermore, the rules dictating housing authority operations would change, sometimes drastically, whenever the Democratic or Republican Party got control of the federal government.

As a result, many authorities had abdicated the role of self-evaluation and self-direction and they saw little relevance in standard real estate principles, such as the notion that each property comes with a unique set of issues, problems, and opportunities. Few metrics were developed to measure the performance of individual properties; the focus was on program compliance and uniformity of standards. The disconnect between the public housing industry and the larger real estate industry also meant that few real estate experts were working in public housing, even at the CEO level.

The government's skewed priorities aggravated the isolation of public housing communities. Behavior that led to rewards in the nation's entrepreneurial, capitalist system got punished in the public housing world. As just one example, the uniform rent system mandated by the Brooke amendment to the Housing Act of 1937 (initially passed in 1969) essentially penalized tenants for working. Under the system, which is still in effect today, public housing tenants generally spend 30 percent of their income on rent. If their income goes up, their rent goes up, without any corresponding improvement in housing. As researchers have noted, additional rent payments combined with an

Behavior that led to rewards in the nation's entrepreneurial, capitalist system got punished in the public housing world.

increased tax burden and costs such as those for caring for a new child could siphon off much of the additional income, significantly undercutting the financial rewards of work.[4]

The severe dysfunction bred by these factors was as evident in the early 1990s as it had been in 1979, when the Department of Housing and Urban Development published its first list of the worst-performing agencies. In the early 1990s, that list still included many of the big city housing authorities, although there were notable exceptions, such as the authorities in New York City and Seattle. Between the time of the list's initial publication and the commission's meeting, too many long-troubled agencies were still doing a poor job of housing the needy.[5]

Bringing Asset Management to Public Housing

Broad reform of public housing management did not take place in the immediate wake of the report of the National Commission on Severely Distressed Public Housing, most likely because the general feeling was that with 86,000 severely distressed public housing units acting as the proverbial millstone around their necks, housing authorities could not be turned around. Nonetheless, the report shaped the 1992 legislation that would become known as HOPE VI, a program that did spur management reform, albeit in a way that perhaps no one had predicted.

HOPE VI offered funds for either rehabilitation or demolition and new construction of public housing properties that were functionally obsolete or beyond repair.[6] Substantial though the grants were, by the mid-1990s housing authorities had realized that they needed additional private investment, such as equity from low-income housing tax credits (LIHTCs), if they were going to create the kind of economically integrated communities that would improve neighborhoods and ensure ongoing investment in public housing. But to lure private investors, they had to operate more like private sector real estate firms.

All of a sudden, it was the property that mattered, not the housing authority as an organization or how well it complied with HUD rules. That portion of a HOPE VI redevelopment project that was funded by tax credit equity was now owned by an entity that had to answer to its investors. As the sole or partner owner in a LIHTC property, the housing authority now had a monetary interest in seeing that the property was managed and protected the way that it would be in the private sector. The result was the adoption of the asset management method for overseeing a project and evaluating its performance.

Broadly defined, asset management is the practice of protecting an asset and maximizing its performance. Day-to-day activities such as collecting rent, enforcing lease provisions, and performing maintenance are conducted in

Charlotte Housing Authority Asset Decision Tree

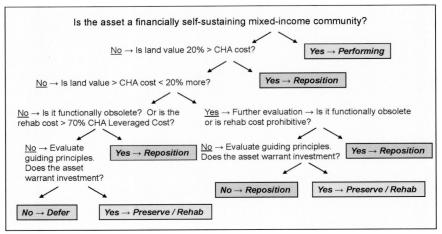

Reprinted with permission from "Building Community, People, and Partnerships,"
Charlotte Housing Authority Report of Achievements, 2006–2007, p. 13.

accordance with established performance goals. By and large, housing authorities were not doing asset management with regard to public housing because
it was, de facto, the federal government's job.[7]

However, under HOPE VI, housing authorities and their partners were
performing site inspections and reviewing quarterly reports on property performance. They assessed such things as rents collected, vacancy rates, outstanding debt, and status of vendor and utility payments. They tracked critical
metrics, such as debt coverage ratio, and performed interventions when necessary. If their cushion after subtracting costs from net operating income fell
below 15 percent, they looked for ways to expand it, such as by reducing vacancies, reducing expenses, and increasing income.

From HOPE VI, then, housing authorities learned asset management and
saw that it worked. Some forward-thinking authorities began applying the
asset management approach tested in HOPE VI more broadly to their operations. For example, in 2002—without any direction from HUD—the Charlotte
Housing Authority in North Carolina began developing an asset management
model that required the organization to maintain balance sheets and income
statements for each property and base decisions for each property on certain
benchmark criteria, such as economic performance and replacement cost.[8] The
"asset decision tree" (above) encapsulates the process followed by the housing
authority when making investment decisions about its assets.

Housing authorities' exposure to asset management through HOPE VI coincided with mounting industry discussions about applying asset management to public housing.[9] Notions about moving to a real estate focus solidified in the late 1990s, when the Quality Housing and Work Responsibility Act of 1998 (QHWRA) established a new operations fund for the management of public housing and stipulated that the formula for allocating the funds would be set through negotiated rulemaking. Confusion and disagreements over how the formula should be set led officials to engage the Graduate School of Design at Harvard University to break the impasse by conducting a study, which ultimately led HUD to launch the phased implementation—now currently under way—of asset management in public housing.[10] Although neither HOPE VI nor asset management was mentioned formally in the study, the property-based focus that resulted surely reflected the thinking that had emerged since HOPE VI was implemented.

Opening the Door to Leveraging Federal Funding

While asset management has not yet been institutionalized in the public housing management system, leveraging, another standard real estate practice brought to public housing by HOPE VI, has.

As Richard Baron discusses in chapter 3, the negotiations over the first mixed-finance, mixed-income HOPE VI redevelopments created the template since codified in QHWRA and now replicated nationwide. Though there are many variations, the basic HOPE VI public housing redevelopment has four key sources of financing: the underlying economic value of the public housing property, the continuing cash flow provided by the public housing operating subsidy from the federal government, HOPE VI funds, and tax credit equity. Under the program, the total non–public housing dollars going toward developments with public housing will reach at least $9.35 billion, even without counting the HOPE VI grants made after 2007 (figure 12-1).

Figure 12-1. Leverage from HOPE VI through FY 2007
Grant Awards, in Millions[a]

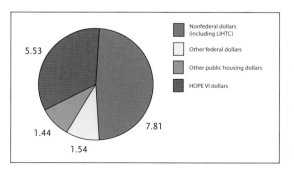

Source: U.S. Department of Housing and Urban Development, *HOPE VI Revitalization Program: Reporting as of September 30, 2008* (Washington: 2008).

a. HUD's most up-to-date report on key indicators for the HOPE VI program covers the 240 grants awarded from 1993 through 2007 and was current as of September 2008. As of December 2008, data for the six FY 2008 grants had not yet been formally entered into HUD's tracking system.

Fueled in part by the need to do more with less, use of this model is growing outside HOPE VI, with other public housing capital funds standing in for HOPE VI dollars as the leveraging tool. But as with HOPE VI, the developments may have a range of housing types, both for sale and rental, that serve residents of various incomes. By August 2008, HUD had reported 643 mixed-finance closings for public housing, 154 occurring outside of HOPE VI.[11] Those non–HOPE VI transactions, approved under what HUD calls the Mixed-Finance Public Housing Program, leveraged nearly $1.5 billion in non–public housing dollars from just over $0.7 billion in public housing funds.[12]

The Capital Fund Financing Program (CFFP), another relatively new tool for meeting the capital needs of public housing, also can be traced, in part, to HOPE VI, in that the shortage of HOPE VI grants helped fuel the industry's search for other redevelopment dollars.[13] A provision in QHWRA allows housing authorities to pledge their expected future allocations of capital funds from HUD to secure loans or to issue bonds. That enables housing authorities to obtain capital funds more quickly in order to meet pressing needs to modernize housing or redevelop distressed properties. The CFFP is being used to rehabilitate public housing and to replace public housing units that have been torn down—sometimes as part of mixed-finance transactions, including HOPE VI–like redevelopments.[14] Some smaller housing authorities that lack the economies of scale required to issue their own bonds are forming bond pools in order to participate in the CFFP as well. Public housing authorities have borrowed about $2.6 billion under the program to date.[15]

Housing finance experts from twenty-one countries taking a tour of Greater Grays Ferry Estates in South Philadelphia in June 2007 listen to the Philadelphia Housing Authority's executive director, Carl Greene (right, foreground) explain how mixed-finance strategies enabled better design of the public housing redevelopment project.

Also slowly catching on is the practice of combining the 4 percent LIHTCs, for which there is less competition than for the 9 percent tax credits, with CFFP funds. While only six such deals were approved in fiscal year 2008, they included a very large deal generating approximately $235 million in equity for the Puerto Rico Housing Authority.[16]

Other recent leveraging innovations include energy-efficiency upgrades, whereby HUD lets a housing authority keep the energy savings it produces through retrofits and those savings are used to back low-interest loans from energy services companies.[17] HUD also has begun implementing—on a very limited basis—the Public Housing Mortgage Program, which allows public housing authorities to mortgage public housing property as security for loans to modernize or develop affordable housing.[18]

Combined, these new opportunities are helping authorities tackle some modernization and redevelopment challenges despite the overall shortfall in public housing capital funds. For example, the Philadelphia Housing Authority raised enough under the CFFP program to redevelop the Tasker Homes public housing site in South Philadelphia as the mixed-income Greater Grays Ferry Estates, and it used the leftover funds to modernize parts of two other public housing complexes.[19]

In Philadelphia and other cities such as Atlanta, Charlotte, and Chicago, the housing authorities are using all the tools at their disposal to form public-private partnerships to transform their entire public housing stock by replacing the more distressed projects with new, mixed-income communities and rehabilitating other family and senior public housing complexes.[20] Among the big city housing authorities, perhaps none has undergone more of a transformation than the Atlanta Housing Authority, where Renée Glover used the catalytic potential of HOPE VI to leverage a broader, more profound change in the way that the authority operates, transforming it from one of the worst big city housing authorities to one of the best (see chapter 9).

Recasting the Role of Housing Authorities

The impact of HOPE VI extends well beyond a new management method and new funding for the public housing stock itself. The asset management approach fostered by HOPE VI, coupled with the new financial tools proliferating in its wake, also have spurred housing authorities to redefine or expand their roles in their community.

Although public housing is a large portion of local housing authorities' inventory, public housing and housing authorities are not, as commonly viewed, one and the same. Local housing authorities are state-created entities that may operate any program and pursue any activity allowed under their enabling legislation.[21] The federal government merely restricts how the housing authority may spend federal dollars and operate federally funded programs.

Local housing authorities are reshaping their image with communications that convey their transformation into full-service real estate development companies providing a quality product. The Housing Authority of the City of Milwaukee presents itself and its offerings in an annual report (here featuring its Townhomes at Carver Park development) and a brochure for the Highland Homes HOPE VI community (bottom). A Philadelphia Housing Authority banner proclaiming its motto, "Building beyond Expectations," flies on a light pole in Wilson Park, a public housing complex in South Philadelphia modernized under the agency's ten-year plan to construct or rehabilitate at least 6,000 affordable housing units (opposite page). The mural shown is one of many painted in PHA neighborhoods under a partnership between the PHA and the Philadelphia Mural Arts Program. Jennifer Gallman, corporate communications officer for the Charlotte Housing Authority, interviews the agency's CFO, Ralph Staley, while taping a segment of *CHA Today*, a new half-hour cable program launched to educate the public about the authority's activities (below).

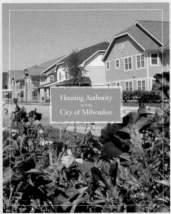

Prior to HOPE VI, some housing authorities—including the Richmond Redevelopment and Housing Authority and the San Diego Housing Commission—had long been operating as diversified contributors to meeting their community's housing needs. Yet by and large, in the early 1990s, housing authorities were not viewed as major players with the capacity to have a major impact on their city's future. Stuck in the compliance mind set, which was reinforced by the disempowering design of federal programs, housing authorities were sidelined, managing the public housing and voucher programs and having little interaction with city government, state government, or the leaders of their community's private and philanthropic sectors.

But then housing authorities engaged in HOPE VI redevelopment started to look at the public housing sites in their portfolio as a series of discrete properties. They began to appreciate the value of their assets, which consist primarily

of the income stream from the federal subsidy plus the real estate itself. That appreciation, coupled with the need to respond to reductions in federal funds for public housing units, has a small but growing number of leaders diversifying their portfolios and acting as lead developer on more development projects, earning fees that can be plowed back into their operations.

Many local housing authorities have become involved in the Low-Income Housing Tax Credit Program to expand the stock of affordable housing within and outside their public housing program. As of 2005, roughly 230 authorities that administer public housing (7 percent of the total number in the country) had developed or were developing 775 tax credit projects comprising 97,930 units—approximately 9 percent of all tax credit units developed.[22] Currently, of the approximately 1,600 LIHTC properties managed by the National Equity Fund, about seventy are sponsored by local housing authorities, and the majority of these properties have no direct public housing subsidy built into their operations. Some are HOPE VI–related, and many have a degree of voucher support, but most are simply straightforward LIHTC properties.

As housing authorities look outward, at the needs and opportunities in their communities, civic and public leaders are beginning to perceive the authorities as a resource to support broader efforts in such areas as reducing homelessness, spurring economic development, and addressing the shortage of affordable housing.

Examples span the country and range from small to large housing authorities. The Northwest Regional Housing Authority, serving seven rural counties in northwestern North Carolina, has produced seven tax credit properties, adding greatly to the stock of affordable housing for an otherwise underserved area. With several successful HOPE VI redevelopments under its belt, the Seattle Housing Authority is now being solicited as a partner in mixed-income developments that do not involve public housing, with two such projects under way. At the city's behest, the authority also is working to win military approval to be the master developer of the Fort Lawton Army Reserve base, to be closed under the BRAC (base realignment and closure) program.

Reintroducing a Mix of Incomes in Public Housing Communities

The same mixed-finance strategy that essentially mandated an asset management approach under HOPE VI also reinforced notions about bringing back to public housing the income mix—and emphasis on working families—that it had to varying degrees in earlier eras. (See figure 12-2; see also the chapters in this volume by Bruce Katz and Alexander Polikoff.) Such notions were certainly percolating before HOPE VI—for example, in the late 1980s and early 1990s in the mixed-income (but technically still all–public housing) Lake Parc Place community, which was developed by the Chicago Housing Authority under Vincent Lane.[23]

HOPE VI theoretically offered a way to address the concerns of both sides of the debate over whom public housing should serve: practitioners who called for "healthy" public housing neighborhoods that reflect a balanced socioeconomic cross-section of the community and resident advocates who championed the cause of serving the most needy.

HOPE VI mixed-income redevelopments created balanced neighborhoods while ensuring that former residents who did not move back into the redeveloped communities found housing elsewhere. And while some decry the loss of physical units, the reality is that the vouchers that replaced them have generally enjoyed more consistent federal funding.

That public housing programs should be free to serve those with a wider range of incomes—and in so doing reduce the concentrated poverty linked to so many ills—has since become federal policy. In addition to formally authorizing HOPE VI and promoting mixed-finance and mixed-income redevelopment,

Figure 12-2. Change in Earned Income of Public
Housing Tenants at Four HOPE VI Sites[a]

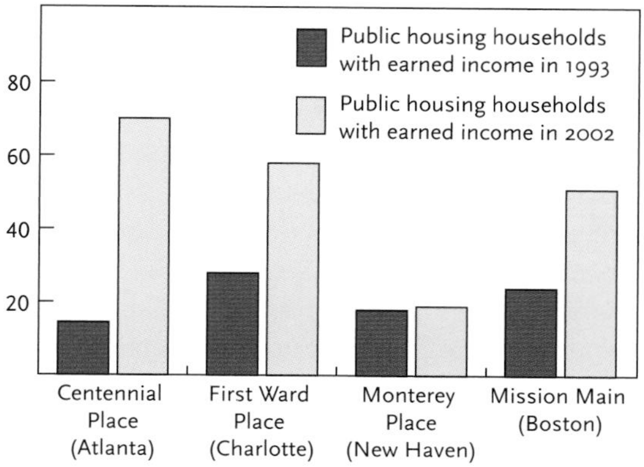

Adapted from Linda B. Fosburg, Susan J. Popkin, and Gretchen P. Locke, *An Historical and Baseline Assessment of HOPE VI,* vol. I: *Cross-Site Report* (Cambridge, Mass.: Abt Associates, 1996), p. 1-24, 1-25; and Mary Joel Holin and others, *Interim Assessment of the HOPE VI Program: Cross-Site Report* (Cambridge, Mass.: Abt Associates, 2003), p. C-5.

a. Sites selected for this chart were the mixed-income HOPE VI sites assessed in the interim report for which type of household income was reported in the baseline report. The 1993 figure for Atlanta is an average of the percent of households with earned income given for the two public housing complexes redeveloped as Centennial Place.

the Quality Housing and Work Responsibility Act of 1998 sought to create a broader income mix within the public housing program and increase assisted households' earned income and self-sufficiency by giving housing authorities greater latitude to vary their admissions, income, and rent-setting policies. Codifying some changes already under way through provisions in appropriations laws, QHWRA formally repealed federal eligibility rules for admission to public housing that favored extremely poor households, instituting instead a provision requiring that a certain percentage of new households be extremely low income. In so doing, it established a lower minimum percentage of public housing residents required to have incomes at or below 30 percent of the area median than is required under the voucher program—40 percent rather than 75 percent. With an eye toward reducing the potential work-disincentive effects of the uniform rent system that exists under the Brooke amendment, QHWRA also required housing authorities to offer flat rents (under which a tenant's rent would not increase as earnings increased) and a two-year phased earnings disregard (under which a rent increase resulting from an increase in earned income would be phased in over two years).[24]

In the wake of that "deregulation," some housing authorities did change their admissions policies to favor working families, likely in part to generate more income for operations as well as reduce the concentrated poverty found in public housing projects, in line with current thinking. And there has been an increase in the percentage of public housing families that are working. A QHWRA progress report released by HUD in 2008 found that the percentage of public housing households with children that had any income from work rose from 39 percent in 1997 to 53 percent in 2006. However, welfare reform and the overall economy probably had more to do with those changes than any changes in public housing rent-setting and admissions policies.[25]

The jury is still out on the impact of the poverty-deconcentrating, income-mixing aspects of QHWRA. Concentrated poverty has been reduced by public housing redevelopment under HOPE VI and by other federal policies allowing public housing authorities to propose and HUD to approve demolition of distressed or obsolete units that no reasonable program of modification can restore.[26] Due to those policies and general economic trends, between 1995 and 2008, the percentage of family public housing units located in extreme poverty neighborhoods fell from 43 percent to 26 percent.[27]

But self-sufficiency, if measured by higher income levels, has not dramatically improved across the board. The causes are wide ranging, but they include the relatively modest nature of some of the QHWRA reforms, delays in and complexities of implementation, and the difficulty of attracting somewhat higher-income families to some of the current public housing sites.[28] Also, in most places very poor people still constitute the bulk of those applying for public housing.[29] Still, the point here is that income-mixing and enhancing residents' self-sufficiency has become a concern of public housing policy. (The last chapter discusses the need to improve the record of self-sufficiency initiatives and other resident services.)

The Future of Public Housing
QHWRA's aims notwithstanding, public housing still overwhelmingly serves very low-income families. In 2006, 73 percent of the families in public housing had incomes of 30 percent or less of area median income (AMI); 91 percent had incomes of up to 50 percent of AMI.[30] Incomes of such families are too low to pay the rent on housing units created through "shallow," or "capital," subsidy programs such as low-income housing tax credits.[31] Accordingly, an operating subsidy, known as a "deep" subsidy, is provided through the public housing program and through housing vouchers. It will remain a critical resource for very low-income families, a segment of the population not otherwise served by housing assistance programs.

Thanks to the elimination of the most distressed and obsolete public housing units, 90 percent of public housing developments are now in good physical shape, meeting or exceeding HUD's physical condition standards.[32] Further, under HOPE VI and other federal policies that have reshaped public housing in the last decade and a half, some of the worst-managed agencies have been

Figure 12-3. **Improved Management of Public Housing**

Condition of public housing developments in 2007

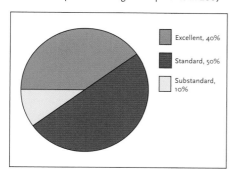

- Excellent, 40%
- Standard, 50%
- Substandard, 10%

Drop in units managed by troubled agencies

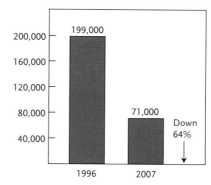

Adapted with permission from Barbara Sard and Will Fischer, "Preserving Safe, High-Quality Public Housing Should Be a Priority of Federal Housing Policy" (Washington: Center on Budget and Policy Priorities, September 2008), p. 9.

turned around, contributing to a 64 percent decline in the number of public housing units owned and managed by troubled agencies (figure 12-3). Today, troubled agencies own and manage less than 6 percent of the public housing stock, down from 16 percent in 1996.[33]

More widespread adoption of asset management is a critical next step to sustaining public housing. As mentioned, HUD currently is developing and implementing an asset management model for use in public housing similar to that used in the private sector.[34] The model is controversial. Opponents say it is overly complicated and will fatally disrupt local operations, given HUD's track record in managing the old system. Supporters say it is time that the public housing industry moved away from its historic insularity and into the larger world of real estate that governs other forms of affordable housing, such as that funded by low-income housing tax credits.

Although arguments on both sides have merit, it is far better to continue moving toward a modern asset management system and fix the inadequacies in the HUD system than to abandon the process.

Housing authorities will need to implement project-based financial systems that measure and evaluate the performance of each property. They also will need to set standards for occupancy rates and compare project performance against those standards as well as the performance of other projects. Rent collection rates, bad debt write-offs, financial reserve levels, and debt coverage ratios also will need to be measured, as applicable. Asset management also will have implications for nonroutine maintenance, major replacements, modernization, and the determination of obsolescence.

An asset management approach, at least as practiced in the private sector, recognizes that all properties have a finite useful life; they do not last forever. Periodic measurements and projections must be made, over time, regarding additional investment in the property, alterations to the property, and eventual redevelopment or alternate reuse of the underlying investment asset. In addition, staff skills must increase, hopefully aiding and aided by more shuttling back and forth by real estate professionals between employment in public housing and the larger real estate industry.

Some people argue that a shift toward project-based asset management somehow subverts public housing's focus on residents or social services. The opposite is true. Resident and social services would remain critical to a property's performance, much like the amenities that help to make any private sector housing work.

As mentioned, a debate also is currently under way with regard to whom public housing should serve and what, if anything, should be required of residents. Some cities, such as Atlanta, Chicago, and Pittsburgh, are requiring work or education coupled with work training or are reconfiguring rent structures so that tenants are not penalized for working. Such measures should be encouraged or, at least, allowed as a local option, either throughout all of a housing authority's projects or for a specific project, at the discretion of the locality. The old entitlement mentality, which historically has resulted in the warehousing of the poor in public housing, harms both residents and their long-term prospects; it also works to the detriment of the surrounding population and the likelihood that it will offer political support to public housing over the long term. Generally, a quid-pro-quo approach toward residents is not unreasonable.

For its part, HUD needs to do more to make it easier for local housing authorities to leverage needed funds to keep up the public housing stock. While QHWRA and subsequent rule changes have given housing authorities new flexibility, many hurdles still exist. Mixed-finance and CFFP transactions have been streamlined somewhat but still require detailed and often extended HUD reviews.[35] Further, if HUD wants housing authorities to act more like private sector property managers, it is going to have to change its still-embedded tendency to dictate from on high. While there have been experiments with tweaking the policies cited earlier in this chapter that have long discouraged proactivity among local housing authorities—such as the exceptions to the Brooke amendment granted to some Moving to Work agencies—such policies remain a barrier to innovation.[36]

Housing Vouchers: Suited to the New Paradigm

Approximately 2 million households are served by the Housing Choice Voucher Program, making it the largest housing assistance program in the country. The program serves households that have basically the same level of income as public housing households; in 2006, 77 percent of voucher households made 30 percent of AMI or less.[37] But because vouchers are much more flexible than public housing, they are very well suited for the new project-based real estate paradigm and will be more important in the years ahead.

Vouchers allow very low-income families and individuals to rent from private landlords, with the voucher generally making up the difference between 30 percent of the voucher-holder's income and the private market rent on the unit. Most vouchers are "tenant-based," meaning they are not attached to any one specific unit but are a subsidy provided to the renter household. But under HUD regulations, local housing authorities may "project-base" up to 20 percent of their voucher funds, meaning that they can dedicate a voucher to a specific unit, thereby allowing them to use the "project-based voucher" as collateral in obtaining a construction loan. Vouchers may be dedicated to an entire property if it is designed for use by the elderly or disabled, or they may be used for only a percentage of the units in a property, depending on a variety of factors.[38]

In collaboration with other local players, housing authorities can tailor voucher use to local needs. For example, the housing authority might decide to dedicate a certain number of project-based vouchers to a particular area in order to help the city target that area for redevelopment or to support the development of specific kinds of housing, such as mixed-income housing, senior housing, or permanent supportive housing (housing coupled with services that often serve formerly homeless people or other special needs individuals). Or the housing authority might decide that its local market already contains a surplus of eligible existing properties and that a fully tenant-based voucher program would be best not only for voucher recipients but also for the local real estate industry.

A significant new development is the ability to combine the voucher program with tax credits to help create new housing that is affordable for people with very low incomes, sometimes as part of a mixed-income community. In that kind of development, the tax credits are the capital subsidy that lowers a property's rent to a level that families at 60 percent of median income can afford. Adding the deep subsidy provided by vouchers lowers the level further, so that households at below 50 percent of median income can afford a unit.

In 2006, approximately 40 percent of the LIHTC partnerships that the National Equity Fund, the nation's largest nonprofit syndicator of LIHTCs, formed with local sponsors included some level of voucher use—most often the local housing authority as a partner rather than as project sponsor. Provisions in the Housing and Recovery Act of 2008 make it easier to use project-based vouchers for development in general and with tax credits in particular.[39] Given the flexibility inherent in the voucher design and the inherent inflexibility of

> A significant new development is the ability to combine the voucher program with tax credits to help create new housing that is affordable for people with very low incomes.

traditional public housing, federal public housing policy should make it easier for local housing authorities to convert federal subsidies attached to specific public housing units into subsidies for vouchers for free-standing or project-based units. Such conversions currently are allowed, but only through a cumbersome two-step process.[40]

Helping Housing Authorities Develop beyond the Traditional Programs

Very little new public housing has been developed over the past 30 to 40 years, and little expansion of the voucher program has occurred over the past 6 to 7 years. Even under a new federal administration in 2009, there is unlikely to be much additional funding for or products developed from these traditional programs. Therefore, in the future, LHAs will not be able to survive if they continue to think of themselves as passive purveyors of only the traditional public housing and voucher programs. The local housing authority of the future must be a locally focused, opportunity seeking, full-service real estate development and holding company, developing and managing the value of its investments for the good of the community.

Going forward, federal policy changes should continue to move in the direction of allowing local housing authorities greater latitude in designing local uses of federal resources. Guidance issued regarding the activities of housing authority subsidiaries has been considered helpful in this regard. Further, legislative and rule changes have loosened some restrictions. But full use of the new tools that are on the horizon requires additional steps. For example, as mentioned earlier, HUD, drawing on statutory authority under QHWRA, recently established a public housing mortgage program enabling housing authorities to borrow funds for certain purposes by obtaining a mortgage on their real estate. But at this writing few such transactions have occurred due to barriers to using the program, namely the decrease in the land valuation created by the stipulation that public housing units that are foreclosed on because of default remain reserved for families that are eligible for public housing.[41] By and large, HUD itself is still stuck in a regulatory, compliance-oriented mindset that poses barriers to the continued evolution of housing authorities.

There is a better way. If an authority wishes to combine the value of its public housing asset base and cash flow with a private sector tax credit investment, the authority should be encouraged to do so. Federal policy should not just allow but encourage local exceptions to regulatory control, diversity of program design, and complex, mixed-finance options for building housing.

Conclusion

Many of the housing authorities once on the troubled list or in receivership are now considered high or standard performers, such as those in Atlanta, Kansas City, Los Angeles, Philadelphia, San Francisco, and Washington,

D.C.—housing authorities in cities that by dint of their size create the national image of public housing.

For these and many other local housing authorities, lifting the barriers to innovation posed by poor public housing program design and the weight of distressed housing stock was the first step toward regaining their perspective as local organizations.

HOPE VI helped to lift those barriers and encourage changes, but more must be done. Tom Kingsley points the way in the last chapter to the new direction that housing authorities must take if they are to remain relevant to their respective localities in the years to come.

····· Endnotes ·····

1. The Public Housing Capital Fund, which enables housing authorities to repair roofs and replace heating systems and tend to other structural needs, fell from $3 billion in fiscal year 2001 to $2.4 billion in fiscal year 2008. At the same time, the gap has been widening between the amount appropriated by Congress to cover routine expenses, such as those for utilities and maintenance, and the amount needed to cover actual costs, as determined by a formula specified in the regulations governing the public housing operating fund. The percentage of the formula-defined needs—referred to by the industry as the "HUD-defined needs"—actually appropriated fell from 100 percent in FY 2002 to 83 percent in FY 2007. Although the latest available calculation from HUD, as reported in "Explanation of Fourth and Final Obligations under Operating Fund Program for Calendar Year (CY) 2008," September 10, 2008 (www.hud.gov/offices/pih/programs/ph/am/of/2008fnlprrtnexplntn.pdf), reports that the proration rose to 89 percent in FY 2008, the National Association of Housing and Redevelopment Officials (NAHRO) had not adjusted its figures pending a review of HUD's calculations. Personal communication between Lora Engdahl and Beth Cooper, NAHRO, November 7, 2008, and "Worth Fighting For: Preserving Our Nation's Affordable Housing Infrastructure," National Association of Housing and Redevelopment Officials, March 2008. The number of public

In the early 1990s, the vacant Ellen Wilson Dwellings (left), located on the edge of the neighborhood that includes the U.S. Capitol, served as the public face of public housing as well as of the District of Columbia Housing Authority, whose terrible performance landed in it receivership in 1995. Under HOPE VI, Ellen Wilson was redeveloped as the Townhomes on Capitol Hill, a new "calling card" for the now high-performing DCHA and the resuscitated public housing industry to which it belongs.

housing authorities and units comes from Barbara Sard and Will Fischer, "Preserving Safe, High-Quality Public Housing Should be a Priority of Federal Housing Policy" (Washington: Center on Budget and Policy Priorities, September 2008), pp. 3–4.

2. A 1998 study estimated an unfunded capital needs backlog of $22 billion and newly accruing needs of $2 billion, while in recent years capital fund appropriations have been sufficient to cover only "somewhat more than accrual needs," according to Rod Solomon, "The Sixth Annual Public Housing Finance Update," *Journal of Housing and Community Development* (September-October 2008), pp. 8–9. The article reported that although renovations and demolitions in recent years under HOPE VI and HUD's capital fund financing and mixed-finance programs have helped clear some of the backlog, the amount of funds needed to bring the portfolio up to par will likely be shown to be "daunting" when the assessment of public housing capital needs mandated under the FY 2008 appropriations act is completed.

3. In her comprehensive overview of the policy evolution of HOPE VI, Yan Zhang quoted from the 1995 NOFA to illustrate the dramatic expansion of HOPE VI goals in the early years of the program. Yan Zhang, "Wills and Ways: Policy Dynamics of HOPE VI from 1992 to 2002," Ph.D. dissertation, Massachusetts Institute of Technology, September 2004, p. 96.

4. The potential rent disincentives of the subsidized housing rent formula are explored in depth in Ed Lazere and Jennifer Daskal, "Will Changing the Rent Formula Encourage Moves from Welfare to Work?" in *A Place to Live, A Means to Work: How Housing Assistance Can Strengthen Welfare Policy,* edited by Barbara Sard and Amy S. Bogdon (Fannie Mae Foundation, 2003).

5. Thirteen of the public housing authorities serving the forty most populous U.S. cities were also on the list of troubled housing authorities as of March 31, 1992. Linda B. Fosburg, Susan J. Popkin, and Gretchen P. Locke, *An Historical and Baseline Assessment of HOPE VI,* vol. 1, *Cross-Site Report* (U.S. Department of Housing and Urban Development, Office of Policy Development and Research, July 1996), p. 1-10 (www.huduser.org/Publications/pdf/hopevi_vol1.pdf).

6. In fiscal years 1993 and 1994, twenty-seven grant awards were made, ranging from nearly $19 million to $50 million, with 17 in excess of $40 million. See appendix B of this volume.

7. Because the federal government was funding the operating subsidies on which housing authorities relied in order to pay for upkeep, the government made decisions relating to the long-term value of each property. That usually was done without knowledge of or regard to the unique characteristics of a particular property.

8. "Building Community, People, and Partnerships," Charlotte Housing Authority Report of Achievements, 2006–2007 (www.cha-nc.org/documents/CHA_Annual_Report.pdf).

9. As Joe Shuldiner, a former assistant secretary for Public and Indian Housing at HUD, noted in a recent opinion piece, by the early 1990s decisionmakers in the industry were discussing the need to focus on the individual properties themselves rather than just the organizations. Joe Shuldiner, "W(h)ither Public Housing," *Journal of Housing and Community Development* (May–June 2007): pp. 6–8, 10.

10. When the public housing program was designed, there was no operating subsidy. Rather, housing authorities would use bond financing to cover the capital costs, and the federal government would make annual contributions to retire the debt. But after the Brooke amendment limited rent payments to a percent of a family's income, housing authorities were severely pinched and began to essentially barter with HUD to cover their losses. An operating subsidy was enacted as part of the Housing and Community Development Act of 1974, but the formula was esoteric and the system came to be viewed as predictable but arbitrary—reflecting not true costs but a base year's expenditures, whether or not housing authorities had been frugal. QHWRA mandated a revised system of operating subsidies to be determined

in a negotiated rulemaking session including both HUD and public housing representatives. When HUD and the industry were unable to come to an agreement, HUD engaged the Harvard University Graduate School of Design to produce a study, the "Public Housing Operating Cost Study," identifying the expenses associated with running well-managed and well-maintained public housing developments. The study recommended that the operating subsidies should be property specific, not derived from an agency-wide formula, an approach more like that historically used by HUD for subsidized FHA properties. That recommendation was in the September 2005 final rule of the Negotiated Rulemaking Advisory Committee. HUD's "Asset Management Overview" web page gives the history of the negotiated rulemakings and rules (www.hud.gov/offices/pih/programs/ph/am/overview.cfm).

11. Personal communication between Lora Engdahl and Tony Hebert, Office of Public Housing Investments, Office of Public and Indian Housing, U.S. Department of Housing and Urban Development, August 5, 2008.

12. Data from the "Mixed-Finance Closing Module" provided by the Office of Public Housing Investments, Office of Public and Indian Housing, U.S. Department of Housing and Urban Development, August 4, 2008. Public housing funds totaled $705,031,457; non–public housing funds (which would include federal and nonfederal, public and private funds) totaled $1,448,299,524.

13. Complaints arose early on in the implementation of HOPE VI that there were too few grants to go around and that, particularly in the first rounds, only the largest or most distressed authorities got grants. Although later rounds expanded eligibility to more housing authorities, they were in fierce competition. That left many local housing authorities that needed a capital infusion for redevelopment without options. Under existing operating and capital grants programs, the amount of funds was derived by formula and was not necessarily sufficient to cover all needs in a timely fashion.

14. An example of a HOPE VI–like development funded without HOPE VI dollars is Greater Grays Ferry Estates in Philadelphia, a $165 million redevelopment of the former Tasker Homes into a mixed-income, mixed-use community. Jack Kemp and others, "Our Communities, Our Homes: Pathways to Housing and Homeownership in America's Cities and States," Harvard University, Joint Center for Housing Studies, 2007, p. 40.

15. Solomon, "The Sixth Annual Public Housing Finance Update," p. 10.

16. Ibid., pp. 8–9. See also Rod Solomon, "The 2007 Annual Housing Finance Update," *Journal of Housing and Community Development* (September–October 2007), p. 8. In the 2007 article, Solomon, a former HUD official, explained that 9 percent LIHTCs, which are allocated by state housing agencies, are very competitive because they generate more equity, sometimes enough to fully cover redevelopment costs. Four percent credits, which are allocated in conjunction with tax-exempt bonds, are easier to get but "raise only about 25% to 40% of the total development costs for public housing improvement, redevelopment, or replacement, and thus debt financing is also needed for such projects."

17. Among the housing authorities pursuing such energy-efficiency upgrades are the Boston and the Allegheny County, Pennsylvania, housing authorities.

18. A fact sheet provided by HUD's Office of Public Housing Investments in the Office of Public and Indian Housing on September 16, 2008, cites the New Bedford, Massachusetts; Cook County, Illinois; and Tacoma, Washington, housing authorities as recent participants in the program, with a total of $19.4 million in transactions approved for the three. However, as Solomon noted in "The Sixth Annual Public Housing Finance Update," the program, which was authorized by QHWRA, "has had limited use." HUD has not issued any regulations, particularly those that would enable "pledging of public housing operating funds, capital funds, and rents on a per-property basis."

19. "First Residents Move in as PHA Completes Renovation of Wilson Park," press release, Philadelphia Housing Authority, November 20, 2003.

20. As Barbara Sard and Will Fischer noted in their September 2008 report, Atlanta and Chicago are among the twenty-eight agencies whose reform and revitalization efforts also have been aided by their designation as Moving to Work agencies. Under the federal MTW program, the agencies were able to apply voucher funds toward public housing rehabilitation efforts; however, recent voucher funding policy changes would prevent that, the authors note. Sard and Fischer, "Preserving Safe, High-Quality Public Housing," p. 31.

21. Depending on the state, they are, indeed, technically local "authorities," which are local public corporations created and controlled by the local government for a particular purpose, or they are a department of a local government.

22. Written statement of Dominique Blom, deputy assistant secretary, Office of Public Housing Investments, U.S. Department of Housing and Urban Development, "Redeveloping Public Housing outside of HOPE VI: Potential Impacts on the Community and Residents of Jordan Downs," Los Angeles Field Hearing before the House Subcommittee on Housing and Community Opportunity, March 15, 2008.

23. For a description of the effort, see James E. Rosenbaum, Linda K. Stroh, and Cathy A. Flynn, "Lake Parc Place: A Study of Mixed-Income Housing," *Housing Policy Debate* 9, no. 4: 703–40

24. Rod Solomon, "Public Housing Reform and Voucher Success: Progress and Challenges," Brookings Institution Metropolitan Policy Program, January 2005, p. 34 (www.brookings.edu/~/media/Files/rc/reports/2005/01metropolitanpolicy_solomon/20050124_solomon.pdf).

25. A QHWRA progress report noted that it would be hard to claim QHWRA as the cause given the general persistence of traditional admissions preferences and rent policies and such broader trends as periods of economic expansion and the passage of welfare policy reforms aimed at increasing the self-sufficiency of welfare recipients. According to the Center on Budget and Policy Priorities, the increase in working public housing families is likely attributable not only to falling welfare rates and the decline in the number of extreme poverty neighborhoods nationwide but also to public housing demolition, which has focused on the biggest developments in the most impoverished neighborhoods, "where welfare-dependent families were more likely to reside." See U.S. Department of Housing and Urban Development, "Seventh Annual Report to Congress on Public Housing and Rental Assistance Programs: Demographics, Income and Work and Rent," 2008, pp. 9, 19, 20, 21; and Sard and Fischer, "Preserving Safe, High-Quality Public Housing," pp. 7–8, 30.

26. After HOPE VI started, Congress implemented a number of other policies designed to eliminate distressed or obsolete public housing. Policies include lifting the one-for-one replacement rule, first in appropriations acts beginning in 1995 and then formally in QHWRA; a QHWRA provision streamlining the process by which housing authorities obtain HUD approval to demolish or dispossess public housing units meeting certain standards of obsolescence; a provision in HUD's FY 1996 appropriations act (Public Law 104-134) establishing under HOPE VI a separate, demolition-only grants program that lasted through fiscal 2003; and a provision in the 1996 appropriations act requiring mandatory conversion to vouchers of costly, dilapidated public housing complexes with 300 units or more and vacancy rates exceeding 10 percent.

27. Those public housing units in complexes exclusively for seniors are not included in this figure. Extreme poverty neighborhoods are those in which 40 percent of families fall below the poverty line. See Sard and Fischer, "Preserving Safe, High-Quality Public Housing," pp. 6–8. Note that Sard and Fischer attribute the reduction in public housing in extreme poverty neighborhoods to the overall decline in extreme poverty neighborhoods nationwide as well

as the elimination of the largest, most distressed public housing developments under HOPE VI and other demolition policies.

28. Rod Solomon, "Public Housing Reform and Voucher Success: Progress and Challenges" (www.brookings.edu/~/media/Files/rc/reports/2005/01metropolitanpolicy_solomon/20050124_solomon.pdf).

29. In 2006, households with extremely low incomes constituted 73 percent of households newly admitted to the public housing program. U.S. Department of Housing and Urban Development, "Seventh Annual Report to Congress on Public Housing and Rental Assistance Programs," p. 3.

30. Ibid., p. 9.

31. Capital, or shallow, subsidy programs such as the LIHTC attempt to correct for the lack of private market housing for households making under a certain income level. (Opinions on the exact level vary, ranging from 60 percent of area median income to 80 to 100 percent.) Under these programs the reduction in cost at the initiation of a housing program lowers the cost to a level that the target population can afford. The rents then are less than market, generally, and by program definition affordable. Opinions differ on the income level of those needing deeper subsidies. Some say it is higher than 50 percent of AMI; some say it is much lower. In general, the lower rents enable a family making 60 percent of AMI to pay no more than 30 percent of its income on rent. (It is generally accepted that rent consuming more than 30 percent of income is unaffordable because it leaves too little for health care, transportation, and other expenses and savings.) For discussion purposes, a family making less than 50 percent of median income and paying 30 percent of its income on rent typically would not be covering the costs of operating the LIHTC unit, even when debt service is excluded.

32. Sard and Fischer, "Preserving Safe, High-Quality Public Housing," pp. 2, 6.

33. Ibid., pp. 8–10. Sard and Fischer attribute the drop in units managed by troubled agencies to new HUD management assessment tools, "HUD's concentrated attention on the most troubled agencies," the strengthened capacity of local housing agencies under HOPE VI, and new partnerships with local and state governments arising from efforts to transform public housing.

34. With asset management for public housing not slated to be fully phased in until 2011, there have been and may be more changes to implementation guidelines between now and then. Under current rules, any public housing authority operating 250 or more units must start converting to project-based funding, budgeting, accounting, management, and performance assessment and must have all systems in place by 2011. (The industry won a provision—not considered by HUD to be permanent law—in the 2008 appropriations bill that exempts agencies with 400 or fewer units and is backing legislation, H.R. 5829, that would set a permanent 500-unit threshold). With project-based budgeting coming online in 2008 (and project-based accounting phased in over 2008 and 2009), HUD already has started the switch from allocating a lump sum for each housing authority based on a formula to allocating funds based on presumed needs of groupings of buildings, called asset management projects (AMPs), of which there are roughly 8,000. The 8,000 AMPs were formed from the roughly 14,000 individual projects previously designated as projects in Annual Contributions Contracts. To address the concerns of public housing authorities slated for large funding cuts under the new system—and to provide an incentive for a prompt shift to asset management by those agencies—HUD created a stop-loss option whereby authorities could keep their losses to 5 percent by converting to asset management more quickly. But authorities have to apply for that option, and in some cases the process has not gone smoothly. In addition to concerns over disruptions in service, the industry has objected to the conflict between HUD's asset management system and management systems already in place within authorities that have Moving to Work authority. (Under the goal of fostering innovation and

efficiency, the Moving to Work program frees some housing authorities from certain rules and regulations.) Another source of disagreement is the requirement that housing authorities charge each AMP a set "reasonable" management fee and pay central office costs out of that fee. The management fees are to be phased in by 2011, but they will apply earlier for stop-loss agencies. The industry and HUD are in disagreement over how a "reasonable" fee should be determined. However, HUD has issued guidance whereby authorities other than stop-loss agencies that elect to use capital fund subsidies for central office costs (as permitted under the fungibility provisions of the 1937 Housing Act) can operate within the old cost allocation system rather than the new fee-for-service system. For more details on HUD's implementation of asset management, visit the HUD website (www.hud.gov/offices/pih/programs/ph/am/). Both the National Association of Housing and Redevelopment Officials and the Council of Large Public Housing Authorities regularly post documents on their websites examining aspects of the program and new developments.

35. Solomon, "The Sixth Annual Public Housing Finance Update," p. 10, notes that HUD has shortened the projected review period for CFFP transactions to sixty to ninety days but that processing requirements still pose a barrier to using the program.

36. The Moving to Work program is a demonstration program that was developed in 1996 to promote greater efficiency in the administration of the public housing and voucher programs; to increase housing choices for low-income families; and to allow housing authorities to provide the families that they assist with incentives to prepare for or seek work and to become economically self-sufficient. MTW agencies have more flexibility to combine funds from different funding steams, develop alternative rent structures, impose time limits, and engage in other activities.

37. U.S. Department of Housing and Urban Development, "Seventh Annual Report to Congress on Public Housing and Rental Assistance Programs," p. 11.

38. With some exceptions, not more than 25 percent of the units in a development can be subsidized by project-based vouchers. Sard and Fischer, "Preserving Safe, High-Quality Public Housing," p. 27.

39. Solomon, "The Sixth Annual Public Housing Finance Update," p. 10, covers some of the changes, which include an increase in the maximum initial term of project-based vouchers to fifteen years to match the initial compliance period of the LIHTC program. Solomon notes that the proposed Section 8 Voucher Reform Act (SEVRA) also has provisions that would further enhance use of project-based vouchers if passed.

40. Local housing authorities that want to convert public housing units to vouchers must first request approval for the demolition or disposition of the units and then request replacement vouchers for the "lost" units; the option of direct conversion through a one-step process should be allowed.

41. The Tacoma [Washington] Housing Authority got around the barrier posed by restrictions on mortgaging public housing real estate by acting as a prior lien on the mortgage. Janet Rice, THA's director of real estate development, explained that the public housing mortgage program was tapped to finance infrastructure improvements to the fifty-acre phase 2 of the seven-phase Salishan HOPE VI redevelopment. Phase 2 included 182 single-family homes and 180 multifamily units. Even though the financing package was funding improvements on the entire fifty acres, the transaction was segregated so that only the fifteen acres that would host the single-family homes were pledged as collateral on the loan. The strategy worked because of the already high value of the land—the last large parcel in the region.

Learning from
Critiques and Planning
for the Future

SHEILA CROWLEY

13

HOPE VI: What Went Wrong

HOPE VI was initiated with the best of intentions, but it is a case study in how badly a government program can run amok. While HOPE VI has resulted in the removal of blighted buildings and the development of some lovely new homes, it also has resulted in the involuntary displacement of tens of thousands of poor, predominantly African American families from their homes and communities, made the housing situation for some of the nation's most vulnerable citizens even more precarious, and exacerbated the shortage of affordable homes for people in the lowest income brackets. The promise (and rhetoric) of HOPE VI as a means of improving opportunities for residents of distressed public housing never matched the reality. Many more displaced residents were promised improved housing *and* economic uplift than have actually received both or are ever likely to.

Andrea Williams stands amid the rubble of the Miami public housing complex that was her home.

© *The Miami Herald*, 2006

Those who have examined HOPE VI refer to "winners and losers," with one study concluding that "the effects have been mixed, with some former residents . . . better off . . . and . . . others at risk" and another asserting that "HOPE VI enhances only a small number of public housing residents."[1] Overall, more people who lived in public housing communities redeveloped under HOPE VI were hurt by the program than helped. Thus, the core tenet of government intervention in the lives of its citizens—"First, do no harm"—has been violated.

Evaluation scholar Egon G. Guba of Indiana University asserts that public policy must be examined and understood from three perspectives: what the policy intended, how the policy was implemented, and what happened to the people whom the policy was supposed to affect.[2] It is a circular, nonhierarchical process of which the written policy that outlines what policymakers seek to achieve is the beginning, not the end. Policymakers examine the results of the programs designed to implement their policies to determine how well-crafted the policies were in the first place. Actual impacts and experiences are continually fed back into the policymaking loop to improve the policies in order to better meet the needs of the intended beneficiaries.

It is in that spirit that this critique of the HOPE VI program is offered, trusting that indeed the intended beneficiaries of HOPE VI are the residents of "distressed" public housing and not the developers, lenders, public housing officials, and politicians who are the program's most loyal advocates. This chapter examines the implementation of the HOPE VI program from the vantage point of the intended beneficiaries and other low-income people in need of affordable homes in their communities. The thesis of the critique is that the implementation was more about the real estate than it was about the people. The chapter closes with recommendations for reform to best address the failings identified and with thoughts about the future of public housing.

For Residents, Displacement and the Loss of Home

The number of public housing households relocated under HOPE VI has now reached more than 72,000.[3] All of those families—even the small number that have or will return to the redeveloped sites—were removed from the place that was their home.

The importance of "home" to the physical and mental health of human beings cannot be overstated. Shelter is one of the most essential human needs. One's house is where one's life is centered and where family life is conducted. One's house is connected to other houses, creating the structure for communal life and the organization of human society.[4] The disruption of a home that occurs when a move is not freely chosen by the people who must move is one of the most serious consequences of any action that a public authority can take, and *forced relocation should be approached with extreme caution.*

FORCED RELOCATION

In the United States, poor and disenfranchised people are disproportionately forced from their homes.[5] Urban renewal in the United States is the story of poor people "pushed out of their neighborhoods to make room for various forms of 'progress' . . . no other group will allow itself to be displaced."[6] So, too, the vast majority of homes that were lost to the construction of the interstate highway system belonged to poor and black people.[7] The displacement of 72,000 families from their homes by HOPE VI is another chapter in this sad history.

Decisionmakers justify forced relocation by defining the community to be demolished as distressed and by marginalizing the people who live there. In a three-stage process, residents are diminished, then they are dispersed, and then their homes and institutions are destroyed to make way for new development that those in power find preferable.[8]

Forced relocation, under any conditions, always causes trauma to those who are displaced. People who are uprooted against their will experience "root shock, the traumatic stress reaction to the destruction of all or part of one's emotional ecosystem."[9] Place attachment is deeply felt, with place including one's actual dwelling and a neighborhood populated with people and services on which one can rely. The longer one has resided in a home and community, the more attached one becomes.[10]

Despite being dismissed as dysfunctional by policymakers and the general public, poor communities nonetheless have intricate webs of social connections that offer communal support and sustain their members through difficult times.[11] In a 2004 article, Sudhir Venkatesh and Isil Celimli introduce the reader to Lee-Lee Henderson, who lived in Chicago's infamous Robert Taylor Homes and left in 2002 under HOPE VI redevelopment. A year later, she wanted to move back. She was glad to be rid of the gang activity but missed the child care and mutual financial support in her old neighborhood. As she explained, "poor people help poor people. They have no one else, so they know how to help each other get by."[12]

Venkatesh and Celimli report that three-quarters of the social network of a public housing resident is composed of other public housing residents.[13] In an interview with the Center for Community Change, a resident who was displaced by HOPE VI in Detroit expressed her loss: "I get real sad sometimes when I know I can't go back to Herman Gardens. It makes me want to cry. I think because I lived there so long . . . I just felt safe there. At Herman Gardens, we just knew everybody."[14]

Elderly people are among the most vulnerable to physical and emotional damage when they are uprooted from their homes and their support systems.[15] The HOPE VI Panel Study found that the mortality rate among black women fifty-five years of age or older displaced by HOPE VI was, shockingly, twice than of older black women in general and higher among HOPE VI Panel Study participants than in a comparison group of public housing women. Although the comparison was imperfect and an overwhelming majority of HOPE VI women had illnesses or chronic health needs before moving, the findings raise serious questions about the impact of the stress of moving on people who already are in frail condition.[16]

Relocation can also have a harmful effect on school-age children, who risk falling behind in their studies when they must move during the school year. It is not just the children who move who are affected. With the churning of students through classrooms over the school year, all students are subject to disruption of the learning process.[17] During a planning meeting for one HOPE VI project, a school official was observed begging the housing authority staff to hold off on relocating residents of the site slated for demolition until the end of the school year. The plea fell on deaf ears; housing authority staff said that the demolition had to go ahead as planned.[18] HOPE VI Panel Study participants who moved to private market housing with or without vouchers experienced significant rates of residential mobility, with half moving twice in two years.[19] It is likely that the children in those households also changed schools during that time.

> Elderly people are among the most vulnerable to physical and emotional damage when they are uprooted from their homes and their support systems.

IS THE "CURE" WORTH THE PAIN?

In the case of HOPE VI, the severing of ties to communities and schools may have been justified if the people who were displaced were guaranteed to be better off as a result. The one improvement that studies of HOPE VI outcomes have consistently shown is that people feel safer. While increased security is an extremely important outcome, the improvements were experienced primarily by residents who relocated with vouchers to better neighborhoods or who were able to reestablish themselves without housing assistance, not by people who were relocated to other public housing. At best, these voucher or unassisted movers constitute little more than half of the affected families.[20]

Residents relocated from HOPE VI sites have not improved their economic and employment status.[21] While families that relocated with vouchers are in safer neighborhoods and higher-quality housing, they also face higher levels of economic hardship and housing instability because, with the addition of utilities to their monthly costs, their housing costs have increased.[22] Indicators of well-being of school-age children in the HOPE VI Panel Study referenced earlier are inconclusive about positive effects on children's health, school engagement, and behavior.[23] And as already noted, the health status of many residents displaced by HOPE VI may have actually deteriorated.

The HOPE VI Panel Study is the only analysis to date to examine the extent of homelessness among people displaced by HOPE VI. The researchers found that just 2 percent had become homeless and concluded that the rate was insignificant.[24] That anyone became homeless as a result of government-initiated forced relocation from their homes is unacceptable. At a minimum, any homelessness of former residents should have been prevented under any HOPE VI project.

Moreover, the analysis includes only families from five HOPE VI sites. Other studies that do not specifically raise the question of homelessness nevertheless show that the whereabouts of some displaced residents was

In 2005, Eva Kelly looks out from the tenth floor of Fairhill Apartments, a North Philadelphia public housing complex to which she was relocated in 2001 when her old home, Cambridge Plaza, was redeveloped. Kelly told the *Philadelphia Inquirer* that she felt trapped at Fairfield and wanted to return to Cambridge Plaza.

David Swanson/The *Philadelphia Inquirer*.

unknown. According to HUD data on HOPE VI households relocated as of June 30, 2003, 20 percent were not able to be assessed.[25] The Miami-Dade Housing Authority cannot account for more than half of the residents displaced by the Liberty City HOPE VI project.[26] After initially relocating with vouchers, many of the Miami families lost their vouchers at the end of the first lease and became homeless when they could not find another home to which to move.[27] In a remarkable example, researchers studying the Atlanta Smith Homes HOPE VI site four years after the relocation of residents received a contact list from the Atlanta Housing Authority for 493 relocated households. A stunning 90 percent of the heads of household could not be reached. Eventually, researchers were able to find just 116 households by word of mouth among former residents.[28]

As noted by the National Housing Law Project in 2002's *False Hope*, the most definitive analysis to date of the flaws of HOPE VI, there is an astonishing lack of data about what has occurred as a result of the program.[29] In the early years, no one was required to track the outcome for each resident, making it impossible to assert that HOPE VI did not contribute to the continued crisis of homelessness in the United States in the 1990s. The number of residents who were simply "lost" should be of enormous concern to the architects of HOPE VI and those who want to continue redevelopment under the program. The failure to plan and carry out the least harmful relocations possible and to follow residents to ensure their well-being is a permanent stain on the HOPE VI record. It certainly supports the thesis that the well-being of public housing residents was not the principal focus of those charged with redevelopment.

Flaws in the Intervention Lead to Disempowerment

Although overused and misused in the discourse of anti-poverty programs, empowerment remains a crucial goal for interventions to improve the social and economic well-being of low-income people. At its core, empowerment is the redistribution of power in a socially and economically stratified society to create greater equality and fairness. Empowerment practice seeks collaboration between the implementers and beneficiaries of social programs to produce both personal and social transformations.[30] It presumes that all people, even the most disadvantaged, have strengths and resources. The most beneficial transformations occur through interventions that are based on maximizing people's gifts.

Poor people, people of color, women, and people with disabilities—and especially people who fall into more than one of those categories—are disadvantaged in U.S. society; therefore they face greater risk of personal limitations that can impede change. As social work scholar Barbara Simon has observed, "Oppression, once internalized, takes a number of self-denigrating forms including the toxic self-hatred and self-doubt that cripple individuals and groups who have been subject over many decades to the contempt of members from more powerful groups."[31] Interventions that focus only on people's limitations or that deny their reality will fail. Interventions that either romanticize or pathologize the people to be helped and that are not based on a complete, accurate assessment of a family or a community are disempowering, reducing chances for positive change. False promises deepen alienation.

Social interventions that strive for real and lasting change are not easy to implement. They require skilled practitioners with the time to follow through on a project, and they must be backed by institutions that are committed to their success. As implemented, HOPE VI did not seek the empowerment of residents; its emphasis was on transforming neighborhoods, not the people who lived in them. HOPE VI has been disempowering in at least three ways. First, resident participation in the planning and implementation of HOPE VI redevelopment has been weak and ineffectual. Second, many residents feel that they were misled to believe that the redevelopment was really for them and that they would benefit from new services and other opportunities. Third, HOPE VI failed to accurately assess the serious challenges faced by many public housing residents for whom any improvement in social and economic well-being would require much more support than HOPE VI has ever offered.

WEAK RESIDENT PARTICIPATION

Since their inception, public housing programs have included more than housing; they also have focused on creating community with the encouragement and support of tenant councils and other forms of resident participation.[32] Resident participation in its ideal form involves residents of public housing collaborating with the staff of public housing agencies in order to improve the lives of individuals and the community. Although that goal was reaffirmed in the HOPE VI rules requiring residents to be active participants in the decision to apply for a HOPE VI grant and in the preparation of the application,implementation was weak.[33]

A GAO study of resident participation in the twenty HOPE VI sites that received grants in 1996 found considerable variation across sites. All held informational meetings, but some engaged residents in actual decisionmaking while others complied with resident participation requirements only after they were threatened with litigation.[34]

The lack of meaningful opportunities for resident participation was one of the five program shortcomings cited by the National Housing Law Project in *False Hope*. A 2003 Center for Community Change study of resident perceptions of HOPE VI in seven cities found that the required resident participation did not occur in the manner promised. Outreach to residents to inform them that their housing authority was considering a HOPE VI application was haphazard. Invitations to meetings usually took the form of flyers delivered the day of the meeting. Residents interviewed in the Center for Community Change

Resident participation in its ideal form involves residents of public housing collaborating with the staff of public housing agencies in order to improve the lives of individuals and the community.

study said that they had to investigate rumors that would spread in the vacuum of accurate information. Sometimes selected residents were suspected of getting special notice and not sharing information with all residents. Sometimes it was outside organizers who helped residents understand the full implications of redevelopment and the importance of attending planning meetings.[35]

Residents reported in the Center for Community Change study that the meetings in which the most important decisions were made were the least accessible; for example, they would be held at the central office of the housing authority during regular business hours. At the meetings that they did attend, residents experienced their role as that of passive recipients of information who were expected to rubber-stamp whatever decision officials had decided to make. In the words of one resident, "instead of residents developing information, the City gives us information and wants us to agree with it."[36] A frequent complaint voiced in the Center for Community Change report was that public housing authorities co-opted selected residents who would go along with the plans and gave them special favors in return.[37]

A serious limitation to true resident participation is the failure of the current HOPE VI statute[38] to allow for private right of action by either residents or the community at large, thus depriving residents of any means of holding housing authorities accountable for how a project is carried out, no matter how different it is from what was promised.[39]

LIES AND DECEIT

A repeated theme in resident complaints about HOPE VI is that they were deceived by the housing authorities and the numerous consultants who were engaged in the HOPE VI projects.[40] Residents report that they were deceived even in the application process, when sign-in sheets for informational meetings about HOPE VI were used as documentation that the people who attended the meeting supported the application.[41]

The most egregious lie was that public housing residents would someday live in the new homes and have new opportunities for economic betterment if they supported a HOPE VI application. Seduced by charettes in which architects flashed sketches of idyllic settings and housing with modern amenities, many residents believed that those sketches represented their future. A resident in Jersey City, New Jersey, said that "at the beginning, they showed us the townhouses that they were going to build, showing us how pretty they were going to be. But they did not tell us that we would be kicked out." A Richmond, Virginia, resident reports that the housing authority told her, "You'll be the first to come back." But, the resident said, "Everything that has been said has been a lie . . . When they sent me the letter that told me I was not able to come back, I was tore up."[42]

Residents who have returned to new homes developed under HOPE VI constitute less than a third of those who were displaced.[43] A primary reason is that the people who are displaced cannot afford most of the new units. For example, the Atlanta Housing Authority's redevelopment of Techwood–Clark Howell Homes displaced 998 households whose median household income was $3,960 a year, and planners did not intend for the vast majority of original residents to return. Reserving only 360, or 40 percent, of the planned 900 units at the new Centennial Place as public housing, authorities targeted households with a minimum income of 40 percent of the area median, much higher than the income of the former residents, to occupy those units. The other 540 units were intended for families with even higher incomes.[44] What actually happened at Centennial Place is an improvement over the plan; about 40 percent of the 738 units built are public housing–assisted units, predominantly serving households with incomes of less than 30 percent of AMI. Nonetheless, there was a significant reduction in units that the people who were displaced could afford. Overall, just over a third of the total units appear to serve extremely low-income households.[45]

Other reasons for permanent displacement include not passing new screening requirements, such as credit checks, and new units not having the same number of bedrooms as the ones that were demolished. In some cases, the lapse of time between relocation and redevelopment has been so prolonged that residents just give up hope.[46]

Some former residents cannot or will not meet the requirements of residency in redeveloped units, which range from work requirements to restrictions on certain kinds of outdoor activities, like barbequing.[47] Anticipating that she would not be able to return, a resident in Washington, D.C., said that she had heard from a former resident of an earlier HOPE VI project that "a lot of residents there didn't try to return because they were afraid if they moved in, the rules were so strict that they would probably be evicted."[48]

In addition to new homes, HOPE VI is supposed to include supportive and community services for residents such as child care, job training and counseling, education, substance abuse treatment, and recreation centers. Indeed, the initial HOPE VI statute allowed up to 20 percent of the HOPE VI grant to be used for such services; in 1998, the amount was capped at 15 percent. Public housing authorities have not spent anywhere near the amount allowed for services for residents, despite the fact that those services have been considered a distinguishing feature of the program. HUD guidelines indicate that services are to be provided to original residents of a project that is redeveloped under HOPE VI, but for the most part, the new residents of a redeveloped site are the ones who will benefit, not the residents who were displaced.[49]

"THE HARD-TO-HOUSE"

Disempowerment under HOPE VI was perhaps most evident with regard to the "hard-to-house," residents for whom "public housing has been a source of stable, if less than ideal, housing."[50] These include residents with multiple and complicated needs and problems, such as disabling physical and mental illnesses, limited education and poor wage-earning ability, substance abuse, criminal background, and large numbers of children. In some instances, grandparents are raising their grandchildren.

Being classified as hard to house has less to do with the particular problems of a family or individual than it has to do with how they are perceived by landlords and other housing providers; if tenants do not conform to standard expectations of tenants, they are at risk of eviction.[51] HOPE VI Panel Study researchers estimated that from 37 percent to 72 percent of the residents in the five HOPE VI sites that they studied could be classified as hard to house.[52] Such families, for whom traditional public housing was truly a safety net, can transition to other housing arrangements only with extensive and sustained support services. These are the families whose housing stability is threatened by redevelopment under HOPE VI and whom HOPE VI, as designed, is unlikely to help. They were set up to fail, deepening their internalized sense of powerlessness and oppression. The failure to accurately assess both the strengths and limitations of such a large percent of the population prior to demolishing their homes and scattering them to the winds is the most serious of all of HOPE VI's defects.

How could there be such a disconnect between what was intended and what happened? It is rooted in the failure to answer this basic question: Is the program about building buildings or about improving lives and building communities? The buildings are not an end in themselves; they are a means to the end of helping people maintain stable homes and improve their social and economic well-being.

Adding to the Housing Shortage

When HOPE VI was first authorized in 1992, public housing law still required a new unit to be built for every public housing unit that was demolished, a practice known as one-for-one replacement.[53] As long as one-for-one replacement was in force, HOPE VI projects had to abide by it. But within a few years, the long-standing failure of Congress to properly fund public housing had forced a change in policy. Evidence that public housing agencies could not keep their stock in good repair and lacked the funds to replace uninhabitable units prompted Congress to rescind the one-for-one rule in 1995.[54] Public housing agencies were now free to pursue plans that would result in a net loss of federally assisted units in their communities.

Remarkably, while the U.S. Department of Housing and Urban Development was requiring state and local jurisdictions that received federal housing and community development funds to identify their housing needs and propose how they would meet them,[55] the department's HOPE VI program was causing the loss of the very housing that was most needed in every jurisdiction— housing that the lowest-income families could afford. HUD also was routinely

Andrea Williams and her children, shown here in 2006, survey the site of their former apartment at Scott Homes, a Miami public housing complex razed for redevelopment. Seven years after receiving a HOPE VI grant, the Miami-Dade Housing Agency had relocated more than 800 families and spent millions of dollars but built just three houses, reported the *Miami Herald*.

© *The Miami Herald*, 2006.

issuing its own reports on the country's shortage of affordable rental housing.[56] The enthusiasm with which HOPE VI was touted by HUD officials, the housing industry, and politicians created considerable dissonance for those who were examining the data on housing needs. It seemed that HOPE VI supporters were ignoring the reality of waiting lists for housing assistance, poor families with unsustainable housing costs, and homelessness.

There is widespread agreement that the United States has an acute shortage of rental housing that extremely low-income households can afford. There are more than 9 million extremely low-income renters, 25 percent of all renters in the country, but there are only 6.2 million rental housing units that these households can afford, according to the standard of affordability that allots no more than 30 percent of household income to housing. The result is a shortage of more than 2.8 million homes. Moreover, many of the units that extremely low-income households can afford are rented by higher-income people, so that the real shortage is 5.6 million units. Nationwide there are just thirty-eight affordable and available rental units for every 100 extremely low-income households. Across states, the number of affordable units per 100 ELI households ranges from twenty-three units in California to sixty-five in South Dakota (figure 13-1).[57]

Because of the shortage, the majority of extremely low-income families pay substantially more for their homes than they can afford. Seventy-one percent of such households pay more than half of their income for shelter, forcing them to forgo other basic necessities and putting them at high risk of eviction and homelessness. No other income group comes close with regard to the percent of income consumed by housing.[58]

Public housing is one of the few sources of rental housing that extremely low-income households can afford. Of the 1,282,099 public housing units available in 2000, 69 percent were occupied by extremely low-income households; 45 percent of those households had incomes of less than $10,000 a year.[59] Because public housing residents pay 30 percent of their income for their homes, they are among the lucky minority of poor families that do not have unsustainable housing costs.

HUD and public housing officials frequently cite the number of units demolished and the number of units that have been or will be rebuilt through HOPE VI.[60] An uninformed reader can be left with the impression that eventually most, if not all, of the units that are demolished will be replaced. This sleight of hand masks the reality that a minority of the new units are actual public housing units that families in the same income group as those that lived there before can afford.[61] HOPE VI developers actually plan for one-for-one replacement of public housing so infrequently that those who do so call special attention to their efforts.[62]

Supporters of HOPE VI will argue that the condition of the public housing that has been demolished under the program was so deplorable that HOPE VI could not wait for Congress to come up with the money to replace all lost housing and address the rental housing shortage. The public housing originally

Figure 13-1. Homes Affordable and Available for Rent for Every 100 Extremely Low-Income Renter Households[a]

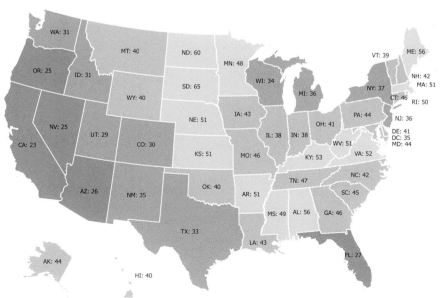

National average = 38 units

- 22.5 - 28
- 28.1 - 38
- 38.1 - 48
- 48.1 - 65

Note: States are classified by their unrounded values.

a. Extremely low-income households earn no more than 30 percent of their state's median family income, adjusted for household size. Affordable means paying no more than 30 percent of household income for housing. 2005 figures. See NLIHC's Research Note #07-01 for the full report (http://www.nlihc.org/docRN07-01.pdf).

As with all surveys, margins of error are associated with all estimates derived from the American Community Survey.

envisioned for HOPE VI probably had deteriorated so badly that it could not be saved. However, the public housing for which HOPE VI was intended was the 86,000 units estimated to be severely distressed by the Commission on Severely Distressed Public Housing. Unfortunately, neither Congress nor HUD has ever concretely defined "severely distressed" or identified the units that would meet such a definition if one existed. The National Housing Law Project cited several different definitions in its 2002 study, noting that the lack of a clear definition of "severely distressed public housing" has allowed the demolition and redevelopment of far more public housing than was originally intended.[63]

The number of units demolished through HOPE VI has now reached more than 91,000, and calls for expanding the program continue to come from the housing industry and elected officials.[64] Some charge that HOPE VI has become a vehicle by which local officials can tear down public housing that stands in the way of new development considered more desirable.[65] HOPE VI likely has caused and in the future certainly will cause the loss of public housing that could have remained viable with proper upkeep and sufficient investment in programs to improve the social and economic well-being of current and future residents. In the absence of reform to once again require one-for-one replacement, public policy will continue to contribute to the scarcity of homes for the poorest people in the United States.

Going Forward

HOPE VI would have been eliminated years ago had the Bush administration had its way, but Congress has kept the program alive with annual, albeit significantly reduced, appropriations. Funding for HOPE VI has fallen from a peak of $755 million in FY1994[66] to just $100 million in FY2008.[67] The program was supposed to sunset in 2002, but Congress reauthorized it until

In March 2008, hundreds of people lined up for Section 8 housing vouchers at the Boca Raton, Florida, housing authority, which had opened its voucher waiting list for the first time in three years. In many communities nationwide, there is an acute shortage of affordable rental housing for extremely low-income families, which make up the bulk of families applying for public housing and vouchers.

© Bob Shanley/The *Palm Beach Post*

2006, adding some protections for residents. Since then, HOPE VI has been reauthorized annually in the HUD appropriations bill, and it is likely to continue to be reauthorized until Congress agrees on reforms to HOPE VI going forward, if it ever does.

The debate about what those reforms should be has been under way for some time. In 2002, the National Low Income Housing Coalition (NLIHC) developed its first position paper on HOPE VI. Hammered out by a diverse group of NLIHC members including tenants, advocates, public housing agency staff, developers, and lenders and informed by the experiences of numerous participants in and observers of HOPE VI projects, the paper reflected NLIHC's core concerns: the shortage of affordable rental housing for the lowest-income people in the United States and the right of all low-income people to be treated fairly and with respect. Accordingly, the paper called for two fundamental reforms, which still define NLIHC's position today.[68]

- HOPE VI should not result in a net loss of public housing units in the jurisdiction in which they are located, and no HOPE VI project should result in a net loss of housing units in the jurisdiction that are affordable and that target extremely low-income families (those with incomes at or below 30 percent of the area median).
- All residents who were eligible to live in a public housing development prior to HOPE VI have the right to return to a redeveloped unit.

More proposed reforms include the following:
- improved resident participation requirements
- a clear definition of what constitutes a "severely distressed" property
- assurance that original residents benefit from new services funded through HOPE VI in addition to new or improved housing
- improved relocation services with better counseling to help families make the best possible choices
- ongoing support services to ensure continued housing stability
- more links between redevelopment of housing and improvement of public schools that serve the new housing
- more focus on the unique vulnerabilities of subsets of original residents, such as elderly people, people with disabilities, and school-age children
- greater commitment to law enforcement and gang reduction in existing public housing
- tracking of 100 percent of residents affected by HOPE VI over extended periods of time.

At this point, the choices seem to be to continue HOPE VI as currently structured, to do away with HOPE VI altogether, or to reform the existing program. The first is the default choice, a function of lack of legislative consensus or even interest, but a position with few, if any, advocates. The Bush administration had been the primary advocate of ending HOPE VI, as part of its strategy to shrink the HUD budget, especially all accounts that support public housing. HUD has noted the delay in implementation of HOPE VI projects and the backlog of unspent HOPE VI dollars, for which HUD holds the housing authorities responsible.[69]

Reform seems the most likely course, but the shape of any reforms remains to be seen. Considerable differences exist among the stakeholders. The core issues of dispute are one-for-one replacement and the right of original residents to new homes and services produced by HOPE VI. Reform will require congressional action, and recent legislative history shows that, at least as of 2008, lawmakers in the House and Senate differed markedly in their support of one-for-one replacement and the right to return.[70] Lawmakers also differ on the need to tighten up requirements for determining whether a potential HOPE VI project is "severely distressed" and to require resident involvement throughout the development process.[71]

Given the intensity of the critique of HOPE VI here and by other low-income housing advocates and residents, it is reasonable to ask why the National Low Income Housing Coalition does not support ending HOPE VI. The pragmatic reality is that the HOPE VI program has considerable support in Congress among both Democrats and Republicans. Moreover, advocates were heartened that the HOPE VI reauthorization bill passed by the House in 2008 reflected many of the reforms that low-income housing advocates and residents have been seeking for years. With hard work and determination, it is possible to change policy for the better.

But there is a fourth choice. Rather than reform and reauthorize HOPE VI as a separate program to be used by a select number of housing authorities, it is time for a serious discussion about the future of public housing as an institution. The housing stock is aging and in too many places suffers from deferred maintenance due to lack of funding or poor management. For too many years, Congress and the administration have turned their backs on public housing.

Yet public housing is a valuable resource in most communities and provides much-needed housing to a very needy population. Nearly one-third of public housing residents are elderly and another 16 percent are disabled non-elderly adults, meaning that almost half of the units are occupied by people whose economic prospects are unlikely to improve.[72] Many other units are occupied by very poor people with complex, multiple needs whose transition to improved economic prosperity will take considerable and intensive services. And every community in the United States has a shortage of housing for its lowest-income members.

The task at hand is much greater than simply seeking compromise on changes to the HOPE VI program. The task is to figure out how the country will ensure good housing for everyone who resides here and what role the federal public housing program will play in meeting the challenge. How does the nation ensure that elderly and disabled residents of public housing will be able to age in place in decent and safe homes in the communities that they know best? How does it ensure that public housing is improved and preserved as a viable option for the generation of aging baby boomers whose future housing needs will not be met by the housing market?

While the myriad questions that arise in examining the future of public housing are beyond the scope of this chapter, the fundamental principles that should guide the analysis can be articulated:

- Funding must be sufficient to do the job right, in terms of providing both human services and housing.
- The best interests of all current and future residents, collaboratively determined and accurately assessed, must be paramount.
- Policy must be informed by both practice and the felt experiences of those most affected.

But first, do no harm.

····· Endnotes ·····

1. The reference to "winners and losers" is from Susan Clampett-Lundquist, "Relocation: Moving to New Neighborhoods and Building New Ties," *Housing Policy Debate* 15, no. 2 (2004), p. 441. The quote about effects being mixed is from Susan J. Popkin and others, "The HOPE VI Program: What about the Residents?" *Housing Policy Debate* 15, no. 2 (2004), pp. 407–08. That "HOPE VI enhances only a small number of public housing residents" is from Michael Brazely and John I. Gilderbloom, "HOPE VI Housing Program: Was It Effective?" *American Journal of Economics and Sociology* 66, no. 2 (2007), pp. 433.

2. Egon G. Guba, "Perspectives on Public Policy: What Can Happen as a Result of Policy?" unpublished manuscript, 1985. As Guba explains, public policy is manifested in three ways that reflect at least three perspectives. First, "policy-in-intent" is the realm of policymakers; it reflects what they want to happen. Second, "policy-in-implementation" is how policy-in-intent is translated into programs. The effects of policies cannot be assessed directly; the effects of programs are the best proxies. Third, "policy-in-experience" is what happens to people and to social problems as a result of the programs that policies generate. Guba is professor emeritus of the Indiana University School of Education.

3. Using HUD data, appendix A of this volume summarizes key indicators through September 2008 for the 240 HOPE VI revitalization grants awarded from 1993 through 2007. According to HUD, 72,265 households had been relocated.

4. Mindy T. Fullilove, "What's Housing Got to Do with It?" *American Journal of Public Health* 90, no. 2 (2000), pp. 183–84.

5. Susan Bennett, "The Possibility of Beloved Place: Residents and Place Making in Public Housing Communities," in *Representing the Poor and Homeless: Innovations in Advocacy*, edited by Sidney D. Watson (Washington: American Bar Association, 2001), pp. 55–88.

6. Herbert J. Gans, *People, Plans, and Policies: Essays on Poverty, Racism, and Other National Urban Problems* (Columbia University Press, 1993), p. 267.

7. Raymond A. Mohl, "Planned Destruction: The Interstates and Central City Housing," in *From Tenements to Taylor Homes: In Search of an Urban Housing Policy in Twentieth-Century*

America, edited by John F. Bauman, Roger Biles, and Kristin M. Szylvian (Pennsylvania State University Press, 2000), pp. 226–45.

8. Bennett, "The Possibility of Beloved Place."

9. Mindy T. Fullilove, *Root Shock: How Tearing Up City Neighborhoods Hurts America and What We Can Do about It* (New York: One World Ballantine Books, 2005), p. 11.

10. Rachel G. Kleit and Lynne C. Manzo, "To Move or Not to Move: Relationships to Place and Relocation Choices in HOPE VI," *Housing Policy Debate* 17, no. 2 (2006), pp. 271–308. See also Edward G. Goetz, "Forced Relocation vs. Voluntary Mobility: The Effects of Dispersal Programmes on Households," *Housing Studies* 17, no. 1 (2003), pp. 107–23.

11. Marc Fried and Peggy Gleicher, "Some Sources of Residential Satisfaction in an Urban Slum," in *Urban Renewal: People, Politics, and Planning,* edited by Jewel Bellush and Murray Hausknecht (New York: Doubleday, 1967), pp. 120–36; Fullilove, *Root Shock;* Gans, *People, Plans, and Policies.*

12. Sudhir Venkatesh and Isil Celimli, "Tearing Down the Community," *Shelterforce 138* (November-December 2004) (www.shelterforce.com/online/issues/138/chicago.html).

13. Ibid.

14. Center for Community Change, *A Hope Unseen: Voices from the Other Side of HOPE VI* (Washington: 2003), p. 62.

15. Sara Sanders, Stan L. Bowie, and Yvonne D. Bowie, "Lessons Learned on Forced Relocation of Older Adults: The Impact of Hurricane Andrew on Health, Mental Health, and Social Support of Public Housing Residents," *Journal of Gerontological Social Work* 40, no. 4 (2003), pp. 23–35.

16. Carlos A. Manjarrez, Susan J. Popkin, and Elizabeth Guernsey, "Poor Health: Adding Insult to Injury for HOPE VI Families," in *HOPE VI: Where Do We Go from Here? Brief No. 5* (Washington: Urban Institute, 2007). The brief concluded that the mortality rate for elderly HOPE VI Panel Study participants was much higher than for black women in general of the same age. The brief also concluded that the mortality rate for HOPE VI Panel Study respondents in general was higher than the rate for a comparison group of public housing residents who applied for but did not receive a voucher under the Moving to Opportunity demonstration and therefore remained in place.

17. Popkin and others, "The HOPE VI Program: What about the Residents?" See also Sheila Crowley, "The Affordable Housing Crisis: Residential Mobility of Poor Families and School Mobility of Poor Children," *Journal of Negro Education* 72, no. 1 (2003), pp. 22–38.

18. That exchange, between officials of the Richmond (Virginia) Redevelopment and Housing Authority and the Richmond Public Schools, was witnessed by the author in the summer of 1998.

19. Jennifer Comey, "HOPE VI'd and on the Move," in *HOPE VI: Where Do We Go from Here? Brief No. 1* (Washington: Urban Institute, 2007).

20. Michael Brazely and John I. Gilderbloom, "HOPE VI Housing Program: Was It Effective?"; Susan J. Popkin and Elizabeth Cove, "Safety is the Most Important Thing: How HOPE VI Helped Families," in *HOPE VI: Where Do We Go From Here? Brief No. 2* (Washington: Urban Institute, 2007).

21. Diane K. Levy and Mark Woolley, "Relocation Is Not Enough: Employment Barriers among HOPE VI Families," in *HOPE VI: Where Do We Go from Here? Brief No. 6* (Washington: Urban Institute, 2007).

22. Larry Buron, Diane K. Levy, and Megan Gallagher, "Housing Choice Vouchers: How HOPE VI Families Fared in the Private Market," in *HOPE VI: Where Do We Go from Here? Brief No. 3* (Washington: Urban Institute, 2007).

23. Megan Gallagher and Beata Bajaj, "Moving On: Benefits and Challenges of HOPE VI for Children," in HOPE VI: Where Do We Go from Here? Brief No. 4 (Washington: Urban Institute, 2007).

24. Debi McInnis, Larry Buron, and Susan J. Popkin, "Are HOPE VI Families at Greater Risk of Homelessness?" in HOPE VI: Where Do We Go from Here? Brief No. 7 (Washington: Urban Institute, 2007).

25. U.S. General Accounting Office, Public Housing: HOPE VI Resident Issues and Changes in Neighborhoods Surrounding Grant Sites, GAO-04-109 (2003).

26. Charles Rabin, "612 Families on Housing List Missing," Miami Herald, December 12, 2006, p. 1A.

27. Charles F. Elsesser, testimony before Senate Banking, Housing, and Urban Affairs Committee, Subcommittee on Housing, Transportation, and Community Development, Reauthorization of HOPE VI, 110th Cong., 1st sess., June 20, 2007; Yvonne Stratford, testimony before House Financial Services Committee, Housing and Community Opportunity Subcommittee, Reauthorization of HOPE VI, 110th Cong., 1st sess., June 21, 2007.

28. Fred Brooks and others, "Resident Perceptions of Housing, Neighborhood, and Economic Conditions after Relocation from Public Housing Undergoing HOPE VI Redevelopment," Research on Social Work Practice 15, no. 6 (2005), pp. 481–90.

29. National Housing Law Project, False Hope: A Critical Assessment of the HOPE VI Public Housing Redevelopment Program (Oakland, Calif.: 2002).

30. Lorraine Gutiérrez and Edith A. Lewis, Empowering Women of Color (Columbia University Press, 1999).

31. Barbara L. Simon, The Empowerment Tradition in American Social Work: A History (Columbia University Press, 1994), p. 15.

32. Rhonda Y. Williams, The Politics of Public Housing (Oxford University Press, 2004).

33. Center for Community Change, A Hope Unseen; National Housing Law Project, False Hope.

34. U.S. General Accounting Office, Public Housing.

35. Center for Community Change, A Hope Unseen.

36. Ibid., p. 89

37. Ibid.

38. Section 24 of the U.S. Housing Act of 1937 as amended by Section 535 of the Quality Housing and Work Responsibility Act of 1998 (P.L. 105-276).

39. Elsesser, testimony before Senate Banking, Housing, and Urban Affairs Committee; National Housing Law Project, False Hope.

40. Stratford, testimony before House Financial Services Committee.

41. Center for Community Change, A Hope Unseen.

42. Ibid., pp. 26, 25.

43. See appendix A of this volume.

44. Jerry J. Salama, "The Redevelopment of Distressed Public Housing: Early Results from HOPE VI Projects in Atlanta, Chicago, and San Antonio," Housing Policy Debate 10, no. 1 (1999), pp. 95–142.

45. The breakdown of incomes served by type of unit comes from a report by McCormack Baron Salazar of St. Louis, Missouri, the private company that manages Centennial Place. As of June 30, 2008, 60 percent of public housing–assisted households reported annual

incomes of less than $20,000, while the 2008 HUD area median income for Atlanta was $69,200, translating into $20,760 for 30 percent AMI. Estimating that some of the 4 percent reporting no data and the 18 percent earning from $20,000 to $24,999 fall into the ELI category suggests that around two-thirds of public housing–assisted households were ELI households. The percentages of households overall in any income category come from a chart provided by McCormack Baron Salazar.

46. Debbie Cenziper, "House of Lies," *Miami Herald,* July 25, 2006, pp. 1A, 20A-21A.

47. Center for Community Change, *A Hope Unseen;* Salama, "The Redevelopment of Distressed Public Housing."

48. Center for Community Change, *A Hope Unseen,* p. 32.

49. National Housing Law Project, *False Hope.*

50. Susan J. Popkin, Mary K. Cunningham, and Martha Burt, "Public Housing Transformation and the Hard-to-House," *Housing Policy Debate* 16, no. 1(2005), p. 2.

51. Penny Gurstein and Dan Small, "From Housing to Home: Reflexive Management for Those Deemed Hard-to-House," *Housing Studies* 20, no. 5 (2005), pp. 717–35.

52. Popkin, Cunningham, and Burt, "Public Housing Transformation and the Hard-to-House."

53. HOPE VI grantees had a little more flexibility in meeting the one-for-one rule than housing authorities in general. Regulations allowed them to replace up to one-third of the demolished or disposed-of units with Section 8 tenant-based certificates.

54. The one-for-one replacement requirement was first suspended in the fiscal 1995 Rescission Bill and suspended again in subsequent years until it was permanently repealed in the Quality Housing and Work Responsibility Act of 1998.

55. The Cranston-Gonzalez National Affordable Housing Act of 1990 (P.L. 101-625) requires that jurisdictions prepare a "comprehensive housing affordability strategy" (CHAS) that includes an assessment of housing needs, the nature and extent of homelessness, and the housing market, among other information, as a condition of receiving housing assistance under the act. The CHAS was later incorporated into the Consolidated Plan, which all jurisdictions that receive community development block grant funds from HUD must prepare every five years and update annually.

56. In 1990, Congress directed HUD to conduct an annual survey of "worst-case housing needs" in the United States, defining as worst cases the housing needs of families whose income is below 50 percent of the area median and who pay more than half of their income for rent or live in substandard housing. These reports, produced by HUD's Office of Policy Development and Research, include *Priority Problems and "Worst-Case" Needs in 1989* (June 1991, HUD–1314–PDR), *The Location of Worst-Case Needs in the Late 1980s* (December 1992, HUD–1387–PDR), *Worst-Case Needs for Housing Assistance in the United States in 1990 and 1991* (June 1994, HUD–1481–PDR), *Rental Housing Assistance at a Crossroads: A Report to Congress on Worst-Case Housing Needs* (March 1996), *Rental Housing Assistance—The Crisis Continues* (April 1998), and *Rental Housing Assistance—The Worsening Crisis* (March 2000). The most recent such report is *Trends in Worst-Case Needs for Housing, 1978–1999: A Report to Congress on Worst-Case Housing Needs, Plus Update on Worst-Case Needs in 2001* (December 2003).

57. Danilo Pelletiere and Keith E. Wardrip, *Housing at the Half: A Mid-Decade Progress Report from the 2005 American Community Survey* (Washington: National Low Income Housing Coalition, 2008).

58. In the next-higher income group (very low-income, 31–50 percent of area median), the percentage of families paying more than half of their income for housing drops considerably, to 32 percent. Just 7 percent of low-income renters (51–80 percent of area median) pay more than half of their income for their homes. Only 1 percent of renters with incomes above

80 percent of AMI, who constitute 37 percent of all renters, have such a high cost burden. Pelletiere and Wardrip, *Housing at the Half.*

59. Lydia B. Taghavi, "HUD-Assisted Housing 101: Using 'A Picture of Subsidized Households: 2000,'" *Cityscape: A Journal of Policy Development and Research* 10, no. 1(2008), pp. 211–20.

60. For example, see Orlando J. Cabrera, HUD assistant secretary, testimony before Senate Banking, Housing, and Urban Affairs Committee, Subcommittee on Housing, Transportation, and Community Development, *Reauthorization of HOPE VI*, 110th Cong., 1st sess., June 20, 2007. Also see Sandra B. Henriquez, testimony before Senate Banking, Housing, and Urban Affairs Committee, Subcommittee on Housing, Transportation, and Community Development, *Reauthorization of HOPE VI*, 110th Cong., 1st sess., June 20, 2007.

61. According to appendix A, table A-1, of this volume, 48 percent of the post-revitalization units will be public housing rentals governed by the Annual Contribution Contract (ACC), offering deeply subsidized assistance.

62. For example, see Michael P. Kelly, testimony before House Finance Services Committee, Housing and Community Opportunity Subcommittee, *Reauthorization of HOPE VI*, 110th Cong., 1st sess., June 21, 2007.

63. National Housing Law Project, *False Hope.*

64. Appendix A, table A-1, of this volume.

65. National Housing Law Project, *False Hope;* Patricia A. Sughrue, "Power, Place, and Social Perceptions: A Comparative Study of Perceived HOPE VI Neighborhood Impacts in Pittsburgh, Pennsylvania," master's thesis, University of Pittsburgh, 2006; Venkatesh and Celimli, "Tearing Down the Community."

66. U.S. Department of Housing and Urban Development, "HOPE VI Program Authority and Funding History," updated March 2007, p. 1; H.R. 2764, Consolidated Appropriations Act, 2008, Division K, Title II, p. 575.

67. National Low Income Housing Coalition, FY09 Budget Chart for Selected Programs (Washington: 2008) (www.nlihc.org/doc/FY09_BudgetChart.pdf [July 22, 2008]).

68. National Low Income Housing Coalition, "Position Paper on HOPE VI Reauthorization," unpublished document, 2002.

69. Orlando J. Cabrera, Office of the President, Office of Management and Budget, "Statement of Administration Policy: H.R. 3524–HOPE VI Improvement and Reauthorization Act of 2007," January 16, 2008 (www.nlihc.org/doc/statement-of-administration.pdf [July 22, 2008]).

70. Legislation passed in the House in 2008 would require both, while legislation introduced in the Senate in 2007 would require neither. National Low Income Housing Coalition, "HOPE VI Legislation Side by Side," January 25, 2008 (www.nlihc.org/doc/NLIHC-HOPE VI-side-by-side_012508.pdf).

71. Ibid. The 2008 House bill would have tightened up requirements for determining whether a potential HOPE VI project is "severely distressed," while the Senate bill would have allowed the HUD secretary to waive evidence of physical distress as a condition of applying for a HOPE VI grant. The House set mandatory threshold criteria that a HOPE VI application must meet to be eligible for consideration, while the Senate bill had a long list of criteria that HUD must consider but is not required to meet. While both bills required resident involvement in redevelopment planning, only the House bill required it for all phases of redevelopment and detailed who should be involved and how.

72. U.S. Department of Housing and Urban Development, "Seventh Annual Report to Congress on Public Housing and Rental Assistance Programs: Demographics, Income, and Work and Rent," 2008, p. 9. Household characteristics provided are as of 2006.

RONALD D. UTT

14

The Conservative Critique of HOPE VI

By reviving the project-based assistance that many believed had ended in 1974, HOPE VI offered a comparatively expensive form of housing assistance for the needy and an incomplete solution to the ills that plague the inner-city poor and the environments in which they live. While it has had some beneficial effects, HOPE VI was perhaps overly broad in scope. With philosophical roots stretching back as far as the New Deal but operating in a far different environment, it aimed for multiple objectives but, by relying on the direct government provision of services, appears to have failed to deliver the value warranted by its expenditures. In that respect, HOPE VI shares many of the same shortcomings as the public housing construction programs preceding it.

Historically, project-based housing assistance has proved incapable of addressing the issue of the limited opportunities provided by inadequate education in many cities.

A New Deal Heritage

When the first public housing program arose under the New Deal, it represented one of the federal government's first attempts to assume some measure of responsibility for the urban environment and to use project-based housing programs to improve it.

While most central cities today are an increasingly insignificant component of the commercial, political, and cultural fabric of American life, in the 1930s and up through the early 1950s, major cities attracted a significant portion of the nation's population and much of the commerce that was not related to agriculture or extractive industries. But those central cities also housed the oldest housing stock, and the economic deprivation caused by the Great Depression left some of it in deplorable condition. The government's response, launched under the Public Works Administration in 1933 and codified in the U.S. Housing Act of 1937, was a program that aimed to create jobs in the beleaguered construction market, provide housing for the displaced, clear slums, improve the urban environment, and, in the process, generate rent revenue to service the debt incurred to build the projects.[1]

In that respect, the program shared the same philosophical underpinning as many other New Deal policies developed during the Great Depression. Despite the massive increase in government spending that it created—which tripled the federal share of GDP between 1929 and 1939—the New Deal produced many programs with a decided element of old-fashioned fiscal rectitude.[2] That fiscal attitude manifested itself chiefly in an implicit benefit-cost criterion that encouraged reliance on programs designed to meet several goals for each dollar spent and, if possible, to be self-funding. For example, the Rural Electrification Administration was established in 1935 to lend money at near market rates to rural co-ops to bring electricity to farms and, in the process, raise farm productivity and income; provide work for installers, linemen, and generator manufacturers; and, in the end, create enough rural prosperity to service the debt used to build the system.

What to Do about Cities

Despite its earlier attempts to improve the urban environment, the federal government in the post–World War II era was swimming upstream against some pretty powerful forces. Material and labor shortages during the war led to further declines in the urban housing stock. And aside from its deterioration, much of the stock was also functionally obsolete in terms of the amenities (square footage and plumbing, heating, and electrical systems) that it could offer under the best of circumstances. As a consequence, the newly prosperous postwar households often opted to live in the newer and more modern houses being constructed in the suburbs.[3]

Thus, over the postwar years, most U.S. cities began to experience the loss of their middle-class population and employment base to the surrounding suburbs or to the suburbs of cities elsewhere in the United States. (And the exodus has continued to this day, producing substantial declines in city populations. Philadelphia, which peaked at 2.1 million in 1950, had fallen to 1.5 million in 2000. Over the same period Minneapolis went from 522,000 to 383,000, while Washington, D.C., dropped from 802,000 to 572,000. With rare exceptions, this pattern was repeated in cities throughout the nation.)[4]

In the post–World War II years, U.S. cities began to lose middle-class households to the suburbs, where the housing was newer and had more modern amenities.

European cities also were losing population in the postwar years, but the racial composition of the cities (at least until recently) remained largely the same.[5] While both U.S. and European central city population declines were concentrated in the middle class, the phenomenon was probably more extreme in the United States. Partly offsetting the loss of middle-income white households in U.S. cities was an influx of lower-income African Americans moving in from the rural South.

While the proportions of the various income classes changed in European cities, the quality of public services and quality of life did not decline as dramatically as in the United States, and the cities' central core remained commercially and culturally vital, albeit less densely populated. Another difference was that most European governments did not view the changes with the same sense of alarm as did their U.S. counterparts. In contrast, beginning in the early 1950s, the federal, state, and local governments in the United States embarked on an ambitious program to demolish the worst (or most inconvenient) of the older, deteriorated housing—now occupied largely by African Americans—and to replace it with federally subsidized and locally managed public housing units, which might be constructed in another part of the city. Although the intention was to replace each razed unit with a new one, in fact production consistently fell short of demolition.

Failures of Project-Based Programs Lead to Bipartisan Support for Vouchers

Behind the postwar raze-and-build program was the presumption—which was to reappear decades later in HOPE VI—that there was more to revitalization than the provision of affordable, safe, and sanitary housing. These tidy, new projects, coupled with social services, were expected to have an uplifting effect on the inhabitants and induce them to advance beyond their existing social and economic station.

This emphasis on the effect on human behavior of what today is often called "the built environment" has characterized U.S. social (and housing) policy since the issue became an organized part of our "social thinking" in the late nineteenth century. The idea was that pathologies arising from the socially toxic environments created by rapid industrialization and urbanization could be eradicated or diminished by placing people in less squalid, more civil environments.

That approach did not seem to work especially well in the 1950s version of the plan. Many of the new public housing projects built to replace the slums often served as regional magnets for economically and socially troubled households. In turn, a number of the public housing projects soon became slums every bit as bad as those that they replaced. Among the many tragic examples was the Pruitt-Igoe public housing project in St. Louis. The project, which included 2,870 apartments in thirty-three buildings, was completed in 1956 and demolished beginning in 1972, after less than twenty years of mediocre service.[6]

In fact it was in the 1970s that the failure of this approach began to lead to a dramatic shift away from the overreaching, project-based programs to a tenant-based program that offered eligible households a rent voucher that could be exchanged for a privately provided housing unit of their choice. In effect, the social problems associated with concentrated poverty were resolved through a federally subsidized process of self-dispersal. And in one of the most extraordinary instances of bipartisan comity, in 1974 a Republican president convinced a Democratic Congress to shift all future federal housing assistance to vouchers that empowered tenants and private sector providers, removing government from the real estate business.[7]

Despite their general skepticism about federal social welfare programs, many conservatives were attracted to vouchers because vouchers

- offered the most cost-effective form of assistance
- empowered individuals, not government bureaucracies
- relied on private sector providers
- utilized the existing market process
- eliminated the role of public officials in the production and operation of housing units.

Within a relatively short period of time, those views became the bipartisan norm, and today many liberals are staunch supporters of tenant-based approaches.

Slum Clearance, Again

The increasing use of vouchers that began in the 1970s still left a stock of inherited public housing, of course, some of which was in deplorable condition and served as the epicenter of a city's worst neighborhoods. Although rent vouchers were expected to largely substitute for all of the project-based housing assistance programs, public housing remained an important component of the system.

In 1989 Congress created the National Commission on Severely Distressed Public Housing to investigate what to do about the worst of the legacy projects—the federally funded incubators of social pathologies that, unlike Pruitt-Igoe, were still standing. In 1992 the commission reported that 6 percent—or 86,000 public housing units—were severely distressed, and in the waning days of the administration of George H. W. Bush Congress enacted the new HOPE VI program.[8] It is to the credit of President Bill Clinton and Henry Cisneros, his secretary of the Department of Housing and Urban Development, that they recognized that HOPE VI could be shaped into a more systematic federal approach to addressing the problems of deteriorated housing projects and the people living in them. Those projects were also an obstacle to the companion goal of revitalizing U.S. central cities, many of which had reached a demographic and commercial nadir by the early 1990s.

Perhaps reflecting the need to compromise with Congress and accommodate influential stakeholders, the package of policies that the Clinton administration assembled into the HOPE VI program could be seen—both conceptually and programmatically—as an updated version of the failed program whose damage it was designed to offset.

Instead of clearing privately owned slums, HOPE VI would clear publicly owned slums, and instead of replacing them with the high-density public housing projects of the past—which were the fashion in the urban planning and design world of the 1940s and 1950s—it would replace them instead with low-rise communities, which were the fashion in the urban planning and design world of the 1990s. The only difference of consequence between the

In the late 1950s, slums on Chicago's South Side were razed and replaced with Stateway Gardens (visible in the background in 1959, one year after its completion) and Robert Taylor Homes (completed in 1962, encompassing the site above).

In the 1960s, girls walk by the Stateway Gardens public housing complex, whose eight high-rise buildings were a product of the urban planning and design fashions of the day.

By the summer of 2007, Stateway Gardens and other decrepit public housing projects on Chicago's South Side had been razed and were being replaced with new, low-rise mixed-income communities, in keeping with current approaches to urban planning and design. Here, in July 2007, a former Stateway Gardens family moves into Park Boulevard, built on the site of Stateway.

© 2007 David Schalliol.

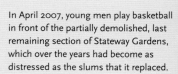

In April 2007, young men play basketball in front of the partially demolished, last remaining section of Stateway Gardens, which over the years had become as distressed as the slums that it replaced.

© 2007 David Schalliol.

past project-based approach and the present project-based intervention was that the updated version included the interim (and sometimes permanent) step of providing the displaced tenants of to-be-demolished public housing projects with HUD-funded housing vouchers or replacement units in another public housing project. Those options were not available to policymakers in the early 1950s. Beyond the programmatic similarities were conceptual similarities that saw housing as not just safe and sanitary shelter but as a "home" in a "neighborhood" that offered a package of intangible nourishments that would make its residents better people.

In 2007 the Congressional Research Service reported that between 1993 and 2006, HOPE VI dispersed $6.2 billion in 560 separate grants to eligible projects. While many demolition-only grants were made, most of the *money* was for revitalization grants—projects that included demolition, renovation or new construction or both, and social services.[9] Although the revitalization grants were intended to help leverage private and local funds, the GAO reported in 2002 that 79 percent of the leveraged funds were from other federal sources.[10]

Measuring the Success of HOPE VI

Among the many ways of assessing the HOPE VI program's success, or lack thereof, in solving the targeted problems is whether it has been more cost effective than other approaches that could have been adopted to solve the same problems.

HOUSING THE NEEDY

While all levels of government are notorious for not knowing how much it costs to do what they do, in the case of HUD's many housing assistance programs this lacuna was partially remedied in the late 1990s when the Quality Housing and Work Responsibility Act of 1998 (P.L. 105-276) required the GAO to conduct a study to determine the federal subsidy cost per household assisted for each of the federal housing assistance programs that still was supporting the construction of new units.

In an unsurprising finding consistent with the findings of internal studies conducted by HUD, the GAO identified vouchers as the least-cost vehicle for delivering housing assistance to eligible households. Table 14-1 presents some of the findings of the GAO's comparative cost study, with the cost of a voucher serving as the benchmark against which each program's cost is compared. For example, the table reveals that over the life of the project (estimated at thirty years), GAO concluded that HOPE VI would cost 27 percent more per household assisted than would a voucher.

From the perspective of a fiscal conservative, the comparative cost analysis of competing government programs is always of value in determining whether the public sector is providing the expected stewardship of taxpayers' dollars. But in the case of federal housing programs—which are means-tested programs, not

Table 14-1. First-Year and Life-Cycle Per-Household Housing Program Cost as a Percentage of the Federal Cost of a Voucher[a]

Percent

Program	First year	Life-cycle (30 years)
Low-income housing tax credits	132	112
HOPE VI	159	127
Section 202	145	119
Section 811	138	112
Section 515	142	125

Source: General Accounting Office, "Federal Housing Assistance Policy: Cost of Housing Characteristics," GAO-01-901R, July 18, 2001.

a. HOPE VI costs include only housing-related construction costs.

entitlements—the cost of fiscal inefficiency can also be measured in terms of the many low-income households that are eligible for HUD programs but nonetheless receive no assistance. Benefits are available on a first-come, first-served basis, and hundreds of thousands of eligible households remain unserved.

Table 14-1 indicates that if the HOPE VI program were terminated and the funds were redeployed to subsidize vouchers, then the number of HUD-assisted households could be increased by 25 percent for the same cost. But, of course, this cold calculus does not *always* consider the possibility that an otherwise costly program may provide additional benefits that would make it the preferred choice if the programmatic goals went beyond mere provision of a cost-effective custodial service—that is, beyond basic shelter—for low-income households.

IMPROVING THE SOCIAL ENVIRONMENT

In the case of HOPE VI, the benefits expected in addition to the provision of housing included improvements in the social environment—reduced crime, increased economic opportunity, financial independence, and other attributes associated with economic advancement and neighborhood revitalization. In particular it was expected that the low-density design of the new structures, combined with the mix of households of different incomes (low-income assisted households would be living in the same development as unsubsidized, middle-income households), would contribute to a better social environment and expedite the process of self-advancement among the poor. Some scholars have defined the added qualitative benefits of income mixing as follows:

– increased social capital
– informal social control leading to safer and more orderly communities
– direct or indirect role modeling of social norms for work and behavior
– gains for the broader community through enhanced social engagement of political and market forces.[11]

HOPE VI thus rests on the presumption that the poor among us are susceptible to certain negative influences from other poor households from which other income classes apparently are immune. HOPE VI therefore was expected to provide low-income tenants with the opportunity to be indirectly mentored by their economic and social betters who also lived in the project. (Now, this goal is also often accomplished by the voucher program, and the outcome is thought to be one of the voucher program's chief attractions. But apparently some federal officials, and most likely some members of Congress, were uncomfortable with the left-to-chance, unmanaged nature of the race and income mixing that the voucher program accomplished.)

But not all scholars in the field are convinced that income mixing yields significantly positive results, a skepticism likely fueled by some reports that low- and moderate-income neighbors in HOPE VI redevelopments have limited interaction.[12] In a recent study, Mark Joseph of Case Western Reserve University drew the following conclusions:

> There is a tremendous amount of hyperbole about and hope for mixed-income development. My analysis suggests that we should lower our expectations about its impact on low-income residents. Short- to medium-term effects in terms of social order and increased quality of goods and services seem to be reasonable. The new developments seem certain to improve the overall living environment for the low-income families that move in and thus will have an indirect effect on their well-being. However, it is also possible that low-income families may experience significant personal and familial challenges in the new environment, including social isolation, stigma, a sense of relative deprivation, increased scrutiny, and competition with more affluent residents for scarce local resources. . . .
>
> Promoting sustainable changes in the lives of low-income residents who move from neighborhoods with concentrated poverty to mixed-income developments will generally require combining housing with investments in social services, education, job readiness, training and placement, and transportation.[13]

As briefly touched on earlier, an issue seldom raised in discussions about the benefits of income mixing is whether social influence moves in both directions—that is, whether the presence of troubled, low-income households in mixed-income projects is likely to have a deleterious effect on families of other income classes, most notably on those just above them, often referred to as the working poor. While housing vouchers have generally received strong support from most conservatives, some conservative-leaning analysts oppose vouchers because they may have an adverse impact (through income mixing) on those who have successfully struggled to escape poverty but nonetheless are still close to the edge, in terms of income and neighborhood, and thus vulnerable to slipping back. Howard Husock of Harvard's Kennedy School argues that

> [O]ut in the blue-collar and middle-class neighborhoods where voucher holders increasingly live, longtime residents hate the program. It

undermines and destabilizes their communities by importing social problems into their midst.[14]

Whether these voucher-related fears are translating into rising crime, middle-class flight, and economic deterioration has probably not been systematically investigated or properly documented; it also is probably too early to tell whether similar fears, concerns, or outcomes characterize any of the HOPE VI projects that rely on income mixing to achieve desired social benefits.

ENHANCING SELF-SUFFICIENCY OF RESIDENTS
AND NEIGHBORHOODS

Even if HOPE VI does make contributions toward improving the social environment, is its approach (beyond the demolition and dispersal components) a cost-effective way to improve the social and economic characteristics of a troubled population—as well as a struggling neighborhood or a city in decline—in ways that will soon lead its members to financial self-sufficiency and a productive role in U.S. society? If not, is HOPE VI little more than an expensive way to revive project-based housing assistance in a more socially hygienic way than its predecessors?

While there is some evidence that HOPE VI leads to a reduction in neighborhood crime and seems (so far) to be free of the problems that had previously infected contiguous neighborhoods (a benefit that may be largely attributable to the demolition and dispersal components of the program), it does not (and neither do vouchers, apparently) seem to lead to the self-betterment that would encourage program beneficiaries to become financially self-sufficient. As Sue Popkin of the Urban Institute and Mary Cunningham of the National Alliance to End Homelessness note in chapter 11 of this volume:

> In addition to providing residents with an improved environment, the HOPE VI program sought to help them attain self-sufficiency. However, while the panel study results document dramatic improvements in quality of life for many respondents, there were no changes in employment or self-sufficiency for private market movers, the few HOPE VI movers, or those who remained in traditional public housing. At baseline, 48 percent of the working-age respondents were not working, even part-time—the same share as at the 2003 and the 2005 follow-ups. Findings from the panel study suggest that standard HOPE VI relocation and community support services are unlikely to affect employment or address the many factors that keep extremely disadvantaged residents out of the labor force.

HOPE VI therefore might be viewed as a more costly, though perhaps tidier and less intrusive, human custodial program performing essentially the same role as the public housing that preceded it. In chapter 10 of this volume, the Urban Institute's Margery Austin Turner wonders whether the positive impact that some HOPE VI projects have on the surrounding neighborhood can be fully credited to HOPE VI:

> [W]hile the revitalization of public housing can have a sizable impact on the revitalization of surrounding neighborhoods, dramatic turn-arounds are not likely to be achieved—and should not be expected—everywhere. Moreover, where neighborhood transformation has occurred, questions remain about the extent to which the HOPE VI investment *caused* the improvements. In many cases, other public sector investments—some of which were launched earlier or in adjacent neighborhoods—may have helped trigger the market turnaround.

Starting Over?

One way to evaluate the efficacy of any government program and its approach more effectively is to pretend that the program does not exist but that the problems and issues that it was expected to address do. In the case of HOPE VI, suppose that the process of policymaking begins with a focus on the problem itself. In this case we recognize that one of the greatest urban challenges is a largely minority, unemployed, uneducated, very poor, financially dependent, unmarried, crime-prone population. Further, we reason that this particular problem is (perhaps) a subset of a broader problem: to wit, that many of the urban centers of which these troubled populations are a part face their own severe challenges from other, more competitive communities. We conclude that the potential solution set may include elements that address both challenges. With the challenges so defined, would an exhaustive vetting of all of the options that clever analysts could devise conclude that HOPE VI was the most cost-effective solution to the puzzle? Indeed, would any project-based housing assistance program be deemed the best way to deal with this set of complex, deep-seated problems? Not likely.

Housing policy debates and discussions of the sort that characterize the chapters in this book often fail to address the more fundamental proposition that the typical social welfare problem—whether related to housing, hunger, health care, or education—is, in fact, an income problem. With rare exception, people living in substandard housing do so because that is all that they can afford; likewise, those who suffer from inadequate health care and nutrition usually do so because their incomes are insufficient to purchase the necessary health care services or foods. Although they inexplicably excepted a good portion of the existing housing assistance programs, federal policymakers long ago recognized that fact and created a series of pseudo–income-enhancement mechanisms to deliver certain social services: the government provides food stamps instead of food commodities; instead of building federal hospitals and hiring doctors, the government has established Medicare and Medicaid to reimburse the cost of privately acquired health care.[15]

While these delivery programs formally acknowledged that inadequate incomes were the problem, little was done to try to enhance the income-producing potential of the programs' beneficiaries. That changed somewhat in 1996 with the passage of the Personal Responsibility and Work Opportunity Reconciliation Act, which offered a more promising approach by mandating stricter work requirements to prod welfare recipients into financial independence.[16] While the Temporary Assistance for Needy Families program had some promising results in its first decade of operation, many of the households that it serves continue to exist in urban environments that are inimical to personal advancement, to receive federal benefits (housing assistance) whose availability is independent of work effort, and to have attitudes and a lack of education and other life skills that discourage financial independence and other social gains even in better environments.[17]

Back to Basics

Under the circumstances and given the finding that HOPE VI projects appear to represent a costly form of housing assistance with a limited impact on many of HOPE VI's quality-of-life objectives, perhaps a more productive approach might be to consider major revisions in the federal housing and welfare programs—revisions based on approaches that emphasize the fundamentals of human advancement and put the burden of improvement on the beneficiary, rather than on the manipulated neighborhood environment.

As others have noted, the HOPE VI program has eliminated the externalities associated with blight and offered many a better living environment. What it has not achieved is the goal of self-sufficiency and financial independence among participants. And as others also have noted, the same outcomes and more can be achieved less expensively with vouchers.

Vouchers also have the advantage of being a service delivery mechanism that can be more readily linked to a tighter work requirement, which should be made a condition of any HUD housing assistance. And more important, vouchers represent a delivery mechanism that recognizes that all human progress follows from people moving to opportunity—unlike HOPE VI, which is based on the implicit belief that opportunity can be moved to people. Unless the nation's vast social service industry can overcome its squeamishness toward efforts that forcefully compel and frighten its wards into doing the right thing, many decades from now our grandchildren will be writing a book much like this one and wondering, with a similar degree of mystification, why they are still in this costly quandary.[18]

With research suggesting a number of reasons to be skeptical of HOPE VI's positive impact on a range of issues and with the quality-of-life improvements

The general mediocrity of inner-city schools (this one, in Chicago, is shown prior to demolition) makes central cities less competitive with the suburbs for middle-class residents.

for voucher recipients reportedly the same as for those moving into new HOPE VI projects, why not stick with the less expensive option—voucher/certificates—and help a larger number of households? And on the larger issues of central city renewal and revitalization, why not consider approaches that rely on something more effective than the blunt instrument of subsidized, project-based, housing units dedicated largely to the poor?

As I have noted in other sources, cities will not be competitive until they offer residents full value for taxes paid.[19] With many older central cities providing mediocre services in areas of compelling importance—public safety and public education to name just two—and at the same time imposing the highest tax rates in the metropolitan area, they are no more competitive in the market than a dollar store charging Neiman Marcus prices. The HOPE VI approach does not, and cannot, address these issues, and there is no reason to expect a population whose opportunities are limited by inadequate education to somehow find salvation in a community in a city that is unable to provide them an adequate education.

····· Endnotes ·····

1. This history comes from Linda B. Fosburg, Susan J. Popkin, and Gretchen P. Locke, *An Historical and Baseline Assessment of HOPE VI*, vol. 1, *Cross-Site Report* (Abt Associates, July 1996) (www.huduser.org/Publications/pdf/hopevi_vol1.pdf).

2. *Budget of the U.S. Government: Fiscal Year 2009, Historical Tables* (Government Printing Office, 2008), table 1-2, p. 24.

3. At the same time, many cities in the South and West used the process of annexation to accommodate suburbanization while keeping the growing population within the city limits.

4. Demographia, "U.S. Population from 1790: Cities Achieving Population 300,000 or More" (www.demographia.com/db-uscity1790.htm [April 14, 2008]).

5. While we tend to look at this central city depopulation pattern as a U.S. phenomenon, the same trend occurred in most of the major cities in Europe and Asia—often for similar reasons—and sometimes began at an earlier date. Paris's population peaked in 1921 at 2.9 million; today it is 2.1 million, as many more millions of French families have opted for the suburbs and their single-family detached homes.

6. Alexander von Hoffman, "Why They Built Pruitt-Igoe," Harvard University, Joint Center for Housing Studies (www.soc.iastate.edu/sapp/PruittIgoe.html [April 18, 2008]). Note that different completion dates and unit counts are found in other sources, such as a completion date of 1954 and a unit count of 2,762 in Alexander Garvin, *The American City: What Works, What Doesn't* (New York: McGraw-Hill, 1996).

7. The Housing and Community Development Act of 1974 (P.L. 93-383) established the Section 8 rental assistance program, which fell into two categories: project-based subsidies, under which developers receiving subsidies had to reserve units for low-income tenants for a specific time period, and tenant-based subsidies, a housing allowance that low-income people could use to pay for private rental apartments, with the government contracting to cover a portion of the rent. Though there had been some use of private market units prior to Section 8, it was the first program in which the private landlord handled all the leasing and maintenance responsibilities.

8. Maggie McCarty, "HOPE VI Public Housing Revitalization Program: Background, Funding and Issues," *CRS Report for Congress,* updated March 30, 2007, p. CRS-2.

9. Ibid., p. CRS-7.

10. U.S. General Accounting Office, "HOPE VI Leveraging Has Increased, but HUD Has Not Met Annual Reporting Requirement," GAO-03-91, November 2002, p. 8. In the report, GAO explains that it counts LIHTCs as a federal outlay while HUD does not.

11. Lawrence J. Vale, "Comment on Mark Joseph's 'Is Mixed-Income Development an Antidote to Urban Poverty,'" *Housing Policy Debate* 17, no. 2 (2006), p. 260.

12. Mark L. Joseph, "Early Resident Experiences at a New Mixed-Income Development in Chicago," *Journal of Urban Affairs* 30, no. 2 (2008), pp. 229–57; Rachel Garshick Kleit, "HOPE VI New Communities: Neighborhood Relationships in Mixed-Income Housing," *Environment and Planning* A 37, no. 8 (2005), pp. 1413–41 (www.envplan.com/abstract.cgi?id=a3796 [October 7, 2008]).

13. Mark L. Joseph, "Is Mixed-Income Development an Antidote to Urban Poverty?" *Housing Policy Debate* 17, no. 2 (2006), pp. 222–23. See also Vale, "Comment on Mark Joseph's 'Is Mixed-Income Development an Antidote to Urban Poverty?'" pp. 259–69.

14. Howard Husock, *America's Trillion-Dollar Housing Mistake: The Failure of American Housing Policy* (Chicago: Ivan R. Dee, 2003), p. 45

15. By the time the voucher program was enacted in 1974, housing assistance was the last of the federal benefit programs relying exclusively on the delivery of a physical product. While vouchers have gained policy share since then, they still coexist with a robust program dependent on the provision of physical units. The HOPE VI program represents the first major (and successful) effort to reimplement project-based assistance.

16. Efforts to apply meaningful work requirements to housing assistance have been consistently rejected by a majority of Congress.

17. In chapter 11 in this volume, Popkin and Cunningham cite the panel study's finding that the major factor affecting employment status is health, that HOPE VI Panel Study respondents are in poor health, and that two of every five respondents rated their health as fair or poor. However, one has to question the validity of a survey in which poorly educated people are asked to conduct a medical self-diagnosis and relate the finding to their ability to participate in a modern economy.

18. The premise of meaningful welfare reform for able-bodied, non-elderly assisted households is that they understand that the benefits that they are receiving will soon end and thus they must become financially self-sufficient or risk hunger and homelessness.

19. Ronald D. Utt, "What to Do about the Cities," *Heritage Backgrounder* 1216, September 1, 1998.

CHAPTER

G. THOMAS KINGSLEY

15

Taking Advantage of What We Have Learned

The HOPE VI story is a striking one. A program conceived as a means of dealing with the devastating conditions in the worst public housing projects grew into what many see as HUD's most impressive neighborhood redevelopment initiative, pumping nearly $6 billion in HOPE VI grants and a total of $8.5 billion in federal investment into 240 neighborhoods and providing 111,059 new and renovated housing units, 59,674 of them affordable for low-income, public housing–assisted families.[1] HOPE VI engaged local leaders and private investors in public housing redevelopment, bringing new constituencies to public housing and allowing many local housing authorities to become players in broader local housing and development systems. And, by deconcentrating poverty in a very visible way, HOPE VI furthered wider public rejection of the notion that a healthy society could leave its poorest members in isolated enclaves.

The Broadway Overlook HOPE VI in east Baltimore occupies a prominent place in a vibrant city neighborhood.

© 2004
J. Brough Schamp/
www.Schamp.com

Innovations that break so substantially from business as usual are rare events in government. Even its critics generally acknowledge that HOPE VI has shattered the conventional wisdom about what public housing can be and has moved the public housing program to a place very different from where it was a decade and a half ago.

But where should policymakers go from here? Some might suggest that HOPE VI has largely finished its job and that it is time to move on to other programs. That would be short-sighted. Now more than ever, the HOPE VI experience deserves prominence in policy debates. HOPE VI offers lessons—learned from its problems as well as its successes—that can make a notable difference in the effectiveness of the overall public housing program if they are fully applied. But perhaps more significant, the HOPE VI experience also has important things to say about how we can strengthen our cities and metropolitan regions.

Accordingly, the first part of this chapter reviews how the context of public housing has changed over the past fifteen years and then recommends ways to take advantage of HOPE VI's lessons to improve public housing overall.

The second part addresses opportunities for applying HOPE VI's lessons in urban policymaking.

HOPE VI and Public Housing Progress

In the early 1990s, public housing was widely considered to be one of the most dysfunctional government programs. Much of its reputation derived from the "severely distressed" projects that were the subject of the 1992 report of the National Commission on Severely Distressed Public Housing.[2] Though a comparatively small share of public housing, those projects were in such deplorable condition that they colored the public's perception of the program. By taking on the challenge that they presented, HOPE VI more than anything else helped change the image and state of public housing.

Public housing and neighborhood conditions improved. Thanks in great part to HOPE VI, most of the nation's large distressed public housing projects have been eliminated. By September 2008, 91,802 public housing units had been demolished under the first 240 HOPE VI revitalization grants. Those grants, made through 2007, had produced 72,196 newly constructed or rehabilitated units, with tens of thousands more units in the pipeline.[3]

The public housing projects that were replaced were not the comparatively stable communities of color broken up by the urban renewal program of the 1950s and 1960s, with which HOPE VI has been compared by a few critics. Although comparatively poor, the minority communities destroyed then typically had a mix of incomes, sizable working populations, strong social ties and institutions, and relatively safe streets. In contrast, the public housing projects selected for HOPE VI represented some of the most hazardous living environments that the nation has ever produced.

Almost all of these developments were racially and economically isolated and inhabited primarily by residents who were extremely poor and dependent on welfare. Statistics from one study of twenty-three early HOPE VI sites tell a story of community instability: 84 percent of residents reported income from public assistance, a majority of the households were headed by single women, and median household income was $5,350.[4] The residents lived in close quarters in structures that at best had unreliable or outdated plumbing or electrical systems and peeling paint and at worst had crumbling foundations, broken windows, and rodents.[5] In many cases, the combination of vulnerable residents living in poorly designed buildings with unsecured public spaces led to graffiti, crime, and drug trafficking in elevators, stairwells, and apartments. A reputation for crime, as well as physical deterioration and poor management, led to vacancy rates averaging 35 percent; in contrast, the rate for public housing projects in general was only 8 percent.[6]

The neighborhoods surrounding the projects also were almost always physically deteriorated and characterized by high unemployment rates, low incomes, and high rates of dependence on public assistance. Though in some communities churches and nonprofit organizations provided valuable services and political leadership, the neighborhoods lacked access to banks, supermarkets, and other goods and services typical of functioning communities.[7]

In the place of such severely unhealthy communities, HOPE VI has created in every region of the country architecturally attractive new communities in which public housing residents and those with higher incomes live side by side. Many of these redeveloped public housing sites have seen substantial increases in per capita incomes and substantial declines in unemployment rates and dependence on public assistance. Many of the surrounding neighborhoods have experienced a marked drop in crime and increases in investment and property values.[8] While only time will tell how sustainable the redevelopments will be, the mixed-financing techniques that fund them create powerful incentives for managers to apply high standards in running them over the long term.[9] And although social interaction between groups of tenants appears limited, the new developments offer powerful images of change, particularly when contrasted to the decaying physical and social environments that they replaced.[10] As argued later in this chapter, that has had a positive effect on public attitudes about the potential for urban improvement more broadly.

HOPE VI projects often seemed expensive.[11] But criticisms of HOPE VI on the grounds of cost generally fail to consider that continuing to operate the existing dysfunctional projects also would have entailed a very high cost. They also generally fail to take into account the net public benefits created when

Below left: In 1995, children run by the building in the Chicago Housing Authority's Ida B. Wells complex where a five-year-old boy was killed a year earlier.

AP Photo/Beth A. Keiser.

Below right: Children play in Oakwood Shores, the HOPE VI–funded community that is replacing the Wells, Madden, and Darrow public housing projects.

Mark Ballogg/Ballogg Photography.

transformed communities substantially improve property values in surrounding neighborhoods. According to one study, the net public benefit—including neighborhood effects—of redeveloping a typical large project under HOPE VI exceeded the long-term costs of continuing to operate the project as it was by $22 million.[12]

In addition to the units demolished under the HOPE VI revitalization program, many more public housing units were demolished or otherwise removed from the inventory under other programs that started later in the 1990s after Congress revoked the one-for-one replacement requirement. Many housing authorities started to demolish other older projects, providing vouchers to the tenants but not replacing any of the buildings.[13] The Center on Budget and Policy Priorities estimates that under all programs, nearly 200,000 units were demolished or disposed of between 1995 and 2008.[14] Less than half of those units were in HOPE VI revitalization projects.[15] Subtracting the replacement units that had been built, the total public housing inventory had declined on net by 165,000 units, a drop of 12 percent from the 1.33 million total at the start of the period.[16]

Since the projects demolished within and outside of HOPE VI generally were the most deteriorated—and located in the most distressed neighborhoods— the average condition of the nation's public housing stock has improved markedly. There are substantially fewer public housing families living in extreme poverty neighborhoods or in large public housing developments.[17] And the overwhelming majority of public housing tenants are now in homes that are in decent physical condition. According to HUD's inspection report for FY 2007, more than 85 percent of the nation's public housing units were in structures that then met or exceeded HUD standards for physical condition.[18]

Quality of life improved for residents who relocated with vouchers. Research shows that the majority of former residents who used vouchers to relocate from distressed public housing sites under HOPE VI experienced meaningful improvements in their quality of life (see chapter 11). They moved to better-quality housing in neighborhoods that were much less poor and dramatically safer, though not much less racially segregated. Typically, they relocated in small numbers to a diverse array of neighborhoods.[19] Most relocatees appear to be quite satisfied with their new neighborhoods and to have no interest in returning, even if they still receive HUD housing assistance.[20] However, the voucher approach did not work for everyone. Some residents— for example, elderly people and those with multiple problems—had a hard time fulfilling the obligations of tenants in private apartments. But they were clearly a minority.

A key to the success in voucher relocation was likely that the numbers moving into any one neighborhood typically were too small to have a noticeable effect on the character of the receiving neighborhoods. Although there were

Figure 14.1. How Public Housing Has Improved

Family public housing units located in extreme poverty neighborhoods[a,b]

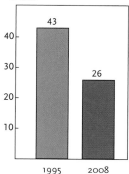

Public housing units in projects with more than 500 units[b]

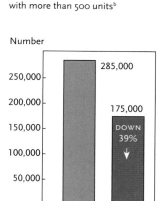

Percentage of families with children in public housing relying on welfare for primary income

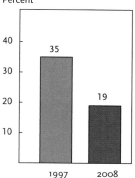

a. Extreme-poverty neighborhoods are defined as neighborhoods in which 2 out of every 5 families live below the poverty line.

b. Data exclude U.S. territories.

Adapted with permission from Barbara Sard and Will Fischer, "Preserving Safe, High-Quality Public Housing Should Be a Priority of Federal Housing" (Washington: Center on Budget and Policy Priorities, September 18, 2008), p. 7.

exceptions, complaints from existing neighborhood residents were comparatively rare. In 2008 one highly publicized article implied that individuals relocated under HOPE VI might have led to increased crime rates in the suburbs of Memphis. However, subsequent reviews raised questions about the methods used to arrive at that inference, and there is no evidence to suggest that rising crime connected to vouchers has become a major concern nationally.[21]

Public housing authorities gained capacity. Under HOPE VI, a large number of housing authorities showed that they could partner with a variety of outside entities; assemble sophisticated development packages that meet the exacting standards of private sector real estate practice; leverage substantial private capital through tax credits, taxable and tax-exempt bonds, and debt financing as well as equity participation; and, although too slowly in some cases, get their projects built and occupied. They also showed that they could ensure sound professional management of completed properties in mixed-income, mixed-finance environments.

Housing authorities have already started to use the same financial tools applied to HOPE VI projects to tackle the renovation of the rest of the traditionally capital-starved public housing inventory. For example, as Rick Gentry noted in chapter 12, the Philadelphia Housing Authority used bonds secured by public housing capital funds and other sources to redevelop the Tasker Homes public housing community into the mixed-income Greater

Grays Ferry Estates and used the remaining funds to modernize sections of two other public housing sites. The past two decades of declining federal public housing appropriations have highlighted the risk of relying solely on government funding for public housing, and housing authorities' demonstrated capacity to secure private capital investment for public housing is a critical safeguard for this national asset.

New consensus built around policy goals. The fundamental themes of HOPE VI—integrating public housing and its residents into the mainstream, leveraging private sector investment, providing more effective planning and management of resources at the local level—have gained wide recognition in the nation's policy community. In 2000, for example, Harvard University's Kennedy School of Government awarded HOPE VI its coveted Innovations in American Government award.[22] And those themes have indeed gained primacy among public housing practitioners and policymakers.

At the local level, leading housing authorities are using the finance tools mentioned earlier to reconfigure their portfolios to better meet local needs and better weather funding trends. In some cases that includes converting subsidies for public housing units to vouchers and pursuing mixed-income redevelopments outside of HOPE VI. It also may include converting tenant-based vouchers to project-based vouchers that can help finance new residences in a range of settings for the neediest households in and outside of traditional public housing developments.

At the federal level, the HOPE VI experience was the basis for most of the key public housing reforms enacted—with strong bipartisan support—in the landmark Quality Housing and Work Responsibility Act (QHWRA) of 1998. A fundamental promise of QHWRA was to improve the managerial performance of the public housing system through deregulation and local capacity building, modeled in many ways on the structured flexibility that was central to the success of the HOPE VI approach.

In addition to QHWRA, a move toward deregulation was taken in 1996 with the development of Moving to Work (MTW), a demonstration program that gave a small number of public housing authorities wide discretion in the design of program fundamentals (for example, rent formulas and time limits on receipt of housing assistance) as well as in the use of funds. Unfortunately, the design of the program did not allow for proper program evaluation.[23] Proposals have been made to extend the MTW approach to a much larger range of agencies. While it might be attractive to do so for some of the managerial flexibility MTW offers, it would be very risky to change program fundamentals without a full evaluation.[24]

Finally, it is important to note the stark difference between today's view of public housing and the climate of opinion that existed in the mid-1990s. The stereotype of menacing housing projects ill-managed by ineffectual public housing agencies no doubt played a role in the call at that time to abolish HUD altogether, which Alex Polikoff recounts in chapter 5. While advocates have rightly focused attention on the loss of public housing units since then, the losses could have been much greater.

The Unfinished Business of HOPE VI and Public Housing Reform

HOPE VI and the management reforms that it inspired have strengthened the condition and image of public housing and created new opportunities for residents and neighborhoods. However, those gains have not come without some costs, nor have they cleared the deck of all challenges. There remain grave threats to the quantity and quality of the housing inventory and to the capacities and well-being of residents.

Reductions in public housing focused attention on sustaining the inventory. In the United States in 2005, 5.54 million low-income renters were receiving housing assistance—1.05 million in public housing and the rest through other programs. Yet there were an additional 12.4 million low-income renters who needed housing assistance but did not receive it—households that were living in physically deficient or overcrowded housing or paying more than 30 percent of their income for rent.[25] That means that our nation was providing housing assistance to less than a third of those who needed it.

Surely, this is a time for expanding rather than cutting back housing assistance, and in that light, the marked reduction of the public housing inventory cited earlier (net decline of 12 percent from 1995 through 2008) is disturbing.

In the 1990s there was a good case for tearing down the worst projects, but now most of those projects are gone and the inventory on average is of much higher quality. While there are still some projects that warrant demolition, preservation generally now would be the more efficient approach. The Center on Budget and Policy Priorities has estimated that, on average, rehabilitating currently available public housing developments and funding their continuing operation for thirty years would cost *8 percent less* than tearing them down and replacing them with vouchers.[26] The call is not for a rigid rule preventing demolitions, but for a new, flexible approach that would allow the inventory to adapt without any further net loss in assisted units.

As things stand, however, the lack of adequate funding for operating and upgrading the stock has created strong incentives for demolition and vouchering out. Federal appropriations for capital expenses—such as the cost of replacing aging heating and cooling systems or nonworking appliances—are consumed by new annually accruing needs. That leaves a backlog of capital needs estimated to cost anywhere from $22 billion to $32 billion or more, depending on how many of the units are so obsolete that they require replacement rather than renovation.[27]

A system in which the cost of deferred maintenance and upkeep far outstrips federal allocations poses the very real risk that currently stable public housing complexes will fall into the same sort of disrepair that had destabilized neighborhoods and much of the overall public housing system fifteen years ago. The challenge calls for more widespread application of the creative approaches to private financing that public housing authorities have started to employ in recent years as well as a more responsible approach by Congress to funding the program.

Inadequate support services revealed inexperience. Few, if any, observers argue that residents of the highly distressed public housing projects selected for revitalization should have been left living in the deplorable conditions that existed there. Allowing those projects to continue to operate at public expense would have been inconsistent with our standards as a nation. However, implementing the relocation and support service programs aimed at enhancing life outcomes for former residents has been a serious challenge for many housing authorities.

Although many former residents of the public housing projects redeveloped under HOPE VI moved to better housing in safer, less poor neighborhoods, a substantial number relocated to other traditional public housing developments that were only marginally better than the distressed developments that they had left behind. Further, despite outcomes that, on net, were positive, relocation under HOPE VI appears to have often been unnecessarily painful. Generally, housing authorities did not anticipate how much counseling and support services would be required to effectively guide residents' transition to new homes and new neighborhoods. Some of them made heroic efforts in that regard, although it was an area in which few had much prior experience.

In some instances, relocation was more blatantly mismanaged; residents were not meaningfully engaged in redevelopment planning and were misled about how they would be affected.[28] In some cases, housing authorities reneged on promises to allow residents to return. While there is no evidence that such problems were widespread, those are serious faults that should be addressed in redevelopment and relocation efforts going forward.[29]

HOPE VI called for the provision of social services but was initially vague about what services should be provided, toward what ends. In the late 1990s, new policies clarified that help should go to original residents, begin before relocation, and focus on helping residents move toward self-sufficiency, consistent with welfare reform themes. A HUD guidance paper promoted case management, whereby "an experienced case manager assesses the needs and circumstances of each family holistically and makes referrals to an appropriate range of service providers based on the priorities these individual assessments suggest."[30]

This approach showed that most public housing residents do not need extensive services to progress along the path to self-sufficiency, but there

Implementing the relocation and support service programs aimed at enhancing life outcomes for former residents has been a serious challenge for many housing authorities.

remains a sizable number of residents with multiple problems whose needs for support services are substantial. HOPE VI housing authorities generally inexperienced in this line of work struggled to hire and manage the requisite staff in house or to contract with existing local social service agencies to help such families. But when housing authorities did partner with other providers, the conflicting regulations and distinct operating styles of their programs often got in the way.

The HOPE VI experience made it impossible to ignore the fact that there are large numbers of families living in public housing that have substantial needs for support services. HOPE VI program managers deserve considerable credit for being the first in the system to recognize those needs explicitly and to make a forceful effort to address them at scale. The challenge now is finding an effective way to address them throughout the existing inventory.

Management reforms were incomplete. While HOPE VI has done much to improve the image and condition of public housing, considerable work remains to transform public housing into the well-functioning system that the United States needs to address its pressing housing challenges. The housing authorities at the forefront of HOPE VI achievements may include those agencies serving the most people, but they still represent a small share of all housing authorities. HUD puts only about 6 percent of all authorities into its "troubled" category, but many more that are in between still have a long way to go before they are managing their housing stock effectively.[31]

Of major concern are the public housing reform efforts under QHWRA, which appear to have stalled a decade after the law's enactment. A review by Rod Solomon in 2004 showed that the path to implementation of the act was far from smooth, and recent developments highlight continuing barriers to improving performance.[32] For example, while HUD has now strongly endorsed the asset management approach to operating the public housing stock systemwide, implementation appears to be heavy-handed. Further progress will require a more flexible approach that will allow taking "to scale" the lessons learned from HOPE VI throughout the public housing program.

HOPE VI's Lessons for Public Housing

Since the early 1990s, considerable progress has been made toward the goal of creating a portfolio of sustainable, well-managed public housing that is an asset to both the families that need assistance and the communities in which the housing is located. But much remains to be done to address the challenges outlined earlier.

Meeting those challenges calls for broader application of the policy principles that have distinguished HOPE VI: flexibility to design and implement federal programs to meet local needs; partnerships among housing authorities and local stakeholders; mixed-income strategies; asset management; and the broad use of mixed-finance tools. It also requires the sensitive application of lessons learned from HOPE VI's shortcomings regarding relocation and support services for original residents. The following are HOPE VI-inspired lessons for sustaining public housing as an asset to needy households and communities.[33]

Reinvigorate public housing regulatory reform. As noted, progress on the deregulation agenda set by QHWRA and modeled in part on the structured flexibility of HOPE VI appears to be stalled. If that does not change, it seems unlikely that any other steps toward preserving public housing can be fully effective. Indeed, leaders from the public housing, real estate development and finance, and policy research sectors pulled together by the Council of Large Public Housing Authorities in mid-2008 identified an outdated regulatory system as one of the key threats to the sustainability of public housing.[34] The final policy framework document that resulted from this high-level summit on the future of public housing noted that the present regulatory regime diverts resources away from property management and modernization and resident services and undermines efforts to bring new partners and their capital investments to the table. The summit calls for a new effort to "redefine the relationship between HUD and PHAs through sensible regulation that achieves both accountability and the flexibility to address local conditions."[35]

Moving forward, HUD should apply different regulatory regimes to different groups of housing authorities, depending on the level of risk that they pose to the system. Under this tiered approach, the smallest authorities, which already have seen their annual plan requirement streamlined, would be relieved of more of the burdensome requirements that apply to larger authorities. Larger authorities judged to be outstanding performers would be exempt from a wide range of current rules and reporting obligations. Instead, they would face a short list of clear performance expectations, with the threat of subsequent audits and serious penalties for noncompliance. This emphasis on flexibility in exchange for accountability would be reinforced by the current QHWRA requirement that housing authorities prepare one- and five-year operating plans and submit them to local stakeholders for review.

HUD supervision would continue for other authorities, with the level of support, technical assistance, and monitoring tailored to the authority's situation and designed to improve performance and prevent deficiencies from sending the agencies into troubled status. Sanctions or threats of sanctions may be needed when performance trends are negative. At the extreme—as provided for in QHWRA but not implemented—troubled authorities would be given firm deadlines to correct their performance problems. Those that fail to demonstrate sustainable improvements would be taken over by HUD, another agency, or a receiver.[36]

This tiered regulatory approach should provide the management flexibility offered under the MTW program to the right housing authorities when they are ready for it. As noted earlier, it would be unwise to extend MTW's flexibility to changes in program fundamentals such as alternative rent rules and time limits until those changes have been carefully tested and evaluated.

Perhaps most important, regulations need to be modified to facilitate housing authorities' ability to transfer subsidy commitments to alternative properties after a project has been demolished. Traditionally, authorities have received funds from HUD under an Annual Contributions Contract (ACC) tied to specific units. When those units are demolished or otherwise disposed of, there has been a commensurate reduction in the subsidy. It would make sense instead to allow the housing authority to transfer the subsidy commitment to another property located where the need is great, particularly to mixed-income environments. For example, there is no reason why the commitment could not be transferred to selected units in privately owned apartment buildings as long as the housing authority continues to manage the units over the long term.

This subsidy-transfer approach offers an alternative to vouchers when demolition is warranted, as for run-down properties in high-poverty neighborhoods. It is consistent with the emphasis on flexible preservation advocated earlier, allowing changes in the inventory managed by the public housing authority without any net reduction in units. Arrangements to transfer subsidies have been made to work under existing statutes, but doing so has been an administrative nightmare.[37] Regulations—and organizational cultures—should be modified so that transfers will be encouraged and facilitated.

Align public housing with broader metropolitan housing strategies. As outlined later in this chapter, the United States needs a new system to ensure that its metropolitan areas will adequately expand the stock of affordable housing and create healthy mixed-income neighborhoods in the suburbs as well as the central cities.

Public housing resources should be included in planning for regional housing strategies, and public housing authorities should actively participate in the process, reflecting regional priorities in their own one- and five-year plans. Given the enormous housing assistance deficit noted earlier, plans should seek to expand assistance using both vouchers and hard units and strive to avoid any net reduction in either form. However, the dramatic variations among metropolitan markets would argue against a national one-for-one replacement rule; rather, regional planners would make the decision if analysis determines that full replacement of hard units is needed.

Besides the effective deployment of affordable housing, a sound metropolitan area housing plan requires entrepreneurial development agencies that can lead local development efforts and provide for a range of types of assisted housing. While few housing authorities might have been considered candidates for such a role in 1990, the HOPE VI experience indicates that many of them could be effective today. Establishing subsidiaries as appropriate, housing authorities have produced other forms of assisted housing, including low-income housing tax credit (LIHTC) developments subsidized by project-based vouchers, to house the lowest-income groups.

The Charlotte, North Carolina, housing authority is one agency that is building on its development capacity to position itself as a leader in community-wide efforts to address affordable housing issues through activities such as co-sponsoring a regional housing symposium.[38] In Aurora, Colorado, the Aurora Housing Authority and its subsidiary development corporation have worked with the city and other partners to identify and fill the gaps in this Denver suburb's housing infrastructure, which includes a shortage of more than 4,000 housing units arising from the redevelopment of a military base into a biomedical center.[39] Deregulation would help equip more housing authorities to pursue a leadership role, as would the provision of technical assistance to those that have the desire to do so but not the capacity.

Engage partners with an interest in preserving public housing. Besides strengthening the regional housing infrastructure, engagement in broader regional housing efforts would help housing authorities strengthen partnerships with other sectors committed to preserving public housing. Indeed, participants in the Future of Public Housing summit identified partnership building—along with reinvestment and institutional reform—as a key strategy for sustaining public housing in today's tough funding environment. Summit participants noted, for example, the natural affinity between public housing and aging in place initiatives that seek "to provide affordable community-based living alternatives to prevent premature institutionalization." One-third of public housing households are headed by seniors. Meanwhile, forecasts predict that 71.5 million people—nearly 20 percent of the U.S. population—will be 65 or older by 2030, and communities are struggling to respond to the stated desire of older Americans to remain in their communities even as their health and service needs increase.[40] In keeping with the summit's recommendations, the public housing sector should work with local and federal partners that focus on the elderly to redevelop or convert some public housing into high-quality assisted-living units.

Similarly, the summit suggested that the public housing sector could help satisfy the country's increasing demand for environmentally conscious development and the push for "green jobs" by funneling public housing repair and construction dollars to partnerships for the development of green affordable housing.[41] Residents would benefit from healthier living environments, agencies from lower energy costs, and communities from reduced greenhouse gas emissions. And the efforts would bring in new constituencies from the environmental movement in support of affordable housing.

The public housing sector could help satisfy the country's increasing demand for environmentally conscious development and the push for "green jobs."

Models for such types of collaboration do exist. The housing authority of the city of Milwaukee developed Cherry Court HOPE VI, a 120-unit green apartment complex for the elderly and people with disabilities, designed in partnership with the nonprofit Independence First. The complex offers residents case management, health, and personal services through an arrangement with another local organization, S.E.T. Ministry.[42]

Expand asset management and mixed-financing techniques. To sustain public housing and build new partnerships, the public housing sector must implement asset management and mixed financing more broadly than has been done over the last decade. Leaders convened recently at the Future of Public Housing summit noted that even a reliable stream of new federal appropriations is unlikely to provide the level of reinvestment needed to eliminate the capital needs backlog and cover the future needs of public housing. While the reforms mentioned earlier will better equip public housing authorities to secure private capital investment, further alignment with private sector norms is needed.

Sunshades that optimize daylight and solar heat gain extend from the corners of Cherry Court, a "green" apartment complex for seniors and people with disabilities developed by the Housing Authority of the City of Milwaukee.

In the past—counter to all responsible real estate practices—housing authorities generally did not keep records, prepare budgets, or monitor performance for individual developments. The public housing system must be structured to allow tough-minded assessment of the financial and market circumstances of individual properties and operating strategies must be shaped by those assessments. Private investors want to see data up front indicating that the property that they are about to put their money into is likely to remain viable.

HUD issued a rule in 2005 requiring that all housing authorities with 250 units or more convert to the asset management system by 2011.[43] As noted, HUD's current approach to implementation appears overly burdensome. Streamlining and expediting the asset management conversion should be the first order of business for the new regulatory reform agenda proposed earlier. Tasks include devising a more flexible approach to implementation and creating a strong technical assistance component. Implementation should occur in stages, with the goal of converting sizable portions of the inventory to the new system every year.

Public housing reforms also must include expediting approvals for mixed-financing deals and developing regulations and guidelines to facilitate pledging of rents and operating subsidies for debt service.[44] Although rule changes have eliminated some key regulatory barriers to mixed financing, many still consider the process too cumbersome.[45]

In addition, Congress should authorize an approach to financing that supports much greater leveraging than is possible under the current methods of funding capital improvements. In 2004 HUD proposed an approach known as the Public Housing Reinvestment Initiative (PHRI), which would allow housing authorities to trade capital and operating subsidies for individual public housing developments and receive vouchers in return. By committing the vouchers to a particular property, the authority could then borrow private capital funds against the expected income stream. Providing a partial loan guarantee also would enhance leverage.

Proponents of mixed financing aim not to relieve the government of its obligation to support public housing but rather to create incentives for maintaining properties over the long term. Rather than diverting housing authorities from the mission of providing decent shelter to America's most needy families, private real estate finance and management approaches help mobilize the resources needed to accomplish that goal. And, by allowing federal dollars to stretch further, private real estate approaches should encourage Congress to pay its fair share. As noted by Michael Kelly, director of the Washington, D.C., housing authority, adequate federal funding is critical to the agency's efforts to issue highly rated bonds and secure other private investment.[46]

Promote mixed-income environments systemwide. As part of their mandatory annual planning process, housing authorities should analyze their inventories to identify viable opportunities for income mixing in existing developments outside of the HOPE VI program. Successful income mixing increases the probability that properties will be maintained in good condition for all residents, raises rental revenues to levels that better attract private investment, and lowers the cost of operating public housing.[47] QHWRA furthered income-mixing opportunities in public housing by liberalizing rent and tenant selection policies and endorsing work requirements, but relatively few agencies have made adequate efforts to take advantage of these opportunities.[48]

Mixed-income environments can be created outside of the HOPE VI context in two ways. First, in improving neighborhoods that attract families able to pay market rent, existing public housing developments can gradually incorporate more such tenants as normal turnover occurs. Market-rate renters are most likely to move into properties that have been rehabilitated to high architectural standards and that enjoy sustained sound management. As units open up and market-rate tenants move in, assistance would be provided to lower-income families elsewhere to further expand mixed-income environments while avoiding any net reduction in the total number of families assisted.

Second, income mixing should be part of any efforts to expand the assisted housing stock. The Dayton, Ohio, housing authority, for example, is purchasing complexes in suburban communities and making the units into public housing.[49]

The Clearwater, Florida, housing authority is incorporating income mixing into its development activities in a different way. It acquired four apartment buildings through bonds sold to investors in neighborhoods with high homeownership rates and no concentrated poverty. Eighty percent of the units are rented at market rates while the remaining 20 percent serve low-income tenants at reduced rents. The authority also is redeveloping another public housing complex as a mixed-income community and continuing to operate two public housing developments.[50]

Use the tenant-based voucher program more effectively to achieve broader integration goals. As the HOPE VI experience has shown, when deployed properly, tenant-based vouchers enable families to relocate if they wish to safer living environments that offer greater opportunities. But as Polikoff argues in chapter 5, the hope that poor families can be integrated into broader society through relocation with vouchers has not been realized. Families have not been given enough help in finding housing in lower-poverty areas, handling private market transactions, or adjusting to unfamiliar neighborhoods—or, after they move, in learning how to remain in integrated, low-poverty neighborhoods and avoid being forced to return to segregated, high-poverty communities.

Housing authorities must be required to reach out to landlords in lower-poverty areas and develop plans for mobility and post-move counseling. Mobility counseling should include credit repair counseling, "financial literacy" training, transportation to see units, hands-on assistance in negotiating with landlords, and financial assistance with security deposits. Post-move assistance could include help with driver education, automobile ownership, employment, and child care programs and referrals to resources that help low-income families pay their utility bills.[51]

Chapter 5 describes a potentially promising housing mobility program in Baltimore under which some 1,100 families had moved by 2007 from public housing and other inner-city areas to higher-opportunity areas in the city and surrounding region. Job training, driver education, and automobile purchase services are now being tested with the support of several national and local foundations. Health and educational counseling programs are to be added in 2008–09.

To support mobility, the federal government should provide strong incentives for coordinated regional administration of the voucher program. Administrators of the program—which are almost always public housing authorities—have a poor record in using the program to support mobility of recipients to low-poverty neighborhoods in other jurisdictions. Supporting an interjurisdictional move entails additional costs and red tape for the housing authorities. But by not supporting such moves, they are curtailing their beneficiaries' access to good schools and employment opportunities.[52] New mechanisms are needed to eliminate barriers to mobility, either by creating effective collaboration among housing authorities or assigning the task to another regional entity.

Provide well-focused support services, including supportive housing environments. Public housing authorities must form strategic relationships with local service

> To support mobility, the federal government should provide strong incentives for coordinated regional administration of the voucher program.

providers to offer support services to assisted families throughout the inventory and do so under a case management approach that recognizes that the service needs of the population vary. The beleaguered efforts to provide social services under HOPE VI taught practitioners that public housing residents—who were presumed to be relatively homogeneous—have widely varied capacities and needs. When given a housing voucher and a modest amount of help in finding a job, some residents found work and a decent apartment in the private housing market. Others faced much more severe and often multiple barriers, such as lack of education, a history of substance abuse, and health problems. They were the "hard-to-house" families that Popkin and Cunningham identify in chapter 11.[53] Trying to push them too quickly into self-sufficiency could be counterproductive. They are likely to need more support for a longer time.

Some agencies took the lessons on case management to heart. For example, the Atlanta Housing Authority's Work Force Enterprise Program emphasizes long-term individualized family coaching that recognizes the variety and depth of problems facing the affected households. Professionally trained family counselors are assigned to each family to coach the family over a five-year period toward the goal of financial independence.

Although Congress must be pressed for more resources, funding is likely to remain a significant challenge. Rather than creating and paying for a new social service system that duplicates existing community systems, housing authorities can form strategic partnerships, seek other public and philanthropic

The Stamford, Connecticut, housing authority's Post House development provides housing and on-site supportive services to families receiving rental assistance through the public housing and project-based Section 8 programs.

support, and channel revenues from other workforce housing programs into needed services.[54] Funding needs can be minimized by reserving intensive services only for those families that need a high level of support.

Finally, housing authorities need to recognize that in some of their family projects the concentration of too many families with the greatest challenges to self-sufficiency effectively precludes adequately addressing their needs. Outcomes for those families would be likely to improve vastly if they were served in smaller-scale, supportive housing.

For example, the Stamford, Connecticut, housing authority used a 2004 HOPE VI grant of just under $20 million, tax credit equity, and project-based Section 8 vouchers to replace a 144-unit, low-rise public housing project called Fairfield Court with a 90-unit, mixed-income rental community on site and two supportive housing facilities off site totaling 76 units. Thanks to an endowment from HOPE VI funds and the involvement of support services partners, former Fairfield Court residents who have mental health problems or other chronic issues now have access to community facilities and on-site case management—in two attractive complexes tucked into solid middle-class neighborhoods.[55] The Seattle Housing Authority is working with service providers and funders to determine whether to retool one of its public housing buildings for people who need support services "that keep them from being housed successfully in SHA's traditional public housing."[56]

Continue HOPE VI with more efficient and sensitive implementation. As the above recommendations imply, the first order of business for public housing now should be to apply the lessons of HOPE VI to the full public housing inventory. But what should happen to the HOPE VI program itself?

Over the first and second terms of George W. Bush's presidency, the administration consistently recommended zeroing out the program, but Congress consistently restored funding for it, although at annual rates well below the program's peak funding in the late 1990s.[57] What should be done with it in the future? It is clear that some severely distressed projects remain standing and that others are likely to deteriorate to a severely distressed state in the future. To deal with such cases, HUD still needs a separate program that offers the flexibility and incentives for creativity offered under HOPE VI.

How great is the need? In 2003 one estimate indicated that there were still anywhere from 47,000 to 82,000 public housing units in severely distressed projects possibly suitable for HOPE VI treatment. However, many of those projects may have been demolished since then. At this point, a serious new assessment to identify remaining developments that warrant HOPE VI treatment should be a priority.[58]

In that assessment, it should be remembered that location matters. As noted earlier, the cost effectiveness of HOPE VI developments depends on the extent to which they help increase property values and otherwise improve surrounding neighborhoods. In keeping with the principles outlined by Turner in chapter 10, HOPE VI redevelopments should involve sites where the blighting effect of public housing is clear and where redevelopment could produce spillover benefits and be undertaken in conjunction with other city investments. Redevelopments should be part of a larger strategy to expand affordable options in mixed-income neighborhoods throughout the city. They must be monitored to ensure that they are both equitable and sustainable and that supplemental investments are made when necessary to sustain neighborhood vitality and preserve affordable housing options.

To correct past weaknesses, HOPE VI's new agenda should also give higher priority to the human side of the process.[59] It should include

- establishment and enforcement of stronger provisions for resident engagement in planning and provisions for keeping residents informed as redevelopment unfolds
- requirements and budgets for stronger and longer-lasting services to help families with relocating and moving toward self-sufficiency
- a preference for grant applications that provide replacement housing that will be appropriate and beneficial for hard-to-house residents.

Finally, housing authorities seeking HOPE VI grants have complained of pressure to spend substantial sums on submissions of lavish grant proposals—funds lost when applicants do not receive awards. Less wasteful would be a two-stage process in which competing authorities meeting basic threshold conditions prepare tightly defined and comparatively brief concept proposals, with the most promising selected to develop full proposals, which would have to meet more stringent requirements.[60]

HOPE VI and New Opportunities for Metropolitan America

The significant improvement in public housing that has occurred over the past fifteen years has been eclipsed by an even more remarkable shift in the circumstances of central cities. In the early 1990s, even many responsible observers seemed to have given up hope on America's cities. Three decades of unrelenting news about job losses in cities and middle-class families moving to the suburbs—along with analyses by William J. Wilson and others documenting the devastating social and economic effects of concentrated poverty—seemed to knock away any residual underpinnings for optimism.[61]

Further tainting the prognosis for urban America was the widely held stereotype of increasingly black, crime-ridden central cities contrasted with increasingly white, low-crime suburbs. Racial polarity seemed intractable. In 1994, Anthony Downs, a senior fellow at the Brookings Institution, outlined several strategies that theoretically might alter metropolitan patterns. But as to whether local leaders were likely to usher those strategies in given the political realities of the day, Downs concluded, "The odds are against it."[62]

Severely distressed public housing projects contributed much to the negative image of cities. They were the most glaring example of urban despair, particularly after accounts of life in some of the most heinous developments were read far and wide.[63] Against that backdrop, what happened in the rest of the 1990s surprised almost everyone.

Concentrated poverty, crime, and other distress indicators fell. Driven in large part by strong economic growth and national policies enabling poor families to benefit from that growth (such as the earned income tax credit and child care subsidies), poverty began to disperse. The share of the metropolitan poor living in high-poverty neighborhoods (those having poverty rates of 30 percent or more), which had increased from 25 to 31 percent in the 1980s, dropped back to 26 percent in 2000.[64] Although results differed markedly across cities, improvements were widespread, with overall drops in concentrated poverty in 83 of the 100 largest metropolitan areas.[65]

There were many other signs of urban improvement over the decade, including general reductions in crime and teen pregnancy and substantial downtown reinvestment in many cities.[66] The population of the central cities of the 100 largest metropolitan areas grew by 7.5 percent in the 1990s, up from 4.5 percent in the 1980s.[67]

Neighborhood diversity expanded. In addition, the rigid black city–white suburbs stereotype began to break down. While the change was small, black-white residential segregation did register a decline in the 1990s, and there was an increase in the number of black families living in the suburbs. More important, with the increase in Hispanics and Asians, many of whom settled directly in the suburbs, America's spatial patterns could no longer be characterized in simple black-white terms. By 2000, 57 percent of all census tracts in the 100

Customers shop for produce at the Food Project's Farmers' Market in the Boston neighborhood of Roxbury, a working-class community that includes a diverse mix of ethnicities and races, as did an increasing number of other U.S. communities in the 1990s. The neighborhood also is home to two Boston Housing Authority HOPE VI redevelopments, Orchard Gardens and Mission Main.

largest metro areas had such a mix of whites, minorities, and immigrants that no single racial or ethnic group dominated the minority population. The share of all tracts whose populations were more than 90 percent white had declined from 38 percent to 26 percent over the decade.[68] Together, those shifts constituted a modest change in what remains a highly segregated urban geography; nonetheless, diversity had clearly made inroads.

Cities regained stature. Public interest in any problem can be mobilized only when there is a reasonable possibility of fixing it. While urban America still had egregious problems in 2000, conditions looked considerably more promising than they had a decade earlier. The positive developments of the 1990s convinced many decisionmakers that urban America was worth paying attention to again.

To be sure, U.S. urban areas have suffered setbacks since 2000. There are indications that poverty may have reconcentrated to some extent in some metropolitan areas, and the foreclosure crisis that began in 2008 threatens many neighborhoods in all sections of the country with significant declines in property values. But these problems are affecting the suburbs and central cities alike.[69] What happened in the 1990s was important to demonstrate that central city decline is not at all inevitable and, even though there are good reasons for concern everywhere, what has happened since in no way suggests that we have returned to a period of widening polarization of outcomes between cities and suburbs.

HOPE VI played a role in this shift in attitudes. By the early 2000s, many of the worst public housing projects had been replaced. Although they represented only a fraction of the total number of deteriorated housing units in poor neighborhoods nationwide, those projects were so visible that their removal had a tremendous psychological impact.[70]

Policymakers started to embrace economic integration. In 1992, people were advocating mixed-income communities, but they had little evidence that the idea was feasible. By 2000, HOPE VI had produced a significant number of highly visible mixed-income communities that earned widespread news coverage because they contrasted so starkly with the deplorable conditions that they replaced. These handsomely designed redevelopments—which in some cases had won architectural awards—also attracted media coverage for improving surrounding neighborhoods, which enjoyed increasing home values, decreasing crime, and other benefits.

The new developments caught the attention of civic leaders and officials throughout the nation. In 1990, most U.S. cities were still channeling what low-income housing development funds they had to their poorest neighborhoods. As HOPE VI progressed, significant numbers of local leaders began to take seriously the goals of deconcentrating poverty and creating mixed-income communities. Integrating lower-income and higher-income housing in neighborhoods citywide is an explicit goal of a number of new local housing strategies.[71]

And city governments are now using their own discretionary funds to develop mixed-income projects, following the HOPE VI model. Leaders in such places as Washington, D.C., Philadelphia, Seattle, and Bremerton, Washington, are using tax credit equity, land sales, and other sources to finance their developments.[72] The San Francisco Housing Authority has the backing of the city, which plans to issue $95 million in bonds to provide HOPE VI–like funds for redeveloping two of the city's most distressed public housing complexes as mixed-income communities, with six more such redevelopments to follow.

Nonprofit housing developers also are getting into mixed-income development.[73] As documented in a report from the Fair Housing Justice Center, nonprofit and for-profit partners are bringing an increasing number of new mixed-income projects to low-poverty neighborhoods, despite challenges ranging from regulatory barriers to opposition from nearby residents.[74] Such challenges would likely have been insurmountable a decade earlier.

Also aiding mixed-income development is the increasing adoption of inclusionary zoning ordinances, which encourage (and sometimes require) developers to offer a certain share of the units in their housing projects at rents or prices that low- and moderate-income families can afford. Generally, the developers receive nonmonetary benefits, such as density bonuses, zoning variances, or expedited permits to compensate for their commitment. Although the first such ordinance was enacted in the mid-1970s, it was not until the turn of the century that the idea caught on. Now, more than 300 cities, towns and counties have adopted inclusionary zoning.[75]

Applying the Lessons of HOPE VI in Metropolitan Policy

Today there is a new recognition of U.S. metropolitan regions as the drivers of the nation's economy and the key to its competitiveness. Although the 100 largest U.S. metropolitan areas cover just 12 percent of the nation's land area, they account for 65 percent of the U.S. population, 75 percent of gross domestic product, 78 percent of high-paying knowledge jobs, and 94 percent of venture capital funding.[76]

The gains made in the health of central cities have been integral in strengthening greater metropolitan areas. Research shows that central cities provide the most fertile environment for certain critical economic functions. For example, technology, finance, and other creative high-level services depend on opportunities for face-to-face interaction and the strong professional networks forged in cities. The ambience of the central city determines how well a region can attract the young, highly educated workers who sustain the strength of the professional services sector.[77]

Fresh produce is displayed outside the corner grocery store in New Columbia in Portland, Oregon, one of the many award-winning HOPE VI redevelopments that have provided lessons on how to create diverse, healthy urban neighborhoods.

But the progress made in U.S. urban areas is incomplete. Clearly, ensuring that metropolitan America reaches its full potential will require new energy and a creative reformulation of a host of economic and social policies at the local, state, and federal levels. The hallmarks of HOPE VI—economic integration and healthy neighborhoods—should be a critical part of the agenda. Metropolitan competitiveness is hindered by the continued existence of severely distressed neighborhoods and the racial and socioeconomic segregation associated with them, which has real costs in the form of bigger outlays for public safety and social services and lost opportunities for people who have not found a way into the economic mainstream. Segregated distressed neighborhoods breed alienation, dissuade investors, provide a poor environment for education, and contribute little to efforts to build up a highly skilled, educated local workforce. A new urban policy must promote inclusion and equity because it is fundamentally the right thing to do and because it is fundamental to the economic interests of all metropolitan areas.

Bruce Katz articulates that goal in his call for "neighborhoods of choice and connection" throughout U.S. metropolitan areas. In such neighborhoods, residents come from all socioeconomic strata and have access to quality education, training, and other avenues to economic opportunity.[78] To move toward that goal, policymakers must apply HOPE VI's lessons about promoting economic integration and creating healthy neighborhoods at three levels:

metropolitan area, neighborhood, and family. Affordable housing resources are most effectively stewarded at the metropolitan area level as part of broader regional housing and neighborhood development strategies. At the neighborhood level, new approaches are needed to guide change consistent with the goal of creating healthy, sustainable mixed-income communities. Finally, healthy communities require new ways to identify and refer troubled families to needed services and to promote partnerships to help low-income families gain self-sufficiency. The following recommendations suggest ways to achieve the kind of neighborhoods that Katz envisions:

Institutionalize regional housing and neighborhood development strategies. The affordable housing shortage in the United States is a huge challenge that will require forceful and well-orchestrated approaches in all metropolitan areas. Katz and Margery Turner have elsewhere recommended that metropolitan planning organizations (MPOs) be given funding and technical assistance to prepare regional housing strategies similar to the regional transportation plans that MPOs already produce under federal law.[79] These strategies would need to set specific targets regarding the number of households to be assisted and work to achieve those targets by deploying all forms of federal housing assistance, including low-income housing tax credits, HOME funds, and community development block grant (CDBG) funds as well as vouchers and traditional public housing. Strategies would also encompass bond financing and various other locally funded programs along with the local deployment of any resources provided through the newly enacted National Housing Trust Fund.[80]

Strengthen fair housing enforcement and mobility opportunities. The nation's existing fair housing laws are powerful tools but commitment to their enforcement has lapsed. Although more than 3.7 million people are discriminated against in housing transactions every year, the Department of Housing and Urban Development issued only thirty-one charges of discrimination in 2007 and the Department of Justice filed just thirty-five cases, according to the National Fair Housing Alliance's 2008 Fair Housing Trends Report.[81] The report blames the continuing pattern of residential segregation based on race and ethnicity on inconsistent case-processing standards and other problems at HUD, failure of the Department of Justice (DOJ) to bring many race-based cases despite the incidence of racial discrimination, and inadequate and inconsistent funding of the private fair housing organizations that shoulder the greatest burden of fair housing education and enforcement.[82]

Fair housing enforcement must be reinvigorated, and enforcement must go beyond rhetoric. Enforcement includes addressing the practices at HUD and the DOJ and expanding and strengthening the local institutions that play critical roles in the enforcement process.[83] An important corollary to fair housing enforcement is strengthening the institutional capacity to provide counseling to low-income families on the benefits of and opportunities for moving to lower-poverty neighborhoods within their metropolitan area, as described earlier.

Cease government practices that further concentrate poverty. Even today, too much government housing assistance—in the form of vouchers and subsidized housing construction and rehabilitation—is allocated to high-poverty, high-minority neighborhoods. [84] While a given amount of housing subsidy funds can generally assist more families if they are invested in high-poverty neighborhoods because housing costs are lower there, concentrating all low-income housing resources in such communities implies much higher social costs, including the public costs of addressing much higher rates of crime, health problems, and unemployment as well as the costs borne directly by the residents.

Local and regional planning processes must include mechanisms for a more equitable distribution of housing resources. To encourage that, HUD must require local jurisdictions receiving CDBG funds to meet their statutory mandate to "affirmatively further fair housing" with specific fair housing strategies in their comprehensive plans.

Reduce barriers to building affordable housing in the suburbs. Suburban zoning and building regulations that prevent the development of lower-cost housing probably are the biggest barrier to deconcentrating poverty in U.S. metropolitan areas today. Such regulations raise costs by requiring large lots and excessive parking and limit the land available for apartment complexes. Some suburbs are recognizing that they may be able to secure a sounder economic future by permitting, for example, higher-density mixed-use developments with housing around transit stops. However, in most areas the barriers created by practices meant to exclude lower-income minority families from the suburbs remain formidable and call for more serious efforts, particularly in state legislation, to address them.

Federal and state governments should create strong incentives for local governments to reduce such barriers. As suggested by Katz and Turner, incentives could be established by authorizing metropolitan planning agencies to review and certify compliance of local jurisdictions with the requirements for equitable housing distribution stated in the metropolitan strategy; giving noncompliant jurisdictions a reasonable amount of time to respond, under threat of the loss of federal CDBG, HOME, and transportation funding; and establishing a new federal incentive fund for jurisdictions, mostly in the suburbs, that do not now qualify for CDBG and HOME grants. Jurisdictions could receive awards from the fund if they "reduced regulatory barriers and expanded the supply of moderately-priced housing within their borders."[85]

Develop more mixed-income projects in high- and low-poverty neighborhoods. Regional leaders should spearhead efforts to apply the HOPE VI model to rundown privately owned properties in poor neighborhoods. Working just with public housing will not bring the mixed-income approach to sufficient scale.

Potential mixed-income redevelopment sites should be located in areas that can attract market-rate tenants, and redevelopments should be designed and financed to ensure long-term viability.

For example, the District of Columbia Housing Finance Agency worked with HUD and private entities to finance the redevelopment of Clifton Terrace, a crime-ridden, privately owned complex in northwest Washington, into a new mixed-income community of 152 apartments and 76 condominiums. The complex had been financed under the project-based Section 8 program but persistently poor conditions prompted foreclosure by HUD. HUD turned it over to the developers who spearheaded the redevelopment, Community Preservation and Development Corporation, a nonprofit known for including services with its housing, and to Michaels Development Company.

It is equally or perhaps more important to expand the number of mixed-income projects in low-poverty neighborhoods, as is being done by nonprofits and some public housing authorities mentioned earlier in this chapter. The Fair Housing Justice Center report documents examples in nine states, all of which are multifamily rental or condominium projects in neighborhoods where poverty rates were below 15 percent in 2000. The projects were most commonly initiated by policy-oriented nonprofits, which often formed joint ventures with for-profits to handle project development and management.[86]

The 120-unit Madison Glen apartment complex in Raleigh, North Carolina, is an example of a well-conceived mixed-income redevelopment in a low-poverty area. The complex is situated in a new growth area that has a 5 percent poverty rate. A significant share of all units (42 percent) are rented at levels afford-able for families earning less than 50 percent of the area median income; the rest are leased at market rents. Developed by the Downtown Housing Improvement Corporation, the largest nonprofit housing developer in the metropolitan area, Madison Glen has a swimming pool, a fitness center, and other amenities, and it is managed by a well-respected private management firm. Those benefits, along with the neighborhood environment, retain the interest of market-rate tenants.

Low-income households and tenants paying market rates enjoy the amenities at Madison Glen, an apartment complex in a low-poverty neighborhood in Raleigh, North Carolina.

Such mixed-income approaches should be integral to metropolitan housing strategies and they should be promoted nationally, with federal assistance to help build the capacity of local governments and builders to develop mixed-income communities.

Undertake protective interventions in transitioning neighborhoods. Together with efforts to promote more mixed-income development throughout met-ropolitan areas, neighborhoods in transition must be guided in the desired directions. Different techniques are required, depending on how the neigh-borhood real estate market is changing.

In neighborhoods where gentrification is under way or likely to occur, the momentum should be harnessed so that many lower-income residents can stay and benefit from the renewed investment rather than be displaced. The goal of preserving affordable housing in gentrifying neighborhoods might have seemed naïve a decade ago, and indeed it is unlikely to work where gentrification is far advanced. However, when efforts begin early enough, new techniques enhance the prospects of success.[87] They include inclusionary zoning along with the facilitation of ownership change and other property-by-property interventions that preserve units at affordable prices, including subsidizing affordable units in market-rate developments. Two preservation techniques in particular should be given a high priority. First, landlords of Section 8 projects who want to opt out of their commitment to provide units at affordable rates when their subsidy contracts expire should be offered extra incentives to remain in the program or encouraged to transfer ownership to nonprofits that will preserve the complexes as affordable housing. Second, tenants should be given the right of first refusal to purchase rental properties about to be converted to condominiums, and they should be given assistance as appropriate to make the purchase.[88]

Local officials also should pay special attention to neighborhoods, mostly in the outer portions of central cities and in inner-ring suburbs, where poverty rates are lower but increasing. As with gentrifying neighborhoods, the goal should not be to prevent the change but to guide it so that the neighborhood continues to work for current and new residents. That means maintaining services and investment in neighborhoods where low-income families are moving in so that many existing higher-income families will not move out and a sustainable, mixed-income community will result.

Extra efforts must be made in such neighborhoods to keep the streets clean and safe, enforce codes governing property maintenance, and deploy community policing to keep the crime rate low. To avoid creating high-poverty enclaves, housing agencies should avoid clustering too many voucher recipients in one place. Services such as youth activities and job training should be offered to newcomers to help them succeed in their new environment. Many of these techniques have been tested in the healthy neighborhoods approach, "a model of stabilizing communities through real estate investment and resident involvement that was pioneered in Baltimore by the Goldseker Foundation."[89]

Thoughtful leaders also recognize the need to address the human side of the equation—the fears and rumors that accompany real or perceived changes in neighborhoods welcoming more low-income residents. In 2007, leaders in Ames, Iowa, responded to rumors that former public housing residents moving from Chicago to Ames were setting off a crime wave by calling a town meeting to discuss race relations head on. The goal was to deal with the "misinformation going around," Mayor Ann Campbell told the *Iowa Independent*. Participants shared their observations and impressions of factors that could be related to the increase in crime, from people who were following the Section 8 residents to the area to an ordinary cyclical rise in crime that was being associated with new subsidized residents although it was due to other factors. New residents were coming to the area because they wanted a better life, Campbell said, and the city established a task force that is working to implement recommendations for better integrating the newcomers.[90]

Develop fresh and focused approaches to assisting the most troubled families. Many seriously troubled families live in distressed neighborhoods in and outside of public housing. The various service providers that come into contact with those families need to coordinate the process of identifying who needs services and what those services must encompass. Homeless services providers, foster care agencies, schools, and other providers need to work together so that families get help *before* they lose their housing or custody of their children. Using a case management approach, programs should offer modest assistance to people who need just a little boost to become self-sufficient and more intensive, longer-term services to those who have multiple problems.

For the former population, agencies that work with low-income families should collaborate to provide case management and asset-building services to their clients. One such effort under way is the Seattle Asset Building Initiative, a pilot project engaging eighteen nonprofit and public agencies in coordinated delivery of asset-building services such as job training, credit counseling, financial education, and assistance with preparing tax returns. The program targets families served by the Seattle Housing Authority.[91]

For more deeply troubled families, lessons can be applied from successes in working with the homeless population. Many communities are successfully assisting chronically homeless people and families with permanent supportive housing. In their 2007 guide to local housing strategies, former HUD secretaries Jack Kemp and Henry Cisneros describe a number of promising partnerships, including those whereby local housing authorities provide project-based Section 8 subsidies to help fund permanent supportive housing projects developed by nonprofits.[92]

It makes sense to house more families whose troubles leave them homeless or at the edge of homelessness in smaller-scale, nonprofit-operated supportive housing than in a larger-scale public housing environment. To generate funding for their efforts, supportive housing partners can cite research documenting the cost savings gained by serving severely challenged people in supportive housing rather than letting them remain on the streets, where they require expensive emergency shelter and medical services.[93]

Local and federal leaders cannot wait for the long-overdue reform of the nation's fragmented social service system to address the needs of such families. Using the lessons learned from HOPE VI about case management, they can develop new ways to identify and refer troubled families to needed services and to promote partnerships to help low-income families gain self-sufficiency.

In Conclusion

HOPE VI is one of the rare government initiatives that has won widespread bipartisan support in Congress in recent years. But its critics, though comparatively few in number, are vocal. They rightly point out that HOPE VI was painful for many original residents. They share credible stories of projects in which residents were treated poorly in the rush to get redevelopment under way. And though the majority of residents benefited tremendously from relocation under HOPE VI, living conditions for those who ended up in other traditional public housing communities were not much better than before.[94]

Children walk down the street in Philadelphia's Greater Grays Ferry Estates, one of the many mixed-income communities that have replaced former public housing projects and created new hope for public housing.

David Swanson/
The Philadelphia Inquirer

Critics who accuse HOPE VI partners of trying to "break up minority communities," however, forget that most who relocated under HOPE VI wound up in another minority neighborhood; they just moved from an unviable minority community to a more viable one. The central motivation for undertaking HOPE VI was the recognition that some public housing projects had simply become intolerable. Sound minority neighborhoods should be supported and uplifted, but that does not mean leaving families with children in highly unsafe and unhealthy places. Doing so would be inconsistent with our standards as a nation. Even the critics have acknowledged that those terrible projects had to go, and HOPE VI Panel Study responses suggest that many residents could not wait to leave them.

While it is too early to know for certain whether these mixed-income environments will be sustained, the mounting evidence on the extraordinary personal, social, and economic costs of polarization by race and income supports continued efforts to strive for mixed-income communities. There should be some urgency in applying the lessons from HOPE VI—drawn from its shortcomings as well as its successes—to reform of the public housing program overall and to a new national policy for metropolitan development.

When historians look back at the last two decades, it seems likely that, despite its imperfections, HOPE VI will at least be credited as a success in solving the deeply troubling problems of more than 240 severely distressed projects. If the visibility of its success transforms it into a catalyst for much broader efforts to reduce the isolation of poor families, HOPE VI may well gain a more significant mention in the history books. If the program's emphasis on economic integration expands to include greater efforts to achieve racial integration, its positive legacy will be ensured.

····· Endnotes ·····

1. These numbers reflect data from HUD's HOPE VI management information system through September 2008 on the status of the first 240 grants awarded from 1993 through 2007 (see appendix A). Since then, six additional grants have been awarded, bringing the total to 246 at the end of 2008, but firm data on their circumstances or plans have not yet been compiled.

2. As discussed by Katz in chapter 2 of this volume, the work of the National Commission on Severely Distressed Public Housing led to the enactment of HOPE VI. See also *The Final Report of the National Commission on Severely Distressed Public Housing; A Report to Congress and the Secretary of Housing and Urban Development* (U.S. Department of Housing and Urban Development, 1992).

3. See appendix A.

4. Linda B. Fosburg, Susan J. Popkin, and Gretchen P. Locke, *An Historical and Baseline Assessment of HOPE VI,* vol. 1, *Cross-Site Report* (U.S. Department of Housing and Urban Development, Office of Policy Development and Research, July 1996), pp. 1-23, 3-10.

5. Ibid., p. iii. Serious physical problems, from mold to cockroach and rodent infestation, also were documented in later HOPE VI sites by the HOPE VI Panel Study. See Susan J. Popkin and others, "HOPE VI Panel Study: Baseline Report" (Washington: Urban Institute, 2002), pp. 3-1 through 3-4.

6. Fosburg, Popkin, and Locke, *An Historical and Baseline Assessment of HOPE VI,* pp. 1-21, 3-4.

7. Ibid., pp. iv–v.

8. As documented by Turner in chapter 10 of this volume.

9. A 2004 report notes that while the short-term viability of mixed-finance HOPE VI developments appears sound, their long-term prospects hinge on each of the public housing, tax credit, and market-rate components being "financially feasible, marketable, and sustainable" over time. They also must have a sufficient mix of residents and the rental income necessary to service financial obligations, including a private mortgage for the minimum forty-year term of the public housing obligation. See Susan J. Popkin and others, *A Decade of HOPE VI: Research Findings and Policy Challenges* (Washington: Urban Institute and Brookings Institution, May 2004), pp. 25–26.

10. For a discussion of social interaction, see Mark L. Joseph, "Is Mixed Income Development an Antidote for Urban Poverty?" *Housing Policy Debate* 17, vol. 2 (2006), pp. 209–34; and Mark L. Joseph, "Early Resident Experiences at a New Mixed-Income Development in Chicago," *Journal of Urban Affairs* 30, no. 3 (2008): 229–57.

11. As explored in chapter 10 of this volume, studies on neighborhood impacts recognize that, depending on the location as well as the design of some projects, they could yield smaller neighborhood benefits and even deficits.

12. Margery Austin Turner and others, *Severely Distressed Public Housing: The Costs of Inaction* (Washington: Urban Institute, March 2007), p. 4.

13. By the mid- to late 1990s, demolition or disposition of deteriorated public housing was eased by the elimination of the one-for-one replacement rule; a HOPE VI demolition-only grant program that ran from 1996 to 2003; the streamlining of approvals for demolition or disposition; and a program, since expanded, requiring the conversion to vouchers of subsidies for large distressed public housing complexes with high vacancy rates that could not be preserved cost effectively.

14. Barbara Sard and Will Fischer, "Preserving Safe, High-Quality Public Housing Should Be a Priority of Federal Housing Policy" (Washington: Center on Budget and Policy Priorities, September 2008), p. 6; p. 30, n. 14.

15. Data from HUD (appendix A, table A-1) shows that as of September 2008, total planned demolition under the 240 HOPE VI revitalization grants made during program years 1993 to 2007 was 96,226 units and that actual demolition was slightly less than planned demolition, leading to the conclusion that the HOPE VI revitalization program accounted for less than half of the 200,000 units estimated by Sard and Fischer to have been demolished throughout the public housing program by 2008.

16. Sard and Fischer, "Preserving Safe, High-Quality Public Housing," p. 30, n. 14.

17. Ibid., p. 7. The report notes that in addition to federal policy changes, the overall drop in the number of extreme poverty neighborhoods has helped reduce the number of family public housing units in such neighborhoods from 43 percent in 1995 to 26 percent in 2008.

18. Ibid., p. 6 n. 12.

19. G. Thomas Kingsley, Jennifer Johnson, and Kathryn L. S. Pettit, "Patterns of Section 8 Relocation in the HOPE VI Program," *Journal of Urban Affairs* 25, no. 4 (2003): 427–47.

20. Also, given the fairly high rate of turnover among families in public housing, it is likely that a notable share of the original residents in the first ten years of HOPE VI projects have by now left the program altogether. It would be valuable for HUD to examine its own records pertaining to this issue—that is, to find out how many HOPE VI relocatees are still in the program and where they now reside.

21. The original article is Hanna Rosin's "American Murder Mystery," *The Atlantic,* July-August 2008. The most prominent response, questioning methods and interpretation, is Xavier de Souza Briggs and Peter Drier, "Memphis Murder Mystery? No, Just Mistaken Identity," *Shelterforce,* July 22, 2008. Rosin herself notes a September 2007 headline in the local paper that reads "Memphis Leads the U.S. in Violent Crime"—indicating that Memphis is by no means a typical U.S. city.

22. Harvard Kennedy School, "Hope VI Mixed Finance Public Housing" (www.innovations. harvard.edu/awards.html?id=3853).

23. Martin Abravanel and others, *Testing Public Housing Deregulation: A Summary Assessment of HUD's Moving to Work Demonstration* (U.S. Department of Housing and Urban Development, May 2004), pp. 4–6 (www.urban.org/publications/311009.html).

24. Barbara Sard and Will Fischer, "Bipartisan Legislation Would Build on Housing Voucher Program's Success but Worthwhile Reforms Bill Holds Risks from Expanded Deregulation Authority" (Washington: Center on Budget and Policy Priorities, September 2007).

25. Calculated from data in *Affordable Housing Needs 2005: Report to Congress* (U.S. Department of Housing and Urban Development, May 2007), pp. 60, 82. Low-income households are defined as those whose incomes are at or below 80 percent of the median income in their locality. From 2003 to 2005, the number of households that had housing problems but no assistance grew by about one-third, mostly because of an increase in the number paying too large a share of their income for rent.

26. Sard and Fischer, "Preserving Safe, High-Quality Public Housing," p. 3.

27. Ibid., p. 2. Sard and Fischer place the estimated backlog of unmet capital needs at $22 billion but note that if 100,000 of the nation's nearly 1.2 million public housing units required replacement rather than renovation, the backlog would be about $32 billion.

28. See discussion by Crowley in chapter 13 of this volume.

29. This issue is discussed further in chapter 13 of this volume. Principles for guiding relocation services can be found in *Responsible Redevelopment: Relocation Roadmap 1.0*, Annie E. Casey Foundation, 2008 (www.aecf.org/~/media/Pubs/Topics/Community%20Change/Neighborhood%20Development/ResponsibleRedevelopmentRelocationRoadMap10Fi/Roadmap_final.pdf).

30. *Community and Supportive Services for Original Residents: General Guidance for the HOPE VI Program* (U.S. Department of Housing and Urban Development, 2000) (www.hud.gov/offices/pih/programs/ph/hope6/css/cssguidance2-18-00c.pdf).

31. According to HUD, 197 agencies (6.2 percent of all agencies) were considered "troubled" by HUD's management assessment system. "Fiscal Year 2007 Performance and Accountability Report," U.S. Department of Housing and Urban Development, November 2007, p. 188 (www.hud.gov/offices/cfo/reports/2007/2007par.pdf).

32. A thorough discussion of the act and its rocky road to implementation is provided in Rod Solomon, *Public Housing Reform and Voucher Success: Progress and Challenges* (Brookings, 2005). See also Andre Shashaty, "Backsliding on Public Housing," *Affordable Housing Finance* (March 2007).

33. See further discussion of many of these ideas in G. Thomas Kingsley and others, *Lessons from HOPE VI for the Future of Public Housing* (Washington: Urban Institute, December 2003).

34. "The Future of Public Housing,"draft policy framework (Washington: Council of Large Public Housing Authorities, September 15, 2008).

35. "The Future of Public Housing," policy framework (Washington: Council of Large Public Housing Authorities, October 30, 2008).

36. For all of that to happen, the system now used to assess housing authority performance needs to be strengthened so that individual authorities can be assigned to categories reliably.

37. Conrad Egan and Jennifer Lavorel, "Preserving Public Housing Subsidies: A Call for Maximum Flexibility," in *Public Housing Transformation and the Legacy of Segregation,* edited by Margery Austin Turner, Susan J. Popkin, and Lynette Rawlings (Washington: Urban Institute Press, 2008), pp. 171–82.

38. "Building Community, People, and Partnerships: Charlotte Housing Authority Report of Achievements 2006–2007" (www.cha-nc.org/documents/CHA_Annual_Report.pdf).

39. "Authority Developing Housing to Meet Needs of Denver Suburb," *HDR Current Developments,* October 27, 2008, pp. 649–50.

40. All data in this paragraph come from "The Future of Public Housing," October 30, 2008.

41. Ibid.

42. "City Unveils Second Green Housing Facility," press release, Housing Authority of the City of Milwaukee, April 26, 2007.

43. For background, see Meena S. Bavan and Shomon R. Shamsuddin, "The Transition to Asset Management in Public Housing," *Cityscape: A Journal of Policy Development and Research* 9, vol. 2 (2007): 185–92.

44. See discussion in Solomon, *Public Housing Reform and Voucher Success,* p. 25.

45. Ibid., p. 27.

46. Michael Kelly, "America's Other Housing Crisis," *Washington Post,* May 24, 2008, p. A21.

47. Sean Zielenbach, a senior consultant at the Woodstock Institute, has been conducting research that compares operating costs in traditional public housing projects with those in revitalized HOPE VI developments as part of a forthcoming study on the economic benefits of

HOPE VI developments. In an interview with Lora Engdahl on November 7, 2008, Zielenbach explained that while the research is not yet final, for the properties examined to date, operating public housing in HOPE VI properties is notably less expensive than operating traditional public housing properties.

48. U.S. Department of Housing and Urban Development, "Seventh Annual Report to Congress on Public Housing and Rental Assistance Programs: Demographics, Income and Work and Rent," 2008, pp. 4–5. Also documented in Solomon, *Public Housing Reform and Voucher Success.*

49. James Cummings, "Public Housing in Region Shifting out of City Limits," *Dayton Daily News,* June 26, 2008; and an interview conducted by Lora Engdahl with Gregory D. Johnson, executive director, Dayton Metropolitan Housing Authority, November 3, 2008.

50. Jose Cardenas, "Site Cleared for New Uses," *St. Petersburg Times,* May 27, 2008; and an interview conducted by Lora Engdahl with Jacqueline Rivera, chief executive officer, Clearwater Housing Authority, November 3, 2008.

51. As Popkin and Cunningham note in chapter 11 of this volume, because utilities generally are included in the rent in public housing, many former public housing residents who move into the private market have trouble coping with the seasonal variation in utility costs.

52. See discussion in Bruce Katz and Margery Turner, *Who Should Run the Housing Voucher Program? A Reform Proposal* (Brookings, 2000).

53. Mary K. Cunningham, Susan J. Popkin, and Martha R. Burt, *Public Housing Transformation and the "Hard to House"* (Washington: Urban Institute, 2005).

54. Examples are discussed in Henry G. Cisneros and others, *Our Communities, Our Homes: Pathways to Housing and Homeownership in America's Cities and States* (Cambridge, Mass.: Joint Center for Housing Studies, Harvard University, 2007), pp. 56, 65–66.

55. Telephone conversation with Vincent Tufo, development director, Charter Oak Communities (the new name for the Stamford Housing Authority), June 11, 2008. The two supportive housing complexes are Post House, which includes ten public housing apartments and fifty apartments receiving project-based Section 8 rental subsidies, and 25 Taylor Street, a development that includes two-story, owner-occupied town houses and sixteen supportive housing rental units.

56. "Jefferson Terrace Considered as Supportive Housing Model," *Building Community E-News,* Seattle Housing Authority, October 17, 2008.

57. QHWRA authorized HOPE VI through 2002. In the debates surrounding reauthorization, the Bush administration argued that HUD and its local housing authority partners were too slow in implementing the program and too slow in spending the money and that funds were needed for other national priorities. HUD altered its 2002 Notice of Funding Availability to lower the cap on award amounts to $20 million and require housing authorities to have private funders lined up before receiving an award. Although President Bush eliminated funding for the program in his proposed FY 2003 budget, supporters in Congress succeeded in restoring funds to the previous year's level of $574 million. But a proposal to zero out HOPE VI arose again the following year, and the funding level fell to $150 million in FY2004 and less in following years.

58. Kingsley and others, *Lessons from HOPE VI for the Future of Public Housing,* p. 8.

59. Weaknesses are discussed in Barbara Sard and Leah Staub, "House Bill Makes Significant Improvements in HOPE VI Public Housing Revitalization Program" (Washington: Center on Budget and Policy Priorities, 2008). The house bill also incorporated a requirement that a new public housing unit be provided for every such unit demolished, but it was more flexible as to how the requirement could be met than the rigid pre–HOPE VI one-for-one replacement

rule. The new approach would permit replacement off site and, consistent with the deconcentration objective, require that any such replacement units be provided in low-poverty neighborhoods.

60. More stringent requirements might include feasibility analyses, involvement of city agencies and citizens, and more fully developed partnering arrangements. As part of an improved selection process, HUD staff should have more latitude to investigate assertions made in the proposals, perhaps making site visits to verify such factors as the support of key actors or the likelihood of securing the required financing.

61. William Julius Wilson, *The Truly Disadvantaged: The Inner City, the Underclass, and Public Policy* (University of Chicago Press, 1987). See also the discussion in chapter 2 of this volume; Janet Rothenberg Pack, "Poverty and Urban Public Expenditures,"*Urban Studies* 35, no.11 (1998): 1995–2019; and Henry G. Cisneros, *Urban Entrepreneurialism and National Economic Growth* (U.S. Department of Housing and Urban Development, September 1995).

62. Anthony Downs, *New Visions for Metropolitan America* (Brookings, 1994).

63. See, for example, Alex Kotlowitz, *There Are No Children Here: The Story of Two Boys Growing Up in the Other America* (New York: Doubleday, 1991).

64. G. Thomas Kingsley and Kathryn L. S. Pettit, "Concentrated Poverty: A Change in Course," Neighborhood Change in Urban America Brief 2 (Washington: Urban Institute, 2003), p. 1. Also see Paul A. Jargowsky, *Stunning Progress, Hidden Problems: The Dramatic Decline of Concentrated Poverty in the 1990s* (Center on Urban and Metropolitan Policy, Brookings, 2003). It is important to point out that the overall poverty rate in U.S. metropolitan areas remained constant over the decade (in the range of 11 to 12 percent), so this change did represent a true, geographical "spreading out" of poverty.

65. G. Thomas Kingsley and Kathryn L.S. Pettit, "Concentrated Poverty: Dynamics of Change," Neighborhood Change in Urban America Brief 5 (Washington: Urban Institute, 2007), p. 4.

66. See, for example, Paul Grogan and Tony Proscio, *Comeback Cities: A Blueprint for Urban Neighborhood Revival* (Boulder, Colo.: Westview Press, 2000).

67. G. Thomas Kingsley and Kathryn L. S. Pettit, "Population Growth and Decline in City Neighborhoods," Neighborhood Change in Urban America Series Brief 1 (Washington: Urban Institute, 2002). See also Edward L. Glaeser and Jesse M. Shapiro, *City Growth and the 2000 Census: Which Places Grew and Why* (Center on Urban and Metropolitan Policy, Brookings, 2001), and Bruce Katz and Alan Berube, "Cities Rebound—Somewhat," *American Enterprise* 13, no. 4 (2002): 47.

68. For statistics cited, see Margery Austin Turner and Julie Fenderson, *Understanding Diverse Neighborhoods in an Era of Demographic Change* (Washington: Urban Institute, June 2006), pp. 2, 32. Also see Lynette Rawlings, Laura Harris, and Margery Turner, "Race and Residence: Prospects for Stable Neighborhood Integration," Neighborhood Change in Urban America Series Brief 4 (Washington: Urban Institute, 2003).

69. Analysis of trends in poverty concentration since 2000 is found in Elizabeth Kneebone and Alan Berube, *Reversal of Fortune: A New Look at Concentrated Poverty in the 2000s* (Brookings, 2008). Research on spatial patterns of subprime lending and foreclosures is presented in Christopher J. Mayer and Karen Pence, "Subprime Mortgages: What, Where, and to Whom," Working Paper 14083 (Cambridge, Mass.: National Bureau of Economic Research, June 2008). Both of these studies give emphasis to data showing that the problems that they discuss are occurring extensively in suburbs as well as central cities.

70. Similarly, HOPE VI's direct effect on reducing concentrated poverty was not large at that point. By April 2000 (the date of the census that provided the data on the reduction in concentrated poverty cited earlier), only 25,600 households had been relocated from HOPE

VI sites and half of those families had moved to interim accommodations in other public housing projects. The long-term number is from the HUD HOPE VI Management Report of March 31, 2006. The totals through 2000 are also from HUD sources, as documented in Kingsley, Johnson, and Pettit, "Patterns of Section 8 Relocation in the HOPE VI Program," pp. 427–47.

71. See G. Thomas Kingsley and Barika Williams, *Policies for Affordable Housing in the District of Columbia: Lessons from Other Cities* (Washington: Urban Institute, January 2007).

72. Philadelphia's "HOPE VI–like" development, Greater Grays Ferry Estates, was profiled in Cisneros and others, *Our Communities, Our Homes,* p. 40. Seattle's mixed-income plans for its Yester Terrace housing project and the Bremerton Housing Authority's mixed-income/mixed-use plans for its Westpark complex were featured in *Washington State Housing Finance Commission Newsletter,* June 2008, p. 19.

73. Carol Hazard, "A New Approach: Nonprofit Plans Its First Mixed-Income Community," *Richmond Times Dispatch,* June 1, 2008. According to the article, the Richmond, Virginia, Habitat for Humanity is building what could be the country's first mixed-income Habitat community, with traditional Habitat homes and some market-rate homes.

74. Diane L. Houk, Erica Blake, and Fred Freiberg, *Increasing Access to Low-Poverty Areas by Creating Mixed-Income Housing* (New York: Fair Housing Justice Center, 2007).

75. "The Effects of Inclusionary Zoning on Local Housing Markets: Lessons from the San Francisco, Washington, D.C., and Suburban Boston Areas," Housing Policy Brief (Furman Center for Real Estate and Urban Policy, New York University, March 2008), p. 1 (www.nhc.org/pdf/pub_chp_iz_brief08.pdf).

76. "MetroPolicy: Shaping a New Federal Partnership for a Metropolitan Nation" (Metropolitan Policy Program, Brookings, 2008), p. 13.

77. See arguments in Richard Florida, *The Rise of the Creative Class and How It's Transforming Work, Leisure, Community, and Everyday Life* (New York: Basic Books, 2002).

78. Bruce Katz, *Neighborhoods of Choice and Connection: The Evolution of American Neighborhood Policy and What It Means for the United Kingdom* (Brookings, July 2004). Note also the relationship of these approaches to emerging ideas about reforming U.S. urban policy more broadly in *Metro Nation: How U.S. Metropolitan Areas Fuel American Prosperity* (Metropolitan Policy Program, Brookings, 2007).

79. Bruce Katz and Margery Austin Turner, "Rethinking U.S. Rental Housing Policy: A New Blueprint for Federal, State, and Local Action," in *Revisiting Rental Housing,* edited by Nicolas P. Retsinas and Eric S. Belsky (Brookings, 2008).

80. The Housing and Economic Recovery Act of 2008 (H.R. 3221), which was signed into law on July 31, 2008, incorporates a new National Housing Trust Fund with a dedicated source of resources: shares in the profits of Fannie Mae and Freddie Mac. At least 90 percent of the funds must be used for the production, preservation, rehabilitation, and operation of rental housing. All of the funds for rental housing must benefit very low-income households and 75 percent must benefit extremely low-income households. Because of the federal takeover of Fannie Mae and Freddie Mac in September 2008, the future of the resource base for the trust fund was uncertain at this writing.

81. "Dr. King's Dream Denied: Forty Years of Failed Federal Enforcement: 2008 Fair Housing Trends Report" (Washington: National Fair Housing Alliance, April 8, 2008), pp. 52, 55.

82. Ibid., pp. 1–5.

83. Those institutions would include Fair Housing Assistance Program agencies, local and state agencies authorized to act as HUD's enforcement counterparts, and the private enti-

ties funded under HUD's Fair Housing Initiatives Program, which processes more than 60 percent of the complaints, according to the National Fair Housing Alliance.

84. For example, 42 percent of LIHTCs end up in census tracts that are 50 percent or more minority, which is 10 percent greater than the percentage of all rental units in such census tracts (March 12, 2008, memorandum from Daniel & Beshara, P.C., to Commissioner of Internal Revenue, Re: Petition for Rulemaking Involving 26 C.F.R. § 1.42-17 Qualified Allocation Plan, p. 11).

85. They could receive awards from this fund if they "reduced regulatory barriers and expanded the supply of moderately priced housing within their borders." See Katz and Turner, "Rethinking U.S. Rental Housing Policy."

86. Houk, Blake, and Freiberg, *Increasing Access to Low-Poverty Areas by Creating Mixed-Income Housing.*

87. Options are described in Diane K. Levy, Jennifer Comey, and Sandra Padilla, *Keeping the Neighborhood Affordable: A Handbook of Housing Strategies for Gentrifying Areas* (Washington: Urban Institute, 2006), and in Policy Link, "Equitable Development Toolkit" (http://policylink. org/EDTK).

88. Washington, D.C., has taken a forceful approach in both areas. See Kingsley and Williams, *Policies for Affordable Housing in the District of Columbia.*

89. David Boehlke, *Great Neighborhoods, Great City* (Baltimore, Md.: Goldseker Foundation, 2001).

90. Jason Hancock, "Ames Strives to Be More Inclusive Community," *Iowa Independent,* July 2, 2008.

91. The program targets families without income or assets and those facing the loss of subsidies when they begin to earn a living wage.

92. Cisneros and others, *Our Communities, Our Homes,* pp. 6–28.

93. Ibid.

94. See evidence presented by Popkin and Cunningham in chapter 11 of this volume.

The younger residents of the Tacoma Housing Authority's HOPE VI redevelopment, Salishan, enjoy treats from an ice cream truck in 2008.

Photo courtesy of www.wshfc.org

APPENDIX A

G. THOMAS KINGSLEY

This appendix presents a quantitative summary of the scope and status of the HOPE VI revitalization program. The numbers are derived from the management information system set up by the HOPE VI staff at HUD to monitor program performance. The system covers all revitalization grants awarded since the program began in 1993, with initial data and quarterly updates provided by the individual housing authorities responsible for the implementation of each grant. The forms and definitions for data submission are well defined and have remained quite consistent over time. HUD has contracted with private consulting firms to assemble the data from the housing authorities and provide a reasonable amount of quality control.

The information in this appendix represents the most reliable portrait of the program and its accomplishments that could be prepared as of December 2008. The data cover the plans and status of the 240 grants made from 1993 through 2007 as of September 30, 2008.

HUD has not yet formally compiled and entered some indicators for the six grants awarded in 2008 into its system, and it is likely that little site work has been completed for those developments at this point. Accordingly, the appendix does not cover the six grants awarded in 2008; planning parameters for all of them have not yet been finalized.

This appendix covers only the HOPE VI revitalization grants that are the subject of this book.[1] Information is not presented on the 287 "demolition only" grants that were made under HOPE VI legislation from 1996 to 2003.[2]

Funds Budgeted and Spent

Through September 2008, budgets had been approved for $5.53 billion of the total $5.92 billion awarded for the first 240 developments (table A-1).[3] However, sizable additional amounts in leverage, adding up to $10.78 billion, were anticipated. Thus, total planned investment amounted to $16.31 billion, an average of $68.0 million per development and approximately three times the HOPE VI amount budgeted. Some of the leveraged investment was expected to come from other public housing and federal outlays, but the bulk ($7.81 billion, or 72 percent) was expected to come from private sources (including tax credit investors) and state and local governments. Table A-1 also shows that by

Table A-1. **HOPE VI Program Status**[a]

	Number planned	Complete Number	Complete Percent
Revitalization grant funds awarded ($ millions)	5,918	...	...
Funds budgeted and expended ($ millions)			
HOPE VI	5,528	4,731	86
Other public housing	1,435	1,169	81
Other federal funds	1,536	855	56
Nonfederal funds	7,809	5,216	67
Total	16,308	11,971	73
Site Preparation			
Households relocated	73,640	72,265	98
Units demolished	96,226	91,802	95
Development (housing units)			
Rehabilitation	11,961	10,651	89
New Construction	99,098	61,545	62
Total	111,059	72,196	65
Type of units provided			
Public housing (ACC)			
Rental	52,951	40,022	76
Homeowner	6,723	4,605	68
Total	59,674	44,627	75
Non-ACC			
Rental	31,821	20,950	66
Homeowner	19,564	6,619	34
Total	51,385	27,569	54
Total	111,059	72,196	65
No. units occupied	110,633	69,317	63

a. Status as of September 30, 2008, of 240 Grants (1993–2007).
... Not applicable.
Source: U.S. Department of Housing and Urban Development, HOPE VI management information system.

September 2008, 86 percent of the HOPE VI budgets and 73 percent of the total expected amount already had been spent.

Planned Production

As shown in table A-1, the developments associated with the 240 grants awarded through the end of 2007 will have entailed the demolition of 96,226 original, on-site public housing units but ultimately will yield a total of 111,059 new and rehabilitated units for occupancy, for an average yield of 463 units per grant. More than half (54 percent) of the post-revitalization units will be public housing units, identified in the table as annual contribution contract (ACC) units for which deep subsidies are provided by HUD. Of the ACC units, 89 percent will be rental units and 11 percent will be homeownership units.[4] Of the remaining post-revitalization units that will not be public housing units (46 percent), 62 percent will be rentals (rented either through other, shallower forms of public subsidy or at market rates), and 38 percent will be homeownership units.[5]

Program Status through September 2008

By September 2008, almost all of the site preparation work (relocation of residents and demolition) under the 240 grants had been completed, and rehabilitation and new construction were catching up. The share of planned units completed had more than doubled since September 2003 (from 31 percent to 65 percent), and the share occupied had increased from only 29 percent to 63 percent.[6] In sum, by September 2008 the program had

- relocated 72,265 households (98 percent of the planned total)
- demolished 91,802 units (95 percent of the planned total)
- rehabilitated 10,651 units (89 percent of the planned total)
- constructed 61,545 new units (62 percent of the planned total)
- occupied 69,317 completed units (63 percent of the planned total).

Relocation of Households

An issue of substantial interest in HOPE VI has been the extent to which original residents returned to the original site after revitalization was complete. When HOPE VI began, it often was assumed that most residents should return. Later, many program operators recognized that sizable numbers of original residents had good reasons to prefer other locations and did not want to move back. Having a low share of original residents ultimately return to the site was no longer seen as necessarily a problematic outcome, although it has to be recognized that there also were some real issues in this regard, particularly when original residents wanted to return but were not allowed to do so.

As indicated in table A-2, only 17,382 households had returned to occupy units in their former projects by September 2008 (24 percent of the total number of original residents relocated to that point). The housing authorities now expect that the ultimate total will be only 27,170 families returning (38 percent of the total number relocated).

Net Change in the Availability of Low-Income Units

HOPE VI frequently is criticized because it has led to a net loss in available public housing units (on-site hard units funded under annual contribution contracts), but often the magnitude of the loss is substantially distorted.

It is logical to assume that the original number of units in HOPE VI developments was equal to the number of units to be demolished plus the number to be rehabilitated: a total of 108,187 units, according to the September 2008 management report (table A-3).[7] The total number of new and rehabilitated units that will be provided in the developments after revitalization, 111,059, is actually 3 percent above the number that were there beforehand. However, the question raised here focuses on the number of low-income families that will be provided for by the ACC units that will be available. ACC units are expected

Table A-2. Relocation and Returns to the Site[a]

	Planned	Completed	Percent
Total households relocated	72,392	72,265	99
Households returning to revitalized HOPE VI community	27,170	17,382	64
Households returning as a percentage of total households relocated	38	24	...

a. Status as of September 30, 2008, of 240 Grants (1993–2007).

Table A-3. Comparison of Pre- and Post-Revitalization Units[a]

	Planned		Completed	
	Number	Percent	Number	Percent
Original projects				
Total units	108,187	100	102,453	100
Occupied units	73,640	68	72,265	71
Total units compared				
Total original	108,187	100	102,453	100
Total post-revitalization	111,059	103	72,196	70
Public housing units compared				
Original occupied units	73,640	100	72,265	100
ACC post-revitalization	59,674	81	44,627	62

a. Status as of September 30, 2008, of 240 Grants (1993–2007).

to total 59,674 when the developments are complete. That implies an ultimate loss of 45 percent of the original total of on-site ACC units.

However, that is not an appropriate comparison. Many of the original units in the projects to be redeveloped were vacant and uninhabitable. If we assume that the number of units "occupied" at the start equaled the total number of families to be relocated (73,640), then the projects had an average occupancy rate of only 68 percent when HOPE VI began—that is, on average 32 percent of the original units were vacant (not a surprising number given the deteriorated state of the projects in question). The 59,674 post-revitalization ACC units can house 81 percent of the 73,640 total. Looked at that way, the loss rate would be only 19 percent; that is, the number of families that can be provided for in ACC units after revitalization under HOPE VI will be just 19 percent less than the number of such families living in ACC units before revitalization.

Still, that is not an appropriate comparison either. Not all of the vacant units on site originally were uninhabitable, although we will never have a fully reliable estimate of that share. All we can suggest is that the loss rate of ACC units is somewhere between 45 percent and 19 percent, probably closer to the lower figure.

Further, as explained earlier in this book, the low-income housing tax credits that financed many of the units in HOPE VI developments also serve low-income households. While tax credit subsidies often were attached to ACC units, many HOPE VI redevelopments also had "tax credit–only" units, which generally are restricted to serving households making up to 60 percent of area median income (AMI).

How Much Housing Is Mixed Income?

HOPE VI did not prescribe standards for income mixing in housing authority plans. However, as the idea caught on, almost all of the plans in later years called for some mixing of income groups in their developments.

Table A-4 shows that recipients of only 32 grants (13 percent of the 240 total) planned to make 100 percent of their post-revitalization units ACC units. The post-revitalization plans for nearly half of grants (117, or 49 percent) call for ACC units to amount to 50 to 99 percent of the total. For the remaining two-fifths (91 grants or 38 percent), ACC units will constitute less than half of the total when the projects are complete. (Note that 100 percent ACC grants were more prevalent in the early years of the program. Since 1999, there have been only six of them.)

A 2003 study by Abt Associates of thirteen HOPE VI developments notes that various research studies have concurred that true mixed-income communities have substantial shares (defined as at least 20 percent) of both very poor households (those making less than 30 percent of the area median income) and relatively less poor households (those with annual incomes of about 50 percent AMI). The study found that the sites that met the broad range of income definition of a mixed-income property were sites in which at least 20 percent of the units were for non–public housing households.[8] Although information on the incomes of households in the 240 HOPE VI sites is unavailable, we can use the 20 percent non–public housing units as a proxy measure. Under that measure, three-quarters (179) of the 240 developments are mixed-income.[9]

The mixed-income share is even higher when measured in terms of housing units. The table shows that only 10 percent of planned units will be in 100 percent ACC developments; 39 percent will be in developments in which the ACC share is between 50 and 99 percent; and 52 percent will be in developments in which the ACC share is less than half. In 82 percent of the developments, at least 20 percent of the units are for non–public housing households.

This analysis of income mixing through non-ACC units is incomplete. Many practitioners and experts consider the promise of income mixing unfulfilled unless the development includes market-rate units. Market-rate units theoretically allow for the presence of unsubsidized renters or homeowners who have greater means to "vote with their feet" if housing or neighborhood conditions fail to meet their expectations. Table A-5 provides an assessment of

Table A-4. HOPE IV Grants and Planned Units, by ACC Percentage of Planned Units

| | Number of grants | | | | | Percent of planned housing units[a] | | | | |
| | | Percent ACC | | | | | | Percent ACC | | |
Grant year	Total	100	81–99	50–80	Under 50	Total	100	81–99	50–80	Under 50
1993	13	5	2	4	2	100	35	10	31	24
1994	14	6	3	3	2	100	22	15	22	40
1995	13	3	5	4	1	100	35	26	24	15
1996	19	2	1	9	7	100	4	4	38	54
1997	23	3	3	11	6	100	7	16	48	30
1998	28	7	2	12	7	100	10	2	38	49
1999	21	0	2	9	10	100	0	10	32	58
2000	18	0	2	6	10	100	0	7	16	77
2001	16	1	0	8	7	100	6	0	31	63
2002	27	2	2	8	15	100	4	5	19	71
2003	24	1	2	6	15	100	1	8	24	68
2004	7	0	3	3	1	100	0	38	36	27
2005	8	0	1	4	3	100	0	7	48	45
2006	4	2	1	1	0	100	52	16	32	0
2007	5	0	0	0	5	100	0	0	0	100
Total	240	32	29	88	0	100	10	9	30	52
Percent	...	13	12	37	38	...	...	...	...	...

a. Totals of some rows may reach 99 percent or 101 percent because of rounding

Table A-5. HOPE IV Grants and Planned Units, by Income-Restricted Percentage of Planned Units[a]

| | Number of grants | | | | | Percent of planned housing units[a] | | | | |
| | | Percent Income-Restricted | | | | | | Percent Income-Restricted | | |
Grant year	Total	100	81–99	50–80	Under 50	Total	100	81–99	50–80	Under 50
1993	13	6	4	3	0	100	44	22	34	0
1994	14	11	2	0	1	100	51	18	0	30
1995	13	7	3	3	0	100	51	18	31	0
1996	19	8	5	4	2	100	20	26	31	22
1997	23	10	8	5	0	100	35	39	26	0
1998	28	14	9	5	0	100	22	26	51	0
1999	21	8	6	5	2	100	26	31	29	14
2000	18	5	6	4	3	100	14	21	39	26
2001	16	3	5	6	2	100	12	22	42	24
2002	27	7	10	8	2	100	15	29	38	17
2003	24	8	8	6	2	100	30	22	36	12
2004	7	4	2	1	0	100	53	33	14	0
2005	8	2	4	2	0	100	29	32	39	0
2006	4	3	1	0	0	100	68	32	0	0
2007	5	1	0	3	1	100	33	56	0	11
Total	240	97	73	55	15	100	28	26	33	13
Percent		40	30	23	6	...	...	...	...	...

a. There was a discrepancy in the total number of units in the HUD spreadsheet breaking down projects by ACC versus non-ACC units (111,059) and the HUD spreadsheet breaking down projects by income-restricted and non-income-restricted units (110,706), but the number was too small (353) to affect the findings of this analysis.

b. Totals of some rows may reach only 99 percent because of rounding.

Source for tables A-4 and A-5: U.S. Department of Housing and Urban Development, HOPE VI management information system.

the percentage of HOPE VI redevelopments that include units with no income restrictions. Two-fifths of grantees (97, or 40 percent) of the 240 developments planned to include only income-restricted units. Nearly a third of grantees (70, or 29 percent) plan to lease or sell at least 20 percent of the units in their developments without income restrictions.

The share of unrestricted units is greater when measured in terms of housing units. The table shows that only 28 percent of planned units will be in 100 percent income-restricted developments; 59 percent will be in developments in which the income-restricted share is between 50 and 99 percent; and 13 percent will be in developments in which the income-restricted share is less than half. In nearly half (46 percent) of the developments, at least 20 percent of the units are for non-income-restricted households.

····· Endnotes ·····

1. Researchers looking at past reports summarizing HOPE VI revitalization grant status may see different figures for the total number of awards made before 2007 because two grantees each had two of their awards combined into one. The 1995 and 1996 awards to the New York City Housing Authority were combined into the authority's 1996 Averne Edgemere grant, and the 1999 and 2002 awards to the Bradenton Housing Authority in Florida were combined into the 1999 grant.

2. Beginning with the fiscal 1996 appropriation act and through fiscal 2003, the HOPE VI program also made demolition-only grants. But most evaluations and analyses of HOPE VI focus on the HOPE VI revitalization grants program because the demolition-only side of HOPE VI is not only managed separately but has a different legislative history and purpose. As Yan Zhang explained, Congress intensified its focus on accelerating the demolition of distressed public housing in 1994, when Republicans won control of the House and Senate and embarked on House Speaker Newt Gingrich's "Contract with America." Proposals to eliminate HUD were forestalled, but HUD and Congress moved forward under a reform agenda that included speeding up the removal of distressed public housing from the inventory. In addition to a provision requiring mandatory conversion of the costliest, most dilapidated stock to funding for vouchers, HUD's FY 1996 Appropriation Act also included for the first time HOPE VI grants for "the demolition of obsolete public housing projects or portions thereof." See Yan Zhang, "Wills and Ways: Policy Dynamics of HOPE VI from 1992–2002," Ph.D. dissertation, Massachusetts Institute of Technology September 2004, pp. 103–115. See also Rod Solomon, "Public Housing Reform and Voucher Success: Progress and Challenges," discussion paper prepared for the Brookings Institution Metropolitan Policy Program, January 2005, pp. 5–6, 13–15; U.S. Department of Housing and Urban Development, HOPE VI Program Authority and Funding History (March 2007), p. 12.

3. After the HOPE VI grant awards are announced, public housing authorities must prepare budgets showing how the grant award will be spent. HUD will only begin dispensing grant funds after it has approved the budget for the use of grant funds.

4. HUD's data system slots as a "homeowner ACC" unit any homeownership unit paid for in whole or in part with HOPE VI program funds (or other public housing capital funds in cases in which those funds are among the leveraged funds for the HOPE VI redevelopment project). The homeownership unit could be a for-sale home that received a construction subsidy or a unit purchased by a buyer who received assistance with closing costs, a second mortgage, or other purchase assistance, including through a lease-purchase arrangement. Before QHWRA was passed in 1998, HOPE VI was authorized under appropriations acts as

an "urban revitalization demonstration program," and some of the replacement units were allowed to be homeownership housing meeting the same eligibility requirements as certain other existing HUD homeownership programs serving households making up to 115 percent of area median income. With QHWRA, HOPE VI was folded into the same authorizing statute as the public housing program and subject to meeting the eligibility requirements of public housing—that is, households could make only up to 80 percent AMI. E-mail and telephone phone communications to Lora Engdahl from Brian Gage, Office of Public Housing Investments, U.S. Department of Housing and Urban Development, September 3 and 11, 2008.

5. It is not exactly correct to identify the homeownership units as owner-occupied units. Conceivably a unit was developed to be sold and was sold, but, in turn, the owner ended up renting it out. Therefore, it is better to call them "for-sale units."

6. The 2003 figures come from Urban Institute analysis of data from HUD's HOPE VI reporting system as of September 30, 2003. See G. Thomas Kingsley and others, *Lessons From HOPE VI For the Future of Public Housing* (Washington: Urban Institute, 2003). The number of units planned to be occupied is slightly less than the number planned to be constructed because of expected vacancies due to normal turnover.

7. This assumption may be off to some extent, but it should not be off by much.

8. Mary Joel Holin and others, "Interim Assessment of the HOPE VI Program: Cross-Site Report," prepared by Abt Associates for the U.S. Department of Housing and Urban Development, September 19, 2003, p. 43 (www.abtassociates.com/reports/20030_RETASK-X SITE_03.pdf).

9. The breakdown of ACC versus non-ACC units provided by HUD covers all units created under the grant, some of which may be off site. Therefore it is impossible from these data to elicit an exact picture of the unit-mix of the "development" arising solely on the footprint of the former public housing site.

APPENDIX B

HOPE VI Revitalization Program Grants, 1993–2008

Award Year	Grant name	Location	Award amount (dollars)	Total units expected at completion	Rental units (ACC/non-ACC income-restricted/ market rate)	For-sale units (ACC/non-ACC income-restricted/ market rate)[a]
1993	Allen Parkway Village	Houston, TX	36,602,761	600	600 (600/0/0)	0
1993	Allequippa Terrace	Pittsburgh, PA	31,564,190	674	660 (467/12/181)	14 (14/0/0)
1993	Bernal/Plaza	San Francisco, CA	49,992,377	353	353 (353/0/0)	0
1993	Earle Village	Charlotte, NC	41,740,155	872	797 (365/191/241)	75 (40/0/35)
1993	Ellen Wilson Homes	Washington, DC	25,075,956	147	0	147 (134/0/13
1993	Elm Haven	New Haven, CT	45,331,593	392	339 (280/44/15)	53 (9/44/0)
1993	Guinotte Manor	Kansas City, MO	47,579,800	610	610 (398/212/0)	0
1993	Hillside Terrace	Milwaukee, WI	45,689,446	456	453 (453/0/0)	3 (3/0/0)
1993	Mission Main	Boston, MA	49,992,350	535	535 (445/0/90)	0
1993	Outhwaite Homes/King Kennedy (combined)	Cuyahoga, OH	50,000,000	503	503 (503/0/0)	0
1993	Pico Gardens & Aliso Apartments	Los Angeles, CA	50,000,000	412	373 (298/75/0)	39 (0/0/39)
1993	Richard Allen Homes	Philadelphia, PA	50,000,000	408	408 (408/0/0)	0
1993	Techwood Homes/Clark Howell Homes	Atlanta, GA	42,562,635	738	738 (301/126/311)	0
1994	Archbishop Walsh Homes	Newark, NJ	49,996,000	463	447 (422/25/0)	16 (16/0/0)
1994	Cabrini-Green	Chicago, IL	50,000,000	2,573	1,351 (610/279/462)	1,222 (0/112/1,110)
1994	Cristantemos y Manuel A. Perez	San Juan, PR	50,000,000	256	256 (256/0/0)	0
1994	Desire	New Orleans, LA	44,255,908	575	425 (362/55/8)	150 (0/150/0)
1994	Homeownership demonstration	Baltimore, MD	18,648,000	814	646 (0/646/0)	168 (0/168/0)
1994	Jeffries Homes	Detroit, MI	39,807,342	972	858 (643/121/94)	114 (0/41/73)
1994	John Hay Homes	Springfield, IL	19,775,000	221	172 (172/0/0)	49 (49/0/0)
1994	Lafayette Courts	Baltimore, MD	31,015,600	338	311 (311/0/0)	27 (0/27/0)
1994	Lakewest	Dallas, TX	26,600,000	336	336 (336/0/0)	0
1994	Lockwood Gardens/ Lower Fruitvale	Oakland, CA	26,510,020	426	426 (426/0/0)	0
1994	McGuire Gardens	Camden, NJ	42,177,229	253	253 (253/0/0)	0

Award Year	Grant name	Location	Award amount (dollars)	Total units expected at completion	Rental units (ACC/non-ACC income-restricted/ market rate)	For-sale units (ACC/non-ACC income-restricted/ market rate)[a]
1994	Quigg Newton Homes	Denver, CO	26,489,288	400	400 (400/0/0)	0
1994	Spring View	San Antonio, TX	48,810,294	349	232 (232/0/0)	117 (31/86/0)
1994	Windsor Terrace	Columbus, OH	42,053,408	500	500 (420/80/0)	0
1995	Arverne/Edgemere Houses	New York, NY	67,700,952	1,827	1803 (1803/0/0)	24 (24/0/0)
1995	Carver Park	Cuyahoga, OH	21,000,000	609	512 (471/38/3)	97 (97/0/0)
1995	Concord/Eagle Creek	Indianapolis, IN	29,999,010	221	221 (190/31/0)	0
1995	Darst-Webbe	St. Louis, MO	46,771,000	1,009	784 (564/49/171)	225 (0/44/181)
1995	Hayes Valley	San Francisco, CA	22,055,000	195	195 (117/78/0)	0
1995	Holly Park	Seattle, WA	48,116,503	1,145	938 (400/334/204)	207 (0/0/207)
1995	Kennedy Brothers	El Paso, TX	36,224,644	414	364 (364/0/0)	50 (50/0/0)
1995	LeMoyne Gardens	Memphis, TN	47,281,182	411	341 (326/15/0)	70 (70/0/0)
1995	Lexington Terrace	Baltimore, MD	22,702,000	391	291 (250/41/0)	100 (0/100/0)
1995	Manchester	Pittsburgh, PA	7,500,000	192	164 (92/0/72)	28 (26/2/0)
1995	Mirasol	San Antonio, TX	48,285,500	390	230 (230/0/0)	160 (160/0/0)
1995	Orchard Park	Boston, MA	30,000,000	511	466 (380/25/61)	45 (45/0/0)
1995	Parkside Homes	Detroit, MI	47,620,227	215	173 (173/0/0)	42 (7/0/35)
1996	ABLA (Brooks Extension)	Chicago, IL	24,483,250	744	511 (455/56/0)	233 (0/74/159)
1996	Bedford Additions	Pittsburgh, PA	26,592,764	380	351 (180/110/61)	29 (29/0/0)
1996	Connie Chambers	Tucson, AZ	14,600,000	320	260 (200/60/0)	60 (0/60/0)
1996	Cotter & Lang Homes	Louisville, KY	20,000,000	1,212	763 (500/160/103)	449 (449/0/0)
1996	Dalton Village	Charlotte, NC	24,501,684	580	533 (247/286/0)	47 (15/0/32)
1996	Durkeeville	Jacksonville, FL	21,552,000	389	361 (361/0/0)	28 (0/0/28)
1996	Heman E. Perry Homes	Atlanta, GA	20,000,000	1,417	700 (228/213/259)	717 (40/124/553)
1996	Henry Horner	Chicago, IL	18,435,300	764	449 (271/91/87)	315 (0/44/271)
1996	Herman Gardens	Detroit, MI	24,224,160	920	457 (234/173/50)	463 (0/98/365)
1996	Hollander Ridge	Baltimore, MD	20,000,000	450	450 (225/225/0)	0
1996	Jackson Parkway	Holyoke, MA	15,000,000	178	100 (100/0/0)	78 (17/61/0)
1996	Lamokin Village	Chester, PA	14,949,554	150	150 (150/0/0)	0
1996	North Beach	San Francisco, CA	20,000,000	341	341 (231/110/0)	0
1996	Riverview/Lakeview	Cuyahoga, OH	29,733,334	260	260 (260/0/0)	0
1996	Robert S. Jervay Place	Wilmington, NC	11,620,655	178	124 (95/29/0)	54 (6/48/0)
1996	Robert Taylor Homes	Chicago, IL	25,000,000	823	663 (251/277/135)	160 (0/40/120)

Award Year	Grant name	Location	Award amount (dollars)	Total units expected at completion	Rental units (ACC/non-ACC income-restricted/ market rate)	For-sale units (ACC/non-ACC income-restricted/ market rate)[a]
1996	St. Thomas	New Orleans, LA	25,000,000	923	800 (346/94/360)	123 (0/0/123)
1996	Theron B. Watkins Homes	Kansas City, MO	13,000,000	226	226 (175/36/15)	0
1996	Tobe Hartwell/Extension	Spartanburg, SC	14,620,369	268	218 (128/90/0)	50 (0/50/0)
1997	Allen Parkway Village 2	Houston, TX	21,286,470	538	324 (201/87/36)	214 (204/10/0)
1997	Blackwell	Richmond, VA	26,964,118	537	229 (75/154/0)	308 (308/0/0)
1997	Christopher Columbus	Paterson, NJ	21,662,344	343	313 (137/176/0)	30 (0/30/0)
1997	College Hill/ Ponce de Leon	Tampa, FL	32,500,000	842	824 (391/215/218)	18 (0/18/0)
1997	College Homes	Knoxville, TN	22,064,125	253	168 (103/44/21)	85 (65/5/15)
1997	Colonel John Warner Homes	Peoria, IL	16,190,907	233	186 (68/118/0)	47 (47/0/0)
1997	Colonial Park	Orlando, FL	6,800,000	149	48 (48/0/0)	101 (35/19/47)
1997	Curries Woods	Jersey City, NJ	31,624,658	553	450 (388/24/38)	103 (103/0/0)
1997	Enterprise Drive	Helena, MT	939,700	14	14 (14/0/0)	0
1997	Heritage House I	Kansas City, MO	6,570,500	124	124 (51/54/19)	0
1997	Ida Barbour Revitalization	Portsmouth, VA	24,810,883	278	117 (117/0/0)	161 (161/0/0)
1997	Jordan Park	St. Petersburg, FL	27,000,000	405	290 (290/0/0)	115 (35/0/80)
1997	Kimberly Park Terrace	Winston-Salem, NC	27,740,850	495	402 (196/166/40)	93 (0/93/0)
1997	Lakeview Homes/Lower West Side	Buffalo, NY	28,015,038	359	359 (339/20/0)	0
1997	McKees Rocks Terrace	Allegheny County, PA	15,847,160	230	211 (130/53/28)	19 (19/0/0)
1997	Murphy Homes, Julian Gardens	Baltimore, MD	31,325,395	260	75 (75/0/0)	185 (185/0/0)
1997	Oak Street	Chester County, PA	16,434,200	290	135 (83/52/0)	155 (82/21/52
1997	Pioneer Homes, Migliore Manor	Elizabeth, NJ	28,903,755	554	468 (281/187/0)	86 (0/10/76)
1997	Schuylkill Falls	Philadelphia, PA	26,400,951	291	135 (135/0/0)	156 (0/28/128)
1997	Southfield Village	Stamford, CT	26,446,063	366	315 (160/70/85)	51 (51/0/0)
1997	Valencia Gardens	San Francisco, CA	23,230,641	260	260 (148/112/0)	0
1997	Valley Green/Sky Tower	Washington, DC	20,300,000	314	180 (148/32/0)	134 (125/9/0)
1997	Vine Hill Homes	Nashville, TN	13,563,876	152	137 (121/16/0)	15(0/15/0)
1998	ABLA Homes	Chicago, IL	35,000,000	2,528	1,413 (1012/399/2)	1,115 (0/320/795)
1998	Aliso Village	Los Angeles, CA	23,045,297	470	377 (242/135/0)	93 (27/0/66)
1998	Caroline Street Apartments	New Bedford, MA	4,146,780	64	64 (58/0/6)	0
1998	Carver Homes	Atlanta, GA	34,669,400	1,153	851 (385/259/207)	302 (62/0/240)

Award Year	Grant name	Location	Award amount (dollars)	Total units expected at completion	Rental units (ACC/non-ACC income-restricted/ market rate)	For-sale units (ACC/non-ACC income-restricted/ market rate)[a]
1998	Central Plaza Towers	Mobile, AL	4,741,800	77	77 (77/0/0)	0
1998	Charlotte Court	Lexington, KY	19,331,116	296	176 (161/15/0)	120 (0/120/0
1998	Chestnut Court and 1114 14th Street	Oakland, CA	12,705,010	168	151 (83/66/2)	17 (0/17/0)
1998	Curtis Park Homes & Arapahoe Courts	Denver, CO	25,753,220	580	323 (135/94/94)	257 (185/20/52
1998	Eastlake Family Public Housing	Wilmington, DE	16,820,350	160	70 (70/0/0)	90 (90/0/0)
1998	Edwin Corning Homes	Albany, NY	28,852,200	376	370 (254/68/48)	6 (0/6/0)
1998	Fairview Homes	Charlotte, NC	34,724,570	1,250	1,179 (263/612/304)	71 (25/0/46)
1998	FDR & Homestead Apartments	Allegheny County, PA	2,549,392	180	180 (180/0/0)	0
1998	Flag House Courts	Baltimore, MD	21,500,000	192	182 (130/52/0)	10 (10/0/0)
1998	Heritage House II	Kansas City, MO	3,429,500	63	63 (28/23/12)	0
1998	John F. Kennedy Apartments	Cambridge, MA	5,000,000	83	83 (44/39/0)	0
1998	Lincoln Court	Cincinnati, OH	31,093,590	503	453 (222/171/60)	50 (50/0/0)
1998	Lincoln Terrace	Roanoke, VA	15,124,712	243	195 (165/30/0)	48(47/1/0)
1998	Martin Luther King Plaza	Philadelphia, PA	25,229,950	245	136 (136/0/0)	109 (109/0/0)
1998	McCaffery Village	Chester, PA	9,751,178	186	110 (110/0/0)	76 (26/50/0)
1998	Morningside Homes	Greensboro, NC	22,987,722	678	415 (216/199/0)	263 (48/162/53)
1998	New Brunswick Homes	New Brunswick, NJ	7,491,656	192	192 (72/120/0)	0
1998	Osage Hills Apartments	Tulsa, OK	28,640,000	405	397 (287/110/0)	8 (0/0/8)
1998	Parklawn Housing Development	Milwaukee, WI	34,230,500	420	380 (380/0/0)	40 (40/0/0)
1998	Prospect Plaza	New York, NY	21,405,213	520	415 (298/80/37)	105 (100/5/0)
1998	Roseland Homes	Dallas, TX	34,907,186	864	825 (472/100/253)	39 (29/0/10)
1998	Roxbury House and Village	Seattle, WA	17,020,880	285	285 (210/75/0)	0
1998	Samuel Madden Homes	Alexandria, VA	6,716,250	100	100 (100/0/0)	0
1998	Ward Tower	Miami, FL	4,697,750	100	100 (100/0/0)	0
1999	Broadway Homes	Baltimore, MD	21,362,223	166	132 (84/0/48)	34 (0/34/0)
1999	Duneland Village	Gary, IN	19,847,454	144	144 (62/49/33)	0
1999	Edgewood Court, Metro Gardens and Metro Gardens Annex	Dayton, OH	18,311,270	191	95 (95/0/0)	96 (53/43/0)

Award Year	Grant name	Location	Award amount (dollars)	Total units expected at completion	Rental units (ACC/non-ACC income-restricted/ market rate)	For-sale units (ACC/non-ACC income-restricted/ market rate)[a]
1999	Frederick Douglass Dwellings & Stanton Dwellings	Washington, DC	29,972,431	600	280 (68/212/0)	320 (0/0/320)
1999	Grandview Manor/Lincoln Homes	Wheeling, WV	17,124,895	122	86 (59/24/3)	36 (13/20/3)
1999	Halifax Court	Raleigh, NC	29,368,114	326	326 (177/90/59)	0
1999	Joel C. Harris Homes	Atlanta, GA	35,000,000	1,072	689 (250/243/196)	383 (69/0/314)
1999	Laurel Homes	Cincinnati, OH	35,000,000	348	328 (132/43/153)	20 (10/0/10)
1999	Longview Place	Decatur, IL	34,863,615	674	654 (526/87/41)	20 (20/0/0)
1999	Metropolitan Gardens	Birmingham, AL	34,957,850	658	658 (435/75/148)	0
1999	Preston Taylor Homes	Nashville, TN	35,000,000	471	338 (314/24/0)	133 (0/133/0)
1999	Rainier Vista Garden Community	Seattle, WA	35,000,000	264	264 (173/91/0)	0
1999	Rogers Garden Park/ Zoller Apartments	Bradenton, FL	23,305,788	449	338 (140/198/0)	111 (74/0/37)
1999	Saxon Homes	Columbia, SC	25,843,793	438	229 (93/116/20)	209 (93/63/53)
1999	Scott/Carver Homes	Miami, FL	35,000,000	419	160 (160/0/0)	259 (0/259/0)
1999	Shore Park/Shore Terrace	Atlantic City, NJ	35,000,000	528	190 (190/0/0)	338 (24/0/314)
1999	Springfield Townhouses	High Point, NC	20,180,647	162	44 (18/26/0)	118 (118/0/0)
1999	Stella W. Wright	Newark, NJ	35,000,000	589	528 (220/308/0)	61 (30/25/6)
1999	Washington Park Homes & Lake Ridge Homes	Lakeland, FL	21,842,801	320	236 (130/106/0)	84 (84/0/0)
1999	Westwood Gardens	Oakland, CA	10,053,254	168	168 (46/122/0)	0
1999	Woodland/Pearce Homes	Greenville, SC	21,075,322	205	82 (34/48/0)	123 (123/0/0)
2000	Bayview Homes/Bayou	Biloxi, MS	35,000,000	387	337 (287/50/0)	50 (39/0/11)
2000	Coliseum Gardens	Oakland, CA	34,486,116	531	393 (141/252/0)	138 (0/106/32)
2000	East Capitol Dwellings	Washington, DC	30,867,337	761	528 (155/373/0)	233 (0/56/177)
2000	Easter Hill	Richmond, CA	35,000,000	382	300 (192/108/0)	82 (13/21/48)
2000	Few Gardens	Durham, NC	35,000,000	415	275 (163/99/13)	140 (0/116/24)
2000	Garden Homes Estates	Savannah, GA	16,328,649	367	306 (87/174/45)	61 (24/15/22)
2000	High Point Garden	Seattle, WA	35,000,000	1600	835 (350/325/160)	765 (0/0/765)
2000	Hurt Village	Memphis, TN	35,000,000	798	286 (102/184/0)	512 (61/0/451)
2000	Lapham Park	Milwaukee, WI	11,300,000	142	122 (51/51/20)	20 (20/0/0)
2000	Liberty View	Danville, VA	20,647,784	176	166 (134/32/0)	10 (0/10/0)
2000	Madden/Wells/Darrow	Chicago, IL	35,000,000	1128	675 (325/173/177)	453 (0/75/378

Award Year	Grant name	Location	Award amount (dollars)	Total units expected at completion	Rental units (ACC/non-ACC income-restricted/ market rate)	For-sale units (ACC/non-ACC income-restricted/ market rate)[a]
2000	McCallie Homes	Chattanooga, TN	35,000,000	317	275 (200/75/0)	42 (42/0/0)
2000	Peter G. Noll, Booke	Newport, KY	28,415,290	376	243 (233/10/0)	133 (133/0/0)
2000	Robert F. Kennedy Homes	Tucson, AZ	12,748,000	306	80 (80/0/0)	226 (0/70/156)
2000	Roberts Village and Bowling Green	Norfolk, VA	35,000,000	967	440 (394/27/19)	527 (0/276/251)
2000	Salishan Housing Development	Tacoma, WA	35,000,000	1,270	898 (553/343/2)	372 (0/18/354)
2000	Steel City Terrace	Mercer County, PA	9,012,288	133	116 (74/42/0)	17 (0/17/0)
2000	Westfield Acres	Camden, NJ	35,000,000	517	298 (279/19/0)	219 (119/100/0)
2001	Arthur A. Blumeyer	St. Louis, MO	35,000,000	789	512 (245/116/151)	277 (0/30/247)
2001	Capitol Homes	Atlanta, GA	35,000,000	1,140	639 (138/308/193)	501 (141/0/360)
2001	Capper/Carrollsburg	Washington, DC	34,937,590	1,781	1,462 (707/0/755)	319 (0/50/269)
2001	Cohansey View	Bridgeton, NJ	10,945,944	310	301 (150/151/0)	9 (9/0/0)
2001	Columbia Villa	Portland, OR	35,000,000	852	622 (297/325/0)	230 (0/0/230)
2001	Lafayette Gardens	Jersey City, NJ	34,140,000	578	532 (338/108/86)	46 (24/18/4)
2001	Matthew Henson	Phoenix, AZ	35,000,000	611	549 (310/134/105)	62 (62/0/0)
2001	Maverick Gardens	Boston, MA	35,000,000	396	396 (305/0/91)	0
2001	Mill Creek	Philadelphia, PA	34,825,000	685	585 (585/0/0)	100 (100/0/0)
2001	North Park Village	North Charleston, SC	30,347,921	724	616 (274/317/25)	108 (108/0/0)
2001	Oglethorpe Homes	Macon, GA	19,282,336	228	203 (134/37/32)	25 (25/0/0)
2001	Park Lake Homes	King County, WA	35,000,000	923	449 (180/269/0)	474 (0/0/474)
2001	Riverview/Dyer	Tampa, FL	19,937,572	346	250 (205/45/0)	96 (0/36/60)
2001	Robert Taylor Homes A	Chicago, IL	35,000,000	894	639 (297/207/135)	255 (0/48/207)
2001	Rockwell Gardens	Chicago, IL	35,000,000	780	520 (260/200/60)	260 (0/60/200)
2001	Westview Homes	Hagerstown, MD	27,357,875	411	330 (206/124/0)	81 (22/59/0)
2002	Arrowhead Apartments/ Thomas Bean Towers	Denver, CO	20,000,000	873	598 (250/223/125)	275 (0/69/206)
2002	Bessemer Avenue Apartments	Prichard, AL	20,000,000	275	160 (160/0/0)	115 (115/0/0)
2002	Bethune Village/ Halifax Park	Daytona Beach, FL	17,242,383	212	207 (94/113/0)	5 (4/1/0)
2002	Brentwood Park	Jacksonville, FL	20,000,000	422	328 (226/102/0)	94 (0/0/94)
2002	Carver Court	Orlando, FL	18,084,255	493	401 (94/307/0)	92 (39/21/32)
2002	Champion Park	Winnebago County, IL	18,847,938	156	52 (41/11/0)	104 (100/4/0)
2002	Clarksdale	Louisville, KY	20,000,000	1,054	811 (399/111/301)	(243 (0/0/243)
2002	Dutch Point Colony	Hartford, CT	20,000,000	190	127 (93/34/0)	63 (28/0/35)
2002	East Boulevard and Oklahoma Street	East Baton Rouge, LA	18,640,495	126	90 (90/0/0)	36 (36/0/0)

Award Year	Grant name	Location	Award amount (dollars)	Total units expected at completion	Rental units (ACC/non-ACC income-restricted/ market rate)	For-sale units (ACC/non-ACC income-restricted/ market rate)[a]
2002	Elizabeth Park Homes	Akron, OH	19,250,000	256	242 (106/58/78)	14 (0/13/1)
2002	Frazier Courts/Frazier Courts Addition	Dallas, TX	20,000,000	356	316 (316/0/0)	40 (0/40/0)
2002	George Foster Peabody Apartments	Columbus, GA	20,000,000	554	515 (164/173/178)	39 (39/0/0)
2002	Happy Hill Gardens	Winston-Salem, NC	18,264,369	445	272 (158/103/11)	173 (32/31/110)
2002	Harbor View Homes	Duluth, MN	20,000,000	551	322 (110/127/85)	229 (54/54/121)
2002	Highland Park	Milwaukee, WI	19,000,000	194	170 (102/68/0)	24 (0/0/24)
2002	John Hanson/Roger Brook Taney Apartments	Frederick, MD	15,889,376	264	157 (86/71/0)	107 (38/0/69)
2002	Munsyana Homes	Muncie, IN	12,352,941	244	244 (136/63/45)	0
2002	Ohioview Acres	Allegheny County, PA	20,000,000	196	181 (134/37/10)	15 (15/0/0)
2002	Quinnipiac Terrace/ Riverview	New Haven, CT	20,000,000	160	160 (114/46/0)	0
2002	Red Oak Townhomes	Fulton County, GA	17,191,544	595	442 (126/316/0)	153 (96/0/57)
2002	Sam Levy Homes	Nashville, TN	20,000,000	275	227 (181/0/46)	48 (0/48/0)
2002	The Bryants	Minneapolis, MN	14,193,604	277	102 (102/0/0)	175 (0/53/122)
2002	Tonomy Hill	Newport, RI	20,000,000	262	255 (122/97/36)	7 (7/0/0)
2002	Victoria Courts	San Antonio, TX	18,788,269	602	455 (99/67/289)	147 (6/53/88)
2002	Washington Courts	Utica, NY	11,501,039	149	113 (50/63/0)	36 (19/17/0)
2002	Westlake Terrace	Youngstown, OH	19,751,896	183	153 (75/72/6)	30 (0/30/0)
2002	Woodland Terrace	Pleasantville, NJ	13,446,700	153	128 (77/51/0)	25 (12/0/13)
2003	Albert Owens/Jesse Thomas Homes	Mobile, AL	20,000,000	487	325 (275/0/50)	162 (125/0/37)
2003	Brokenburr Trails	Indianapolis, IN	16,778,288	217	179 (60/99/20)	38 (36/0/2)
2003	Chavis Heights	Raleigh, NC	19,959,697	223	223 (141/55/27)	0
2003	Chester Towers	Chester, PA	20,000,000	279	255 (180/75/0)	24 (0/24/0)
2003	Clarksdale Phase II	Louisville, KY	20,000,000	857	503 (302/76/125)	354 (0/0/354)
2003	Cochran Gardens	St. Louis, MO	20,000,000	243	223 (90/76/57)	20 (0/20/0)
2003	Eastgate Gardens	Washington, DC	20,000,000	286	161 (136/25/0)	125 (0/61/64)
2003	Fairfield Court	Stamford, CT	19,579,641	275	179 (49/95/35)	96 (8/88/0)
2003	FDR Manor	Camden, NJ	20,000,000	663	561 (389/172/0)	102 (0/102/0)
2003	Hendley Homes	Columbia, SC	10,755,952	187	132 (66/0/66)	55 (19/0/36)
2003	John Henry Hale Homes	Nashville, TN	20,000,000	268	228 (188/0/40)	40 (0/35/5)
2003	Lamar Terrace	Memphis, TN	20,000,000	320	320 (152/101/67)	0
2003	McDaniel Glen	Atlanta, GA	20,000,000	1,133	836 (318/262/256)	297 (67/0/230)
2003	MLK Jr. Apartments	Daytona Beach, FL	7,639,191	113	103 (50/53/0)	10 (10/0/0)

Award Year	Grant name	Location	Award amount (dollars)	Total units expected at completion	Rental units (ACC/non-ACC income-restricted/ market rate)	For-sale units (ACC/non-ACC income-restricted/ market rate)[a]
2003	Mulford Gardens	Yonkers, NY	20,000,000	410	380 (102/278/0)	30 (0/30/0)
2003	Phyllis Goins	Spartanburg, SC	20,000,000	520	385 (183/202/0)	135 (119/16/0)
2003	Piedmont Courts	Charlotte, NC	20,000,000	804	504 (252/112/140)	300 (45/0/255)
2003	Scattered Sites	Milwaukee, WI	19,500,000	77	73 (73/0/0)	4 (4/0/0)
2003	Tuxedo Court	Birmingham, AL	20,000,000	331	220 (110/110/0)	111 (25/86/0)
2003	Valley View Homes	Cuyahoga, OH	17,447,772	201	189 (95/60/34)	12 (0/12/0)
2003	Victory Village	Meridian, MS	17,281,075	242	242 (95/147/0)	0
2003	Whitfield I	Benton Harbor, MI	15,947,404	326	168 (94/74/0)	158 (48/22/88)
2003	William J. Fischer Homes	New Orleans, LA	8,127,632	55	20 (20/0/0)	35 (0/32/3)
2003	Yosemite Village	Fresno, CA	20,000,000	168	80 (80/0/0)	88 (82/0/6)
2004	Alamito Apartments	El Paso, TX	20,000,000	452	397 (397/0/0)	55 (0/38/17)
2004	Hanover Acres and Riverview Terrace	Allentown, PA	20,000,000	322	269 (190/79/0)	53 (29/0/24)
2004	Jesse Jackson Townhomes	Greenville, SC	20,000,000	622	472 (200/272/0)	150 (0/150/0)
2004	Lincoln Park	Springfield, OH	20,000,000	157	132 (132/0/0)	25 (0/25/0)
2004	Ludlow Scattered Sites	Philadelphia, PA	17,059,932	192	89 (89/0/0)	103 (50/53/0)
2004	Martin Luther King Apartments	Tucson, AZ	9,825,000	321	288 (192/13/83)	33 (0/8/25)
2004	McKenzie Court	Tuscaloosa, AL	20,000,000	273	245 (234/11/0)	28 (0/28/0)
2005	Bluegrass/Aspendale	Lexington, KY	20,000,000	483	332 (332/0/0)	151 (0/141/10)
2005	Dixie Homes	Memphis, TN	20,000,000	404	374 (145/74/155)	30 (0/30/0)
2005	Edgewood Homes	Akron, OH	20,000,000	225	176 (90/86/0)	49 (0/20/29)
2005	Grady Homes	Atlanta, GA	20,000,000	947	778 (243/368/167)	169 (55/0/114)
2005	Iris Court	Portland, OR	16,895,528	155	130 (100/30/0)	25 (0/21/4)
2005	Jeffry Wilson	Portsmouth, VA	20,000,000	500	399 (399/0/0)	101 (0/101/0)
2005	Michigan Court/Flossie Riley	Ft. Myers, FL	20,000,000	521	386 (279/107/0)	135 (0/135/0)
2005	Seaview	Long Branch, NJ	20,000,000	247	216 (204/0/12)	31 (0/31/0)
2006	Center Court	Niagra Falls, NY	20,000,000	282	240 (150/90/0)	42 (30/0/12)
2006	Delaware Terrace & Delaware Terrace Annex	Easton, PA	20,000,000	144	96 (96/0/0)	48 (42/6/0)
2006	Magnolia Gardens	Beaumont, TX	20,000,000	401	401 (401/0/0)	0
2006	Riverview	Kingsport, TN	11,900,000	62	38 (38/0/0)	24 (24/0/0)
2007	A.L. Krohn (aka Krohn West)	Phoenix, AZ	8,855,000	220	83 (42/25/16)	137 (13/15/109)
2007	C. J. Peete	New Orleans, LA	20,000,000	510	460 (193/144/123)	50 (0/50/0)

Award Year	Grant name	Location	Award amount (dollars)	Total units expected at completion	Rental units (ACC/non-ACC income-restricted/ market rate)	For-sale units (ACC/non-ACC income-restricted/ market rate)[a]
2007	Delona Gardens and Campbell Terrace	Fayetteville, NC	20,000,000	673	673 (249/424/0)	0
2007	Sheridan Terrace	Washington, DC	20,000,000	344	183 (110/73/0)	161 (0/46/115)
2007	Washington Beech	Boston, MA	20,000,000	262	191 (104/87/0)	71 (0/15/56)
2008	Westpark	Bremerton, WA	20,000.00	...	...	...
2008	Stateway Gardens	Chicago, IL	20,000,000	...	...	...
2008	Park Lake II	King County, WA	20,000,000	...	...	...
2008	Scattered Sites	Milwaukee, WI	6,759,852	...	...	...
2008	Lake City Village and House	Seattle, WA	10,486,839	...	...	...
2008	Covington/Stevens/ Griff King Homes	Texarkana, TX	20,000,000	...	...	...

Source: U.S. Department of Housing and Urban Development, HOPE VI management information system, as of September 30, 2008

a. Unit totals and breakdowns are not available for the 2008 grants. ACC = annual contributions contract. Market-rate units are those that, whether subsidized or unsubsidized, impose no income restrictions on who buys or rents a unit. The unit counts and breakdown provided by HUD and shown in this chart may differ slightly from the units reported to the public and press at any one time because production plans may change during the course of redevelopment.

CONTRIBUTORS

HENRY G. CISNEROS is executive chairman of the CityView companies, which have partnered with leading homebuilders in developing more than forty communities in twelve states. Cisneros served as secretary of the Department of Housing and Urban Development during the first Clinton administration. Previously he served four terms as mayor of San Antonio, a position to which he was originally elected in 1981, becoming the first Hispanic American mayor of a major U.S. city.

BRUCE KATZ is vice president and director of the Metropolitan Policy Program at the Brookings Institution. Katz regularly advises national, state, regional, and municipal leaders on policy reforms that advance the competitiveness of metropolitan areas, particularly reforms that promote the revitalization of central cities and older suburbs. Before joining Brookings, Katz served as staff director of the Senate Subcommittee on Housing and Urban Affairs and then as chief of staff to Henry Cisneros when he was secretary of the U.S. Department of Housing and Urban Development.

RICHARD D. BARON is cofounder, chairman, and chief executive officer of McCormack Baron Salazar, a development company that focuses on rebuilding distressed urban communities. Baron has founded or cofounded a number of other enterprises, including the Center of Creative Arts, a visual and performing arts center in University City, Missouri; the Vashon Education Compact, a partnership of the St. Louis Public Schools and major corporations to transform ten St. Louis schools from low- to high-performing institutions; and the Center for Urban Redevelopment Excellence at the University of Pennsylvania.

PETER CALTHORPE has helped solidify a national trend toward adoption of the key principals of New Urbanism through his thirty years of practice in urban design, planning, and architecture. He helped found the Congress for New Urbanism and was its first board president. During the Clinton presidency, Calthorpe provided direction for HUD's empowerment zone and consolidated planning programs as well as the HOPE VI program. He recently was selected by the state of Louisiana to lead its long-term growth and redevelopment planning following hurricanes Katrina and Rita.

ALEXANDER POLIKOFF was executive director of BPI (Business and Professional People for the Public Interest), a Chicago-based public interest law and policy center, having held that position for twenty-nine years. He continues to serve on the BPI legal staff and retains responsibility for BPI's ongoing Gautreaux public housing litigation as lead counsel for the plaintiff. Polikoff is the author of *Waiting for Gautreaux: A Story of Segregation, Housing, and the Black Ghetto.*

LORA ENGDAHL is a Washington, D.C.–based writer, editor, and housing consultant to government agencies, nonprofits, and media outlets. Her articles have appeared in trade journals, magazines, and newspapers, including the *Chicago Tribune* and *Washington Post.* From 2003 to 2008, she kept the affordable housing and community development industry abreast of news from around the country as writer and editor of KnowledgePlex *Week in Review.*

RENÉE LEWIS GLOVER joined the Atlanta Housing Authority as chief executive officer in September 1994. At AHA, Glover pioneered the development of master-planned, mixed-use, mixed-income communities in which families from all socioeconomic backgrounds live next to each other in the same amenity-rich community. The model Glover created at AHA is now used as the redevelopment blueprint by the Department of Housing and Urban Development, and Glover has been nationally recognized for her role in transforming U.S. urban policy. Prior to joining the Atlanta Housing Authority, Glover was a corporate finance attorney in Atlanta and New York City.

MARGERY AUSTIN TURNER is vice president for research at the Urban Institute. Her research focuses on the forces that create and sustain racial and economic segregation in neighborhoods, why it matters, and what public policies can do about it. From 1993 through 1996, Turner served as deputy assistant secretary of research at the Department of Housing and Urban Development, where she launched three rigorous demonstrations testing potential strategies for overcoming concentrated poverty and racial segregation.

SUSAN J. POPKIN is a principal research associate at the Urban Institute's Metropolitan Housing and Communities Policy Center. A nationally recognized expert on assisted housing and mobility, Popkin directs the Roof over Their Heads research initiative, which examines the impact that the radical changes in public housing policy over the past decade have had on residents' lives. Popkin is a coauthor of *The Hidden War: Crime and the Tragedy of Public Housing in Chicago* and of the recently published *Public Housing and the Legacy of Segregation.*

MARY K. CUNNINGHAM is a senior research associate at the Metropolitan Housing and Communities Policy Center at the Urban Institute. Her research focuses on homelessness and affordable housing in the United States. Before joining the Urban Institute, Cunningham was founding director of the Homelessness Research Institute, the research and education arm of the National Alliance to End Homelessness. Prior to that, she was at the Urban Institute, managing research studies with a focus on public housing, HUD's voucher program, and family self-sufficiency programs.

RICK GENTRY is president and chief executive officer of the San Diego Housing Commission. The commission administers Section 8 and other traditional housing programs, finances affordable housing, and provides policy advice to the mayor and city council regarding housing development incentives and regulations. Previously, Gentry served as senior vice president of asset management with the Chicago-based National Equity Fund, the nation's largest nonprofit syndicator of low-income housing tax credits. Gentry has been involved in the affordable housing industry for thirty-six years, including as chief executive officer of the Austin Housing Authority (Texas) and the Richmond Redevelopment and Housing Authority (Virginia).

SHEILA CROWLEY is president and chief executive officer of the National Low-Income Housing Coalition, a membership organization dedicated solely to ending the affordable housing crisis in the United States. She came to the coalition in December 1998 after serving two decades in Richmond, Virginia, for various organizations in the areas of organizational leadership, direct service, policy advocacy, and scholarship. She serves as an adjunct faculty member at the School of Social Work at Virginia Commonwealth University as well as in George Mason University's Department of Social Work, teaching social policy, social justice, policy advocacy, and community and organizational practice.

RONALD D. UTT is the Herbert and Joyce Morgan senior research fellow for the Thomas A. Roe Institute for Economic Policy Studies at the Heritage Foundation, where he conducts research on housing, transportation, and the federal budget. He also works in cooperation with scholars across the United States to evaluate the success and failure of policies for urban revitalization, land use, and growth management. Utt is a veteran of budgetary politics in Washington, having served in senior positions at HUD, where he was director of the Housing Finance Division in the 1970s; the Office of Management and Budget; the National Association of Real Estate Investment Trusts; and the U.S. Chamber of Commerce.

G. THOMAS KINGSLEY is a senior researcher in housing, urban development, and governance issues at the Urban Institute, where he served for more than a decade as director of the Center for Public Finance and Housing. Previously he was director of the RAND Corporation's Housing and Urban Policy Program and assistant administrator for the New York City Housing and Development Administration, where he was responsible for the agency's budget and policy analysis functions. He also has taught in the graduate urban planning programs at the University of California–Berkeley and the University of Southern California.

INDEX

PHOTOGRAPHY CREDITS

(Photographs from newspapers and visual media providers such as Corbis and AP have a credit line adjacent to the photo and are not repeated here.)

Page 2: Baltimore's Broadway-Overlook community; photo by J. Brough Schamp, provided by Urban Design Associates, project architect.

Page 5, left: Roosevelt dedicating Techwood, courtesy of Kenneth Rogers Photographs/Kenan Research Center at the Atlanta History Center.

Page 5, right: Street in the Mexican quarter of San Antonio in 1939, reproduced with permission from the Library of Congress.

Page 6: Alazán Courts 1942, from the San Antonio Light Collection, University of Texas at San Antonio Institute of Texan Cultures, #L-2433-M, courtesy of the Hearst Corporation.

Page 8: Lexington Terrace before redevelopment, courtesy of Torti Gallas and Partners, project architect.

Page 11: Lexington Terrace after redevelopment, courtesy of Torti Gallas and Partners.

Page 13: City West in Cincinnati; photo by Steve Hall of Hedrich Blessing, provided by Torti Gallas and Partners, project architect.

Page 14: Youngsters in front of Lincoln Heights (reappears on page 19); from the Washington Star Collection, DC Public Library; ©Washington Post.

Page 18, top row left: Edward Vaughn family, March 1942; photo by Jack Delano, reproduced with permission from the Library of Congress.

Page 18, top row right and detail on back cover: Ida B. Wells housing project from above; March 1942 photo by Jack Delano, reproduced with permission from the Library of Congress.

Page 18, bottom row: North Philadelphia in the 1970s; photo by Dick Swanson, courtesy of the U.S. National Archives, from the EPA Documerica Series, 1972–1977.

Page 19, top row: Curtis Park in 1941, from the Denver Public Library, Western History Collection, RMN 1937, call number X-29037.

Page 19, bottom row right: Garbage outside Arthur Capper in Washington; from the Washington Star Collection, DC Public Library; ©Washington Post.

Page 20: Stairwell of Martin Luther King Plaza in Philadelphia, from Temple University Archives, courtesy of the Philadelphia Housing Authority.

Page 30: Renaissance Place in St. Louis; photo by Lora Engdahl.

Page 34: Crawford Square in Pittsburgh, courtesy of McCormack Baron Salazar, project developer.

Page 35: George L. Vaughn in St. Louis, courtesy of McCormack Baron Salazar.

Page 37: Murphy Park in St. Louis, courtesy of McCormack Baron Salazar, project developer.

Page 38, left: Teacher in Murphy Park's Jefferson Elementary school, courtesy of McCormack Baron Salazar.

Page 38, right: Jefferson Elementary, courtesy of McCormack Baron Salazar.

Page 48: Villages of Curtis Park cottage homes, courtesy of Denver Housing Authority.

Page 50, left: Le Corbusier's Plan Voisin (www.nyu.edu/.../sem/city/lecorbu_img.html).

Page 50, right: Pruitt-Igoe in 1955; photo by Ted McCrea, courtesy of Missouri History Museum, St. Louis.

Page 51, left: Stateway Gardens in 1973; photo by John White, courtesy of the U.S. National Archives, from the EPA Documerica series, 1972–1977.

Page 51, right: Stateway Gardens in 1959; photo by Clarence W. Hines, courtesy of the Chicago History Museum.

Page 54: Martin Luther King Plaza in Philadelphia, from Temple University Archives, courtesy of the Philadelphia Housing Authority.

Page 55, top left: MLK redevelopment rental homes; photo by Steve Hall of Hedrich Blessing, provided by Torti Gallas and Partners, project architect.

Page 55, top right: MLK redesign sketch, from Torti Gallas and Partners, project architect.

Page 55, bottom: Juniper Street houses; photo by Jan Pasek, courtesy of the Philadelphia Housing Authority.

Page 56: Broadway Homes in Baltimore before redevelopment, courtesy of the Housing Authority of Baltimore City.

Page 57: Broadway Overlook before-and-after sketches, courtesy of Urban Design Associates, project architect.

Page 58: Broadway Overlook streetscape; photo by J. Brough Schamp, provided by Urban Design Associates.

Page 60, top row: Curtis Park street and alley before redevelopment, courtesy of the Denver Housing Authority.

Page 60, bottom left: Villages of Curtis Park street after redevelopment, courtesy of Calthorpe Associates, master planner and phase 1 architect.

Page 60, bottom right: Villages of Curtis Park lane after redevelopment, courtesy of the Denver Housing Authority.

Page 62: High Point drainage system, courtesy of the Seattle Housing Authority.

Page 69: Dorothy Gautreaux, courtesy of Business and Professional People for the Public Interest.

Page 84: Rosa Parks Elementary School; photo by Gary Wilson Photography, provided by Dull Olson Weeks Architects, project architect.

Page 85: New Villages of Eastlake in Delaware, courtesy of the Wilmington Housing Authority and Leon N. Weiner and Associates, project codevelopers.

Page 86, left: Cascade Village in Akron; photo by Sarah Wolf, courtesy of Community Builders, Inc., project developer.

Page 86, right: HOPE VI in Wheeling, West Virginia, courtesy of Urban Design Associates, project architect.

Page 87, left and right: North Beach Place in San Francisco; photo by Bob Canfield, provided by BRIDGE Housing, project developer.

Page 88: JFK Apartments in Cambridge, courtesy of the Cambridge Housing Authority.

Page 92: New Holly library, courtesy of the Seattle Housing Authority.

Page 95, left: Holly Park before redevelopment, courtesy of the Seattle Housing Authority.

Page 100: New Holly site map, courtesy of the Seattle Housing Authority.

Page 101: Upper New Holly site plans, 1996 and 1999, courtesy Weinstein A/U Architects + Urban Designers LLC, New

Holly phases 1 and 2 project planners and architects.

Page 102, left and right: New Holly duplexes and single-family homes, courtesy Weinstein A/U Architects + Urban Designers LLC.

Page 103: Boys on bikes in New Holly, courtesy of the Seattle Housing Authority.

Page 104: New Holly back yards, courtesy of Dan Solomon of WRT/Solomon E.T.C., Othello Station (New Holly phase 3) project architect.

Page 111 and spine: High Point houses, photo by Lora Engdahl.

Page 120: Yellow house in Villages of Park DuValle, Louisville; photo by Lora Engdahl.

Page 122, left: Quiet residential street in Villages of Park DuValle; photo by Lora Engdahl.

Page 124, top row: Algonquin Manor and Cotter Homes, courtesy of Urban Design Associates, project architect of the Villages of Park DuValle.

Page 124, bottom: Park DuValle area map, courtesy of Community Builders, Inc.

Page 127: Six-flat apartment house and single-family house in the Villages of Park DuValle, courtesy of Community Builders, Inc.

Page 129: Villages of Park DuValle site map, courtesy of Community Builders, Inc.

Page 130: Park DuValle street with school, courtesy of Urban Design Associates.

Page 132, left: Mix of home styles on Park DuValle street; photo by Lora Engdahl.

Page 132, right: Craftsman-style homes in Park DuValle, courtesy of Urban Design Associates.

Page 133: Park DuValle town square, courtesy of Urban Design Associates.

Page 135: Liberty Green in Louisville, courtesy of Urban Design Associates, project architects.

Pages 144, 149, 151, 156, 157, 159: Before-and-after photos of Atlanta Housing Authority redevelopments, courtesy of the AHA.

Page 168: Capper-Carrollsburg redevelopment in southeast Washington, D.C. (reappears on page 184), courtesy of the District of Columbia Housing Authority.

Page 170, top left: Washington slums razed for urban renewal, courtesy of the Washingtoniana Division, District of Columbia Public Library.

Page 170, top right and bottom: Public housing and neighborhood east of the Anacostia River in 1969 and 1971, Washington Star Collection, DC Public Library; ©Washington Post.

Page 173: Orchard Park in Boston before redevelopment, courtesy of Trinity Financial Inc., project codeveloper of Orchard Gardens.

Page 174: Orchard Gardens redevelopment; duplicate images of photo, by Peter Vanderwarker, provided by Domenech Hicks & Krockmalnic Architects (project architect) and Trinity Financial (codeveloper).

Page 175, top: Earle Village, courtesy of Charlotte Housing Authority.

Page 175, bottom: First Ward, photo by Jennifer Gallman, courtesy of Charlotte Housing Authority.

Page 180: Wheeler Creek Estates in Washington, D.C., courtesy of the District of Columbia Housing Authority.

Page 184, bottom: Washington Nationals ballpark; photo by Lora Engdahl.

Page 190: Phyllis Williams and her family (also appears on page 195), courtesy of the Chicago Housing Authority.

Page 193, left and right: Children in Robert Taylor Homes and outside Ida B. Wells; photo by John White, courtesy of the National Archives, from the Documerica Series, 1972–1977.

Page 204: Kitchen of unit in Lincoln Heights Dwellings in Washington, D.C.; Washington Star Collection, DC Public Library; ©Washington Post.

Page 210: Tour of Greater Grays Ferry Estates in Philadelphia; photo by Maurice Browne, Philadelphia Housing Authority.

Page 212 left: Taping of *CHA Today* program, courtesy of the Charlotte Housing Authority.

Page 212, top and bottom right: Housing authority and Highland Homes brochure covers, courtesy of the Housing Authority of the City of Milwaukee (annual report cover photograph by Rocky Marcoux, commissioner of the City of Milwaukee Department of City Development).

Page 213: PHA light-pole banner; photo by Maurice Browne, Philadelphia Housing Authority.

Page 221, left: Vacant Ellen Wilson Dwellings, courtesy of Amy Weinstein, project architect for the Townhomes on Capitol Hill development.

Page 221 right: Townhomes on Capitol Hill; photo by Lora Engdahl.

Page 248: Boy in front of school; iStock photo.

Page 250: Postwar suburban house; iStock photo.

Page 253, top left: Vacant Chicago lot with Stateway Gardens housing project in background; photo by Mildred Meade, courtesy of the Chicago Public Library, Special Collections and Preservation Division.

Page 253, top right: Girls walking by Stateway Gardens in 1960s, courtesy of the Chicago Housing Authority.

Page 260: Abandoned Chicago school; iStock photo.

Page 262: Aerial view of Broadway Overlook in Baltimore; photo by J. Brough Schamp, provided by Urban Design Associates.

Page 275: Sunshades on Cherry Court, courtesy of the Housing Authority of the City of Milwaukee.

Page 278: Post House development, courtesy of Charter Oak Communities.

Page 281: The Food Project's Farmers' Market in Roxbury; photo by Greig Cranna, courtesy of the Food Project.

Page 284: Corner grocery in New Columbia, Courtesy of Housing Authority of Portland, Oregon.

Page 287: Madison Glen in Raleigh, courtesy of Downtown Housing Improvement Corp. Inc.

Page 290: Children in Philadelphia's Greater Grays Ferry Estates; photo by David Swanson, *The Philadelphia Inquirer.*